THE NEW EDUCATIONAL
TECHNOLOGIES AND LEARNING

ABOUT THE AUTHOR

Ibrahim Michail Hefzallah has been on the faculty of Fairfield University since 1968. At present, he is a professor of educational technology and the chair of the Educational Technology Department of the Graduate School of Education and Allied Professions. He received his Ph.D. from Ohio State University in educational media in 1959. Since then he has been engaged in teaching, research, and writing. He has authored and/or coauthored numerous articles, five Arabic textbooks, and three English textbooks in the areas of television, curriculum planning, and learning and communications media in the information age. His latest book publication was a spiritual novel titled *I Have Grown in His Love* (2003).

His articles have appeared in such publications as *Babel, The National Association of Secondary School Principals Bulletin, Educational and Industrial Television (EITV), International Journal of Instructional Media, Journal of Advertising Research, The Journal of the University Film Producers Association,* and *Vocational Guidance Quarterly.* Some of his research has focused on critical viewing of television, electronic publications, and the use of the World Wide Web in education.

In addition to teaching, research, and writing, Dr. Hefzallah is a producer and director of educational and cultural television programs. A sample of programs he has produced include *The Fairfield Gallery, Photographic Vision, Transcribing Jazz, Teaching Children About Families,* and *Design for Life,* all of which have been shown on Connecticut Public Television. *Design for Life* focuses on teenage smoking and received the American Cancer Society 1980 Connecticut Media Award. His latest production, *If These Stones Could Speak,* focuses on the story of Fairfield University as told in its buildings. It won The Communicator Crystal Award for Excellence in 1996.

Second Edition

THE NEW EDUCATIONAL TECHNOLOGIES AND LEARNING

Empowering Teachers to Teach and Students to Learn in the Information Age

By

IBRAHIM MICHAIL HEFZALLAH, PH.D.

Professor of Educational Technology
Chair, Department of Educational Technology
Fairfield University

CHARLES C THOMAS • PUBLISHER, LTD.
Springfield • Illinois • U.S.A.

Published and Distributed Throughout the World by

CHARLES C THOMAS • PUBLISHER, LTD.
2600 South First Street
Springfield, Illinois 62704

© 2004 by CHARLES C THOMAS • PUBLISHER, LTD.

ISBN 0-398- 07492-5 (hard)
ISBN 0-398-07493-3 (paper)

Library of Congress Catalog Card Number: 2003070320

Printed in the United States of America
JW-R-3

Library of Congress Cataloging-in-Publication Data

Hefzallah, Ibrahim M. (Ibrahim Michail)
  The new educational technologies and learning : empowering teachers to teach and students to learn in the information age / by Ibrahim Michail Hefzallah. — 2nd ed.
     p. cm.
  Includes bibliographical references and index.
   ISBN: 0-398-07492-5 — ISBN: 0-398-07493-3 (pbk)
     1. Education technology—United States.   2. Telecommunication in education—United States.   I. Title.

LB1028.3.H43 2004
371.33—dc22

                                                              2003070320

To my family

PREFACE

When the first edition of this book appeared, the size of the web was estimated at 320 million web pages. Only 34% (108 million pages) of those pages were indexed. Pages that are not indexed stay invisible to search engines. Today, the web has over 17 billion web pages. Although only approximately 18% of those pages are indexed, the number of searchable pages has increased to over 3 billion web pages!

The increase in the size of the indexed web pages is just one example of the tremendous and fast pace of technology development that is affecting every phase of our lives and, of course, our educational practice. More and more technologies are introduced (software and hardware) providing the vehicles and tools through which excellence in teaching and learning may occur.

Statesmen, legislators, business leaders, parents, and educators are constantly advocating the infusion of technology in education. *The CEO Forum on Education and Technology* (2000) stated: "As part of our efforts at school reform, we should apply technology's resources to develop the full academic abilities of all our students."

Professional organizations interested in studying requirements for teaching certifications have recognized literacy in technology as an essential standard for teaching certification. Standards for technology-literate students have also been developed and practiced by many schools.

In light of recent studies, educational technology developments, and emerging educational needs of the twenty-first century, the chapters in the new edition have been revised and updated. A new section on children and youth's safety on the Internet was added, and a new chapter on television in education was introduced.

In the preface to the first edition (1999), I wrote: "Prior to the accelerated evolution of information technologies, educators advocated the need for individualized, flexible, interactive, interdisciplinary and up-to-date learning environments in which students control their own learning—necessary conditions to enable students to become educated persons. However, with reliance on textbooks and audiovisual supplements it was difficult, if not impossible, to implement such progressive educational practices. Today, the new learning and telecommunications technologies can help realize educators' pedagogical dreams." Five years later, that statement is still true; teachers are required to infuse technology in their teaching.

Ibrahim M. Hefzallah

PREFACE TO FIRST EDITION

As the world prepares to enter the 21st Century, the goal of education has become more focused than ever on cultivating truly educated persons. On the threshold of a new millennium, the drive for educational reform should not be propelled by business needs only. Emphasis should also be put on graduating people who can deal with change in our world— a change that is accelerated by the technologies of the Information Age. An *Educated Person* in this Age is one who is capable of maintaining a high quality of life, and of contributing to the betterment of the community and the world as a whole.

Information technologies have proven to be a significant advantage to the teaching/learning process. Developments in these technologies provide more powerful and versatile applications in education. One can look at our current era as the golden era of technology in education. Never before have educators had the wide and effective range of instructional and telecommunications technologies that are available to them and their students in and out of class. Educators have at hand very efficient tools to structure learning environments conducive to achieving the goal of education: the cultivation of the *Educated Person*.

Prior to the accelerated evolution of information technologies, educators advocated the need for individualized, flexible, interactive, interdisciplinary and up-to-date learning environments in which students control their own learning—necessary conditions to enable students to become educated persons. However, with reliance on textbooks and audiovisual supplements it was difficult, if not impossible, to implement such progressive educational practices. Today, the new learning and telecommunications technologies can help realize educators' pedagogical dreams.

This book examines these new learning and telecommunications technologies and their potential applications to enrich the learning process, to ensure educational equality for all students and to help cultivate the *Educated Person*.

Ibrahim M. Hefzallah

ENVIRONMENT, REFORM, TECHNOLOGY, AND TWENTY-FIRST CENTURY CHALLENGE

"We never educate directly, but indirectly by means of the environment."

John Dewey

"I have learned to undertake reform of the environment and not to try to reform man."

Buckminster Fuller

"We are unlikely to obtain the schools we want until we take greater advantage of the power of modern technology and its appeal to youth."

Howard D. Mehlinger

"Our economic survival and leadership in the free democratic world rest on the educated individuals of our nation. The need to achieve excellence in education and educational equity for everyone is urgent. Only when our quest is multilateral and targets the student as a whole person will we realize excellence in education."

Ibrahim M. Hefzallah

INTRODUCTION

Since man perceived the need to educate the young, educational goals and practices have been examined to assess the efficiency of the educational system. As a result, different views of educational reform have emerged. These views reflect the values and aspirations of those who express them, as well as their perception of the economic, social, political, national, and international conditions of the time. However, the road to educational reform has many paths, and one must consider a broad range of educated points of view to formulate a comprehensive vision of the goal of educational reform. Reforming education should not be driven by business needs only. It also should target the cultivation of well-rounded educated persons. Education for earning and education for learning are two sides of one coin, which form the goal of education: the cultivation of the *educated person.*

Since we educate by means of the environment, special attention must be given to the design of learning environments conducive to the cultivation of the educated person. An essential element of that design is ensuring the learner's interactivity with models of excellence, both in human resources and in learning materials. Fortunately, the technology of the information age provides students and teachers with the tools and vehicles through which models of excellence can be accessed.

This book is divided into four sections: *Education in the Information Age, The Learning Environment, The New Learning and Telecommunications Technologies*, and *Necessary Conditions for Effective Utilization of the New Learning and Telecommunications Technologies.*

Section I examines the need for educational reform, the goal of that reform, and the role of technology in realizing that goal.

Section II addresses the significance of the learning environment and the necessary conditions for providing teachers and students with access to models of excellence in human resources and in learning materials.

Section III presents the new learning and telecommunications technologies with emphasis placed on their potential applications in education.

Section IV focuses on necessary conditions conducive to the empowerment of the teachers to teach and the students to learn in the Information Age. Among these conditions are the cultivation of technology-literate teachers, technology-literate students, and effective school media specialists.

I.M.H.

CONTENTS

SECTION III—THE NEW LEARNING
AND TELECOMMUNICATIONS TECHNOLOGIES

Part One—Computers In Education

Part Four—Video Telecommunications

Part Five—Distance Education

SECTION IV—EFFECTIVE UTILIZATION OF THE NEW LEARNING AND TELECOMMUNICATIONS TECHNOLOGIES

THE NEW EDUCATIONAL
TECHNOLOGIES AND LEARNING

SECTION I

EDUCATION IN THE INFORMATION AGE

Chapter 1: Educational Reform
Chapter 2: The Educated Person in the Information Age

INTRODUCTION

Chapter 1, "Educational Reform," addresses the need for a comprehensive view of educational reform. It reviews various studies focusing on reforming education and presents the goal of educational reform as the cultivation of the "educated person."

Chapter 2, "The Educated Person in the Information Age," examines the basic characteristics of the modern age in an attempt to identify the qualities that an educated person should possess. Identifying these qualities is essential to the effective design of learning environments conducive to the achievement of these qualities.

Chapter 1

EDUCATIONAL REFORM

THE NEED FOR A COMPREHENSIVE VIEW OF EDUCATIONAL REFORM

Since man perceived the need to educate the young, educational goals and practices have been examined to assess the efficiency of the educational system. As a result, different views of educational reform have emerged. These views reflect the values and aspirations of those who express them, as well as their perception of the economic, social, political, national, and international conditions of the time.

Toward the end of the twentieth century, various studies and reports addressed the need for educational reform. One major report was the 1982 National Science Foundation's *Today's Problems, Tomorrow's Crises.* In this report, the National Science Foundation (NSF) alerted the nation to potential crises resulting from citizens not being prepared to participate fully in the technological world:

> We appear to be raising a generation of Americans, many of whom lack the understanding and the skills necessary to participate fully in the technological world in which they live and work. Improved preparation of all citizens in the fields of mathematics, science, and technology is essential to the development and maintenance of our nation's economic strength, military security, commitment to the democratic ideal of an informed and participating citizenry, and leadership in mathematics, science, and technology.[1]

In 1985 and 1992, The National Center for Education Statistics (NCES) conducted assessments of adult literacy. (A 2003 study, *The National Assessment of Adult Literacy* [NAAL], is under way[2]). The 1992 study indicated that almost half of the American adult population was much less likely to respond correctly to the more challenging literacy tasks that require higher-level reading and problem-solving skills.[3]

Proficiency scores of young adults who participated in the 1985 literacy survey were higher than the 1992's scores. The *National Adult Literacy Survey* (NALS) study suggested that this might be due to changes in the demographic composition of the population with an increase in the percentage of participants who learned English as a second language.[4]

The study referred to a current report from the American Society for Training and Development, which indicated that those individuals with poor skills "are condemned to low earnings and limited choices."[5] The 1992 data appeared to support this view. The report indicated that,

> On each of the literacy scales, adults whose proficiencies were within the two lowest levels were far less likely than their more literate peers to be employed full-time, to earn high wages, and to vote. Moreover, they were far more likely to receive food stamps, to be in poverty, and to rely on non-print sources (such as radio and television) for information about current events, public affairs, and government.[6]

Commenting on the study findings, Madeleine M. Kunin, former Deputy Secretary of Education said,

> The overall education level of Americans has increased in terms of schooling and even in fundamental literacy. But the demands of the workplace simultaneously have vastly increased. We simply are not keeping pace with the kinds of skills required in today's economy.[7]

Suffering from a workforce with a poor level of literacy, businesses estimated, then, "that they lose between $25 billion to $30 billion a year nationwide in lost productivity, errors and accidents attributable to poor literacy."[8] Driven by the need for employable and productive workers, businesses have been assuming assertive roles in education. These roles include adopting a school, offering training opportunities to students, providing teaching expertise to schools, donating money and/or equipment, and maintaining comprehensive training and development programs within their organizations. Davis, et al. (1994) noticed that Motorola spent $120 million dollars a year on employee education.[9]

No Child Left Behind Act 2001

Driven by the need to reform education, President Bush signed into law on January 8, 2002 the *No Child Left Behind Act of 2001*. The Act redefines the federal role in K–12 education. "It is based on four basic principles: stronger accountability for results, increased flexibility and local control, expanded options for parents, and an emphasis on teaching methods that have been proven to work."[10]

The Act emphasizes:

1. Support of learning in the early years to prevent learning difficulties that may arise later.
2. Providing more information for parents about their child's progress and important information on the performance of their child's school.

3. Providing parents options to ensure that their children receive high-quality education in the event of a school's continued poor performance. That might mean that children can transfer to higher-performing schools in the area or receive supplemental educational services in the community, such as tutoring, after-school programs or remedial classes.
4. Hiring and employment of qualified teachers.
5. Measuring students' learning in English, mathematics, and science.
6. Providing more resources to schools, and focusing on what works.[11]

The *No Child Left Behind* (NCLB) Act states that American schools are not producing the science and math excellence required for global economic leadership and homeland security in the twenty-first century.[12,13] Explaining that claim, NCLB referred to the 2000 National Assessment of Educational Progress (NAEP) science test that revealed that 82% of our nation's 12th graders performed below the professional level.[14] In math, although the average math scores of 4th and 8th graders have slightly improved, still only one-fourth of our 4th and 8th graders are performing at or above proficient levels.[15]

The NCLB Act considers reading, writing, and speaking English to be at the root of any success an individual could achieve in society. However, only one-third of 4th graders are able to read at a proficient level.[16] The 2000 NAEP reading assessment showed that 40% of white 4th graders scored at or above proficient level compared to 12% of their African American peers, 16% of their Hispanic peers, and 17% of their Native American peers.[17–19]

Level of Students' Achievement and Employment

"Evidence strongly suggests that students who fail to read on grade level by the fourth grade have a greater likelihood of dropping out of school and a lifetime of diminished success," NCLB stated.[20] Correlation between level of education and a higher standard of living is also indicated in the U.S. Department of Education and the NCES *Digest of Education Statistics, 2000.* The digest reports:

> Adults with higher levels of education were more likely to participate in the labor force (including those who were employed and those actively seeking employment) than those with less education. About 79 percent of adults, 25 years old and over with a bachelor's or higher degree, participated in the labor force in 2001 compared with 64 percent of persons who had completed high school. In contrast, 44 percent of those 25 and older, who were not high school completers, were in the labor force.[21]

For ages 20 to 24, the picture is similar to those who are 25 years of age and older. About 85% of adults 20 to 24 years old with a bachelor's or higher degree participated in the labor force in 2001 compared with 81% who had completed high school and 70% of those who had not completed high school.[22] The correlation between unemployment and lower level of attainment is reported as follows:

> Persons with lower levels of educational attainment were more likely to be unemployed than those who had higher levels of educational attainment. The 2001 unemployment rate for adults (25 years old and over) who had not completed high school was 7.3 percent compared with 4.2 percent for those with 4 years of high school and 2.3 percent for those with a bachelor's degree or higher. Younger people with high school diplomas tended to have higher unemployment rates than persons 25 years old and over with similar levels of education. Four years after graduating from college in 1992–1993, 89 percent of individuals receiving bachelor's degrees were employed (81 percent full time and 8 percent part time), 2.7 percent were unemployed, and 8.1 percent were not in the labor force.[23]

Moreover, the correlation between level of educational attainment and participation in voting is evidenced by the NCES, *The Condition of Education, 2003.* The report states, "The more education people have, the more likely they are to vote in presidential and congressional elections. Thirty-eight percent of U.S. voting-age citizens who had not completed high school voted in 2000, compared with 77 percent of those with a bachelor's degree or higher."[24]

To raise the educational standards of K–12 students, NCLB has setup key performance goals for states:

- All students will be taught by highly qualified teachers by 2005–2006.
- All students will attain "proficiency" in reading and mathematics by 2014, including students with disabilities and English learners.
- All English learners will become proficient in English.
- All students will learn in schools that are safe and drug free.
- All students will graduate from high school.[25]

In the words of President Bush,

> ". . . the *No Child Left Behind Act* requires every state in our country to submit an accountability plan that leads to measurable gains in student performance. . . . The era of low expectations and low standards is ending; a time of great hopes and proven results is arriving. . . . Under the *No Child Left Behind Act*, every student in this country will be held to high standards, and every school will be held accountable for results. Teachers will get the training they need to help their students achieve. Parents will get the information and choices they need to make sure their children are learning. And together we will bring the promise of quality education to every child in America."[26]

Making Schools Accountable for Results

NCLB requires each state to establish its own:

1. Unique set of standards for reading, math, and science.
2. Annual tests aligned with state standards for grades three through eight to measure how successfully students are learning what is expected by the standards.[27]

The Act's dual incentive to schools is, first, "taxpayers dollars will only go to states that have standards and expectations for improving schools or teaching a solid academic curriculum."[28]

Second, under the Act parents have options to ensure that their children receive high-quality education. In the event of a school's poor performance, parents could transfer their children to a higher performing school in the area or see to their children's receiving supplemental educational services such as after-school tutoring.[29]

Comments on No Child Left Behind Act of 2001

Projected Effects of Testing on Educational Practice

There is concern that emphasis placed on testing might force teachers to teach their students to pass tests. Teaching, then, will be characterized by drill and practice to prepare the students for testing while due attention is not given to crucial aspects of educating the whole person.

The fear is that schools will emphasize the subjects in which their students are tested and deemphasize or neglect other subjects that are needed for comprehensive educational programs. Addressing the need for developing students' economic and financial literacy, the National Summit on Economic and Financial Literacy, May 13–14, 2002, noted:

> Economic education wording is included in the Education Bill, *No Child Left Behind*, signed by President Bush. Title V: Innovative Education Programs provides for funds to be made available to local educational agencies to be used for programs that may include the following: ". . . activities to promote consumer, economic, and personal finance education, such as disseminating information on and encouraging use of best practices for teaching the basic principles of economics and promoting the concept of achieving financial literacy through the teaching of personal financial management skills, including the basic principles involved with earning, spending, saving and investing.
>
> How will this be accomplished? In today's environment it is difficult to add courses to the school curriculum except in language arts, mathematics and science.[30]

One also fears that schools will hesitate experimenting with new teaching strategies that could have the benefits of educating the students beyond the basic skills required to pass state tests. An example of creative and innovative teaching strategies that foster students' interest in learning and at the same time prepare the students to pass state tests is "Environmental Literacy." Michele L. Archie (2003) of The Harbinger Institute, explained how linking the environment to education could just achieve the dual goal of helping students to pass state exams and assume their societal responsibilities. In her words:

> As education reform efforts continue, substantial agreement is emerging about what to teach in our schools. Education reform experts have identified essential content and skills. In large part through the process of developing national and state educational standards for the core academic disciplines, as well as state assessments that measure student performance. For the most part, these assessments are designed to measure not only students' knowledge of facts, but also their ability to write well, think critically, solve problems, and integrate knowledge.
>
> Now the question in the forefront of many educators' minds is how best to teach. Which instructional strategies will best help students gain the knowledge and skills that will prepare them to pass state exams and meet the demands of future schooling, jobs, and societal responsibilities? How can curricula, school days, and teacher responsibilities best be organized to support this essential knowledge?
>
> Many educators and schools are answering these questions by linking education and the environment.[31]

Gene R. Carte, executive director of the Association for Supervision and Curriculum Development explained the value of environmental literacy and what it means.

> In today's world, environmental literacy is not a luxury. Simply defined, environmental literacy means understanding how human decisions and actions affect environmental quality as well as using that understanding as the basis for responsible and effective citizenship. Increasingly, people are asked to grapple with decisions ranging from land-use zoning to consumer choices that can affect air and water quality. Personal choice and societal policies have consequences for the natural world. People need the knowledge and skills to seek sound decisions that maintain public health and the quality of the environment. Students must be prepared for those responsibilities, as well.[32]

Meeting Standards Naturally is a CD-ROM featuring free activities focusing on promoting academic excellence and environmental literacy. They focus on a wide range of subject matter areas including social studies, language arts, mathematics, fine arts, science, and health. "This broad focus speaks to the diversity of educators who are using the environments as a focal point for top-quality education."[33]

Developing teaching strategies such as the one just described helps achieve four major objectives of today's education. First, it helps the students to learn the skills set up by experts that are needed to live a functional life in the twenty-first century. Second, it helps establish interesting and exciting learning environments that would eventually lead to the development of life-long learners. Third, it provides the students with up-to-date information required for assuming intelligent citizenry. Fourth, in the process of achieving the preceding points they develop the required skills to pass state tests.

The Need to Emphasize Development of Values in Education

Satisfactory attainment of reading, writing, speaking, mathematical, and scientific skills are definitely needed for a successful life. However, as stated earlier, they are not enough. Developing values and proper attitudes toward self and society is the second side of that coin. The following incident illustrates the struggle that bright students might face in their competition to excel. Sara Rimer (2003) in her *New York Times* article, "Finding That Today's Students Are Bright, Eager and Willing to Cheat," reported:

As a high school student working in a university professor's neurobiology laboratory, a 17-year-old Manhattan girl endorsed a strong code of scientific values. Honesty was essential, she said.

But she also wanted to be a winner in the fiercely competitive Intel Science Talent Search. She had been told that the judges did not look favorably on experiments involving live mice. So when she presented the findings of her experiment on estrogen and learning, she concealed the fact that she had worked with live mice.

"Maybe it was wrong, lying, in a way," she said. "But I didn't think that it was wrong because I deserved to be rewarded." She was rewarded: she was an Intel semifinalist, won a college scholarship and got into an Ivy League university, where she plans to pursue scientific research.

The Manhattan student was one of more than 100 promising young scientists, journalists and stage actors interviewed by Harvard researchers in a study of how young professionals perform and think about their work. The researchers, directed by Howard Gardner, a Harvard professor of cognition and education, asked probing questions about their subjects' goals and aspirations, their strategies for overcoming obstacles and their mentors and values.

One finding was that the Manhattan student was not unusual. A number of the other people 15 to 35 acknowledged a willingness to compromise their values and to cut corners ethically and professionally to advance their careers. They said they knew right from wrong and intended to follow a strict code of values after they gained power and authority.

"We might be tempted to say they've lost their moral compass," Professor Gardner said. "But it's probably better to say that their teachers and mentors and the rest of society never helped them construct and internalize a moral compass in the first place."[34]

A COMPREHENSIVE EDUCATIONAL REFORM GOAL

The question now becomes how can we emphasize a proper value system and provide for K–12 students to proficiently attain needed information and skills in a variety of subject matters? The answer to this crucial question is threefold:

1. Insightful revision of school curricula to eliminate unnecessary items and to maximize the implementation of integrated and noncompartmentalized information taught in K–12.
2. Design teaching strategies so that students learn more, learn it more efficiently, retain it longer, and apply it more effectively.* All of this should happen within the K–12 period; and
3. Adopting the goal of education as the cultivation of the educated person.

Revision of school curricula is beyond the scope of this book. Designing teaching strategies is within the scope of this book since it addresses a variety of information technologies and their potential applications to enrich learning environments conducive to the cultivation of the educated person, the goal of educational reform.

THE EDUCATED PERSON—A DEFINITION

The drive for reforming education should not be driven by earning needs only. It should target, as well, the cultivation of well-rounded persons. Education for earning and education for learning are two sides of one coin, which form the goal of education: the cultivation of the educated person.

An educated person is a self life-long learner. There is not a limit to what an educated person would learn, since learning becomes synonymous with living. The following are basic merits an educated person possesses:

1. An educated person rejoices in discovering new facts and learning new material, in always recognizing learning as a lifelong process, and in seeing formal education as a foundation upon which further self-education will occur.

---

*This is in line with the 4th basic principle of the NCLB, "emphasis on teaching methods that have been proven to work."

2. An educated person develops the ability to examine change carefully and objectively.

3. An educated person has also articulated values, paramount to which is deep concern for freedom and justice for all, and love of mankind.

4. An educated person has compassion toward other people, respecting all individuals and finding delight in communicating with fellow men. He or she takes the time to express joy for others' joy and concern for their problems.

5. An educated person defines *community* not only in parochial terms but also in global terms.

6. An educated person takes care of mind, body, and spirit.

TECHNOLOGY AND THE CULTIVATION OF THE EDUCATED PERSON

Cultivation of the educated person ought to be the prime goal of education. The application of instructional technology has to aim at achieving that goal. In many teaching situations, technology is treated as an afterthought or as an addition to a teaching plan that could be executed without the use of technology.

Instructional technology should not be an afterthought, nor is it a fad. It is firmly grounded in educational technology. Educational technology is a technology of the mind, which may or may not use hardware or a highly technical teaching strategy to achieve the stated goals of education. It requires systematic planning based on our knowledge of human learning.[35] It examines accessible communication and information technologies to determine those most appropriate for the achievement of the desired objective in a cost-effective manner. It considers the unique characteristics of each technology, the purpose of using it, with whom it will be used, and under what circumstances. Under no circumstances should technology be used just for the sake of using technology. We must keep the goal of education always in focus.

Visionaries believe that formal education should be structured to energize learners to learn. Alfred North Whitehead (1955) wrote,

The justification for a university is that it preserves the connection between knowledge and the zest of life, by uniting the young and the old in the imaginative consideration of learning. The university imparts information, but it imparts it imaginatively. At least, this is the function, which it should perform for society ... this atmosphere of excitement, arising from imaginative consideration, transforms knowledge. A fact is no longer a bare fact: it is invested with all its possibilities. It is no longer a burden on the memory: it is energizing as the poet of our dreams, and as the architect of our purposes.[36]

To energize learners to learn we should take into consideration the individual's multiple intelligence profile and his or her learning style. This would require the application of a variety of learning materials packaged in different formats.

Reflecting on the future task of the teacher, Dale (1969) observed that it would be "more complicated, more challenging, more professional, more worthy of respect. The new curriculum demands more thinking by teachers and students and will result in less deadening routine."[37] He anticipated greater range in choice of instructional materials and concluded "the teacher must learn how to use new media as a part of a modern learning system, not merely to enrich or supplement methods."[38]

Sound applications of information technologies can help achieve the school reform that we all seek. In addressing school reform in the information age, Howard D. Mehlinger (1993) indicated that "we are unlikely to obtain the schools we want until we take greater advantage of the power of modern technology and its appeal to youth."[39] He further explained, "When thinking about schools of the future, it is difficult to imagine a vision of schooling that ignores the role that computers, video and other technology will play in shaping our system of education."[40]

In the field of educational technology, we have come a long way from emphasizing a variety of learning materials to providing for individual differences in learning styles and aptitudes, to the creation of an interactive, flexible, and rich in resources learning environment. A flexible, rich, and interactive learning environment engages the student in a self-rewarding learning experience in which the student discovers the joy of self-learning. Moreover, learning with and about information technologies provides the learner with the survival tools needed for efficient living in the Age of Information. Mehlinger explained:

> It is . . . a time of global communication and relatively inexpensive, rapid transportation, permitting multinational corporations to produce goods abroad and transport them for sale in the United States less expensively, in some cases, than to produce them here. If the future requires that people be able to operate successfully in such an environment, how can any credible vision of future schooling ignore the tools and skills required to work in such settings?[41]

CONCLUSION

There is an urgent need to reform education. The goal of that reform is the cultivation of the educated person who not only is capable of earning a decent living in the information age but also is capable of becoming a caring citizen. Information technologies can provide essential components of a learning environment conducive to the achievement of this goal and, at the same time, educate the student in the use of information age tools for self-development and actualization.

REFERENCES

1. National Science Board, National Science Foundation. *Today's Problems Tomorrow's Crises*, A Report of the National Science Board Commission on Pre-college Education in Mathematics, Science and Technology, Washington, D.C., 1982, p. 1.
2. NCES, NAAL 2003: Overview, http://nces.ed.gov/naal/design/about02.asp, downloaded 7/7/03.
3. U.S. Department of Education, Office of Educational Research and Improvement (OERI), National Center for Education Statistics. *Adult Literacy in America, A First Look at the Results of the National Adult Literacy Survey*, Stock No. 065-000-00588-3, September 1993, p. 18.
4. *Ibid.* p. 19.
5. *Ibid.* p. 22.
6. *Ibid.* p. 22.
7. William Celis, 3rd, *The New York Times*, Thursday, September 9, 1993, pp. A1, A22.
8. *Ibid.*
9. Davis, Stanely. *Monster under the Bed.* New York: Simon & Schuster, 1994. p. 16.
10. *No Child Left Behind Act of 2001*, http://www.ed.gov/offices/OESE/esea/, the page was modified July 11, 2002, downloaded 7/6/03.
11. Introduction and Overview: *No Child Left Behind*, http://www.nochildleftbehind.gov/next/overview/index.html, pp. 3–5, downloaded 7/6/03.
12. No Child Left Behind, The Facts About . . . Science Achievement, http://www.nochildleftbehind.gov/start/facts/science.html, p. one, downloaded 7/6/03.
13. No Child Left Behind, The Facts About . . . Math Achievement, http://www.nochildleftbehind.gov/start/facts/math.html, p. one, downloaded 7/6/03.
14. No Child Left Behind, The Facts About . . . Science Achievement, *op.cit.*
15. No Child Left Behind, The Facts About . . . Math Achievement, *op.cit.*
16. No Child Left Behind, The Facts About . . . Reading Achievement, http://www.nochildleftbehind.gov/start/facts/reading.html, p. one, downloaded 7/6/03.
17. No Child Left Behind, Reaching Out . . . Raising African American Achievement, http://www.nochildleftbehind.gov/start/facts/achievement_aa.html, p. one, downloaded 7/6/03.
18. No Child Left Behind, Reaching Out . . . Raising Hispanic Achievement, http://www.nochildleftbehind.gov/start/facts/achievement_hisp.html, p. one, downloaded 7/6/03.
19. No Child Left Behind, Reaching Out . . . Raising American Indian Achievement, http://www.nochildleftbehind.gov/start/facts/achievement_native.html, p. one, downloaded 7/6/03.

20. No Child Left Behind, The Facts About . . . Reading Achievement, op. cit.

21. U.S. Department of Education, National Center for Education Statistics. *Digest of Education Statistics, 2002,* NCES 2003–060, by Thomas D. Snyder. Washington, D.C.: 2003. pp. 441–442.

22. *Ibid.* p. 442.

23. *Ibid.* p. 441.

24. U.S. Department of Education, National Center for Education Statistics. *The Condition of Education 2003,* NCES 2003-067.Washington, D.C., 2003, p. vi.

25. No Child Left Behind, State of California, http://www.cde.ca.gov/pr/nclb.background.html, downloaded 7/4/03.

26. President Highlights Progress in Education, Reform Remarks by the President on the No Child Left Behind Act, The Rose Garden, June 10, 2003, http://www.whitehouse.gov/news/releases/2003/06/200306_10-4.html, p. one, downloaded 6/25/03.

27. *Ibid.*

28. *Ibid.*

29. Introduction and Overview: *No Child Left Behind,* http://www.nochildleftbehind.gov/next/overview/index.html, 3 of 5, downloaded 7/6/03.

30. *Ibid,* p. 1.

31. Archie, Michele L. *Advancing Education through Environmental Literacy,* Alexandria, Virginia: Association for Supervision and Curriculum Development, 2003, p. 5.

32. *Ibid.* p. 4.

33. *Ibid.*

34. Sara Rimer, "Finding That Today's Students are Brighter, Eager and Willing to Cheat, *The New York Times,* June 2, 2003.

35. Association for Educational Communications and Technology, *Educational Technology Definition & Glossary of Terms,* Volume 1, Washington, D.C., 1977, pp. 164–165.

36. Whitehead, Alfred North. *Aims of Education,* New York: A Mentor Book, 1955, p. 97.

37. Dale, Edgar, *Audiovisual Methods in Teaching,* 3rd ed., New York: The Dryden Press, 1969, p. 6

38. *Ibid.* p. 6.

39. Mehlinger, Howard D. *School Reform in the Information Age,* Bloomington, IN: Center for Excellence in Education, Indiana University, 1993, p. v.

40. *Ibid.* p. 6.

41. *Ibid.* p. 7.

Chapter 2

THE EDUCATED PERSON IN
THE INFORMATION AGE

INTRODUCTION

In designing effective learning environments, it is imperative to examine the world in which the individual will live. Identifying basic characteristics of the world today helps clarify the qualities that an educated person should possess; hence, we can identify the specific goals of education in the information age. Once we identify these goals, learning environments designed to achieve these goals could be designed using the technologies of the information age.

BASIC CHARACTERISTICS OF THE MODERN AGE

Accelerated Rate of Scientific Developments

Scientific research extends to all fields of human knowledge and activities. It advances at an accelerated rate because of improvements in research tools and in methods of storing, sorting, analyzing, and sharing information. For instance, the computer has become an indispensable tool of research in all fields of knowledge. Computers facilitate conducting research, analyzing data, and storing and retrieving information with tremendous savings of time. The potential use of computers to link people together and to provide them with access to information when they need it led to the development of the Internet. The Internet revolutionized how information can be stored, sorted, accessed, shared, and distributed. Comparing the Internet to the printing press, Stanek and Purcell, et al. (1995) wrote:

Five centuries ago the printing press with movable type brought society past an impasse with elitist control of knowledge and caused a revolution. It made possible the spread of knowledge to anyone with a passion to learn, and what is more important, it gave society an information base independent of a limited number of scholars. Today, the Internet is again causing a revolution in the way knowledge and information can be accessed.[1]

Dale (1969) observed that

> . . . scientists and other specialists have produced ideas faster than they are being communicated, absorbed, and applied. Hence there is an increasing gap between what is known and what is done. Not only are there more ideas than ever before, but they are complex.[2]

To meet the challenge of the vast growing body of knowledge, Dale advocated, "As teachers or as students we must learn more, learn it more efficiently, remember it better, and apply it more effectively."[3] With today's technology tools and rich learning resources that both teachers and students have at the their command, the likelihood that students will learn more, learn it more efficiently, remember it better, and apply it more effectively is much greater than a few decades ago prior to the information age. School curricula have to be restructured to assist students in becoming self-learners and to develop their abilities to search for information and to judge its validity and appropriateness to the learning task at hand. When the school emphasizes self-learning and research skills, learning will extend beyond the regular school day.

Access to information from homes is increasing, with more families realizing the importance of tapping the Internet's wealth of information. The U.S., Department of Education, National Center for Education Statistics (NCES) reports:

> Sizable percentages of students in 2001 used computers at home, though fewer actually used them for school work. In 2001, 66% of elementary and secondary school students used computers at home, compared to 43% in 1997. During the same period of time, the proportion of students using computers at home for school work rose from 25 to 45%.[4]

Availability and use of computers at home is associated with income. "About 64% of students from families with an income of $75,000 or more used a computer at home for schoolwork compared to 28% of students from families with incomes of $20,000 to $24,999."[5] Alternative ways for providing computer access after school hours to students with no access at home should be studied by every community. As businesses, government offices, colleges, and schools upgrade their computers, the discarded ones could be just enough for doing grades K to 12–related information-seeking projects. Other options are providing public libraries with more terminals and extending the hours of the school library to accommodate students who lack access to computers and the Internet from their homes.

Accessibility to technologies of information is one issue that is not difficult to solve, especially since the cost of new technologies is dropping everyday. NCES reported on the growing base of information technologies
facilities in schools. It stated:

> There has been widespread introduction of computers into the schools in
> recent years. In 2001, the average public school contained 124 instructional
> computers. One important technological advance that has come to schools
> following the introduction of computers has been connections to the
> Internet. The proportion of instructional rooms with Internet access
> increased from 50 percent in 1998 to 85 percent in 2001. About 99 percent
> of schools had access to the Internet in 2001. The proportion of elementary
> and secondary school students using computers at school rose from 70 per-
> cent in 1997 to 84 percent in 2001. Students in elementary and secondary
> schools who were 10 years old or older were more likely to use computers at
> school than younger children. Schools provided access to computers for
> most students.[6]

The real issue facing the efficient use of technologies of instruction in
education is twofold: restructuring school curricula and training teachers in
creative methods of teaching in which information technologies are
infused. Schools should urgently address this issue. Lack of equipment no
longer hinders the use of technologies in instruction. What may be hindering the use of new technologies is the outdated curricula and the lack of
understanding of how technology can be infused in teaching.

Education for Change

Sharing information is greatly facilitated by advances in telecommunication and information processing and dissemination technologies. For
instance, satellite, terrestrial, and telephone communications have diminished the distance between researchers. Instant interaction and sharing
information is not limited to face-to-face communication. Mediated conferences employing both audio and visual elements surmount the geographical separation between researchers and provide channels of
communication for sharing information. The Internet has become a major
source of information that people all over the world can share. It also has
become a medium of interaction among people in delayed or real time
through e-mail, web pages, instant messaging, and web conferencing.

Sharing information facilitates further developments. Scientific, economic, psychological, and educational theories are constantly introduced
and tested. New learning disciplines and new careers are emerging. A few
years back the life cycle of an individual was equivalent to preparation for
and assuming a career. Today retraining and retooling are musts in the
working lifetime of an individual. As Winston Hindle (1983) explained,

> We can almost guarantee that a person we hire today will not be performing the same job in five years, or even two years in many cases. The problem is that the working lifetime of our employees is not very much greater than the development and support lifetimes of our products. . . . Right now a typical employee in industry or in business can look forward to a career that consists of cycles with alternating periods of training and productive contributions.[7]

Today, the frequency of training-productive contributions is much higher than 20 years ago.

Change is synonymous with life. When change is accelerated, our survival will depend on education, which will prepare individuals to deal with change. According to Carl Rogers (1969):

> We are, in my view, faced with an entirely new situation in education where the goal of education, if we are to survive, is the facilitation of change and learning. The only man who is educated is the man who has learned how to learn; the man who has learned to adapt and change; the man who realized that no knowledge is secure, that only the process of seeking knowledge gives a basis for security. Changingness, a reliance on process rather than upon static knowledge, is the only thing that makes any sense as a goal for education in the modern world.[8]

As we educate ourselves for living in the twenty-first century, we must develop an ability to recognize and examine change. Not every change is desirable. Objective analysis of a change in terms of its total effect on human lives, human interaction, justice, freedom, and the fulfillment of a happy and content life for all can result in fostering, diverting, or opposing that change.

Serious World Problems

Environmental pollution, deterioration of values, inflation, world hunger, terrorism, spread of Aids, and military confrontations are some of the problems that need immediate attention of the world community. An educated person is able to address these problems and exert the necessary efforts toward their alleviation. It is beyond the scope of this publication to address all of these problems as they relate to the cultivation of the educated person. For the sake of giving an example, one problem only, world hunger is briefly addressed.

As a result of scientific developments and the discovery of antibiotics and immunization, infant mortality has decreased and the average life span of the individual has increased. There is an alarming increase in the world's population, especially in Third World nations, where supplying adequate food and jobs is particularly challenging.

While the population increase is a serious problem for developing nations, it is the responsibility of developed nations to help alleviate the problem. We are all living on one planet as the family of man. Interests of nations overlap as the human race strives for world peace. Peace cannot be built while members of poor nations are hungry for the basic foods needed to survive. Four avenues can be followed by developed nations to help solve that problem. First, help developing nations to develop their economic infrastructure that would lead to increasing national productivity and creating more jobs for their citizens. Second, help developing nations establish a national policy to preserve and increase their national resources. Third, set an example of how they can respect national resources and not destroy them. Fourth, provide food for areas suffering from acute shortages in food supplies.

Education can help prepare today's youth for this by developing in them the following:

1. An understanding of the world's hunger problem and sensitivity toward helping the unfortunate populations.
2. A concept of "a neighbor" to include all human beings on earth and not just our fellow citizens.
3. A respect for natural resources and the environment.
4. A commitment to leave the world in better shape than when they came in for future generations to enjoy. This entails developing their understanding of how natural resources can be used without harming their inherent ability to renew themselves.

Technology and the Changing Family Lifestyle

"Football widow" is a colloquial phrase used to denote a married woman whose husband watches long hours of telecast football games. "Computer widow" is a relatively new phrase coined in 1980s to refer to a wife whose husband has become a computer addict, spending a great deal of time with the computer. Both phrases simply point to a very important fact. When technology enters the home, especially at an early stage of that technology, family lives are affected. As time passes and the product proves to be apparently useful, people develop a strong, close relationship with the product. For instance, people have developed very strong ties with TV. A TV set is usually placed where it can be easily seen and comfortably watched, occupying a prominent place in living rooms, family rooms, playrooms, bedrooms, and even in the kitchen. It has become the new fireplace around which the family gathers. Watching television has become a ritual, during which certain conduct is expected of individuals viewing a program with a group of people. With some programs people watching together have to be quiet in order to follow the program. Comments about the program, if any, might be shared after its conclusion.

Just as the presence of a technology product can affect family life and family dynamics, changes in society and in the world may also have an effect. For example, in some families where both spouses are working to maintain a desirable standard of living, young children might be spending less time with their parents than in earlier generations.

In preparing young people for happy, productive lives, we must teach them about families. One thing that stays fresh in my memory is my experience in producing a six-part television series on families in 1985 with Fairfield University's Media Center. As the series producer, I was moved as we examined a single-parent family as well as families with a handicapped, mentally retarded, learning-disabled or gifted child. The love and concern that each member of these families demonstrated for each other under difficult circumstances was heartwarming. Observing families such as these can teach us important lessons—lessons that could greatly benefit young people, especially with the distorted image they see so often in television programs. An educated person has developed an appreciation of family dynamics and of family members' demonstrated caring, love, and mutual respect.

Increased Automation

Understanding the Limitation of Automation

Automation can help make life much easier. It can eliminate the mundane efforts one might spend in performing one function or another. It can speed up communication between people, and it can shorten the physical distance between people. It can increase the speed and efficiency with which a service is offered. Automation, however, has its limitations and sometimes its drawbacks.

Computers are as good as the programs that run them. Certainly the advances in computer technology are going to improve the efficiency and the ease of using computers, but they are still only machines. They can break down and cause problems.

People seem to find it easier to grasp the advantages that machinery and automation offer than the associated limitations and dangers. Cell phones are wonderful for staying in touch regardless of where we are; however, one must observe a certain etiquette in using them in enclosed public places such as restaurants. There is a limit to how much one may expose people trying to relax to one-sided conversation. More dangerous is their use while one is driving a car. When we do that, we are overestimating our ability to concentrate on driving and at the same time carry on a conversation on the phone. More terrifying is dialing a number when one is driving. This constitutes a form of reckless driving. When people drive recklessly, they are putting more trust than they should in the car and in themselves. Reckless driving is an indication of a poor understanding of what the car and the driver can do under certain circumstances. Extending the capability of man and machine beyond reality is dangerous and can cause terrible accidents. In a Third World country I was visiting, an elevator claimed many lives. The cause was crowding the elevator beyond the posted load. Some passengers thought that somehow the machine could handle the overload. In another instance, a luxury ferryboat capsized because of overloading. Machines have limitations and can cause problems even when used according to the manufacturers' suggestions. The same can be said about drugs, vitamins, and dietary pills in which unwarranted use can be harmful.

Scientific and technological products can always be improved. Even after testing a product or a procedure, unexpected, undesirable, and sometimes fatal outcomes may occur. Man does not have to abandon technological development because of mishaps. Instead, constant evaluation of a product or a procedure should be practiced with an eye to what might go wrong. Although the responsibility lies heavily with the producers and the manufacturers, the public has to avoid blind trust in a product or a procedure. Like anything in life, the critical mind of the user is a prerequisite for the advantageous use of automation and technological products.

Automation and New Careers

As a result of automation and scientific development on all fronts of human knowledge and activities, some existing careers will diminish and new ones, of which no one ever thought, will be introduced. The new generation has to be flexible to adopt new careers. They should be able to study emerging needs and explore new possibilities.

A free and sound choice of a career is a by-product of self-awareness, the attendant condition for a productive and satisfying life. In this sense, education addressing careers should be designed to develop a clear perspective of the student's self. Self-awareness is a dynamic lifetime goal. As a person develops values, interests, aptitudes, and abilities, he is actually changing and developing his self-awareness. In structuring education to foster and develop self-awareness, the following five objectives were recognized by Maloney and Hefzallah (1974) as relevant:

1. RECOGNITION AND ARTICULATION OF INDIVIDUAL DIFFERENCES AND SIMILARITIES IN TERMS OF APTITUDES, VALUES, INTERESTS, AND ABILITIES. This recognition includes respect for one's own individuality and accords respect to others' individuality. Achieving this objective would help develop understanding of the need for unity and diversity in a dynamic technological society.

2. RECOGNITION OF CHANGES IN SELF AND SOCIETY. The development of new technology continuously accelerates the rate of change in all aspects of our national life. New occupations develop and create changes in the economy.

Personal changes, likewise, are taking place. Therefore, there are changes within and outside of the individual. There are also three basic modes of dealing with these changes. First, the individual may seek change within himself and society. Second, he may accept change and be moved by it without active participation. Third, the individual could be passive toward change and may attempt to maintain the status quo. To exemplify these three modes, there are those who swim, those who float, and those who stay on the beach watching swimmers and floaters without participating in the exercise.

3. DECISION MAKING BASED ON CRITICAL THINKING. For too many years, educators have been advocating decision-making ability as an important objective of general education, yet the achievement of this objective is usually left to incidental development. If education is to foster self-awareness, decision-making ability based on analytical thinking should be stressed. Continued self-awareness necessitates decisions about the self, the environment, and the relationship between the two. Through preparation in decision making, students are educated to identify alternatives and to make free choices based on comprehensive, analytical, and evaluative thinking.

4. THRUST FOR CONTINUED LEARNING. Self-awareness is a dynamic and continuous process that necessitates continued learning. To develop the ability for self-renewal entails the development of motivation and skills for continued learning. The individual must keep pace with new technology, processes, and developments within his or her area of expertise to ensure the upgrading of his or her competence. In addition, the individual as a responsible citizen must understand the dynamics of continued personal growth, learning, and development, which facilitate additional in-depth relationships with others and provide more self-insight and understanding.

5. USE OF LEISURE TIME. More leisure time will be available in the future to working individuals. Since there is a correlation between self-awareness and purposeful use of leisure time, students today should be prepared for the constructive and purposeful use of leisure time through participation in varied activities.[9]

An educated person develops and maintains a clear perspective of self and his role for a productive and satisfying life. The emphasis on education in the twenty-first century, therefore, should shift from job training to developing self-awareness for all students.

The Need for a Common Shared Information

To foster communication in a society, there is a need for shared information among citizens. Advancements in information and technology necessitate adult specialized training. Lacking common information, communication among community members suffers. Hirsch (1987) talked of the need for achieving a national literacy. In his words: "The complex undertakings of modern life depend on the cooperation of many people with different specialties in different places. Where communications fail, so do the undertakings. . . . The function of national literacy is to foster effective nationwide communications."[10]

Hirsch believes that more and more young people lack the information we assumed they knew.[11] He explains:

> They (young people) know a great deal. Like every other human group they share a tremendous amount of knowledge among themselves, much of it learned in school. The trouble is that, from the standpoint of their literacy and their ability to communicate with others in our culture, what they know is ephemeral and narrowly confined to their own generation. Many young people strikingly lack the information that writers of American books and newspapers have traditionally taken for granted among their readers from all generations.[12]

Hirsch's claim is well supported by various studies. For instance, the *World Almanac* reported in a study about teenagers' heroes, which was based on a survey of about 4,000 teenagers in 145 cities, Michael Jackson was the number one hero of high school students. Eddie Murphy ranked second, followed by President Reagan. Actors Kevin Bacon and Clint Eastwood were fourth and fifth, followed by basketball star Julius Erving, film stars Tom Cruise and Mr. T., rock artist Eddie Van Halen, and Katharine Hepburn. Of the ten heroes, only two, President Reagan and Julius Erving, were not in show business.[13] "The world still has heroes," says Donna Woolfolk Cross (1984), "but the glare of celebrity often casts them into the shadows." She explains:

> The shift from hero- to celebrity-worship occurred around the turn of the century and was closely tied to the rise of new forms of media—first photography, and later moving pictures, radio, and television. These media gave fame in America an entirely new dimension—physical recognition. . . . Slowly, the focus of public attention began to shift away from knowing what such people did to knowing what they looked like.[14]

Young people need models, a service that the media and schools can offer. Celebrities gain expanded exposure through their work in the media. Heroes who endure and achieve are not well known to young people.

Polls show that Americans are not well informed. Based on some of those studies, Donna Woolfolk Cross (1984) reported:

> Over half the population doesn't know who their senators or congressmen are and almost as many don't even know how many senators there are from their own state. Half of all seventeen-year-olds think that the President can appoint

members of Congress. One survey revealed that almost 70% of the people surveyed could not identify the three branches of government, nor the Bill of Rights, and could not say what important event happened in America in 1776.[15]

In addition, knowledge of international affairs is limited, superficial, and incoherent. In a joint survey conducted in cooperation with the Soviet Academy of Sciences in 1989, interviewees were asked to identify 16 places on a world map. The interviewees were citizens of ten countries: Canada, Italy, France, Japan, Mexico, the Soviet Union, Sweden, the United Kingdom, the United States, and West Germany. The Soviets averaged only 7.4 correct answers, while the Americans averaged 8.6 correct answers. The highest score was achieved by Sweden (11.6 correct answers). Soviet youth, however, did much better than their U.S. counterparts, sharing fourth place with Canadians and Italians. U.S. youth came in last with a score of 6.9. Another interesting finding in this study showed that Americans were the only nationality whose youth 19–24 years did worse than those over 55 years of age.[16]

The need to broaden the knowledge base of young people is urgent. Technological advances could complicate the problem of the lack of shared information among citizens in two ways. First, educational inequality among the American population will be increased. Schools that can offer better teachers, advanced facilities, and administrators with vision will continue to graduate students at higher educational and cultural levels than less-advantaged schools. Second, people might tend to be narrowly trained, and lack a broad vision of life. Addressing the problem of narrow vocational training Hirsch (1987) stated:

> . . . a directly practical draw-back of such narrow training is that it does not prepare anyone for technological change. Narrow vocational training in one state of technology will not enable a person to read a manual that explains new developments in the same technology. In modern life we need general knowledge that enables us to deal with new ideas, events, and challenges. In today's world, general cultural literacy is more useful than what Professor Patterson terms "literacy to a specific task," because general literate information is the basis for many changing tasks.[17]

Advanced technology dictates the need for highly specialized personnel and the need for interdisciplinary research. Crossing disciplines requires the broad understanding of different disciplines and at the same time an ability of the researchers to work cooperatively with researchers from other disciplines. Cultivating students to work efficiently in a cooperative environment should not be left to chance. Schools have to plan educational environments in which students work for the same cause, each attacking a problem or an issue from his field of interest and expertise.

The New Literacies

A few decades ago an illiterate person was one who could not read nor write and was incapable of handling basic arithmetic operations. Then, literacy programs around the world aimed at training the uneducated masses in basic reading, writing, and arithmetic skills. As the pace of modern life became faster and life itself became more complex, the need to expand the concept of basic literacy to include cultural topics was recognized. Literacy programs experimented with offering cultural topics in an attempt to increase the illiterates' social awareness. The emphasis shifted from narrow literacy skills to cultural literacy. What constitutes cultural literacy changes from one nation to another and from one era to another.

The new media/telecommunication/computer technology has introduced to us what might be defined as the "new literacies." To be an educated person in this modern communication technology age, one has to possess basic information about these technologies. Most importantly, one has to have an open mind about the potential applications of these technologies and to acquire basic skills that empower one to use these technologies to enrich one's information. As the Libraries and the Learning Society (1984) reported: "By knowing how to find, analyze, and use information today, they (children) certify their readiness to become reasoning, thoughtful adults tomorrow as citizens of the Information Age."[18] The following is a brief discussion of the new literacies of the modern age.

1. Visual Literacy

Visual literacy is the ability to understand and use visuals in expressing oneself and in understanding visual messages composed by others. In other words, visual literacy includes two basic competencies: competency in critical analysis of visuals perceived and competency in communicating through the visual medium.

A. CRITICAL ANALYSIS OF VISUALS. Pictures play a very significant role in today's communications. Magazines, newspapers, books, posters, bulletin boards, web pages, flyers, mail advertising, television, and motion pictures use pictures to inform, to entertain, and to persuade. An educated person is able to read between the lines and to analyze the written and the spoken word. He should also be able to interpret a picture to reveal its intended message whether it is explicit or implied. Even when the image looks like a real event, a critical viewer understands that there is a marked difference between reality seen and reality photographed. It is that marked difference that makes photography, still or motion, and television artistic media. Guided by the purpose of the shot, the camera assumes the task of composing the image to magnify or reduce certain aspects of what is seen in reality. A photograph is by no means a complete and whole reflection of reality.

In motion pictures and television, the show is a continuous flow of visual images supported by sound. An action in a television program or a motion picture is conceived as a series of shots taken from different points of view. Each point conveys its own separate "picture statement." Each statement is structured to move the story of the program. Andreas Feininger (1955) explained what he meant by "picture statement:" "In comparison to the eye, the lens sees too much—rather than trying to say everything in one picture, subdivide complex subjects and set-ups and show them in the form of a short series in which each picture clearly illustrates only a single point."[19]

Images, therefore, even when they look like what they represent, are interpretations of the image maker of what he sees and wants to communicate to the viewer. Many times we are confronted with images that, through the power of symbolism, imply meanings, feelings, and a lifestyle of the characters shown in the picture. As an example, one of my early encounters with implied images in outdoor advertising was a poster advertising a menthol cigarette. As I was getting off the highway, the poster caught my attention. I felt that there was something strange about that ad. A second look revealed the implied message. The poster did not have a picture of the package of cigarettes, nor were the characters smoking. It seemed that the advertiser was trying to say something through the power of suggestion. A simple analysis of the poster revealed that message. The poster depicted a healthy man and a woman in bathing suits splashing out of the water. From the big smiles they had, they seemed to be having a lot of fun. The dominant color of the poster was a cool green color. The name brand of cigarettes was printed in letters large enough to be read from a distance. The advertiser used the symbols for health, youth, beauty, happiness, fun, and coolness to make a visual statement: "Smoking brand X is healthy, clean, and fun."

Television, which is primarily a visual medium, often uses images to imply claims and statements without explicitly stating them. Studies by media scholars have indicated the need to educate viewers to become critical consumers of the mass media.[20] Comparing people who know how to observe with others, Arnheim, a scholar in the field of visual communication wrote:

> . . . people who know how to observe and to draw conclusions from what they see will profit greatly. Others will be taken in by the picture on the screen and confused by the variety of visible things. After a while, they may even cease to feel confused: proud of their right to see everything and weaned from the desire to understand and to digest, they may feel great satisfaction.[21]

An educated person has to be able to accept or disapprove, according to his will and reasoning, a message presented through the power of visual presentations or implications. Goldman and Burnett (1971) in *Need Johnny*

Read? urged teachers to make room in the conventional established human-ities curriculum for study of the visual language because

> . . . *without* such training, young people will get less and less from school, even-tually becoming ciphers as citizens; brainwashed, manipulated, and motivated by the mindless spellbinders of films and television; whereas *with* such train-ing, students will get more out of their normal, in-school educational experi-ence rather than be passive passengers on a conveyor belt.[22]

B. USING VISUALS IN COMMUNICATION. In today's culture, both the printed and spoken words are often integrated with visuals to maximize the impact of the message. On almost all levels of communication the image, whether it is a graph, a photograph, a computer image, or a moving image, is used extensively in published work or presentations in both the classroom and the boardroom. An educated person should know how and when to use the visual element to enhance his or her message. This does not mean that each person will learn photography, video production, or computer imaging. If any of these skills could be developed, it is all for the good. The important thing is that the educated person should be able to identify the elements of communication that can best be communicated visually and to request tech-nical and professional personnel to produce the most efficient image that helps communicate the message.

2. Media Literacy

Media surround us. The media help shape our thinking, our attitudes, and the type of information we possess. The media are a force that affects almost every phase of our lives. We are instructed, informed, entertained, and persuaded by media. Unfortunately, many people affected by media do not know this. For instance, many people think that they are not affected by television commercials and that they really make up their own minds. In their view, advertising in television is irrelevant, foolish, and ineffectual. These are the people who purchase the most. They are the largest con-sumers without knowing why. As Wilson Bryan Key said, ". . . like it or not, each one of us is continuously and strongly affected by advertising."[23] It is incredible that assertion of not being influenced by a commercial is exactly what advertising intends to happen; as Key (1975) wrote, ". . . a very neces-sary illusion media must perpetuate in order to succeed in making up their minds for them."[24] He also wrote, ". . . they (audience) react to television commercials with a feeling of superiority that permits them to believe they are in control. . . . People are prone to trust anything over which they believe they have control."[25]

Studies on the effects of mass media on individuals and the society as a whole are extensive. An educated person has to:

a. Understand the role of media in modern society, its social, political, psychological, economical, educational effects on the individual, the society, and the world as a whole.

b. Understand the advantages and limitations of different types of media, especially those that are dictated by the business aspect of media production and distribution.

c. Understand the techniques of persuasion practiced by different types of media.

d. Become an activist and interact with civic and scholarly organizations that monitor the media.

In short, an educated person is a critical consumer of the media.

3. Computer Literacy

There are two levels of this type of literacy: user's level and programmer's level. An educated person has to develop the user's level. This entails developing a basic understanding of what can be done with computer technology in one's field, a favorable attitude toward using what is available, and a basic skill in the use of computer software. There are certain skills that many agree are essential for computer literacy at the user's level. Heading the list are familiarity and working knowledge of word processing, use of simple spreadsheets, and graph software. Basic skills in those areas can help the user develop written documents including visual diagrams and charts.

4. Information Processing and Retrieval Literacy

Information is growing exponentially. New information is generated every day in almost every field of knowledge. The cliché "knowledge explosion" is now becoming meaningless. We have been living in an information age.

Associated with this generation of information are more effective methods of storing, sorting, and retrieving information. All of these phases of managing information are carried out at a very high speed as compared with that of previous years.

An educated person should be able to access vast amounts of information in both print and electronic formats. He or she should also be able to locate the specific information being sought, assess the pertinence of the information gathered and weigh it against other sources. To be able to do that, the educated person should be capable of formulating questions to which he tries to find the answers. To put it in a few words, the educated person should possess the qualities and skills of an original investigator and researcher. Included in those qualities are a professional research attitude, ability to formulate questions, and knowledge of databases and sources of information that might provide the answers to the questions. Heading those qualities, however, is the professional attitude, which dictates the need to find all the information pertinent to the problem under study, especially if that information promises to be in contradiction to previous knowledge.

Borderless Information

The Internet has its roots in connecting people to share ideas and information. This was primarily the real reason for its initiation and the present reason for its accelerated tremendous growth today.

Key to sharing information is connectivity. During the past decade the growth of Internet connectivity worldwide has been astounding. Any one, almost anywhere in the world with a computer and phone connection could connect to the Internet. The speed of retrieving information from almost anywhere or posting information for the world surfers or researchers to read has made information borderless. As a result of this astounding growth of the Internet, the people of the world have created the first electronic global library in cyberspace! This library has the following unique features:

1. *Universal Borderless Access.* The Internet can be accessed simultaneously by millions of people in different parts of the world.
2. *Rich in Multimedia Resources.* The Internet is the first global library that disperses information in integrated multimedia formats.
3. *A Publishing Medium.* The Internet is the first library in the history of civilization to which any client can add a document.
4. *An Interactive Medium.* The Internet is the first and the only library whose patrons can interact with each other in real or asynchronous time, resulting in collaborative work among Internet users.

An educated person should be able to intelligently interact with this library. There are two sides to this intelligent interaction: critical analysis of information retrieved and practicing high professional standards in using the Internet to communicate. (These points are further discussed later in the book.)

CONCLUSION

To conclude, the world today necessitates cultivating the educated person who has:

1. Mastered basic understanding of scientific knowledge as it relates to daily living, and most of all, has developed the ability to employ problem-solving skills in dealing with a variety of issues.

2. Developed an ability to recognize and examine change objectively. Objective analysis of a change includes studying its total effect on human lives and interaction.
3. Developed an understanding of the problems and challenges facing the world and a commitment to contribute to the betterment of the standard of living of all of the world citizens.
4. Developed an appreciation of family dynamics and of family members' demonstrated caring, love, and mutual respect.
5. Developed a critical consumer mind to intelligently interact with products and services offered by various organizations in the community and worldwide.
6. Developed a recognition and appreciation of individual differences and similarities in terms of aptitudes, values, interests, and abilities.
7. Developed ability to recognize changes in self and society and objective ways to interact with those changes.
8. Developed ability for decision-making based on critical thinking.
9. Developed a personal thrust for continued self-learning.
10. Developed constructive and purposeful use of leisure time.
11. Mastered the literacy skills of the modern age including visual, media, computer, and information processing skills.

Prerequisite to the achievement of these abilities is the mastery of reading, writing, basic mathematical logic, and technologies of the age of information.

Visionaries spoke of the significance of structuring the environment to reform man. As Buckminster Fuller wrote, "I have learned to undertake reform of the environment and not to try to reform man."26 Special attention has to be given to the design of learning environments conducive to the cultivation of the educated person who possesses the aforementioned qualities and skills. The learning environment should not be a chance environment. It should be planned and programmed to achieve designated educational objectives.

An essential element of that design is ensuring the learner's interactivity with models of excellence, both in human resources and in learning materials. Very often, access to models of excellence can be achieved through mediated interaction. Fortunately, the technology of the information age provides students and teachers with the tools and vehicles through which models of excellence can be accessed.

This book examines the new learning and telecommunications technologies and their potential applications to enrich the learning process and to ensure educational equality for all students. The following section addresses the significance of the learning environment, the unique characteristics of the educational technology environment, and the types of mediated interaction in use in education and training practices.

REFERENCES

1. Staneck, William R. and Purcell, Lee, et al. *Electronic Publishing Unleashed.* Indianapolis, IN: SAMS Publishing, 1995, p. 418.
2. Dale, Edgar. *Audio Visual Methods in Teaching,* 3rd ed., New York: The Dryden Press, 1969, p. 6.
3. *Ibid.* p. 6.
4. U.S. Department of Education, National Center for Education Statistics, *Digest of Education Statistics, 2002,* NCES 2003–060, by Thomas D. Snyder. Washington, D.C.: 2003, p. 486.
5. *Ibid.*
6. *Ibid.* p. 485.
7. *Ibid.*
8. Rogers, Carl R. *Freedom To Learn,* Columbus, Ohio: Charles E. Merrill, 1969, p. 104.
9. Maloney, W. Paul and Ibrahim M. Hefzallah. "Career Education: The Student in Focus," *NASSP Bulletin,* September, 1974, pp. 93–96.
10. Hirsch, E.D. Jr. *Cultural Literacy, What Every American Needs To Know,* Boston: Houghton Mifflin, 1987, p. 2.
11. *Ibid.* p. 2.
12. *Ibid.* p. 7.
13. PARADE, May 5, 1985, p. 21.
14. Cross, Donna Woolfolk. *Mediaspeak: How Television Makes Up Your Mind,* New Jersey: New American Library, 1984, pp. 135–136.
15. *Ibid.* p. 58.
16. Grosvenor, Gilbert M. "Superpowers Not So Super in Geography," *National Geographic,* vol. 176, no. 6, December, 1989, pp. 816–818.
17. Hirsch, *op. cit.* p. 11.
18. Libraries and the Learning Society, *Alliance For Excellence—Librarians Respond To A Nation At Risk,* Washington, D.C.: United States Department of Education, July 1984, p. 10.
19. Feininger, Andreas. *The Creative Photographer,* New York: Prentice-Hall, 1955, p. 20.
20. Hefzallah, Ibrahim M. *Critical Viewing Of Television—A Book For Parents And Teachers,* Lanham, Maryland: University Press of America, 1987.
21. Arnheim, Rudolph. "A Forecast of Television," in *Film As Art,* Los Angeles, California: University of California Press, 1947, p. 196.
22. Goldman, Frederick and Linda Burnet. *Need Johnny Read?* New York: Pflaum, 1971, p. xvii.
23. Key, Wilson Bryan. *Subliminal Seduction,* NJ: A Signet Book, New American Library, 1975, p. 80.
24. *Ibid.* p. 79.
25. *Ibid.* p. 158.
26. Buckminster, Fuller. "What I Have Learned, How Little I Know," *Saturday Review,* vol. 49, no. 46, November 12, 1966, p. 70.

SECTION II

THE LEARNING ENVIRONMENT

INTRODUCTION

We never educate directly, but indirectly by means of the environment.

—John Dewey

Chapter 3, "Significance of the Learning Environment," addresses the role of the learning environment in achieving the goals of education, the role of the teachers as designers of the learning environment, and the necessary conditions for structuring effective learning environments.

Chapter 4, "The Educational Technology Environment," focuses on the unique characteristics of a learning environment that is structured with precision using conventional and new technologies of instruction to achieve clearly stated goals and objectives. Understanding the strengths and limitations of each technology of instruction is essential to the achievement of an effective design.

In an effective learning environment, students should have access to models of excellence. Very often that presence can only be achieved through mediated interaction. Chapter 5, "Mediated Interaction," addresses the reasons for mediated interaction and its various types.

Chapter 3

SIGNIFICANCE OF THE
LEARNING ENVIRONMENT

ACCESS TO EXCELLENCE

In one of his inspiring articles, "Access to Excellence," Edgar Dale (1970) underlined the significance of the learning environment in achieving objectives of education:

> To learn to think we must be in the presence of thinking people—parents, teachers, principals, fellow students. To learn to love literature we must have easy and continued access to persons who are excited about literature. To become responsible citizens or parents or students we must see responsibility abundantly exemplified all around us.[1]

According to John Dewey we never educate directly but indirectly by means of the environment. In his classic work *Democracy and Education*, he wrote:

> . . . the only way in which adults consciously control the kind of education which the immature get is by controlling the environment in which they act, and hence think and feel. We never educate directly, but indirectly by means of the environment. Whether we permit chance environments to do the work, or whether we design environments for a purpose makes a great difference. Any environment is a chance environment so far as its educative influence is concerned unless it has been deliberately regulated with reference to its educative effect. . . . But schools remain, of course, the typical instance of environments framed with express reference to influencing the mental and moral dispositions of their members.[2]

Addressing the importance of the environment in reforming man, Buckminster Fuller wrote, "I have learned to undertake reform of the environment and not to try to reform man."[3] He explained, "It is possible to design environments within which the child will be neither frustrated nor hurt, yet free to develop spontaneously and fully without trespassing on others. . . . If we design the environment properly, it will permit child and man to develop safely and behave logically."[4]

A learning environment has to be structured to achieve the ultimate goal of education: the educated person. Often when we talk about a learning environment we focus on learning resources available in that environment. However, learning resources are one component of the learning environment. Teachers, school administrators, parents, the community, mass media, information utilities, and the physical school surroundings affect the management and the outcome of the learning environment. It is beyond the scope of this chapter to discuss all of these factors. However, we focus on two factors: teachers and learning resources.

TEACHERS AS DESIGNERS OF THE LEARNING ENVIRONMENT

To cultivate educated persons, educators managing the learning environment have to possess the attitudes and master the skills of an educated person. For instance, in addressing the need to develop students' critical viewing skills, Hefzallah (1987) wrote:

> Critical viewing of television is an outcome of planned activities in which understanding the medium of television and what it offers, and thinking about one's relationship with television are underlined. It is a skill that can and should be taught to the younger generation. However, before we can foster critical viewing in our children, we have to develop the skill and wholly believe in its necessity to provide our children with models of intelligent use of television.[5]

In the same fashion, to be capable of designing learning environments conducive to the cultivation of educated citizens, teachers have to possess the attitudes and master the skills of an educated person. Those attitudes are reflected in their daily interaction with the students.

In the following few pages, major traits of teachers that influence the structure of effective learning environments conducive to the cultivation of the target of educational reform, the educated person, are briefly discussed.

Creativity

When children interact with creative thinking teachers, they have a good chance of developing their own creativity. A creative teacher respects every student's needs, aspirations, talents, style of thinking, and method of communicating. He or she does not disregard an idea on the grounds that it is strange and unconventional. Instead the creative teacher encourages the research of new ideas and provides the opportunities for vague ideas to develop. He or she attempts to structure a flexible learning environment that leads to students' achievement of information, skills, and attitudes needed for effective living and at the same time permits the individual growth of every student. To realize such a structure, the creative teacher has to build a learning environment characterized by continuous interaction between the learner, the teacher, other creative human resources, and rich learning materials. To be able to design and implement such an environment, teachers have to experience creative learning environments in their teacher preparation programs. On the school front, teachers need the support of creative school administrators and the diversity of creative interactive teaching and learning materials.

Learning to Learn

The educated teacher sets "learning to learn" as an extremely important educational objective. He or she knows that for students to live effectively in this age, they have to master the process of learning. Dale argued that the chief product of learning may well be the process of learning. He said:

> In an unpredictable world, all of us must learn to learn and develop a taste for learning. Indeed, the chief product of learning may well be the process of learning. Every learner must develop the motivation to learn—the *want-to*—and he must couple this with the methods and the materials of learning—the *know-how* and the *know-why*. . . . He must, in short, consciously learn how to process information, ideas, and subject matter.[6]

Carl Rogers expressed the same idea by saying, ". . . if we are to have citizens who can live constructively in this kaleidoscopically changing world, we can *only* have them if we are willing for them to become self-starting, self-initiating learners."[7] In his opinion, "The significant learnings are the more personal ones—independence; self-initiated and responsible learning; release of creativity; a tendency to become more of a person."[8]

In discussing the principles of facilitating learning, he pointed out that, "The most socially useful learning in the modern world is the learning of the process of learning, a continuing openness to experience and incorporation into oneself of the process of change."[9]

Emphasis on the process of learning does not and should not deemphasize the product of learning. The question is not process versus product, as Dale put it:

> . . . the issue is not process versus product, form versus content, or method versus subject matter. It is rather the kinds of processes used to produce certain products. . . . Indeed product and process must not be separated, any more than we would separate form and content . . . the purpose of the process is progressively to create a product. . . . The issue is not whether there are basic facts and ideas but how they should be learned.[10]

As one masters the process of learning, he or she experiences the enjoyment that comes from self-discovery, the *eureka* experience, and from clear understanding of a subject matter. The enjoyment of learning propels the person to pursue further learning and thus to become a self-motivated learner. A teacher who enjoys learning can benefit his students in two ways. First, his enjoyment of learning becomes apparent to his students. Hence, he or she sets up a model for the pleasure that comes from learning. Second, such a teacher is more inclined to understand and practice his teaching role as a guide and a counselor for his students in their own learning.

Critical Mind

Faced with unpredictable and accelerated change in almost every phase of our lives and faced with alternative points of view and a vast amount of information, developing the ability of citizens to think critically becomes a condition for survival. The more choices a person has, the more he or she is in need of a reliable system of thinking to make the right choice. Critical thinking is a reliable system. It is an objective process that considers all possible alternatives in a situation and the consequences of those alternatives. It withholds judgment until all the facts are gathered and analyzed. It evaluates not only the facts but also the goals of the investigation and the methods followed to achieve those goals. Some aspects of critical thinking are taught in traditional classrooms (mostly in science and mathematics classes). However, such an essential educational objective should not be considered only in a specific course of study with occasional mention in other areas. Critical thinking is an outcome of intense educational situations in which critical thinking becomes the standard procedure of interacting with the situations. Accordingly, especially designed environments where critical thinking becomes the mode of operation is the only guarantee to ensure the development of that skill and, most importantly, to develop the ability of the students to transfer those skills to diversified human activities outside the classroom and beyond the schooling years.

Prerequisites to the implementation of a learning environment conducive to the development of students' critical thinking are critical-thinking teachers and administrators and a curriculum that aims to develop students' critical thinking.

Self-Evaluation

In practice, evaluation is primarily concerned with testing the ability of the students to recite facts, perform previously learned skills including reading, writing, speaking, and problem solving. If our interest is cultivating the total educated person, the learning environment has to employ a comprehensive system of evaluation, which can test the achievement of that goal in a non-threatening fashion.

A comprehensive evaluation system is concerned with:

1. Measurement of factual learning.
2. Measurement of the ability of the student to learn to learn.
3. Measurement of the ability of the student to practice critical thinking not only in his field of study but also in general life situations.
4. Assessment of whether students have developed their ability to deal with change and to foster desirable change.
5. Development of the culturally literate person who has mastered the needed information to live in modern society.
6. Development of the ability of the students to use new communication and information technology and to locate and select the needed information.
7. Assessment of whether students have articulated their values and the quality and the soundness of those values.
8. Assessment of whether students have developed a sense of community and caring for other members of their community and the world as a whole.
9. Assessment of the mental, emotional, and physical status of the students and of values and habits that might hinder their growth in any of those areas.
10. Assessment of the ability of the students to evaluate themselves.

This type of comprehensive assessment requires more than written or oral testing, especially if we consider the multiple intelligence profile of each student. It also should be an intricate component in the design of the learning environment. A significant component of that system is fostering students' self-evaluation. Usually, traditional evaluation systems embody a threat to the students. Student participation in self-evaluation can help eliminate that threat. Moreover, student self-evaluation has two more values. First, learning is facilitated, as Carl Rogers (1969) explained: "Learning is facilitated when the student participates responsibly in the learning process." Second, it helps develop student independence and creativity, as Carl Rogers put it: "Independence, creativity, and self-reliance are all facilitated when self-criticism and self-evaluation are basic and evaluation by others is of secondary importance."[11]

Teachers and school administrators who have developed their ability for self-evaluation can become more functional in fostering the development of students' self-evaluation.

Real People

One of the big mistakes that teachers and administrators make is putting on a mask behind which they hide their real personalities before facing their students. There is nothing more disturbing to students than detecting superficiality and pretension in their teachers. Through my experience as a student for many years, I encountered teachers who wanted to give the impression that they were "with the times," others who wanted to look serious and unapproachable, and others who were the same people whether in class or outside the class.

In one assignment at Ohio State University, we were asked to reflect on our experience and write a short account of whom we considered a good teacher and whom we considered a bad teacher. Years later, I still recall that assignment. As I reflected on my experience, I found out that the real teachers were the good teachers and the fake teachers were the worst.

The educated person is a real person who knows his strength as well as his weakness. He understands, too, that no one is perfect. Based on that understanding, an educated person is not afraid to be really known. Rogers cited realness of the teacher as a condition for facilitating learning.[12] There is no need for double standards, one for the classroom, and one for outside. If we are interested in helping young people to achieve self-actualization, it becomes imperative to have them experience a learning environment staffed with real people. In selecting persons for the teaching profession, extra care has to be taken to select those who can set up models of educated persons and exemplify emotional and mental stability.

Clear Understanding of the Teacher's Role

As an educated person, a teacher finds delight in teaching others. He or she approaches a teaching or an information situation not with a feeling of superiority but with a drive to share and to participate in the growth of others. The teacher recognizes his or her main role in the teaching and learning environment as being a learning facilitator, a counselor, and a good communicator.

As a learning facilitator, the teacher assumes a host of responsibilities to provide a rich, exciting and enjoyable learning environment. Carl Rogers (1969) advocated the following guidelines for the role of the teacher as a facilitator of learning:

1. The facilitator has much to do with setting the initial mood or climate of the group or class experience.
2. The facilitator helps to elicit and clarify the purposes of the individuals in the class as well as the more general purposes of the group.
3. He relies on the desire of each student to implement those purposes, which have meaning for him, as the motivational force behind significant learning.
4. He endeavors to organize and make easily available the widest possible range of resources for learning.

5. He regards himself as a flexible resource to be utilized by the group.
6. In responding to expressions in the classroom group, he accepts both the intellectual content and the emotionalized attitudes, endeavoring to give each aspect the approximate degree of emphasis, which it has for the individual or the group.
7. As the acceptant classroom climate becomes established, the facilitator is increasingly able to become a participant learner, a member of the group, expressing his views as those of one individual only.
8. He takes the initiative in sharing himself with the group, his feelings as well as his thoughts, in ways that do not demand nor impose but represent simply a personal sharing that students may take or leave.
9. Throughout the classroom experience, he remains alert to the expression indicative of deep or strong feelings.
10. In his functioning as a facilitator of learning, the leader endeavors to recognize and accept his own limitations. He realizes that he can only grant freedom to his students to the extent that he is comfortable in giving such freedom.[13]

As a counselor, the teacher guides and stimulates the growth of his student. In this process he or she integrates well-planned teacher-student activities. In those activities, the teacher undertakes a variety of functions such as assessing learning needs, designing teaching strategies, motivating students, implementing an effective learning environment, and evaluating student progress.

As a communicator, the role becomes less than that of an authoritarian dispenser of information. He pays particular attention to the fulfillment of a successful communication process. Lack of communication causes confusion in even a well-designed teaching situation. Moreover, the enjoyment of teaching and learning is reduced to a mere chore. On the other hand, good communication fosters understanding and clears away confusion and uncertainty and makes the teaching and learning process enjoyable for both teachers and students.

Effective communication is not limited to teachers' classroom presentations. It includes the way in which teachers conduct a one-to-one situation, how classroom interaction is guided, and how actively and knowingly appropriate channels are used to communicate effectively with students.

Traditionally, to communicate is to convey one's feelings or ideas through verbal language, either in its written or spoken format. Traditional teacher-training programs emphasize communication through the written and spoken word. While such training is extremely essential, it is not sufficient for effective teacher-student communication. There is a need to adopt an expanded view of communication to foster successful communication in the teaching process. This view calls for considering and integrating a variety of communication forms and channels. These channels and forms include verbal communication, vocal communication—the manner in which words are spoken, the volume, rate, tone, pitch, and inflections— media communication, body language and situational messages.[14] In situational messages, the individual manipulates his distance from others, the use of time, and the setting of the environment. For example, in a situation of a student's coming to see his or her teacher in the teachers' room, the manner in which the teacher conducts himself and the time he gives to the student definitely affects their interrelationship and subsequently the effectiveness of the teaching and learning environment.

Clear Understanding of the Educational Technology Concept

To structure an effective learning environment, clear understanding of educational technology is essential. In many teaching instances, technology is treated as an afterthought or as an addition to a teaching plan that can be executed without the use of technology. In other instances, use of technology in instruction is considered to be a practice of a teacher who is keeping pace with the times.

Instructional technology should not be an afterthought, nor is it a fad. It is firmly grounded in **educational technology**. Educational technology is a technology of the mind, which may or may not use hardware or a highly technical teaching strategy to achieve the stated educational objectives.[15] Its main goal is to achieve excellence in education. It requires systematic planning based on our knowledge of human learning. It examines accessible communication and information technologies to determine those most appropriate for the achievement of the desired objective in a cost-effective manner. The choice of technology of instruction is determined not only by economic considerations but also by the unique characteristics of each technology, the purpose of using it, with whom it will be used, and under what circumstances.

To be effective, an instructional program has to be designed and engineered with precision. Basic to the design of an instructional program are the following ten points:

1. Determination of clear and precise teaching objectives. In stating those objectives, vague terminology should be avoided. Instead, specific clear statements should be developed to describe precisely the intended outcome of the teaching and learning situation.
2. Identification of the target students including social, psychological, physical, and environmental factors that might hinder or foster their development.
3. Determination of the body of information, skills, and attitudes pertinent to the achievement of the stated objectives.
4. Selection of the appropriate instructional technology that will be incorporated in the teaching system.

5. Design of learning strategies taking into consideration the above points.
6. Allocation of funds needed to design and implement the program.
7. Acquisition and preparation of software and hardware needed for the implementation of the program.
8. Implementation of the program with continuous feedback from the learner to evaluate the program's effectiveness and to assess the learner's achievement.
9. Assessment of the program to identify its strong and weak points in terms of achieving the stated objectives and of involving the learner in the program.
10. Refinement of and/or redesigning the program if necessary for implementation with other groups.

Effective teaching and learning systems employing information and media technologies have proved to be advantageous to the learners as well as to the teachers. These advantages are due to their provision of the following:

1. Well-prepared interactive teaching materials jointly produced by experts in subject matter, methods of teaching, media and instructional technology.
2. A variety of learning experiences to accommodate varying needs, learning styles, and learning abilities of the students.
3. A flexible learning environment to accommodate the learning needs of the individual learner.
4. Interdisciplinary learning materials; this is especially significant as more fields of knowledge are integrated within the curriculum.
5. Expert human resources through mediated interaction.
6. Multimedia learning resources that not only appeal to a variety of learning styles but also provide the appropriate medium of expression for a point of study.
7. Extension of the learning environment beyond the school physical space and time; for example, use of the Internet at home and tuning-in to special channels on television to view educational and cultural programming related to the curriculum or for individual self-enlightenment.
8. Creative visualization of abstractions and difficult concepts.
9. Extension to human senses in studying physical phenomena.
10. Effective methods of storing and retrieving information; and
11. Professional assistance to teachers to become better teachers by:
    a. providing good teaching materials;
    b. demonstrating efficient communication and teaching methods;
    c. providing rich resources of information for the teacher to expand his or her knowledge of the subject under study; and
    d. allowing more time for the teachers to attend to neglected aspects of the teaching and learning process.

STRUCTURING THE LEARNING ENVIRONMENT

Pedagogical Dreams Come True

Information technologies have proved to be of significant advantage to the teaching and learning process. Developments in these technologies provide more powerful and versatile applications in education. One can look at our current era as the golden era of technology in education. Never before have educators had the wide and effective range of technologies of instruction that are available to them and to their students in and out of class. Educators have at hand very efficient tools to structure learning environments conducive to the achievement of the goals of educational reform.

Prior to the accelerated evolution of information technologies, educators advocated the need for individualized, flexible, interactive, interdisciplinary and up-to-date learning environments. However, with reliance on textbooks and audiovisual supplements it was difficult, if not impossible, to implement such progressive educational practices. At present, the new learning and telecommunications technologies can make the educators' pedagogical dreams come true. Roger C. Schank and Chip Cleary (1995) reflected on how progressive reformers of education could not carry out their programs earlier in the twentieth century:

> One primary reason progressive reformers could not carry out their program earlier in the 20th century is that they did not have the means to deliver such individualized instruction. Although the progressive movement acknowledged the importance of students controlling their own learning it had no way to create an environment that would allow such self-management to occur. The computer has the power to change all this.[16]

In the hands of educators, the new learning and information technologies can be used to design learning environments that educators have been advocating but were not sure how to go about structuring. Today's technologies of instruction can be used to structure flexible, interactive, interdisciplinary, and up-to-date learning environments, necessary conditions of an effective learning environment.

NECESSARY CONDITIONS FOR AN EFFECTIVE
LEARNING ENVIRONMENT

A Flexible Learning Environment

Over the past few decades, different educators advocated what was considered progressive educational movements. Nongraded school system, programmed instruction, individualized instruction, career education, going-back-to basics, and open education are some of the movements we have experienced within the past 30 years. Common among these movements are the emphasis on the individual learner and the provision of exciting and interesting learning experiences, which are to prepare the student for an effective and fulfilling life.

To achieve the balance between learner-centered education and what educators, parents, and the community consider to be important, flexible teaching strategies supported by rich and diversified instructional materials are essential components in planning and administering effective learning environments.

An effective learning environment should motivate *all* students to learn. Since success is the best motivation to learn, the learning environment should be designed to help every student experience success in learning. A flexible environment, rich in learning resources can help every student experience success, as Dale (1972) explained: "Certainly we can provide a range of experiences wide enough to allow everyone to achieve success in learning. We know that students schooled in failure reject themselves, feel worthless, drop out of school, and become cynical, belligerent, or indifferent."[17] He further indicated that, "Temporary failures in an atmosphere of success are inevitable, and of no lasting harm, but a daily diet of failure is a discouraging and debilitating experience."[18]

A flexible learning environment, rich in resources can provide exciting and appropriate learning experiences to all students involved. It also helps achieve a balance between students' individual needs and the study of systematic sequenced curricula that experts and educators consider essential for effective and productive living. No longer can we rely on one textbook for every student to study. Nor can we use printed material only for instruction. A systematic approach in which a variety of resources in different formats are integrated can provide a flexible learning environment to suit the needs and learning levels of every student.

An Interactive Environment

We learn to drive a car by being behind the wheel and driving the car, not by reading about it. We learn to speak a foreign language by speaking the language. We learn to think by practicing critical thinking skills. We learn to be compassionate persons by experiencing caring behavior that can help others with their needs for affection and encouragement. We learn by taking an active role in life situations. We learn by doing. Sometimes, it is essential to motivate the learner to start. Yet the actual learning occurs when the learner assumes his or her responsibility and becomes an active learner.

An instructional environment has to be an interactive environment. According to Edgar Dale (1972), "The instructional environment . . . is an interacting situation in which the continuity of experience and the relating of experience are critically important."[19]

If we examine the teaching process, we find it to be primarily a communication process. If we accept Dewey's definition of communication as "a process of sharing experience till it becomes a common possession,"[20] then teaching as a communication process should emphasize interaction between the learners and the teacher.

David Berlo (1960) indicated that one necessary condition of human communication is an interdependent relationship between the source (the teacher) and the receiver (the student). "Each affects the other."[21] He identified four levels of interdependence.

At one level, communication involves only a physical interdependence. In this level, both the source and the receiver require each other for its very definition and for its existence.

At a second level, interdependence can be analyzed as an action-reaction sequence. The receiver responds to a message initiated by the source.

At a third level, the source is concerned with how others respond to a message. The source projects himself into the internal states of personalities of others to predict how they will behave. "We infer the internal states of others by comparing them to our own attitudes and predispositions."[22]

The final level of interdependence between the source and the receiver is *interaction*. Berlo (1960) explained the term *interaction* as follows:

> The term interaction names the process of reciprocal role-taking, the mutual performance of emphatic behavior. If two individuals make inferences about their own roles and take the role of the other at the same time, and if their communication behavior depends on the reciprocal taking of role, then they are communicating by interacting with each other.[23]

Berlo believed that the concept of interaction is central to the understanding of the concept of process in communication. In his words, "Communication represents an attempt to couple two organisms, to bridge the gap between two individuals through the production and reception of messages, which have meanings for both. At best, this is an impossible task. Interactive communication approaches this ideal."[24]

The goal of interaction in communication is "the merger of self and other, a complete ability to anticipate, predict, and behave in accordance with joint needs of self and other."[25]

To put it in a few words, to teach is to communicate, to communicate is to interact, to interact is to learn.

Socrates realized the importance of interaction in learning. He invented the tutorial method. In this method, the teacher asked questions, and the student responded. Gilbert Highet (1957) describes this method:

> . . . the questions are so arranged as to make the pupil conscious of his ignorance, and to guide him towards a deeper truth, which he will hold all the

more firmly because it has not been presented to him ready-made but drawn out of his own mind by the joint efforts of his teacher and himself. It is important here that there should be some basis of discussion, so the pupil usually does some work in preparation, which his teacher then examines, criticizes and by constructive questioning attempts to deepen.[26]

Comparing the sophists with Socrates, Highet explains that the sophists were the first lecturers. They said that they knew everything and were ready to explain it. On the other hand, Socrates said he knew nothing and was trying to find out and train people to think. His method stimulated his students to think. Highet explains Socrates' method:

Questions are asked, gently and almost casually. As the answers are given, Socrates draws them together and asks further questions about their apparent inconsistencies. Under his patient interrogation, irrational judgments are thrown aside and shallow ideas re-plumbed and discarded and objections are raised and countered and slowly, slowly, under the guidance of Reason alone, we are carried through the labyrinthine paths of learning until we arrive at a positive result, which we could by no means have foreseen when we started and could not have reached except by cool rational discussion.[27]

Aristotle thought of research and teaching as two sides of the same coin. To him knowledge was a constant process of discovery.[28] In a more recent writing, Dale (1978) indicated that: "A good mind must do more than discover the already known; it must also produce." To produce, education has to choose creative interaction of the learners over "rote imitative reaction."[29]

One of the most significant characteristics of the new learning and telecommunications technologies is putting the learner in control of his or her learning. Through pedagogically guided steps, students proceed in their learning at their own pace and follow avenues of their interest. Slow, fast, and learning disabled students could navigate through well-designed programs to master the basics of the learning task at hand. They also could go beyond learning the basics.

An Interdisciplinary Environment

The quest for human knowledge is multifaceted. In the early days of civilization, man attempted to find answers to phenomena, problems, or difficult tasks. As a result of struggle with daily life, human knowledge expanded. As more and more information accumulated, compartmentalization was introduced and certain bodies of information were called a discipline. Because the amount of information is always on the increase, more compartmentalization seemed logical to implement. Regular schooling meant offering classes in different disciplines almost one after the other.

The fact is, however, that knowledge is interrelated. Facts in mathematics, science, history, geography, social sciences, language, etc. are intricate components in the weave of human knowledge.

As research in different disciplines progressed, the need to interrelate these disciplines became imperative. We cannot produce an efficient automobile fuel without assessing its potential effects on the environment. Nor can we introduce a pesticide without studying its potential effect on the life cycles not only of insects and animals but also of humans. The effect of a chemical, chlorofluorocarbon, which was used in refrigeration and as aerosol spray propellants, is a powerful example of how a household product can harm life on earth by destroying the ozone layer. The use of this chemical has been banned.[30] (For a full story on this chemical and its effects on the ozone layer please refer to *Encarta 2001 Encyclopedia Deluxe, Ozone Layer," Microsoft® Encarta® Encyclopedia 2001. © 1993–2000 Microsoft Corporation. All rights reserved.*)

Advanced technology dictates the need for more interdisciplinary research. Crossing disciplines requires a broad understanding of different disciplines and an ability to retrieve information from other disciplines that have a bearing on the task on hand. In teaching, this entails two important measures. First, emphasizing interdisciplinary approach in teacher preparation; second, providing schools with high-quality interdisciplinary-based learning environments. Multimedia programs prepared by a team of experts from different disciplines provide the teachers and the students with rich interdisciplinary-based learning resources.

An Up-to-Date Learning Environment

Electronic publications tend to be more current and up-to-date than printed information. For instance, a few weeks or months can elapse from the time an article is submitted for publication to the time the article appears in print. During that time information can change drastically, rendering the article out-of-date the day it is published.

An article published on the Internet can be updated more readily than a printed article. Whenever new information is made available, the author can retrieve his or her published article to update and to repost it. The same can happen if feedback from readers requires editing the article for better readability. The ease with which Internet articles can be updated and republished is a tremendous challenge to print publishers. At present, many book and magazine publishers are making use of the Internet's connectivity to update their print material. In this case, the publisher provides the address of a site, which the reader can link to for updated information.

The same is happening with the CD-ROM. Some publishers of CD-ROMs maintain a site for their product. Links embedded in the CD-ROM can connect the user to the Internet site for obtaining updated information.

Usually, multimedia program publishers update their products on a regular basis. Because most of the production cost of a multimedia program is incurred in the publication of the first issue, updating the product is less costly. Publishers offer updates to their programs at a fraction of the cost of the original version. Moreover, some publishers provide an update of the program if a new version is issued within a short period from the date of the purchase of the original version. As a result of these efforts, multimedia environments tend to be current and up-to-date, necessary conditions for providing effective learning in the Age of Information.

All of the preceding conditions for an efficient learning environment could be present in an educational technology environment, the topic of our discussion in the next chapter.

REFERENCES

1. Dale, Edgar. Access to Excellence, *The Newsletter*, Columbus, OH: Bureau of Educational Research, Ohio State University. May 1970, vol. XXXV, no. 8.
2. Dewey, John. *Democracy and Education*, New York: Macmillan, 1916, p .2.
3. Fuller, Buckminster. What I Have Learned, How Little I Know, *Saturday Review*, vol. 49, no. 46, November 12, 1966, p. 70.
4. *Ibid.*
5. Hefzallah, Ibrahim Michail. *Critical Viewing of Television, A Book for Parents and Teachers*, Lanham, MD: University Press of America, 1987, p. ix.
6. Dale, Edgar. *Building a Learning Environment*, Bloomington, IN: Phi Delta Kappa, 1972, p. 51.
7. Rogers, Carl R. *Freedom to Learn*, Columbus, OH: Charles E. Merrill, 1969, p. 126.
8. *Ibid.* p. 120.
9. *Ibid.* p. 163.
10. Dale, Edgar. *op. cit.* pp. 81–82.
11. Rogers, Carl. *op. cit.* p. 163.
12. *Ibid.* pp. 106–09.
13. *Ibid.* pp. 164–166.
14. Hennings, Dorothy Grant. *Mastering Classroom Communication—What Interaction Analysis Tells the Teacher.* Pacific Palisades, CA: Goodyear, 1975, pp. 2–32.
15. Association for Educational Communications and Technology. *Educational Technology Definition & Glossary of Terms,* volume 1, Washington, D.C., 1977, pp. 164–165.
16. Schank, Roger C. and Chip Cleary. *Engines for Education.* Hillsdale, NJ: Lawrence Erlbaum Associates, 1995, p. 67.
17. Dale, Edgar. *op. cit.* p.111.
18. *Ibid.* p. 111.
19. *Ibid.* p. 16.
20. Dewey, John. *op. cit.* p. 9.
21. Berlo, David K. *The Process of Communication—An Introduction to Theory and Practice*, New York: Holt, Rinehart and Winston, Inc., 1960, p. 129.

22. *Ibid.* p. 130.
23. *Ibid.* p. 130.
24. *Ibid.* pp. 130–131.
25. *Ibid.* p. 130.
26. Highet, Gilbert. *The Art of Teaching*, New York: Vintage Books, 1957, p. 88.
27. *Ibid.* p. 161.
28. *Ibid.* pp. 163–165.
29. Dale, Edgar. *The Good Mind*, Bloomington, IN: Phi Delta Kappa Educational Foundation, Fastback 105, 1978, p. 24.
30. "Ozone Layer," *Microsoft® Encarta® Encyclopedia 2001.* © 1993–2000 Microsoft Corporation. All rights reserved.

Chapter 4

THE EDUCATIONAL
TECHNOLOGY ENVIRONMENT

An educational technology environment is a learning environment that is structured with precision using conventional and new technologies of instruction to achieve clearly stated goals and objectives. Understanding the strengths and limitations of each technology of instruction is essential to the achievement of an effective instructional design.

There is a tendency among some educators to view new technologies of instruction as a panacea to current shortcomings of teaching. However, the newness of a medium should not determine its appropriateness to the structure of a learning environment. Since the late 1970s, technologies of instruction have been examined under new light, resulting in new understanding of instructional design.

PARADIGM SHIFT IN ASSESSING ADVANTAGES AND LIMITATIONS OF TECHNOLOGIES OF INSTRUCTION

Media Comparison Studies

Educators' reactions to a new instructional technology have ranged from great skepticism to enthusiastic advocacy of the use of the new technology as a panacea to shortcomings in educational practice. Prior to the mid 1970s, to assess the educational value of a new medium, research was usually conducted using two groups of students—an experimental group exposed to the use of the new technology and a control group taught without the new technology. The purpose was to compare the effectiveness of the new medium with conventional media. A great deal of research was conducted employing that strategy, which is often called "media comparison studies."

Media comparison studies dominated the research field of instructional media until the mid 1970s. In most of these studies, the newer medium appeared to be more effective than traditional means. For instance, on the basis of film research studies from 1918 to 1950, Charles Hoban, Jr., and Edward Van Ormer (1950) summarized the value of motion pictures in teaching:

1. People learn from films. They learn factual knowledge, concepts, motor skills, attitudes, and opinions. Probably, films are useful in achieving other educational objectives, such as appreciation and creative imagination, but there is little evidence available on these outcomes.
2. When effective and appropriate films are properly used, people learn more in less time and are better able to retain what they have learned.
3. Instructional films may stimulate other learning activities (such as discussions, voluntary reading, investigation, artwork, etc.).
4. Certain films may facilitate thinking and problem solving.
5. Appropriate films are equivalent to at least an average teacher, and sometimes even to an excellent instructor insofar as the instructor's function is communicating the facts or demonstrating the procedures presented in the film.[1]

During the late 1950s and 1960s, television became the prime medium of media comparison studies. In *Educational TV the Next Ten Years*, Wilbur Schramm (1967) summarizes the results of 393 comparisons on TV teaching of various subjects K to college. The summary shows that in 21% of the studies, television was superior, in 65% of the cases there was no significant difference between the experimental and control groups, and in 14% of the studies television was inferior to traditional classroom teaching.[2]

The impetus behind these studies was to examine television as an instructional medium to extend the expertise of a qualified instructor to reach classes with large numbers of homebound students and/or adult learners. Probably what those studies and others actually revealed was that television could be used with great success to reach out to off-campus students.

A great deal of time and funds were spent during the 1960s to employ television to improve education. For instance, the Midwest Program on Airborne Television Instruction, MPATI, used a DC-6 airplane circulating above Montpelier, Indiana, to transmit on two channels instructional television programs to schools within a radius of 150 to 200 miles in six states. The program demonstrated potential cooperation among different school systems and resulted in the production of good instructional television programs. The program ceased to operate in 1968 because of a variety of reasons, among which were logistics of transmission.[3]

Media comparison studies continued in full momentum until the mid 1970s. Regardless of the media tested, the studies tended to favor the new medium. The new medium was either significantly better or there was no substantial difference between learning through the new medium and learning through "traditional" methods of teaching. Some studies are still directed at comparing learning from new technology with learning from commonly used technologies. Richard Clark (1988) indicated,

. . . each new medium seems to attract its own set of advocates who make claims for improved learning and stimulate research questions that are similar to those asked about the previously popular medium. Most of the radio research approaches suggested in the 1950's were very similar to those employed by the television movement of the 1960's and to the more recent reports of the computer-assisted instruction studies of the 1970's and 1980's.[4]

This phenomenon is also common in instructional technology research in developing nations. When the field of instructional technology is in its infancy, researchers tend to prove the values of adopting new technologies.

To conclude that learning benefits are due to the use of the medium alone is inaccurate. A medium is just one important component of the learning environment. The newness of the medium can add an element of interest in the learning process that might make students more attentive to the material being studied. Teachers too can be fascinated by the possibilities that a new medium can offer that which older media could not. The key question is not the delivery technology, however, but what is being delivered to whom and under what circumstances, and which medium is more suitable for the situation at hand.

A Paradigm Shift

Since 1975 there has been a shift from behavioral to cognitive theories in instructional media research. Based on behavioral theory of learning, instructional media research focused on the means of instruction as an independent variable. The cognitive theories acknowledge the interaction between the media of instruction and the internal cognitive process that affects learning. Accordingly, learners' backgrounds affect the way they experience the medium used in instruction. Based on this point of view, each medium has its advantages and limitations within the context and conditions of its use. An instructional designer's main responsibility is to engineer a learning environment with precision to help students achieve the objectives of the learning situation. He or she has the advantage of using conventional and new technologies of instruction, each having its advantages and limitations, to structure learning environments leading to educational excellence.

From media comparison studies we have learned specific characteristics of each medium that make it unique. We learned best possible ways of presenting information through each medium. We learned that information can be stored for easy access and in a manner to facilitate its understanding by specific learners. We learned that learners are not only recipients of learning material, they can also be authors. We also learned that "literacy" is more than verbal literacy. The term has been expanded to include visual literacy, media literacy, computer literacy, and information retrieval literacy.

From media market analysis we learned that homebound and off-campus students can learn and prepare for college degrees and continuing education diplomas through distance teaching technologies. Their high level of motivation to receive instruction through distance channels compensates for the lack of face-to-face communication with the instructor.

Finally, we come to grasp that knowledge is independent from its "container." Accordingly, "The medium is the message" is an inaccurate statement. A container (medium), however, can limit or foster learner's interaction and comprehension of the information it carries for two reasons: (1) the nature of the medium itself in displaying specific aspects of the information, and (2) the learner's preference for one medium or another. Accordingly, one must package a broad range of information in a variety of formats to meet different learning styles and backgrounds of the learners.

UNIQUE CHARACTERISTICS OF THE EDUCATIONAL TECHNOLOGY LEARNING ENVIRONMENT

An Extended Environment

The educational technology learning environment is an extended environment since it encompasses more than textbooks, notebooks, chalkboard illustrations, teachers' lectures, and occasional use of videotape recordings. It is an environment in which a variety of technologies of instruction are integrated, such as planned museum visits, invited guest speakers, searching the Internet for information, and posting classwork on the World Wide Web for others to view and comment.

The educational technology learning environment is also an extended environment because it reaches beyond the school physical space and time. From homes, schools, or public libraries, students can access information they need.

Extended learning environment beyond the school's physical space and time helps develop students' knowledge and appreciation of the rich learning resources of the age of information. Becoming familiar with these resources and how to use them to search for information are basic skills of self-learning, an important objective of education in the twenty-first century. Moreover, the information they acquire is more permanent than information memorized from textbooks.

A Multimedia Environment

The term *multimedia* has its origin in the audiovisual movement of the late 1950s. The term was used to describe an integrated use of a variety of media in presenting and/or teaching a topic of study. The unique characteristics of each medium were believed to reinforce each other in presenting students with exciting and rich learning experiences. It was also believed that there are individual differences among students in terms of their media preferences. While one can learn faster through the spoken word, another finds visuals assisting him in learning the material at hand.

Based on these understandings, educators advocated for providing students with a broad range of information in a variety of formats to meet different learning styles and backgrounds of the learners. In the early 1960s, Edgar Dale, an internationally acclaimed educational technology educator wrote: "To achieve access to excellence we must increase the range and quality for available choices. . . . The aspiring learner should have direct access to models of excellence in critical reading, listening, observing, and thinking."[5]

Sound and slide presentations in which a recorded tape was played in synchronization with changing slides were an early form of multimedia. Other formats included sound filmstrips, multimedia displays, and audiovisual displays especially those inviting the viewer to push buttons to listen to a narration explaining the visual aspect of the display. Multimedia kits that incorporated a variety of media focusing on one topic became popular, especially in elementary grades.

As microcomputers became more powerful, they made the orchestration of a variety of media much easier to handle. Using authoring and presentation software, computers can present at the learner's demand information packaged in different formats including text, still picture, moving images, sound, animation and graphics. This astonishing capability of the computer has resulted in associating multimedia with computers. Accordingly, the term *multimedia* has come to mean to many "computer multimedia."

Reflecting on the above, a twofold question presents itself. Why does the use of new technology in instruction look like a fad that comes and goes, and shall we expect the same to happen with computer multimedia?

To answer the first part of the question, there is a great deal of knowledge that we have gained from media comparison studies. Now we know that each medium is unique and has a definite place in an engineered design of a learning environment. No longer do educational technologists tend to favor a new technology and reject an older one. An instructional designer selects the most appropriate technology of instruction, which contributes to the effective structure of the learning environment for target students under specified learning conditions.

To answer the second part of the question, one must explain computerized multimedia and its unique characteristics. Computerized multimedia uses the computer to orchestrate the use of information stored in a variety of formats, including text, still images, graphics, video, voice, music, and sound effects. Essential to this orchestration are authoring and presentation systems, which implement a hypermedia environment. Hypermedia authoring and presentation software have tremendous flexibility in structuring, arranging, linking, accessing, and displaying units of information to provide a learning environment in which knowledge is networked and displayed in different formats at the command of the learner.

Hypermedia empowers the learner to learn. A learner can set up his or her goal and proceed in a nonlinear progression through rich, interesting, attention holding, and interrelated units of information stored in different formats to satisfy his or her learning needs and self-planned query.

Hypermedia provides the learner with a nonthreatening environment, which encourages self-discovery. I still recall my personal experience with *Electromap,* an electronic atlas on a CD-ROM.[6] Clicking a statistics icon, I was prompted to choose among a list of topics. Choosing "Per Capita Income" produced on the screen in an ascending order the per capita income for all the countries of the world. I was surprised to notice that in 1987 the Falkland Islands had the highest per capita income. As I scrolled the list, I noticed that a country Nauru had a $20,000 per capita income, greater than that of the United States that year. Having no prior knowledge of this country, a few clicks of the mouse revealed Nauru to be a tiny island in the South Pacific. Its wealth came from mining phosphates. When *The New York Times* carried a front-page story on the fishing rights conflicts between Japan and Nauru, I probably was one of a few readers who appreciated the motive behind this conflict since Nauru is facing the depletion of phosphate, its major mineral resource.

Hypermedia provides the learner with an efficient means to learn how to search for information—an essential skill in the age of information. The hypermedia affords the user the freedom to question a database in any way that seems desirable and in any order needed without losing track of where the search is heading. Immediate evaluation of query results can help the researcher refine his or her search strategies including refining questions asked and locating pertinent information.

Hypermedia could be designed to assist the student to achieve mastery of the learning material through step-by-step guidance. Many hypermedia environments do not allow the student to proceed to a new step unless the one at hand has been mastered.

Finally, hypermedia allows the learner to be in a relatively greater control of the learning process. Gradually, individuals become seekers of information and not only recipients. With increased access to loads of information available through networking, hypermedia provides the opportunities for learners to delve more deeply into their areas of interest.

We have come a long way from emphasizing a variety of learning materials to provide for individual differences in learning styles and aptitudes to the creation of a hyperlearning environment that has the unique and advantageous characteristics discussed above. Because of these educational values, multimedia is not an instructional technology fad. Although hardware and software used to create, present, and access multimedia learning material will change, the concept of providing the learner with a hyperlearning environment is not only educationally sound, but also has been the dream of many educators for many generations. Probably the name *multimedia* will change since it does not reflect the aforementioned characteristics. Maybe we will use the expression *hyperlearning environment* since it is more descriptive.

An Engaging Environment

Multimedia interactive programs usually engage the user for many hours. Surfing the Net can take hours for many people as they browse or search for captivating information. Children can spend numerous hours playing games on the computer or using their PlayStations. A visitor to video arcades can see how young people become so engrossed playing different machines and different programs. While most, if not all of these, are claimed to be for entertainment, in principle we have to guide our young generation to be in control of their media or technology of entertainment. The same would apply to avoiding extensive hours on the computer either for study or for playing games. (More about this point in upcoming chapters.)

An Educational Equality Environment

The educational technology learning environment is an environment that can foster education equality for two main reasons. First, an educational technology learning environment may be structured to be flexible and rich in resources. As discussed in Chapter 3, a flexible learning environment rich in resources can provide exciting and appropriate learning experiences to *all* students involved. Slow and fast learners can proceed according to their pace. Students with learning disabilities can select the approach most suitable to their needs. In the privacy of their workstations they can achieve a satisfactory level of achievement. Accordingly, all students can have equal opportunities to learn according to their needs, learning styles, and abilities.

Second, applying telecommunications technologies, including the Internet, students, regardless of the geographical location of their school, can gain access to rich learning resources. The National Center for Education Statistics (NCES) reported the widespread introduction of computers and Internet access:

There has been widespread introduction of computers into the schools in recent years. In 2001, the average public school contained 124 instructional computers. One important technological advance that has come to schools following the introduction of computers has been connections to the Internet. The proportion of instructional rooms with Internet access increased from 50 percent in 1998 to 85 percent in 2001. About 99 percent of schools had access to the Internet in 2001.[7]

An Interactive Environment

Educational technology learning environments are usually structured to be interactive. Since the early days of the audiovisual movement, and later the programmed instruction movement, educators have attempted to achieve some level of interactivity between the learner and the learning material. For instance, "card readers" used 10" x 3" cards of the same weight as an index card. A strip of magnetic tape was adhered along the long side of the card. When a student slid the card into the slot of the card reader, he or she listened to the recorded material on the tape. The student was given the option of recording his or her voice on the same card. To do this, he or she had to slide the card into the machine while pressing the record button. Speaking into the built-in microphone in the machine, the student recorded his or her voice. That simple technology was very effective in teaching foreign languages. The student's recorded voice was compared with the teacher's prerecorded voice on the card. The student could record over and over until the pronunciation matched that of the teacher.

Today, the new learning technologies have the potential of being interactive. The strength of computer-assisted instruction and multimedia programs on a CD-ROM relies heavily on their interactive features. Well-developed software attempts to provide a seamless interactive environment. Even help options in some software are becoming interactive question-and-answer sessions. For example, Microsoft IntelliSense provides the user with a dialog box. A question is typed in the question field using plain English. Hitting "Search," the program returns a list of options under a heading "What would you like to do?" Selecting an option opens a window with the information pertaining to the question asked.

The new learning and telecommunications technologies empower the teacher to design interactive learning environments, a dream that progressive educators attempted to achieve and could not prior to the new age of information. Basically, there are two types of interaction: face-to-face interaction and mediated interaction. Face-to-face interaction occurs in the presence of both the student and the teacher in the learning environment. Mediated interaction occurs when space and/or time separates the source of information or of the teaching program or material from the student. Face-to-face interaction was briefly discussed in Chapter 3. Chapter 5 focuses on mediated interaction.

REFERENCES

1. Hoban, Charles Jr. and Edward van Ormer. *Instructional Film Research (Rapid Mass Learning) 1918–1950. Technical Report No. SDC 269-7-19*, Port Washington, NY: U.S. Naval Training Devices Center, December 1950, Chapter 9, pp. 1–2.
2. Schramm, Wilbur. *Educational TV the Next Ten Years*, Stanford, CA: The Institute for Communication Research, 1962.
3. Saettler, Paul. *The Evolution of American Educational Technology*. Englewood, CO: Libraries Unlimited, 1990, p. 369.
4. Clark, Richard E. Research on Instructional Media, 1978–1988, in Elwood E. Miller (Ed.), *Educational Media & Technology Yearbook*, 1988, Littleton, CO: Libraries Unlimited, 1988, pp. 19–36.
5. Dale, Edgar. Access To Excellence, *The Newsletter*, Columbus, OH: Bureau of Educational Research, Ohio State University. May 1970, vol. XXXV, no. 8.
6. *World Atlas*, Fayetteville, AR: Electromap, 1990.
7. U.S. Department of Education, National Center for Education Statistics. *Digest of Education Statistics, 2002, NCES 2003–060*, by Thomas D. Snyder. Washington, D.C.: 2003, p. 485.

Chapter 5

MEDIATED INTERACTION

TYPES OF MEDIATED INTERACTION

Mediated interaction can take a variety of forms depending on the technology used to bridge the space-time gap between the learner and the instructor. Based on the degree of presence or absence of feedback, mediated interaction could be classified as one of three major types: (1) immediate feedback (live) mediated interaction; (2) delayed feedback mediated interaction; and (3) indirect feedback mediated interaction

Live Mediated Interaction

In this type of interaction, there is an immediate feedback between the teacher and the students, who are separated only by space. Telecommunications technology provides them with the means to interact live. Live interaction when separated by space has four basic types:

Audio Interaction

Examples of audio interaction include telephone conversations and audio telelectures using regular telephone lines or special audio arrangement between the originating and the receiving sites. Participants on both sites can interact by conversing back and forth.

Visually Augmented Audio Interaction

In this type of interaction, the parties are provided with supplementary materials, charts, graphs, or photographs that are sent in advance to the receiving site. Supplementary materials such as graphics can be transmitted over the telephone lines by way of facsimile machines or audiographic equipment during the actual time of the conference. They could also be e-mailed through the Internet.

Slow-scan video can also be used to augment an audio conference. A television camera is used to transmit a still image of an object from one site to the other. Transmission can take anywhere from 10 to 30 seconds. The picture can either be painted (developing gradually line-by-line) on the receiving monitors or can appear instantaneously after each scan line has been recorded in a frame-store device that projects only completed images.

Live Video Interaction

In this type of interaction, the teacher and the students interact through audio and video channels. Under this type, there are two basic technologies. The first, such as PictureTel Video Conferencing[1] (PictureTel has been bought by Polycom),[2] utilizes compressed video and uses ISDN, Integrated Services Digital Network, telephone lines or the Internet to conduct audio and video teleconferencing between sites. The participating sites must have identical equipment. A remote control pad is used by the instructor to select the video for transmission. That video can be that of the instructor or one of the participants either in the instructor's site or the receiving site. A stationary graphic camera is used to capture an image of a document, a circuit board, or any other visual.

The second technology commonly used in live video conferencing transmits full-motion video and audio between the originating site(s) and the receiving sites. A two-way, full-motion, live video interaction is the most sophisticated and expensive system of teleconferencing. Origination and receiving sites have television cameras and transmission and television receiving devices.

There are different transmission options between the originating and the receiving sites. One option is to install permanent transmission lines between the points of origination and reception. A second option is to use cable television channels, which are assigned to the event. A third option is to use satellite transmission and reception. Satellite dishes could be temporarily or permanently installed to allow transmission and reception of both audio and video signals. A fourth option is to use interactive television fixed service (ITFS), which utilizes line-of-sight microwave transmission and reception.

To minimize the cost of teleconferencing. a two-way audio and one-way video setup is usually used. The recipients of the conference receive video and audio signals from the originating site. To communicate their feedback to the presenters they usually use dedicated phone lines, which are reserved for the event, and the number that the recipients could use to call in is frequently presented on the television receivers.

Computer Interaction—Synchronous Mode

Interaction through the use of computers has two modes, synchronous and asynchronous. In a synchronous mode, parties interact in real time, and in asynchronous mode feedback between parties is delayed in time.

Examples of synchronous mode are chat rooms and video desktop conferencing. In chat rooms, or as it is called "keyboard conversation," once connected, participants communicate by typing their messages on the computer. A message typed by any participants is relayed to all participants in the chat room. The message appears on the computer screen identified by the nickname chosen by the participant sending the message.

Video desktop conferencing can take different configurations from the simple to the more sophisticated systems. On a local area network (LAN) system or on the Internet, it is possible to use software that allows a number of participants to communicate as they see and hear each other. A small camera is usually mounted on the top of the monitor in each location to transmit the image of each participant. The software used can allow splitting the screen in every location to see a thumbnail video of each of the participants. It is also possible to select one video to fill up the whole screen. **See-You-See-Me** is a well-known technology that is often used in desktop video teleconferencing.

During the past decade, new software, such as WebCT[3] and Blackboard,[4] has been introduced to allow for real-time interactivity using the Internet.

Delayed Feedback Mediated Interaction

In this type of interaction, the teacher and students are separated by space and time. They cannot see or hear each other. Examples of this type of interaction are e-mail, discussion groups, mail lists, radio, and television programs telecast on open, cable, and satellite channels. With this type of interaction, communication is not in real time. Both students and teachers take time to respond. Accordingly, the feedback in this type is delayed.

Indirect Feedback—Totally Mediated Interaction

In this type of interaction the teacher and the students are separated by both space and time. The instructional material is designed and produced based on the assumption that feedback from the learner to the teacher, and vice versa, is not practically possible. This can be best illustrated by the following example.

Reading a book is a form of a totally mediated interaction between the author and the reader. Among the many readers a very few would write to comment on the book to the author. However, the readers might express indirect feedback to the author. Examples of indirect feedback to the author would be the readers' recommendation to other people to read the book or to the school library or the public library to purchase a copy. This indirect feedback is translated in terms of number of copies being sold or circulated.

Technology of totally mediated interaction varies in its degree of sophistication. On top of the list are multimedia-assisted instruction, interactive video programs, and multimedia CD-ROM and DVD programs. At a less sophisticated level are programmed instruction using simple tools from the paper-and-pencil type to the listen/view—respond—listen/view type. With the advancement in computer and telecommunications technologies we are seeing more and more sophisticated applications and less and less of simple mediated packages.

MEDIATED INTERACTION AND EDUCATIONAL TECHNOLOGY

While mediated interaction is technology-based, one must understand that successful mediated interaction is firmly grounded in **educational technology** (see Clear Understanding of the Educational Technology Concept" in Chapter 3). In addition to the principles of designing an instructional program discussed earlier, there are guidelines for the design of mediated interactive learning programs. Following is a brief discussion of these guidelines that is grouped under two major headings: (1) live mediated interaction, and (2) totally mediated interaction.

General Guidelines for the Design of Live Mediated Interaction

1. There is a need to establish a strong rapport with students in remote sites. In regular classrooms, special attention is given to encourage interaction between the instructor and the students. That attention also has to be emphasized in live mediated interaction. Lorne Parker (1984) indicated that, "'Getting to know someone' in teleconferencing is not as easily accomplished as in a face-to-face setting."[5] Students in remote sites should not feel that they are left out there. Some school systems experimenting with distant learning attempt to employ different measures to encourage students' interaction. Some of the strategies used are scheduled visits by the instructor to the remote sites, arranged social gatherings between classes, addressing students in the remote sites by their first name, and acknowledging students' special occasions.

2. There is a need to overcome the reluctance of students to speak in a distant teaching situation. A striking phenomenon is people's hesitation to participate in a discussion when it is mediated. Being unsure of how one sounds on the system or uncertain about the validity of one's question, people tend to be reluctant to speak in a distant teaching situation. Questions given in advance to students to answer in class could help some students to speak during the telecast. Continuous encouragement of students to interact is vital to the success of live mediated interaction.

3. There is a need to design the teaching events in a live telecast to avoid idle time. Inactive time during a live telecast is deadly. Experience in telecasting instructional materials has indicated that more information can be presented in a telecast than in a regular classroom setting. Management of telecast time is crucial to the success of live mediated interaction.

4. There is a need to examine methods of teaching and classroom presentations and adapt the most appropriate to distant teaching. Some of the traditional classroom methods of teaching might be applicable under certain circumstances. However, use of interactive technologies in distant teaching provides means for developing new teaching strategies unavailable in traditional classroom environment (see Chapters 13 and 14).

5. Feedback cannot be overemphasized. Immediate feedback can help change the pace and clarify points in the presentation. It can give the teacher immediate assessment of the success of his presentation. Some schools employing distant teaching installed fax machines that the students use in the remote site to send in their written assignments given during class time (see Chapter 14).

6. Origination and receiving sites facilities have to be designed and equipped for quality transmission and reception of signals. There is no excuse for a bad audio transmission or an out-of-focus and distorted television image.

7. All audiovisual and computer materials have to be professionally designed and executed to ensure clear and pleasant reception of interesting and informative displays.

8. The medium of telecast and reception in live mediated interaction has to be transparent. Teachers and students should not be distracted by equipment and personnel operating the equipment. In many school systems, the origination facility is handled by the broadcast teacher from his desk. All cameras are placed in unobtrusive positions and can be switched back and forth by a simple switcher placed on the teacher's desk.

General Guidelines for the Design of Totally Mediated Interaction

1. Choice of appropriate technology has to be done in terms of what it can offer to the learning tasks at hand. A hi-tech medium is not suitable for every teaching and learning purpose. In the early days of the computer literacy movement, many computer-assisted instruction programs were poor examples for what computers could be used for. The technology has to be used to its full capacity; otherwise, other methods might be chosen.

2. The content of the program should be current and relevant to the tasks being learned. An advantage of mediated learning programs is the ability to update the information more readily than the printed page.

3. There should be a clear statement of the program's objectives. The learner has to know and understand the purpose of the encounter with the mediated interaction.

4. Learning tasks should be well defined. The learner should be clear on what he is supposed to do. He should also be clear on the criterion of judging what he has learned.

5. The learner should have continuous access to help options. There is nothing more frustrating to a learner than to get stuck in a program without knowing how to proceed or circumvent the snag in the program.

6. The learner should have continuous access to the exit and reentry options. The learner should be given the option to exit the program at any time he desires. He should also have the option of reentering the program either at the point of his earlier departure, at the beginning of the program, or at a specific point in the section he covered.

7. The learner should be offered assistance in locating additional information. If the outcome of learning is the desire to learn more, mediated interaction programs should guide the students to ways of accessing more information.

8. The program should be designed to ensure active participation of the learner. In addition to the aforementioned guidelines, the following are designing criteria for the achievement of the learner's active participation:

   a. The learner should be able to learn how to use the program in a very short time. Tutorial instructions have to be concise, accurate, and clear.

   b. The program should be designed to have different entry levels to meet the different levels of students' backgrounds. Also, it should move at a pace adjustable to the learner. For instance, to slow down, the learner might have a pause option. To speed up, the learner should have the option to by-pass a section that has already been mastered in a previous setting.

   c. Students should be allowed to ask questions to which the program presents the answers.

   d. The program should acknowledge the user's input. In doing that, negative feedback should be avoided. Instead, gentle corrective feedback ought to be used.

   e. The program should be designed to include self- assessment tools.

   f. A modular design helps increase the flexibility of the program. It also helps the learner to achieve a sense of accomplishment when a module is mastered, and he or she is allowed to proceed to a second module.

g. The program should allow the students to move between sections of the program to accommodate individual differences in style and ability to learn.

h. the program should provide default options to prevent the crashing of the program if the learner inadvertently makes a mistake; it should also provide for help options at any time.

i. The program should have a pleasant appearance. Graphics should be artistically executed, video portions should be professionally structured, and computer screens should be aesthetically designed. Text should be easily read, and the color and letter styles should enhance screen readability.

Mediated interaction can help meet the educational needs dictated by the information age and other economical, cultural, social, and political factors affecting our lives. The following is a brief discussion of the reasons for using mediated interaction in the modern age.

REASONS FOR USING MEDIATED INTERACTION

To Help Achieve Excellence in Education

Education has to aim at achieving excellence. Teaching for excellence helps and guides the individual to grow to maximum potential and to become a self-generated better person. To achieve this goal, the learner has to have direct access to models of excellence in his or her learning environment. The presence of excellent teachers and community resource people is a necessary condition for the achievement of excellence in education. Very often that presence can *only* be achieved through mediated interaction.

In addition to models of human excellence, rich integrated use of teaching and self-learning materials are essential to stimulate the learner and to provide him or her with suitable material to meet individual needs. Addressing the effectiveness of professionally packaged instructional materials, Robert Heinich (1985) wrote:

> Our technologies of instruction were demonstrated to be effective 25 years ago. They are even more effective today. In addition to adding more technologies such as the computer, we know much more today about how students learn and how to design effective instruction. With expert teams of curricular and instructional designers planning, developing and packaging reliable instructional systems, even the average classroom teacher can achieve superior results.[6]

Learning resources of an effective teaching and learning environment include teaching materials used by the teacher, self-teaching programs used by the students, and information resources used by the teacher and the students.

To Support Evolving School Curricula

In response to advancements in knowledge, school curricula must undergo change to include new information presented in an interesting manner. New information tends to be rooted in different disciplines. In some instances the teacher might not be well versed in all of the areas significant to the study of a certain topic. Mediated programs prepared by scholars and specialists from different disciplines can help overcome that problem.

In addition to updating school curricula to reflect the new body of information and skills, there is a need to employ the best teaching methods that utilize information processing technology and the most efficient presentation methods. The National Science Foundation report (1982) indicated:

> There is evidence that many students who have an interest in mathematics, science, and technology are not being reached through instructional approaches currently used in the classroom. Whereas many students do not like school science—and form this opinion by the end of third grade—many do like the science and technology that they see on television. They also like what they encounter at science and technology museums, planetariums, nature centers, and national parks.[7]

The report recommended that innovative instructional approaches used in exhibits and television programs should be examined and, where possible, applied to the classroom setting.

To present up-to-date and interdisciplinary educational material in a creative and interesting manner requires a great deal of planning, research, and production time and effort from many creative professionals. In many instances, teachers might not have the time or the access to resources needed for the original development of quality interdisciplinary teaching and learning materials. Prepackaged mediated programs can provide the teachers with those components of the learning environment that are significantly needed for the implementation of the ever-changing school curricula.

To Meet Various Needs, Interests, and Learning Styles of Individual Students

When we discussed the flexibility and richness of the learning environment, we indicated that individual differences exist not only in the ability to learn and the desired level of achievement but also in the style of learning and the preference for the medium that promises to be more effective in studying a certain topic. Mediated instruction can help provide varied learning experiences presented in different formats and styles to meet the individual differences and interests of the students.

To Educate Students in the Process of Self-Learning

In the information age, learning is a life-long process. It does not end with the completion of the school day nor the school years. The educated person continues to learn for the rest of his or her life. Some of that learning is achieved within formal education and training programs, but most of it occurs on informal and individual basis. Well-designed mediated programs can be effective teaching tools in both cases. Unless schools educate their students at an early stage of their education, the values and the skills needed to use intelligently mediated instructional programs on their own, continuing education on the informal and individual basis will suffer. On the other hand, offering students that education can help develop their information retrieval skills. Also, it helps them experience the pleasure resulting from self-discovery and self-learning. Such a healthy environment helps develop their attitude toward self-learning and the skills associated with it. Eventually, that attitude and skills transfer to their extended life-learning situations.

To Educate Students in the Use of New Communications and Information Delivery Systems

The Internet

The Internet revolutionized how information can be stored, sorted, accessed, shared, and distributed. It is causing a revolution in the way we conduct research, spend our leisure time, correspond with others, virtually travel the world to interesting places, and do business.

The number of people using the Internet is on the increase. Due to its accelerated growth in various countries, it is difficult to determine the exact number of online active users. An educated guess put online users worldwide at 605.60 million as of September 2002.[8] Nielsen/NetRatings put it at 580 million as of 2002, with 165.7 million in the United States alone.[9,10]

According to the National Center for Education Statistics (NCES), *Digest of Education Statistics 2002*, 99% of American schools had access to the Internet in 2001.[11] The percentage of workers 18 years old and over using a computer on the job rose from 45.8% in 1993 to 49.8% in 1997 and to 54.2% in 2001 (71,782,000 workers). The percentage of on-the-job computer workers using specific computer applications was 72.2% for e-mail and the Internet, 67.2% for word processing, 62.5% for spreadsheets and databases, 53.2% for calendar schedule, 28.9% for graphics and design, 15.3 for programming, and 13% for other uses. The percentage of workers who used four or more use categories was 43.9%.[12]

These figures indicate without doubt that computer skills and skills associated with the Internet are desirable, if not required in the world of work today. It becomes imperative, then, that students should master these skills.

Online Information

With the rapid technological developments in microprocessors, telecommunications, optical recording of information, technology of storing, sorting, and retrieving information, learning outside a traditional classroom will increase. The availability of alternative delivery and distribution systems of information will change the concept of the library. Libraries are no longer places for storing cataloged printed material and nonprint material. Access to a variety of data and information banks through electronic means is a common practice in many libraries. Homes, too, can have the same advantages.

The World Wide Web (WWW) has made it easy for many to access information from the vast Internet resources for various reasons. Learning how to use Web browsers and Internet tools to access data banks are important skills that students should master if they are ever going to survive in the Information Age.

Television

Never before in the history of communication has there been a medium as popular and intimate as TV, and nor has there been a medium that captures the attention of millions of viewers for long viewing hours every day. It has been reported that children spend more time watching television than the time they spend in regular schooling K–12 (Chapter 12, p. 237). The abundance of television programs through cable, satellite, video recording, and Web TV broadcast makes it more pertinent these days to develop audiences', especially young peoples', television discriminating abilities.

Critical viewers of television are capable of analyzing what they see and hear on television, distinguishing between reality and the world of television, making informed judgment and expressing thoughtful evaluation of programs watched, and making intelligent use of leisure time in which television viewing is among other enjoyable activities. Critical viewing of television is an outcome of planned activities in which understanding the medium of television and what it offers and thinking about one's relationship with television are underlined. It is a skill that can and should be taught to the younger generation.[13]

In addition to planned activities targeting the development of young people's abilities of critical viewing of television, schools have to incorporate the rich television materials available through educational and special channels. *Alternative TV* is a term used to denote rich television programming available on cable and satellite channels such as CNN, the Discovery Channel, and PBS. Students should be made aware of educational and cultural programs available on various channels. Schools should aim at helping students to recognize that television is more than an entertainment medium.

Satellites for Learning and Training

The world of satellite communications is gaining ground in education, especially in higher and continuing education. An alphabet soup has emerged: acronyms of satellite and distance learning consortia. A considerable amount of programming is available through consortia. Most of those programs provide the participants with learning and training experiences unavailable through other means.

In the world of work, telecommunication technology offers effective alternatives to conventional training and business meetings. Teletraining, in the words of Lorne Parker (1984), "has the ability to revolutionize the way companies train their employees, making it noticeably more effective from cost, learning, and productivity standpoints."[14]

Most of the programs carried by telecommunication services attempt to implement interactivity between the receiving audience and the originating sites. An observer of teleconferences notices that often participants are too shy to participate. Indicating that "discussion does not just 'happen'" in teletraining, Lorne Parker (1984) wrote:

> No matter how many students may want to make use of the opportunity to ask questions and no matter how easy it may be technically, some students are reluctant to interact at first—they may feel they are infringing on program time, other people's time, or that their questions or comments may be not worded correctly.[15]

To overcome this problem, the designer of the telecommunication program must first recognize the importance of achieving interaction with the audience. Second, there is a need to educate people on how to interact in teleconferences and teletraining situations instead of being passive recipients of information.

At present, some school districts are employing telecommunication strategies to use the expertise of available resource people in one location to reach more students in other locations. If attention is given to planning the lesson to ensure students' interactivity, students will leave high school with an ability to interact with a distant source. This ability can be enhanced further in the world of work when the student goes through teletraining programs or through college education and when the student becomes an active participant in a variety of teleconferences and telecourses originated by a growing number of telecommunication consortia.

To Ensure Educational Equality for All Students

Every student has the right to an education that will foster maximum development of his or her talents. Mediated interaction can help implement this principle by providing special courses for small groups of students and achieving educational equality for all students regardless of their geographical areas. These two topics are discussed in more detail when addressing the topic of distance education in Chapter 14.

CONCLUSION

To assume that conventional teaching guarantees that students will seek electronically published information on their own after finishing their formal education is false. Unless formal education strives to educate students to use effectively electronically published information and mediated instruction programs on their own, there will be many whose continuing education will be undermined. To achieve this type of education, schools must offer their students ample opportunities to experience mediated instruction and information processing and retrieving media.

REFERENCES

1. PictureTel Video Conferencing, http://www.tribecaexpress.com/PictureTel.htm, accessed 7/13/03.
2. Polycom Video Conferencing, http://www.tribecaexpress.com/polycom.htm, accessed 7/13/03.
3. WebCT, http://www.webct.com/, accessed 7/12/03.
4. BlackBoard, http://www.blackboard.com, accessed 7/12/03.
5. Parker, Lorne A. *Teletraining Means Business*, Madison, Wisconsin: Center for Interactive Programs, University of Wisconsin–Extension, 1984, p. 26.
6. Heinich, Robert. Legal aspects of alternative staffing patterns and educational technology, Synthesis, Southwest Educational Development Laboratory, 6(2), 3, quoted by Lyn Gubser, Public Education in a Year of Transition, in Elwood

E. Miller (Ed.), *Educational Media and Technology Yearbook*, 1985, Littleton, CO: Libraries Unlimited, 1985, p. 6.

7. National Science Board, National Science Foundation. *Today's Problems Tomorrow's Crises*, A Report of the National Science Board Commission of Pre-college Education in Mathematics, Science and Technology, Washington, D.C., 1982, p. 7.

8. Jupitermedia Corporation, NUA Internet How Many Online, http://www.nua.ie/surveys/how.many_online/ p. 1, downloaded 7/14/03.

9. CyberAtlas, Population Explosion! http://cyberatlas.internet.com/big_picture/geographics/article/0,,5911_151151,00.html, downloaded 7/1/03.

10. Nielsen NetRatings, http://www.nielsen-netratings.com/, downloaded 7/14/03.

11. U.S. Department of Education, National Center for Education Statistics. *Digest of Education Statistics, 2002, NCES 2003-060,* by Thomas D. Synder, Washington, D.C., 2003, p. 485.

12. *Ibid.* Table 424, p. 495.

13. Hefzallah, Ibrahim. *Critical Viewing of Television—A Book for Parents and Teachers.* Lanham, MD; University Press of America, 1987, p. 11.

14. Parker, Lorne A. *op. cit.* p. 1.

15. *Ibid.* p. 26.

SECTION III

THE NEW LEARNING AND TELECOMMUNICATIONS TECHNOLOGIES

PART ONE: COMPUTERS IN EDUCATION

PART TWO: COMPACT DISC READ-ONLY-MEMORY

PART THREE: THE INTERNET

PART FOUR: VIDEO TELECOMMUNICATIONS

PART FIVE: DISTANCE EDUCATION

Part One

COMPUTERS IN EDUCATION

Chapter 6: Forerunners to Computers in Education
Chapter 7: Current Applications of Computers in Education

INTRODUCTION

At the root of the new information technologies is the computer. Chapter 6, "Forerunners to Computers in Education," surveys educational attempts to increase the efficiency of the learning environment through applications of programmed instruction and teaching machines. With the advent of computers, shortcomings of programmed instruction and teaching machines programs were eliminated, and pedagogical dreams of many education reformers became realities.

Chapter 7, "Current uses of Computers in Education," addresses creative applications of computers in education. These applications extend beyond the 1960s to 1970s computer assisted instruction. They include the use of the computer as a storyteller, a multimedia producer and presenter, an interactive medium of communication, a gateway to the information world, an electronic publishing medium, a desktop tool for managing instruction, and a virtual reality environment.

Chapter 6

FORERUNNERS TO COMPUTERS
IN EDUCATION

INTRODUCTION

Over the centuries, educators have been concerned with the issue of increasing the efficiency of the learning experience. One thought that has prevailed for centuries is using small successive steps in learning. The tutorial method, invented by Socrates, is based on this thought. In this method, he asked questions arranged so as to make the student conscious of his ignorance. The questions were asked gently and almost casually and moved the student toward deeper understanding.[1]

At the turn of the twentieth century, educators and learning psychologists determined basic concepts for increasing the efficiency of the learning process. These concepts can be summarized as:

1. The learning environment has to engage the learner, and the learner has to be an active and not a passive recipient of learning material.
2. The learning material can be taught in small successive steps to which the learner responds.
3. Presentation of subsequent steps depends on the learner's response.
4. It is important to supply the learner with immediate evaluation of his progress.
5. An efficient learning environment should recognize students' individual differences in terms of background, interest, learning pace, and levels of achievement for the materials being learned.
6. The learning environment should lead the students to the mastery of the material.
7. Since education is a life-long process, the learning environment must foster the development of the learner's ability for self-learning.
8. Since education is more than imparting factual information, an ideal learning environment should allow for some time for the teachers to counsel and guide the students.

With these ideas in mind, educators and learning psychologists have been examining a variety of approaches for the implementation of some or all of them. Before the computer age, however, we lacked the technological means through which the above concepts could be implemented successfully. To fully understand the potential role of the computer in the learning process, we must trace some of the major educators' attempts to put into practice the aforementioned ideas.

PROGRAMMED INSTRUCTION AND TEACHING MACHINES

A Definition

Two interrelated movements, programmed instruction and teaching machines, were attempts to increase learning efficiency through emphasizing the learner's active role, use of small successive steps, immediate feedback to student response, and allowing the student to proceed at his or her own pace.

Programmed instruction is a planned sequence of experiences leading to the student's mastery of a topic of study. Tools for presenting the planned sequence of experiences varied from that of paper-and-pencil type to teaching machines. During the late 1950s and early 1960s, there was a quite variety of teaching machines. In 1960, Lumsdaine gave the following generic definition of teaching machines:

> Despite great variation in complexity and special features, all of the devices that are currently called "teaching machines" represent some form of variation on what can be called the tutorial or Socratic method of teaching. That is, they present the individual student with programs of questions and answers, problems to be solved, or exercises to be performed. In addition, however, they always provide some type of automatic feedback or correction to the student so that he is immediately informed of his progress at each step and given a basis for correcting his errors.[2]

This definition implied the implementation of four important teaching practices:

1. Continuous student response to subsequent steps;
2. Explicit practice and testing of each step;
3. Immediate feedback to student's response; if the student's response was incorrect, he was led directly or indirectly to correct his errors; and
4. The student proceeded at his own rate; faster students moved rapidly in the instructional sequence, and slower students were tutored as slowly as necessary.[3]

Historical Review of Programmed Instruction and Teaching Machines

In 1912, Thorndike, a professor of psychology at Columbia University anticipated programmed instructions controlled by a machine:

> If by a miracle of mechanical ingenuity, a book could be so arranged that only to him who had done what was directed on page one would page two become visible, and so on, much that now requires personal instruction could be managed by print. Books to be given out in loose sheets, a page or so at a time, and books arranged so that the student only suffers if he misuses them, should be worked in many subjects.[4]

In the early 1920s, Sidney L. Pressey, a professor of psychology at Ohio State University, designed several machines for the automatic testing of information using multiple-choice questions. The machine advanced to the next question after the student chose the right answer for the first question.[5,6]

Skinner (1968) explained the use of Pressey's device in the following:

> In using the device the student refers to a numbered item in a multiple-choice test. He presses the button corresponding to his first choice of answer. If he is right, the device moves on to the next item; if he is wrong, the error is tallied, and he must continue to make choices until he is right.[7]

Pressey pointed out that such machines "could not only test and score, they could teach."[8] Skinner commented on the value of immediate report of the student's performance when using Pressey's machines. He said, "When an examination is corrected and returned after a delay of many hours or days, the student's behavior is not appreciably modified. The immediate report supplied by a self-scoring device, however, can have an important instructional effect."[9]

Pressey's teaching machines also allowed for self-instruction, which could increase the efficiency of instruction, as Skinner explained:

> Even in a small classroom the teacher usually knows that he is moving too slowly for some students and too fast for others. Those who could go faster are penalized, and those who should go slower are poorly taught and unnecessarily punished by criticism and failure. Machine instruction would permit each student to proceed at his own rate.[10]

The education world was not ready for Pressey's machines. As Skinner explained,

> Pressey's machines succumbed in part to cultural inertia; the world of education was not ready for them. But they also had limitations which probably contributed to their failure. Pressey was working against a background of psychological theory which had not come to grips with the learning process.[11]

Nevertheless, Pressey's pioneering work emphasized four important conditions for effective instruction:

1. Immediate feedback to student's responses.
2. Active student participation in learning.
3. Self-paced instructional tasks.
4. The need for capital equipment in realizing the above.[12]

Edgar Dale (1969) noted another movement in education that converged with that of using self-instructional materials. The movement, called "activity analysis," was developed by Franklin Bobbit and W. W. Charters. Activity analysis was concerned with discovering the activities performed by the individual student and with his behavior analysis. According to Bobbit (1926): "The curriculum is that performance of the activities in their earlier stages out of which the mature performance grows."[13] Bobbit also noticed that, "It is good to state each activity in terms of what the pupil will do or experience. One should avoid stating what he will know or be, since these latter are neither activities nor experiences."[14]

Self-instruction using teaching machines received little attention from educators until the 1950s. Two reasons for the loss of impetus were given by Lysaught and Williams (1963):

> First, no provision was made for systematic programming of materials to be used in these machines, and second, the onset of the depression and its impact on social conditions and education offered an unfavorable environment for an "industrial revolution" in the nation's schools.[15]

By the 1950s, more demand was put on education to improve its quality to graduate effective citizens in a technological world that had experienced its first attempts at space travel. In the late 1950s, teaching machines and programmed instruction were revived. This revival was based on the work of two Harvard psychologists, B. F. Skinner and James G. Holland.[16] In 1960, a comprehensive study by the Department of Audio-Visual Instruction (Association of Educational Communications and Technology—AECT at present) predicted the following regarding the use of teaching machines and programmed instruction in education:

> Teaching machines and programmed learning can have a major impact on education. Their use can effectively and dependably guide the student's learning-by-doing as he proceeds, as rapidly as his abilities permit, through carefully pretested instructional programs. It can thus be made economically feasible to provide every student with many of the benefits of a skilled private tutor, since auto-instructional materials can anticipate and be responsive to his needs for mastering each aspect of a subject matter. Not only do programmed materials themselves thus have the potential for producing much more efficient learning than has hitherto been generally possible, but their wise use should make possible the much more constructive use of the teacher's talents.[17]

In the 1960s, programmed instruction came into the limelight. Its promise to individualize instruction, to ensure mastery of the subject being learned, and to relieve some of the teachers' time to attend to other areas of teaching, such as counseling, challenged many educators to develop programmed materials. Basic to the development of those materials was a recognition of seven key principles of design:

1. A clear identification of the learner, his learning abilities and background as they relate to the program material.
2. Well-stated objectives in measurable terms indicating what the learner would be able to perform or to demonstrate after experiencing the program.
3. A sequence of small steps that guides the learner from introductory information to more in-depth information.
4. Continuous learner interaction with the program; after giving the right response to a step, the following step is revealed.
5. Immediate evaluation of the learner's response to an item; a correct response is rewarded and the learner is permitted to advance in the program; a wrong response leads the learner to remedial steps until the right response is made.
6. Self-instruction to allow the learner to advance in the program according to his own pace.
7. Evaluation of the program to ensure clarity of its items, as well as its suitability to the target learner and the intended objectives of the program.

Two basic approaches of programmed instruction were utilized. The first, a linear approach, was developed by Skinner. In this approach, learning material was organized in a series of successive segments called frames. After each frame, the student was required to answer a question and on the basis of that answer additional frames were presented. Each subsequent frame contained minimal additional information and led the student a step forward toward the achievement of the program's objectives. If a frame did not lead the student forward, either by introducing new material or by expanding the use of information in previous frames, it was considered a wasteful frame that had to be changed, revised, or discarded.[18]

The second approach, developed by Norman Crowder, was called branching. This approach presented to the student after each learning sequence a diagnostic multiple-choice array. Depending on the student's choice, he was prompted to advance to another sequence or to branch to a corrective or remedial sequence. After the successful completion of the corrective or remedial sequence, the student was brought back to the point of his previous branching. In this approach the presentation of the learning material was adjusted to the student response. Accordingly, it allowed different students to follow different paths in learning the material depending on their backgrounds and performances.

Programmed instruction was received with a varied degree of enthusiasm from some educators and with skepticism from others. Proponents of programmed instruction perceived it as an instructional method that would save the teacher's time to attend to valuable and yet neglected objectives of teaching. At the same time it would help individualize instruction.

Those who opposed it thought of it as a cumbersome and mechanical instructional method that was probably more suited for training than for education environments. At the same time, there were those who viewed programmed instruction as a way to replace not only textbooks but also the teacher.

The polarized reaction to new instructional methods and technology, such as programmed instruction, is common among educators. Usually, there are two opposing points of view. One dictates complete advocacy of the new technology, and the other is exactly the opposite. Somewhere between these opposing points of view are educators who can objectively examine the new technology to determine how best it may be used. In 1960, Jerome S. Brunner addressed the opposing points of view on teaching machines and programmed instruction:

> It is still far too early to evaluate the eventual use of such devices (teaching machines), and it is highly unfortunate that there have been such exaggerated claims made by both proponents and opponents. Clearly, the machine is not going to replace the teacher—indeed, it may create a demand for more and better teachers if the more onerous part of teaching can be relegated to automatic devices. Nor does it seem likely that machines will have the effect of dehumanizing learning any more than books dehumanize learning. A program for a teaching machine is as personal as a book: it can be laced with humor or be grimly dull, can either be a playful activity or be tediously like a close-order drill.[19]

Later, in 1969, Dale addressed the claim that programmed instruction will replace textbooks as well as the teacher:

> The view that programmed instruction will replace not only textbooks but also the teacher is unsound. Programmed instruction will take over some of the jobs done by teachers and textbooks, just as the textbook replaced some oral instruction by the teacher. Adjunct or supplementary programming will save the teacher time for the intangibles, for guidance in critical thinking and problem solving, for carefully planned large and small group discussion, for developing the independent learner.[20]

Despite the controversy about programmed instruction and teaching machines, significant learning and teaching concepts have been emphasized. It became clear that to design and administer effective learning environments the following points should be considered:

1. There is a need to examine, revise, and redesign the school curricula in the light of the goals of education and the specific objectives of school offerings and in the light of what instructional technology can offer. The real issue in instructional technology implementation is not how it can fit into the existing curriculum, but rather how an updated curriculum can benefit from its application.

2. A new instructional technology should not be used for its own sake. The student should remain the focus of instruction.

3. Significant attention has to be given to pretesting to determine the student's background and the initial competencies he brings to a learning situation and to posttesting to determine what the student has achieved. Accordingly, subsequent learning experiences can be planned.

4. There are individual differences among learners not only in their level of intelligence and educational background but also in which medium of instruction one can perform better. While others can do well with oral presentations and readings, others might find visualization of concepts to be most helpful. Accordingly, learning and teaching materials, especially those designed for self-instruction, have to incorporate a variety of communication media.

5. There is a need to implement an integrated approach to teaching and learning in which a variety of teaching and learning strategies are engineered and implemented with precision. Rich varied learning experiences administered under the guidance of skilled teachers include conventional learning and teaching materials, such as textbooks, and new material that utilizes new communications technologies.

6. Educators have to continue examining new communications and information technologies that can enhance and extend the instructional capabilities of the teacher. While programmed instruction and teaching machines of the past had certain limitations, new instructional technologies can overcome those limitations.

In 1960, predicting new developments in technology that can improve the shortcomings of teaching machines, James Finn wrote:

. . . I see several developments. First, it is reasonable to expect that programming for teaching machines will move from the verbal Socratic-Skinner type to the audio-visual-branching type. That is, the machine will present, based upon student pretests, conceptual content using films, slides, filmstrips, tapes, and/or video tape as the medium. The presentation sequences will be longer and the student will be given an opportunity to select additional sequences for further explanation if the machine, through testing, informs him that he needs it. Records, of course, will be maintained instantaneously by miniaturized computers.[21]

Today, Finn's prediction is a reality. Prior to computers, instructional tools, including teaching machines, lacked the potential of implementing the significant teaching and learning principles previously discussed. Dale (1969) advocated that computers "can individualize instruction in a way never before done and it can provide valuable data about how students learn. Thus computers can make contributions both to a theory of teaching and to curriculum development."[22]

Recent developments in computer and telecommunications technologies have expanded and enhanced the use of computers in teaching, research, and curriculum development. In the next chapter current uses of computers in education are discussed.

REFERENCES

1. Highet, Gilbert. *The Art of Teaching*, New York: Vintage Books, 1957, p. 88.
2. Lumsdaine, A. A. Teaching Machines: An Introductory Overview, in Lumsdaine, A. A. and Robert Glaser (Eds.). *Teaching Machines and Programmed Learning—A Source Book*, Washington, D.C.: National Education Association of the United States, 1960, p. 6.
3. *Ibid.* p. 6.
4. Saettler, Paul. *A History Of Instructional Technology*, New York: McGraw-Hill, 1968, p. 52.
5. Pressey, S. L. A Simple Apparatus Which Gives Tests and Scores—and Teaches, in Lumsdaine, A. A. and Robert Glaser (Eds.). *Teaching Machines And Programmed Learning—A Source Book*, Washington, D.C.: National Education Association of the United States, 1960, pp. 35–41.
6. Pressey, S. L. A Machine for Automatic Teaching of Drill Material, in Lumsdaine, A. A. and Robert Glaser (Eds.). *Teaching Machines And Programmed Learning—A Source Book*, Washington, D.C.: National Education Association of the United States, 1960, pp. 42–46.
7. Skinner, B. F. *The Technology of Teaching.* New York: Educational Division, Meredith Corporation, 1968, p. 30.
8. *Ibid.* p. 30.
9. *Ibid.* p. 30.
10. *Ibid.* p. 30.
11. *Ibid.* p. 32.
12. *Ibid.* p. 32.
13. Dale, Edgar. *Audiovisual Methods in Teaching*, 3rd ed., New York: The Dryden Press, 1969, p. 628.
14. *Ibid.* p. 628.
15. Lysaught, Jerome P. and Clarence M. Williams. *A Guide To Programmed Instruction*, New York: John Wiley & Sons, 1963, p. 6.
16. *Ibid.* p. 6.
17. Concluding Remarks, A Technology of Instruction, in Lumsdaine, A. A. and Robert Glaser (Eds.). *Teaching Machines and Programmed Learning—A Source*

Book, Washington, D.C.: National Education Association of the United States, 1960, p. 572.

18. Brethower, Dale M. *Programmed Instruction: A Manual of Programming Techniques*, Chicago, IL: Educational Methods, 1963, p. 195.

19. Bruner, Jerome S. *The Process of Education*, Cambridge, MA: Harvard University Press, 1965, p. 84.

20. Dale, *op. cit.* p. 649.

21. Finn, James D. Technology and the Instructional Process, *Audio-Visual Communication Review*, Department of Audio Visual Instruction, Winter 1960, pp. 5–26.

22. *Ibid.* p. 650.

Chapter 7

CURRENT USES OF COMPUTERS
IN EDUCATION

INTRODUCTION

Arthur C. Clarke wrote: "Developments in the field of computers have been so swift that yesterday's miracle is today's obsolescent junk."[1] With more powerful computers, seamless software suites, and advanced connectivity, conventional applications of computers in education are enhanced, and new creative applications are discovered.

A decade ago, computers in education primarily meant the use of computers to assist and to manage instruction, to conduct research, and to administer the school. Today, computers in education mean much more than that. Computers are interactive storytellers, excellent means to produce and present multimedia programs, vehicles for interactive communications among people, gateways to the information world, electronic publishing media, tools for managing and assessing instruction, resources for teaching and learning, windows on virtual reality, and private multimedia tutors. In the following pages we discuss these features and their applications in education.

A STORYTELLER

When my granddaughter was three-and-a-half years of age, I was interested in observing her reaction to children's stories published on CD-ROM format. We started with a copy of *Interactive Story Time.*[2] The experience was fascinating to both of us.

Avery Anne was pleased that she could choose one of the three books on the same CD-ROM. This was a new experience to her since most, if not all, of her children books have only one story each. Opening the book was fascinating as she not only viewed colorful images but also listened to the music and to the narrator reading the lines on the page. As the narrator read, the words were highlighted. Now came my turn as a grandparent. I started clicking on different words to hear their pronunciation. As we kept doing that, I realized that a potential outcome is the recognition that a block of letters form a word, words are separated by blank spaces, and a series of words communicate the story. Of course, a young child cannot articulate this kind of realization; however, I think that recognition could happen. Borrowing from the field of photography, we can name it a "latent" recognition. In photography, a latent image is one that is formed on a film after exposure occurs. When the film is developed, the latent image appears. As children become more exposed to a variety of reading materials, the concept of discursiveness of the written language develops gradually.

Going back to my granddaughter's experience with the computer as a storyteller, interactivity with the material on the computer screen was delightful. She learned that as we move the mouse pointer on the screen it changes from the shape of a pointer to the shape of a small hand. Clicking the left button of the mouse, the name of that object appeared and the narrator pronounced the word. Interacting with the objects on the page suddenly became fun as we attempted to find out what objects are linked to words and sound.

Once we exhausted discovering the different objects on the page, we clicked on the right arrow at the bottom of the screen to move to the next page. Avery Anne also learned that clicking on the left arrow took her to the previous page. As we continued reading the stories, she developed some appreciation of certain pages that she wanted to revisit. This was the time that I showed her the "GO TO" option. I was pleased that she grasped the idea that on a computer you jump directly to a page without the need to move to it page by page, a very important recognition of the computer hyperenvironment.

Educators always alert us to the importance of follow-up activities after going through a learning experience. The program was efficient in this aspect as it allowed us to print a coloring book version of the story. I was surprised later when she asked for certain pages that she wanted to color. Using the print option, we printed the pages she wanted.

Avery Anne has used that CD-ROM many times, sometimes reading the same story twice in one sitting. Then, it was time to look into other children's stories software. *Just Grandma and Me*[3] was her second story. This program provided more interactivity as more objects were linked with sound. Some of the objects were animated, which was a new feature to her since *Interactive Story Time* used still images only. The feature that she missed in this software was printing a coloring book; however, she discovered hidden actions as she started clicking the mouse on different objects. There was an element of discovery since the mouse pointer did not change its shape when it landed on a linked object. It became interesting as she clicked the mouse in an attempt to see if any action would happen. A few times, an excited call brought me to the computer to see what she discovered. Most important I thought was the reinforcement of what she gained from the previous program in terms of the "latent" concepts. Moreover, the computer became a friendly interactive storyteller.

A year and a half later, she learned to listen, view, and interact with other stories. *Just Me and My Dad*,[4] *Arthur's Teacher Trouble*,[5] and *Arthur's Birthday*[6] were among her favorites. Storytelling software led to educational and entertainment software such as *Reader Rabbit's Kindergarten*[7] and *Let's Start Learning*,[8] which provided her with the opportunity to learn the alphabet and numbers and to practice the recognition of shapes while playing. The familiarity with the computer that resulted from her storytelling experience definitely helped her through exploring new software.

MULTIMEDIA PRODUCER/PRESENTER

The term *multimedia* goes back to the audiovisual movement of the late 1950s. The term was used to describe an integrated use of a variety of media in presenting and/or teaching a topic of study. It was believed that the unique characteristics of each medium could reinforce each other to present students with exciting and rich learning experiences. It was also believed that there are individual preferences among students for media. While one can learn faster through the spoken word, another finds visuals assisting him in learning the material at hand. Based on these understandings, educators advocated providing students with a broad range of information in a variety of formats to meet different learning styles and backgrounds of the learners.

The overhead projector became a popular tool for presenting visuals as well as text information. Innovative methods of using the overhead projector became a favorite topic of presentation in many teachers' meetings. To simulate an animation effect, a piece of a polarized film was pasted over the section of the transparency to be animated. A rotating polarizing filter was mounted close to the projection head of the overhead projector. The combined effect of the rotating filter and the pasted polarizing film gave the impression of something moving. Animated transparencies were produced either locally or by professional production houses to show animated diagrams of procedures and events such as the flow of blood in and out of the heart or the passage of an electric current in a circuit.

Sound and slide presentations were another form of multimedia programs. In this system, a recorded tape was played in synchronization with changing slides. Other formats of early multimedia technologies included sound filmstrips, multimedia displays, and audiovisual displays, especially those inviting the viewer to push buttons to listen to a narration explaining the visual aspect of the display. Multimedia kits that incorporated a variety of media focusing on one topic became popular, especially in elementary grades. Their sale started to drop, however, in the early 1980s with the growing interest in microcomputers.

With the advancement in microcomputer and presentation technologies, an average user could orchestrate the integration of a variety of media in a presentation. Essential to the orchestration of the variety of information inputs are authoring and presentation systems, which implement a hypermedia environment. Hypermedia authoring and presentation software have a tremendous flexibility in structuring, arranging, linking, accessing, and displaying units of information to provide a learning environment in which knowledge is networked and displayed in different formats at the command of the learner.

Hypermedia authoring systems range from the simple to learn and use to the more sophisticated software that can track students' progress as they individually interact with the program. With easy to use software, such as Microsoft's PowerPoint, an average user can produce artistic computer presentations. Animation and transition effects between the slides, sound, pictures, and video segments can be easily incorporated to produce an attention-holding presentation. Moreover, PowerPoint allows the producer/presenter to establish links between any object on the slide and an object on another page or in another presentation. PowerPoint can also link the slide with Internet sites or activate a CD player.

After a relatively short time in training on software such as PowerPoint or HyperStudio, students and teachers can produce artistic presentations that may be:

1. Easily updated in terms of information and the order of the presentation.
2. Produced as an interactive program in which the learner is in control of the pace as well as the order of presentation.
3. Printed to produce a handout copy to the students.
4. Linked to other applications on the desktop or to sites on the World Wide Web.
5. Exported to other applications on the desktop.
6. Saved as a hypertext markup language (HTML) file for publication on the WWW.
7. E-mailed across the Internet to one or more recipients.

INTERACTIVE MEDIUM OF COMMUNICATION

It has been said that computers are as good as the programs they run. To engage in that "goodness," however, the user has to interact with the computer.

Effective communication is a two-way process. Even if we communicate with machines, man and machine have to interact. This happens all the time when dealing with today's modern technology. In a routine activity like driving a car, the driver pushes the accelerator down and the car responds by increasing its speed. Applying the brakes, the car reacts and slows.

A computer is a special machine designed to respond to input from its users. It can accept a variety of input devices to accommodate students with special needs. When the computer is turned on, it goes through its self-booting. The user is then presented with a colorful screen that has a number of icons depending on what applications are loaded and how the computer desktop is configured. The opening screen persists until the user enters his or her command. Without that command, the opening screen stays the same until the computer is logged off. To save the screen of the computer, a screen-saver device that introduces animated shapes flying on the screen is used, and sometimes puts the screen to sleep to save energy and prolong the life of the computer monitor.

Another example illustrating the dependability of the computer on the input of the user is the Office Assistant. The Office Assistant gallery contains several animated figures. I selected "The Genius," which looks like Einstein. If I had chosen, this figure would stay overlaid on top of my document as I develop it waiting for a help question to be asked. To seek help from the Genius, I would click that figure to generate a dialog box with space to enter a question in plain English. Hitting "Return," the Genius returns another dialog box with options. Each option is linked to "Help" information. Clicking on the option that seems closest to the question asked, the Genius returns the "Help" information. Without any request from the Assistant, the figure stays waiting for a command.

The computer reacts instantaneously to the user's interaction with the programs. Moreover, it keeps track of all the responses made. It is also capable of complex decision making and can adjust its response in light of the trend of the user's interaction.

Interaction with users can happen simultaneously with many individuals. Loading a program on a server can be accessed simultaneously by many workstations within the local area network or even a wider base of networks.

GATEWAY TO THE INFORMATION WORLD

The computer unlocks the doors to the information world. Millions of information documents are stored in digital forms on the Internet, CD-ROMs, magnetic disks, and drives that can be accessed with a personal computer.

The marriage between computers and other forms of communication like TV is enhanced almost every day. If the computer is equipped with a special TV board, TV channels can be viewed on the computer monitor. WebTV is a relatively new computer product that was released in 1995. The founders of WebTV attempted to provide family audiences with access to information and entertainment available on the Internet right in their living room. Their idea was to develop an easy to use product that works with a television set and phone line. Their success initiated WebTV, "a natural extension of the TV viewing experience."[9] The following is a short history of that invention that revolutionized TV viewing for audiences subscribing to the service and at the same time provided them with access to Internet information related to the shows they watch.

> The company's first product, the WebTV-based Internet Terminal, created an entirely new product category when it appeared in consumer electronics stores in October 1996. When coupled with the Microsoft® WebTV Network™ Classic service, this product makes accessing the Internet as simple as turning on the television. By using a remote control or an optional wireless keyboard, subscribers to the WebTV™ Classic service are able to keep in touch with family and friends through e-mail, participate in chat discussions on topics ranging from parenting issues to financial planning, and do research for everything from school projects to planning a family vacation.
>
> A year after revolutionizing the industry, WebTV Networks introduced its second-generation product, the WebTV-based Internet Receiver. This device, in tandem with the Microsoft® WebTV Network™ Plus service, seamlessly integrates television programming with Internet content and services, providing viewers with a better way to choose which shows to watch and new ways to enjoy more entertainment, information, and services that uniquely relate to those shows. With advanced features in areas such as television and Internet integration, personalization and multimedia e-mail creation, WebTV™ Plus service provides a new level of interactivity for television viewers. With features such as Interactive Television (ITV) Links, subscribers to the WebTV Plus service have the ability to enrich their television-viewing experience with related information from the Internet. When viewers watch programs that feature ITV Links, a transparent "i" icon appears on the screen offering viewers the option to visit a related Web site. WebPIP™ (picture-in-picture) technology enables users to watch television and enjoy interactive Web content related to the broadcast by bringing picture-in-picture capability to standard television sets.[10]

At the heart of this revolutionary integration of the Internet and TV broadcasting is the computer technology that brings the world of information to the user in his or her living room.

DIGITAL PUBLISHING MEDIUM

The computer is often used to produce digital publications. Computer digital publications can be as simple as a term paper e-mailed by a student to his or her professor or as highly sophisticated as a multimedia publication.

Digital publications produced by a computer have the following values:

1. The publication can be e-mailed to interested readers for their feedback. Remarks can be input in the publication and re–e-mailed to the author. Accordingly, a dialogue can ensue between the readers and the author. This type of feedback can be helpful to the author to edit his or her publication for better readership and clearer communication.

2. Digital publications can integrate graphs, pictures, clipart, video, and audio. In other words, digital publications are multimedia publications.

3. Digital publications can employ hypertext coding, which offer the reader the option to read the article in a nonsequential order according to his or her interest. Hypertext coding also facilitates the retrieval of related information. Related pieces of information are defined by the author or searched for by the reader. The author or publisher can establish links between key words in the article and other related information that appears in the article or in other sources. The user can search for related information by using search options. To facilitate locating related information, some authors and publishers include a search option within the published article.

4. Digital publications can provide access to some of the references cited in the publication. Many times a reader becomes interested in a reference cited by an article. If that reference is available online, the author can establish a link between the title of the reference and the Internet location of that reference. Clicking that link takes the reader to the site where the whole reference is published. One can look at this feature as a way of expanding the desktop to open a number of related resources to a topic of study.

5. Digital publications can be posted on the Internet and can be updated more readily than a printed article. Whenever new information is made available, the author can retrieve the published article to update and repost it. The same can happen if feedback from readers requires editing the article for better readability. The ease with which Internet articles can be updated and republished is a tremendous challenge to print publishers. In the print world, a few weeks or months may elapse from the time an article is submitted for print to the time the article appears in print. During that time, information can change drastically, rendering the published printed article out-of-date the day it appears in print.

Tools for Digital Publications—Word Processing

Available to the computer user is a variety of software that can be used for developing documents for publication. At the top of this list is word-processing software. The following, with a focus on MS Word 2002, are some of the major benefits of using word processing in developing documents.

Versioning

Writing is a process that sometimes starts with a vague idea. As the author labors to clarify the idea, he or she might revise the first draft several times. Saving each revision and comparing them, the author can reach a final draft that best expresses his or her ideas. Word-processing software makes the revision and the saving of the progressive rough drafts easy to do. Versioning allows the user to save in the same file multiple copies of a document to keep track of the progressive versions and thus makes it easy to view different versions by opening one file.

Spell and Grammatical Checking

By eliminating the worry about spelling, grammatical mistakes, and vague expressions, the author can concentrate on presenting a smooth flow of clear ideas. Word-editing features can help direct the writer's attention to spelling mistakes and awkward sentence structure.

Word-processing editing features have improved tremendously over the past few years. Spelling and grammatical checking can be done as the author enters the information. A wavy red line underneath a word indicates a spelling mistake or a word that is not in the dictionary of the software, which eventually can be added, thus eliminating the wavy red line when the word is keyed in again. A light-green wavy line indicates a grammatical mistake or poor sentence structure. Usually the program suggests a correction. If not, it at least draws the attention of the author to a sentence that might need editing.

Two other features in Word 2002 can help in ensuring the correct spelling as well as enhancing the speed of keying in text. These two features are AutoComplete and AutoCorrect.

AutoComplete

Autocomplete allows the user to insert entire items such as dates and AutoText entries when a few identifying characters are typed. A screen tip is then displayed at which point the user could accept the tip by pressing "Enter", or continue typing. Word XP explains:

> An AutoText is a storage location for text or graphics the user would like to use often such as a mailing address, a signature, a list of names of a specific group of people, etc. Each selection of words or graphics is assigned a unique

name. To insert an AutoText, first you have to click where you want to insert the AutoText entry. Then, on the Insert menu, point to AutoText, and click the name of the AutoText entry you want.[11]

AutoCorrect

Autocorrect automatically corrects common typing mistakes. The program comes with a list of common typing errors. The user may add to this list his or her personal list of typing mistakes and their corrections. Word then replaces the mistyped word with its correction. Word XP explains AutoCorrect:

> To automatically detect and correct typos, misspelled words, and incorrect capitalization, you can use AutoCorrect.
>
> For example, if you type teh plus a space, then AutoCorrect replaces what you have typed with "the." Or if you type **This is theh ouse** plus a space, AutoCorrect replaces what you have typed with "**This is the house.**"
>
> You can also use AutoCorrect to quickly insert symbols that are included in the built-in list of AutoCorrect entries. For example, type (c) to insert ©.
>
> If the list of built-in entries does not contain the corrections that you want, you can add entries.[12]

Integrated Seamless Software

Microsoft Word XP is a component of seamless integrated MSOffice XP software. This makes it possible to import and export material from other components into and out of Word. For instance, Excel can be used to create tables or graphs, which could be inserted into a Word document. One may also import a Word document into PowerPoint XP.

This feature also makes it easy to develop Word documents as multimedia documents. Audio, video, animation, and picture files can be imported and pasted into a text document. If one has a connection to the Internet, importing documents or sections of a document from a web site into a Word document is also possible.

Easy Navigation

Word XP has two features that can help one navigate long documents faster and easier. These features are Document Map and Browse Object.

Clicking on the **Document Map** icon on the tool bar, a hyperlink outline—headings and subheadings—of the document is displayed in the left pane of the screen with the corresponding text of the document in the right pane. Clicking on the hypertext heading scrolls the text in the right pane of the screen to the text of that heading. This makes it easy to navigate through longer documents.

On the bottom of the right side bar of Word XP there is a **Browse Object** navigation tool that provides a quick way to navigate to different objects within a document. Users can browse their documents by page, section, graphics, comments, tables, field, endnote, footnote, headings, and edits. Two other navigation tools are available in Browse Object navigation, "find," and "go." If you click on "find," a dialogue box appears. Typing the word(s) you would like to find in the document and hitting "Return" take you to where the word appears in the document. With the dialogue box still over-laid on the screen, you can continue clicking on "Find Next" to go to the next occurrence of the word(s) in the document until you search the whole document.

Clicking on the "Go" navigation icon, an arrow produces a dialogue box. In the left scroll windowpane in that dialogue box, "Go to What," you may scroll down to the item you are interested in going to. These items are Page (number), Section, Line, Bookmark, Comment, Footnote, Endnote, Field, Table, Graphic, Equation, Object, and Heading.

Collaborative Authoring

Word processing can facilitate cooperative learning. Students can work together to develop an article in which they incorporate their ideas. Sharing the digital version of the article, they can make comments on it and e-mail it back to the team members. "Comments" was a new feature of Word 97, and it became a standard feature in Word 2000 and Word XP. "Comments" is defined as "electronic yellow sticky notes that can be added to a document without altering the original text. Comments appear when users pause the pointer over the highlighted text."[13] *Microsoft XP Inside Out* explains:

> You can add comments that refer to specific blocks of text within a Word doc-ument without altering the main document text. You can use comments to store alternative text, criticisms, ideas for other topics, research notes, and other information useful in developing a document. Or, you can use them for communicating ideas, corrections, requests, or other information to others who are working on the document.[14]

Teachers and students might find these electronic yellow sticky notes helpful in the process of developing their documents. Teachers as well as peers could leave comments on the work of a student to consider. This could be in the form of the need to elaborate, delete, insert a piece of infor-mation, or direct the student to another reference pertaining to the text. They could also help the teacher in progressively assessing the work of the student.

Another feature of Word XP that can help in collaborative work among students is "Change Tracking." The feature was introduced in Word 97, and again it became a standard feature in Word 2000 and Word XP. XP has revamped the change-tracking feature of previous Word versions and offers new ways to display and work with tracked changes including tracking and marking changes as one edits a document and reviewing tracked document changes made by coworkers on the document.

Microsoft XP Inside Out explains the basics of "Change Tracking" (tracking and reviewing):

> You can have Microsoft Word 2002 track and mark all changes you make to a document so that you or a co-worker can later review these changes and either accept them to make them permanent or reject them to restore the original text. When Word tracks changes, it always stores the details on every change made to the document—the exact modification that was made, the name of the person making the change, and the date and the time of the change. (The name used to indicate the author of a change is the name that was contained in the Name box on the User Information tab of the Options dialog box at the time the revision was made.) You can display this information when you review the revisions. You can also have Word mark the revisions on the screen in various ways so you can see at a glance the proposed corrections and changes to the document. Or, you can temporarily hide the markings, letting Word store the change information internally only.[15]

Clicking on <u>V</u>iew, <u>T</u>oolbars, and <u>R</u>eviewing reveals a **Reviewing Toolbar** with icons helpful in collaborative review of documents. The Reviewing Toolbar has several icons that may be used to insert, edit, delete, and navigate through electronic comments. Also, there are icons to track, accept, or reject changes. Other icons are included in the Reviewing Toolbar to highlight text, create Microsoft Outlook Task, save the reviewed version of the document, and send the document to a mail recipient.

Tools for Artistic Page Layouts

Word XP has integrated easy-to-use tools to lay out documents in an expressive manner. Among these tools are:

1. **Arranging Text with Tables.** Tables are a highly versatile tool for arranging text in rows and columns. They have more advantages than arranging text on a page using tab characters or inserting spaces by the space bar. For instance if a particular text item doesn't fit on a single line, Word automatically creates a new line and increases the height of the row. The width of the column could also be adjusted. Moreover, table items could be emphasized by using borders, background shading, and color.[16]
2. **Text Wrap.** Users have greater flexibility in laying out their documents and wrapping text around objects.

3. **Office Art.** Office Art drawing tools allow users to create more visually effective documents, including three-dimensional effects, shadows, multi-colored fills, textures, and curves.
4. **Page Borders.** Users can add page borders around documents.
5. **Text Borders, Shading, and Font Effects.** Users can add borders around text within paragraphs in addition to applying shading and font effects.
6. **Wizards.** A wizard asks questions, and depending on the answers, automatically lays out and formats a document such as a letter, a newsletter, a fax, a calendar, or a Web Page. By automating common elements in the document, the Wizard allows the user to focus on the content of the document rather than on its format.

Web Publishing

Word XP can save documents as HTML documents for posting on the WWW. The ability to save a Word document as an HTML document eliminates the need for mastering HTML encoding. Users can also embed hyperlinks in a Word document to connect to other documents on the PC, server, or to a web site.

Using web publishing features of Word XP, a teacher can post an article on the school home page for his or her students to study. The article may have links to related references and interesting web sites. It may also have links to articles previously published by the teacher or by some students on the school home page. In assuming this practice, the teacher expands the learning resources for the students.

Word Supportive Software

MSOffice Bookshelf is a versatile reference companion for writers. It supports Word 97, 2000, and XP. MSOffice Bookshelf is a CD-ROM that contains nine major reference books. Bookshelf enhances the information provided by these books with images, audio, animations, word pronunciations, and videos as well as links to the Internet to provide up-to-date information on the topic under study.

Bookshelf can be installed to work as integrated software with Word. Clicking the right mouse button on a word in a Word document produces a drop menu. Clicking on Define at the bottom of this menu box evokes Microsoft Bookshelf. The program locates the word in the dictionary and brings its definition to the screen. A small loudspeaker icon indicates that the program can pronounce the word. To get into the other books of the Bookshelf requires clicking the Microsoft Bookshelf icon in the Status Bar, which brings the opening page of Microsoft Bookshelf to the screen. The nine major reference books are:

1. **The American Heritage Dictionary of the English Language, 3rd Edition.** Some of the entries in the Definitions category of Bookshelf come from *The American Heritage Dictionary of the English Language,* Third Edition. This dictionary brings you the richness of American English with more than 3 million words, 90,000 entries, and 350,000 definitions. To help you learn how to say a word correctly, the dictionary contains more than 80,000 audio pronunciations. Your knowledge is further enhanced with audio clips, illustrations, photographs, animations, and videos.[17]

2. **The Microsoft Press Computer and Internet Dictionary.** Some of the entries in the Definitions category of Bookshelf come from *The Microsoft Press Computer and Internet Dictionary.* This contemporary dictionary contains over 7,500 terms more terms than most computer dictionaries on the market. It features the latest computer- and Internet-related terms and abbreviations. Bookshelf enhances the information with audio and images.[18]

3. **Roget's Thesaurus of English Words and Phrases.** The entries in the Synonyms category of Bookshelf come from Longman's *Original Roget's Thesaurus of English Words and Phrases.* This thesaurus is a vast resource of over 250,000 words and phrases classified according to underlying ideas and meaning. Each entry contains many more related terms than the typical thesaurus. This thesaurus can be an indispensable companion for writers and speakers and can help you expand your vocabulary, avoid repetition, or simply recall a word that has slipped your mind.

   The words and phrases in the Longman version of Roget's Thesaurus are categorized into six classes. Dr. Peter Mark Roget developed this classification system in the 1800s for the first thesaurus, and his system has proven capable of absorbing new concepts and new vocabulary. Dr. Roget used a logical progression from abstract concept, through the material universe, to humanity itself, culminating in what he saw as humanity's highest achievements: morality and religion. First published in 1852, this complete unabridged edition is fully revised to reflect the English language of the 1990s.[19]

4. **The Columbia Dictionary of Quotations.** The entries in the Quotations category in Bookshelf come from *The Columbia Dictionary of Quotations.* This book contains more than 18,000 remarks, witticisms, judgments, and observations that reflect the range of human experience. The quotations in this collection were spoken or written by both the famous and the forgotten figures, modern as well as old, who collectively constitute the shapers of our modern cultural landscape. These memorable, funny, or profound quotations were chosen not for their familiarity but for their relevance.[20]

5. **The Encarta Desk Encyclopedia.** The entries in the Concise Encyclopedia category in Bookshelf come from *The Encarta 99 Desk Encyclopedia.* This streamlined version of the popular *Encarta® Encyclopedia* is a quick reference source for a wide range of information. It contains more than 17,000 entries and features audio clips, illustrations, photos, animations, and videos. To further enhance your learning, more than 6,000 entries contain audio pronunciations.[21]

6. **Encarta Desk World Atlas.** The entries in the World Maps category in Bookshelf come from the *Encarta 99 Desk World Atlas*, based on *Encarta® Virtual Globe*. This atlas contains a map of the world, topographic maps of the world's continents and countries, and state and regional maps of the United States and Canada.

   Bookshelf enhances this information with audio pronunciations of country, city, U.S. state names, and Canadian provinces; full-color examples of country and state flags; and audio clips of the national anthems for many of the world's nations. The Atlas is also linked to the Encyclopedia and the Almanac, so access to detailed information about a particular region is only a click away.[22]

7. **The Encarta® 1999 New World Timeline.** The entries in the Timeline category of Bookshelf come from *The Encarta 99 New World Timeline*. The Timeline documents social and historical events by year. It covers 24 areas of human endeavor in more than 68,000 entries, providing concise details about the milestones that have been reached throughout the ages. This reference work is both a quick portrait of the world and a chronicle of the people and events that have shaped it.[23]

8. **The Encarta 99 New World Almanac.** The entries in the Facts and Figures category in Bookshelf come from *The Encarta 99 New World Almanac*. This almanac provides statistical data, contemporary facts, geographic information, and trivia on people, places, and events throughout the world. Much of the information is displayed in lists, tables, and charts. Bookshelf enhances the information with photos, charts, and calendars.[24]

9. **Encarta® Manual of Style and Usage.** The entries in the Style Guide category of Bookshelf come from *The Encarta Manual of Style and Usage*. This concise but comprehensive guide explains the fundamentals of grammar, punctuation, spelling, word choice, document design, and business communication. It is easy to understand and contains many examples. Whether you are a novice or a professional, the Style Guide will help improve your writing. It even guides you through the elements of electronic communication by offering advice on spelling checkers, e-mail, and online etiquette.[25]

Searching for Information in Microsoft Bookshelf

The first search option is searching the Bookshelf's reference books. The user can search through all the books at once or select a particular book from the Books menu on the Tool Bar. Two ways of searching are available: (1) searching by keyword, and (2) full-text searching by word or phrase.

The second search option is searching for "Multimedia." Under this option, the user can search All Media or a media type. Media types are classified under three categories: Audio; Images; and Animation Videos.

The third search option is searching online references. To search online, you type a word or a phrase in the search box. Then, you click on one of three buttons. The first button, Web Search, expands the search to the

Bookshelf's preferred web sites, the second button is for searching Bookshelf News, and the third button, extends the search to *Encarta Online Library.*[26]

The use of such a supportive reference work provides the user with resources, which he or she could incorporate in the development of his or her document. Importing information in the form of pictures, audio, video, animation, and charts can enrich the process of writing. Since some ideas can best be communicated visually, the use of appropriate visuals within a document can enhance the communication process. The use of multiple media will also develop students' understanding of the advantages and limitations of each medium and help develop their ability to choose the most appropriate medium of communication to achieve the task at hand.

DESKTOP MANAGEMENT OF INSTRUCTION

Many educators explore innovative uses of PC software in managing instruction. Word processing, spreadsheets, graphic presentations, and database software are constantly assessed and used in managing various instructional activities. Some of these uses include creating attendance charts, grade books, student reports, student portfolios, assessment checklists, worksheets, newsletters, publicity items for school activities, attractive visual presentations focusing on school activities and issues, classroom schedules, and book and equipment databases. The list can go on and on. However, for showing how basic software can be used beyond what many consider its main utilization, the following is a simple application of Word in building test items.

At Fairfield University we offer a Master of Arts degree in education with a major in educational technology. One of the requirements for the completion of the program is passing a comprehensive exam at the end of the program. The written examination aims at accessing the candidates' comprehensive understanding of the chosen discipline. Questions are not designed to measure the student's ability of recalling information studied in the program. They are designed to invite the student to address educational technology issues. To be able to do that, they have to draw and capitalize on their understanding of a variety of issues discussed in several courses. Since the program is individually tailored to each student's background with a limited number of core courses, it becomes essential that each student receive an examination paper reflecting his or her courses of study.

Word was used to develop a simple database of questions listed under each course we offer. In this simple database, the course numbers were formatted as "Heading 1," and the questions pertaining to that course as "body text." Choosing "Document Map" view under the <u>V</u>iew option, the screen splits in two sections. The left-hand pane has the course number listing, and the right-hand pane has the corresponding course questions. Either pane has its independent scroll bar. Scrolling the course number section and clicking on a course brings the questions listed under the course number onto the right section of the screen. To generate a question sheet for a student, his or her record is studied carefully to determine what areas should be covered. While having the database open on the desktop, a "new" document of Word is opened. The new document is then saved under the student's name such as name.comp.sp 03.doc. "Name" is the student's name. "comp" means comprehensive, "sp" stands for spring semester, and "03" stands for the year. The examiner then switches to the database window.

Scrolling through the course number list, one can select a question on the list by dragging the mouse over the question's text. Pushing Ctrl+C copies that question to the computer clipboard. Switching to the name.comp.sp 03.doc window and pushing Ctrl+V pastes the text of that question into the student's examination sheet. The procedure is repeated until six to eight questions are pasted on the student's examination sheet.

Student Portfolios

The National Education Association (1993) defined a student portfolio as "a record of learning that focuses on the student's work and her/his reflection on that work. Material is collected through a collaborative effort between the student and staff members and is indicative of progress toward the essential outlines."[27] Other definitions of student portfolios have been given in which authors put their emphasis on the why, the what, and the how of planning and developing portfolios. However, according to Danielson and Abrutyn(1997), most of these definitions share essential characteristics:

> For all their differences in emphasis, most definitions share certain essential characteristics. First, portfolios consist of *collections* of student work: a number of pieces of work produced by individual students. Second, the collections are *purposeful* rather than random.
>   Third: most descriptions of portfolios include the opportunity for students to comment or reflect on their work.[28]

Danielson and Abrutyn identified three major types of portfolios. *Working Portfolios* contain work in progress and finished samples of work. *Display Portfolios* contain the best work of the student. *Assessment Portfolios* document what a student has learned. In discussing innovative uses of portfolios, Danielson and Abrutyn identified examples of portfolios that "allow students to document aspects of their learning that do not show up well in traditional assessments."[29] The examples they gave were Interdisciplinary Unit Portfolios, Community Service Portfolio, Subject Area Portfolios, College Admissions Portfolio, Employment Portfolio, and Skill Areas Portfolio.[30] Reflecting on the different types of portfolios, the authors said:

Portfolios may take many different forms and may be used for many different purposes. They may be used to diagnose, document, or celebrate learning. Regardless of their primary purpose or audience, they have the power to transform the learning environment in the classrooms where they are used. The magic of portfolios lies not in the portfolios themselves, but in the process used in creating them and the school culture in which documented learning is valued."[31]

In discussing the benefits of portfolios, they noted:

The benefits of portfolios result principally from the process of building and using them. While the portfolios themselves have value, particularly in the area of assessment (permitting the evolution of a wide range of outcomes and documenting growth over time), it is the process of creation that offers great power to educators. Students become highly engaged in their own learning through the steps of selection and reflection, assume considerable responsibility for that learning, and enter into a different relationship with their teachers, one characterized as more collegial than hierarchical."[32]

Reflecting on the above, for portfolios to be effective, certain conditions have to be met. First, students, teachers and parents have to have access to the student portfolios. The purpose of student's access to his or her portfolios is twofold: first, to continue building and improving his or her products; second, to review the teacher's comments on the work done, as well as assignments related to the portfolios. The purposes of the teacher's access to student portfolios are to monitor student's progress, assess student's achievement, advise on certain action to be taken by the student, and maintain constant communication with the student as well as his or her parents. Parents' access to their sons' and daughters' portfolios helps establish school-parent-student partnership in the education system and maintains interest in their children's progress in learning.

Second, portfolios have to be stored in a way that makes access to them by students, teachers, and parents possible. The logistics of portfolio management could be overwhelming. Just reflecting on the various types of portfolios and the variety of items that they contain and the number of students engaged in developing portfolios, storage, let alone access, is practically impossible. I think that the management of student portfolios can best be achieved through the application of digital technology.

Student Portfolios Management through Digital Technology

Multimedia authoring systems, or advanced word-processing software such as Word XP, can be easily used to organize, store, and access student portfolio products. Student products can be stored as computer files. For students' 3-D products, pictures, or videos can be taken and stored as digital files. Using the link capability in PowerPoint 2002 or Word XP, the files can be accessed for review. For the purpose of illustration, we discuss the use of PowerPoint 2002, an easy-to-learn authoring system, which could be a viable system for storing and accessing student portfolios.

PowerPoint 2002 is a component of MSOffice XP that can be used to create audio and visual presentations. The presentation in PowerPoint is usually composed of a series of slides. Each slide can contain text, graphics, audio, video, and animation objects. Transition between slides can be done automatically or by the click of the mouse. Many interesting techniques are employed in the program, which can allow for special transition effects such as dissolve, fade-in, fade-out, or different wipe effects.

Slides can contain navigation icons, which can help the user in navigating a hypermedia presentation. Any of the objects on any slide can be linked to any computer file or to a web site. Clicking the mouse on a link to a computer file, the file is retrieved and displayed on the computer monitor. Clicking the mouse on a link to a web site, the user is connected to that site on the web, providing that the computer has access to the web.

Using these effective and easy-to-learn presentation features, a PowerPoint slides program can be used as a container for a student portfolio. Since the portfolio is digital it can be accessed like any other computer file. Also, the file can be saved as an HTML file for posting the portfolio on the web or the school home page. Since digital files can be stored on diskettes, the size for space needed for storage of portfolios is minimized. Accordingly, the problem of accessing and storing student portfolios could be resolved.

In the following paragraphs, a possible scenario for a student portfolio is presented.

The first slide could contain the title of the portfolio, the name of the student, the school's name, the grade level, and the academic year. All of the objects on the first slide could be linked to other slides containing more detailed information about that object. For instance, the name of the student could be linked to a student biography slide, which contains a short biography of the student as well as a color portrait. Other objects on this slide can then be linked to other slides such as "my hobbies are." With the possibility of hyperlinks, the student can include a number of slides to introduce him/herself to potential reviewers of the portfolio. Similarly, links can be established between the rest of the objects on the first slide and slides that can present more information about each object.

Through navigation icons, the reviewer can be guided through an interactive visit of the student's portfolios. For instance, an icon can be established on the first page to take the reviewer to a table of contents of the portfolio. Since we are dealing with a seamless, integrated environment, links can also be established to access text, picture, sound, videos, animation and spreadsheet files. It is also possible to establish links to the student's home page on the web if he or she has one or to other related web sites.

If the student's digital portfolio is posted on the school home page, providing that this does not jeopardize his or her safety, parents and interested community agencies and individuals can view the student's portfolio. Having the student's e-mail address, as well as the teacher's e-mail address, reviewers can make their comments directly to the student or to the teacher.

From this scenario, one could see that the use of affordable digital technology can help solve the storage and accessibility problems of students' portfolios.

Lesson Plans

One of the early and interesting CD-ROMs was *Science Helper K–8*.[33] The CD-ROM contained 919 lesson plans for grades K to 8 that were selected from eight elementary science curriculum projects funded by National Science Foundation. The disc included abstracts of each lesson, the full contents of each lesson plan, the philosophy of each curriculum project, and retrieval software that allows the user to locate lessons for a certain grade to address a certain curriculum objective. For example, one can enter a search to satisfy the following search query:

Steps of the Query	Menu Selection	Number of Lessons That Match the Query
1. Pick Up a Grade	3 or 4	583
2. Academic Subject	Physical Science	239
3. Content Theme(s)	Interaction/Change in Systems	112
	and	
	Instruments	3
4. Process(es) of Science	Operationally Defining	1
	or	
	Measuring	2
	or	
	Predicting	3

5. View Lesson Titles:
   A. Measuring Rate of Evaporation of Water
   B. Patterns and Predicting: Temperature Change
   C. Forces: Weight—A Gravitational Force
6. Selecting a lesson produces the abstract of the lesson on the screen, and pushing F9 retrieves the whole lesson plan.

One of the benefits of using this CD-ROM is helping the teacher focus on goals and specific objective of a lesson, its content theme(s), and employed processes of science.

The CD-ROM had a number of drawbacks by our present standard of CD-ROM design and production. Although you could print the lesson plan, you couldn't save it to a diskette. The quality of the text on the screen and on the printed version was that of the early days of microcomputer technology. The visuals and the illustrations were relatively poor. However, some of the concepts presented are still valid and creative. Even with these drawbacks, studying a variety of lesson plans could enhance teachers' attempts to design creative lessons.

Today, computer and telecommunications technologies can assist in bringing to the teacher's desktop a wealth of up-to-date lesson plans from a variety of resources. This can be done using a variety of approaches.

Connecting to Web Resources on Teaching Plans

There is a wide range of web sites focusing on different disciplines that can provide valuable information on designing teaching plans. The following five sites are selected to demonstrate lesson plan materials that are available to teachers through computer technology. Searching the web, one can locate other rich resources in addition to the ones selected for this discussion.

The Educational Resources Information Center (ERIC)

ERIC is "a federally funded national information system that provides, through its 16 subject-specific clearinghouses, associated adjunct clearinghouses, and support components, a variety of services and products on a broad range of education-related issues."[34]

AskERIC is one of the rich online resources for educators, K through college. It is a personalized Internet-based service providing education information to teachers, librarians, counselors, administrators, parents, and anyone interested in education throughout the United States and the world. It began in 1992 as a project of the ERIC Clearinghouse on Information and Technology.[35] At present, it is with the ERIC Clearinghouse, a component of the Information Institute of Syracuse[36] at Syracuse University. Today, AskERIC encompasses the resources of the entire ERIC system and beyond, using the subject expertise of the 16 ERIC Clearinghouses[37] to respond to education requests.

AskERIC includes:[38]

Question & Answer (Q&A) Service[39]

"Personal e-mail response to questions submitted is usually received within two business days from one of the network information specialists in the ERIC system. The inquirer will also receive a list of ERIC database citations, and will also be referred to other Internet resources for additional information."[40]

Resource Collection[41]

"In response to questions we've received at AskERIC, our network information specialists have compiled over 3000 resources on a variety of educational issues. This collection includes Internet sites, educational organizations, and electronic discussion groups. We will continue to add new resources as we find them."[42]

Question Archive[43]

"Got an education question? Perhaps it's been asked before. Check out our Question Archive! We have created a collection of over 110 responses to questions received through the AskERIC Question & Answer Service. These responses may include ERIC citations, Internet sites, discussion groups, and/or print resource information."[44]

Lesson Plans[45]

"The AskERIC Lesson Plan Collection contains more than 2000 unique lesson plans which have been written and submitted to AskERIC by teachers from all over the United States. Contributions from individuals are essential to the collection; it is how it grows! If you have a great lesson plan you would like to share with educators all over the world, please *send it*[46] to us."[47]

ERIC Database[48]

"The ERIC database, the world's largest source of education information, contains more than one million abstracts of documents and journal articles on education research and practice. By searching AskERIC's web-based version of the ERIC Database, you can access the ERIC abstracts which are also found in the printed medium, *Resources in Education and Current Index To Journals in Education*. The database is updated monthly, ensuring that the information you receive is timely and accurate."[49]

Mailing Lists[50]

"AskERIC maintains the archives of 25+ education-related discussion groups, including K12Admin, a school administrator discussion; LM_NET, a world wide discussion group for school library media topics; and EDTECH, a discussion of educational technology issues. You can search the archives or browse through each month sorting by date or thread."[51]

Teacher's Edition Online—Teachnet.com

"Teachnet.com was started in August 1995 by the husband and wife team of Lee Shiney (graphic designer and writer) and Lajean Shiney (4th–5th grade teacher at Lawrence Elementary School, USD 259, Wichita, Kansas). After being introduced to the Internet, they immediately saw the potential for this technology as a communication vehicle for educators."[52] Among the features of this site is "Lesson Plans." It publishes lessons in language arts, math, science, social studies, health and physical education, technology, and arts.

Another feature, "Take 5 Micro Activities," is a frequently updated list of classroom activities "to fill up five minutes." The following is the list retrieved on July 23, 2003 from Teachnet.com:

- Brainstorm inventions to be foot operated.
- Read a given text. Find as many synonyms and/or antonyms as possible. Work in groups if you like.
- Find the average shoe size of your class.
- A student shares something that stresses them out, then other students can brainstorm suggestions to relieve the stress.
- Sketch an idea for an art project you can eat.
- Brainstorm uses for a brick.
- Pull a long word from the dictionary, then see how many other words can be made from it.
- List all the birthdays in your class on the chalkboard by month, then discuss the idea of "randomness."
- When lined up to leave the room, with backs to the wall, pass a baseball bat or yardstick from the front to the back of the line by using their feet (without kicking). Two or three students carefully lift it up on the tops of their feet at the same time and pass it toward the back, down the line without it touching the floor.
- Think of ways food can make noise.
- Think of 10 ways to get rid of junk mail.
- Discuss how water might be made to go uphill with buckets, through a pipeline, forced through a sprayer, even from a tornado or hurricane; anything's possible in a brainstorming exercise. Fill up a couple of minutes discussing how pumps might work with pistons and valves, or with rotating turbines or blades.
- For those of us still stuck in the clunky non-metric world, on 1 inch wide strips of paper, using a ruler, students can make 6 in/15 cm (or longer) rulers, with centimeters on top and inches on the bottom. Tape to the tops of their desks where they'll stay all year, and when giving assignments or discussing measurements, switch back and forth between inches and centimeters. Over time they will develop a feel for **both** systems, where, when asked "how long is 40 cm?" they will be able to hold up their hands and say "about that long".
- Give students examples of square roots, if they don't know the term already, then have them estimate the square root of some large numbers, like 540, 27,000 or 8,000,000.
- Have students describe the first place they would take a foreign visitor and explain why that place is important to them.
- Discuss mascots or symbols that would be more appropriate for political parties. Need more? Come up with two or three new political parties and what they would stand for.

- What if buildings were made of flexible materials? What are some advantages and disadvantages? What would it be like to be in one? What effect would weather have?
- Think of different symbols for clock faces.
- Have students make their own "business cards" (use the school's address and phone for privacy if you like) using their own paper, pens and markers. They can even include a "business" of their own creation. Then staple them all to a bulletin board and repeat the exercise periodically. Working within the five-minute parameter gives them a tight, real-world "deadline" to focus on.
- Ask a student to describe a Global Positioning System device. Brainstorm interesting uses for one.
- Have students brainstorm how the world seems to be designed for adults, and explain what they would like to see to make them feel more comfortable or important.
- What If: falling rain suddenly froze in mid-air?
- Give each student a meter of string and a piece of heavy paper or cardboard. Let them cut a 10 cm. circle, punch a couple of holes toward the center (like a button) and thread the string through to make one of those things you made as a kid out of real buttons, that spins and whizzes when the string is pulled just right. Have them color the paper with markers or crayons, trying spiral patterns or primary colors that will blend into third colors.[53]

The Collaborative Lesson Archive

Bill and Dee Chapman explained the purpose of The Collaborative Lesson Archive (CLA) to be a forum for the creation, distribution, and archive of education curricula for all grade levels and subject areas. They explained the purpose of the site saying:

> We realize that a teacher's life is a busy one. This tool has the potential to be a time-saver for all educators if it is used responsibly. If everyone who visits this site submits one or two of their favorite lessons to the archive, it will grow into a very useful resource. The responsibility does not end there, however. If you decide to use the lessons or ideas from someone's posted lesson, please return to the archive and use the collaboration/comment posting capabilities of the archive and submit comments about what did and/or did not work well in the classroom environment. This collaboration feature will help refine the current ideas and augment each posted lesson with fresh new ideas.[54]

The archive is nonprofit. Teachers are encouraged to submit their best lesson plans on a non-copyright basis. Teachers are asked to submit their feedback if they select to copy a lesson plan. This makes this site a great meeting place for teachers to collaborate in developing lesson plans.

Teachers Helping Teachers

The home page of this site describes the site as "a free, non-profit service. It costs nothing to access the information, and no money is made from teachers who contribute. Material on this service is updated weekly during the school year."[55]

The goals of the service are:

1. To provide basic teaching tips to inexperienced teachers; ideas that can be immediately implemented into the classroom.
2. To provide new ideas in teaching methodologies for all teachers.
3. To provide a forum for experienced teachers to share their expertise and tips with colleagues around the world.[56]

Lesson plans include classroom management, language arts, math, science, social studies, and special education. One of the interesting links provided on this site is Educational Resources on the Web. The Educational Resources on the Web site includes links to rich teaching and learning resources for teachers: "Arts" Resources Online, Early Childhood Resources Online, Language Arts Resources Online, History/Social Studies Resources Online, Multi-Cultural Resources Online; Science & Math Resources Online; Social Action—Taking Care of Our Society, Special Education/Gifted Resources Online, and some of the best teacher resources available on the web.[57]

Busy Teachers' Web Site K–12

Carolyn Cole began this site. In her words:

During my winter break from school (Georgia Institute of Technology in 1994), I spent some time exploring the Internet (about a gazillion hours!). I began to think of the Internet as a vast electronic library whose materials were scattered about in cryptic places. In this unchartered and uncatalogued space, total democracy existed. Anyone could author materials as well as decide which materials would be made available to others.

I found what one might expect under these circumstances, that the Internet contained a range of materials from useless junk (at least to me) to incredibly rich and fascinating source materials. The Internet held the possibility for wasting my time as well as the potential for enriching my life.

I then put on my teacher's "hat" from my prior years as a public school teacher. I was curious to see what resulted from trying to use the Internet as an educational tool. What I discovered was informative for the eventual design of the Busy Teachers' Website.[58]

She stated two goals for the site:

1. To provide teachers with direct source materials, lesson plans/classroom activities with a minimum of site-to-site linking.
2. To provide an enjoyable and rewarding experience for the teacher who is learning to use the Internet.[59]

VIRTUAL REALITY

A. S. Akins (1992) defined visual reality as "the concept of computer generated three-dimensional simulated models combined with devices that track the movement of a user's eyes, head, hands or body. The system monitors changes in user's movement or in the model and updates the model."[60] Nicholas Negroponte (1995), the founding director of the MIT Media Lab, explains the idea behind virtual reality (VR) as delivering a sense of "being there." In his words:

> The idea behind VR is to deliver a sense of "being there" by giving at least the eye what it would have received if it were there and, more important, to have the image change instantly as you change your point of view. Our perception of spatial reality is driven by various visual cues, like relative size, brightness, and angular movement. One of the strongest is perspective, which is particularly powerful in its binocular form in that your right and left eyes see different images. Fusing those images into one 3-D perception is the basis of stereovision.[61]

James R. Fruchterman (1992) defined virtual reality as "the science of creating artificial worlds."[62] He believed that the cartoon-quality images of VR programs are "the beginning of our move into cyberspace, the artificial realm inside our computers."[63] He defined cyberspace as a "universe where all sights, sounds, tastes, smells, and touches are created by computer but seen as real as our everyday world."[64] Predicting the future, he said, "To many twenty-first century business people and technologists, cyberspace will be the everyday world."[65]

Negroponte (1995) predicts future generations of adults as well as children entertaining themselves through VR experience:

> Jurassic Park would make a fabulous VR experience. Unlike the book or movie of the same name, it would not have a story line. Michael Crichton's job in this case would be that of stage-set or theme-park designer and the one who imbues each dinosaur with appearance, personality, behavior, and purpose. Put the simulation in motion. Then you enter. This is not television, and it need not be as antiseptic as Disneyland. There are no crowds, no queues, no popcorn smells (just dinosaur dung). It is like being in a prehistoric jungle and can be made to seem more dangerous than any real jungle.
>
> Future generations of adults as well as children will entertain themselves in this manner. Since the imagery is computed, not real, there is no need to limit

oneself to life-size or real places. VR will allow you to put your arms around the Milky Way, swim in the human bloodstream, or visit Alice in Wonderland.[66]

Negroponte indicated that "Game companies are driving display technology so hard that virtual reality will become a 'reality' at very low cost, . . . On November 15, 1994, Nintendo announced a $199 virtual reality game called 'Virtual Boy'."[67]   .

To enter the virtual reality world, typically, the visitor wears a head-mounted display (HMD). The HMD includes two small TV monitors, one for each eye. Integrating the two images in the brain, the visitor perceives a 3-D image. In addition to the visual component, the HMD has internal headphones to receive sound, and tracking sensors to track the visitor's head movement around the perceived 3-D world allowing the perceived image to change in synchronization with the head movements. To simulate whole body movement, the visitor wears a glove connected to the computer. Gentle hand movements can bring the visitor closer or farther away from objects in cyberspace. The combination of the HMD and the gloves allows the visitor to travel inside the computer cyberspace.

At present, the quality of VR images is relatively poor, especially in low-cost VR systems. Worse than the poor image quality, VR is not yet fast enough.[68] As the visitor moves his or her head, the image does not change rapidly enough; it lags.[69] Negroponte thinks that the slightest delay in responding to the visitor's motion can ruin the VR experience.[70]

A second type of VR is "lab simulator" like an aircraft simulator. In an aircraft simulator, the trainee is seated inside a simulated cockpit, which has a console similar to that of a real airplane. Instead of the front window, large TV monitors or screens project an image of a flying environment. Negroponte indicates that flight simulations are "the most sohisticated and longest-standing application of VR." [71] He explains:

> (Flight simulation) is more realistic than flying a real plane. Newly trained but fully able pilots take the controls of a completely loaded passenger plane for their first flight in a "real" 747, because they have learned more in the simulator than they could have learned in the actual plane. In the simulator, a pilot can be subjected to all sorts of rare situations that, in the real world, could be impossible, could require more than a near miss, or could rip apart an actual plane.[72]

HMD and flight simulators are just two types of VR worlds. Brill (1994) defined three types of virtual reality worlds: Stage World, Desktop World, and Mirror World.[73] In the Stage World he identified three technologies: HMD, Cab, and the Chamber World. HMD was explained earlier, and "Cab" technology is what is used in flight simulators. Brill explains the Chamber World virtual environment:

> A virtual world in this environment is projected into a room surrounding all walls and ceiling. The viewer enters and by wearing special 3-D glasses is able

to become completely immersed within the virtual world. One of the unique characteristics of this world is that many people can participate in the same virtual world simultaneously.[74]

The second type of VR that Brill explained is the Desktop World. In this type he identified two VR environments: Desktop Virtual Reality and Head-Coupled Display. In the Desktop Virtual Reality situation, "a virtual world is created and then experienced from a desktop monitor with the assistance of a mouse, dataglove, or spaceball input system."[75]

In the virtual world of the Head-Coupled Display, Brill explains:

> . . . participants use a mobile binocular display that is suspended from an articulated arm and that allows participants to encounter a virtual environment without the encumbrance of wearing an HMD. The articulated arm is flexible enough that it visually corresponds to movement in any direction as well as upwards or downwards viewing as defined by the virtual experience.[76]

The third and the last type of virtual worlds is the "Mirror World." In this virtual world, viewers watch themselves move through a virtual environment. Brill explains this type:

> Participants create this experience by moving into a specially prepared virtual center that photographs their image and reproduces a real-time counterpart with a televised virtual world environment. Users are able to see their image within the virtual world and to move accordingly to direct their image in relationship to that world.[77]

Virtual Reality on the Internet

The Internet has a number of sites focusing on virtual reality. Some of them address applications in education, such as Virtual Reality in Education[78] and Virtual Reality Resources for K–12 Education.[79] Others focus on programming for VR environments and advanced articles such as Televirtuality. Televirtuality-based educational process is defined as "a personalized active navigation through unbounded HyperWorld constructed by smoothly linking a myriad of specialized virtual environments."[80] It is conceived that Televirtuality "will replace television, telephony, personal computing and video games. This integration process has already started (e.g., video-on-demand and other first tests of interactive television), is expected to deliver the VRTV prototypes three to five years from now, and will continue in the twenty-first century."[81]

Regardless of the VR technology, the VR objective is to immerse the visitor in a rich and interactive cyberspace environment. Stephen Marcus (1992) explains VR technologies are used to create "a simulation that you seem to enter physically."[82] He quoted Randall Walser, of the Autodesk

Research Lab, who suggests that "text tells, video and film show, and virtual reality *embodies* the world it creates."[83]

Virtual reality provides a safe environment for learning and practicing highly technical skills such as landing an airplane or performing surgery. Virtual reality environments can be effective in exploring 3-D models. One of the uses in architecture is to construct a virtual environment of a building from the blueprints. Then, a physically challenged person in a wheelchair can perform a simulation in this VR to determine accessibility problems within the building.

With all the positive potential effects, there are concerns due primarily to the high degree of realism students experience and the inability of some of them to differentiate between VR and the real world. Diane Andolsek (1995) explains: "The same technology that will let students learn to perform dangerous tasks or experiments through simulation is already letting them experience in great realism the thrill of killing a simulated opponent."[84] Accordingly, educators should constantly address developing young people's abilities to differentiate between real life and depicted life either in a VR environment or on conventional television.

THE COMPUTER AS A TUTOR—TEACHING STRATEGIES

There are several teaching strategies used in conjunction with the use of computers in education: drill and practice, tutorial, simulation, and games. These strategies often have been called computer-sssisted instruction (CAI). CAI refers to "any use of a computer to present instructional material, provide for active participation of the student, and respond to student action."[85] Usually, in one CAI program more than one strategy is employed.

In the following few pages, commonly used strategies are briefly discussed.

Drill and Practice

Drill and practice programs are "designed to integrate previously learned material through practice on the computer. They provide immediate feedback, individualization, and self-pacing. They are usually a supplement to other instruction and are the most common type of CAI found."[86]

Drill and practice teaching strategy is a direct outgrowth of programmed instruction movement discussed in the previous chapter. Four basic principles of programmed instruction are usually employed in drill and practice exercises:

1. The learning material is presented in small successive steps with explicit practice and testing of each step.

2. Presentation of subsequent steps depends on the learner's response.
3. Immediate feedback to student's response is provided, if the student's response was incorrect, he or she is led to correct the errors.
4. The student proceeds at his own rate; faster students move rapidly in the instructional sequence, and slower students take a longer time.

In addition to these principles, drill and practice exercises are applicable to a variety of subject matter. They aim at drilling the learner in basic subject matter skills such as basic arithmetic operations. The idea behind drill and practice exercises is to pose a question to the learner to which he or she has to give the correct answer before advancing to the next question. Usually, drill and practice exercises have different levels of complexity to suit the needs of different learners and to provide the opportunity for the learner to gradually advance to higher levels at his or her own pace.

Most drill and practice programs provide a record-keeping option, which the teacher can use to assess the progress of the students in achieving the intended objectives of the exercises. Some exercises also have the option to print, at the command of the learner, the score achieved. However, drill and practice exercises cannot determine the cause of mistakes made by the student. When the student makes a mistake, he or she is told to try again. If the student does not provide the correct answer after a limited number of attempts, the correct answer is revealed. With the expected development of artificial intelligence and more powerful computers, one can foresee drill and practice exercises that prescribe and lead the student in remedial steps leading to the mastery of the learning task.

Some drill and practice programs incorporate game strategies. Mastery of the targeted skills is a prerequisite to the winning of the game. Thus, as the learner plays, he or she reinforces the skills he or she acquired. With the current advancement in computer technology, drill and practice exercises make use of the multimedia capabilities of computers. Colorful pictures, animation segments, and audio clips, in playing a game that requires the mastery of subject-matter skills, make learning fun and exciting.

Tutorials

Tutorials are similar to drill and practice in the matter of guiding the learner through small steps until the learner understands the information the program is designed to teach. The information in a tutorial is presented through a series of colorful frames. Images, video clips, animated sequences, and sound clips are used to guide the learner through subsequent steps leading to the mastery of the information presented. The emphasis in tutorials is not on questioning the learner but on providing an interactive presentation during which the learner develops an understanding of the program's information.

Computer software tutorials, in some programs, are an option the user might install when installing the software. Some major producers of software implement an integrated media approach to instruct novice users in the basics of the software and expert users in the new features of updated software. To this end, colorful printed illustrated guides and video programs are developed.

Subject matter tutorials cover a variety of subject matter designed for various schooling levels. A record-keeping capability is incorporated into the program to allow the teacher to monitor the student's progress and to inform the student on his/her progress. Sophisticated programs employ a branching strategy to guide the student, if he or she repeats a mistake, to "remedial" exercises or demonstrations and then back to the point where the student left off.

Simulations and Demonstrations

Simulation programs present to the student a hypothetical or a virtual situation and allow the student to make decisions and safely experience the outcome of these decisions. This strategy "allows the student to experiment with and experience situations, which might otherwise be dangerous or impractical to manipulate directly. With the advent of the computer, the flexibility and quality of simulations has greatly improved."[87] Most of the VR programs utilize simulations. (Please refer to Virtual Reality discussion.)

Demonstration programs are different from simulations. The demonstration of a procedure is recorded. The student can view the demonstration as many times as he or she would like. If the demonstration is loaded on a server, students can retrieve it any time they would like. In this approach two values are realized, reducing the cost of running a demonstration more than once, and providing access to absent students, or to students who need to study the material at their own pace. If the demonstration is saved as an HTML document, links can be established to other interesting demonstrations and valuable text information.

Games

Games are fun. A visitor to a video arcade experiences the excitement demonstrated by young and old people as they play with computerized video games. In most, if not in all of the arcade games, the emphasis is on eye and hand coordination to win against your opponent (if more than one person is playing the same game on the same machine) or to reach a high score with the computer. Educational games are different. They present a problem. To solve it, the student has to master a body of information. According to Budoff et al. (1995), "other skills such as eye, hand coordination and quick responses are also taught in a way that students do not even realize that they are learning."[88]

To be effective, educational games should be designed to achieve the following:

1. The student should be able to easily understand the objective of the game.
2. The game has to be challenging. At any point in the game, the student should be able to track back to where he came from and to exit at any time he or she chooses to do so.
3. Success in the game should depend on the mastery of the information the program is set to achieve.
4. The game should have different levels of complexity including a beginner's level and advanced level.
5. Multimedia technology ought to be used to provide an interesting game setting.
6. The game should have a record-keeping function. Some games allow the user to print a certificate of completion.

To summarize, common among the various CAI are the basic four principles of programmed instruction: (1) presenting the learning material in small successive steps, (2) progress from one step to the next based on the successful completion of the step, (3) self-paced learning, and (4) immediate feedback. In addition, CAI programs provide consistency of instruction; the same exact instruction can be provided to many students time after time.

MULTIMEDIA-ASSISTED INSTRUCTION

With the advent of powerful computers and the development of the hypermedia concept, CAI integrates a variety of media. Accordingly, "multimedia-assisted instruction" is a more accurate expression than "computer-assisted instruction." Multimedia-assisted instruction (MAI) is an enriched learning environment employing the principles of structuring effective learning environments, which are discussed in Chapters 3, 4, and 5.

Comparing learning experiences of special students in a conventional classroom with that of computer enriched environment through the application of MAI, Amani Hefzallah wrote:

Johnny fidgets at his desk as he reads and rereads his assignment. It is not making sense to him. As he looks round the room, most of his classmates are finished . . . Mary is embarrassed by the red markings on her paper. She has more misspellings than the other children; even though she is trying very hard . . . Joey is trying to sound out the word. He knows all the letters, but he cannot seem to pronounce the word the way the teacher wants him to. The class is waiting for him. While every student experiences these feelings at one time or another, learning disabled students experience problems like these on a constant basis. In school, where most activities require reading, having a disability in this area puts a student at a serious disadvantage.

Now imagine this scenario instead . . . Johnny sits at a computer in his classroom. As he reads the text presented on the computer screen, he comes across a word he does not understand. Using the mouse, he selects the confusing word. The computer generates an alternate word with the same meaning. He can also click on an icon to see a definition of the word, or click on another icon and have the text read to him by a pre-recorded voice. He completes his assignment at his own pace, not troubled by the speed of those around him. The computer at various points in the assignment quizzes him to check his understanding, and he is given immediate feedback. He will not move onto the next lesson until he has mastered what is being taught.[89]

The above is an example of what a computer-enriched environment using MAI can offer the student. MAI empowers the student to learn. The student becomes in control of his or her learning. Through programmed directions incorporated in the program and teacher counseling, the student advances in learning according to self-pace.

Multimedia programs usually require a great deal of disk storage. Animation, audio, pictures, and video files are much larger files than text files. CD-ROM technology offers a solution to the storage of huge programs. A single CD-ROM disc can store up to 700 mb of information, which makes a CD-ROM equivalent to over 500 1.4mb floppy disks. The large capacity for storage is one of the main reasons that the CD-ROM became the distribution medium of MAI.

In the following chapter on CD-ROM technology, we review samples of MAI published in the CD-ROM format.

REFERENCES

1. Clarke, Arthur C. Foreword, *Technology 2001, The Future of Computing and Communications.* Derek Leebaert (Ed.), Cambridge, MA: The MIT Press, 1995, p. xi.
2. Multimedia Production Group, *Interactive Story Time*, vol. 2. 1992.
3. Mayer, Mercer. *Just Grandma And Me*, Broderbund Software, 1993.
4. Mayer, Mercer. *Just Me and My Dad*, Broderbund Software, 1997.
5. Brown, Marc. *Arthur's Teacher Trouble*, Living Books, A Random House/ Broderbund Company, 1993.
6. Brown, Marc. *Arthur's Birthday.* Living Books, Broderbund Software, 1997.
7. The Learning Company. *Reader Rabbit's Kindergarten*, Version 1.01, 1997.
8. The Learning Company. *Let's Start Learning*, 1995.

9. WebTV Info Center, http://wtvhelp.hypermart.net/about.html, accessed 7/16/03.

10. *Ibid.*

11. Microsoft Corporation, *In and Out of the Classroom,* Microsoft Office 97, 1998.

12. Microsoft Corporation, Word XP, Help Option, What Is Autocorrect? 2002.

13. Microsoft Corporation. *In and Out of the Classroom, Microsoft Office 97,* 1998.

14. Microsoft Corporation, *Microsoft Office XP Inside Out e-Book,* Copyright Michael Halvorson and Michael J. Young, 2001.

15. *Ibid.* Tracking and Reviewing.

16. *Ibid.* Tables

17. Microsoft Corporation. *The American Heritage Dictionary Microsoft BookShelf* 99, 1999.

18. *Ibid.* Computer and Internet Dictionary.

19. *Ibid.* Roget's Thesaurus of English Words and Phrases.

20. *Ibid.* The Columbia Dictionary of Quotations.

21. *Ibid.* Encarta Concise Encyclopedia.

22. *Ibid.* Encarta Desk Atlas.

23. *Ibid.* TimeLine.

24. *Ibid.* World Almanac.

25. *Ibid.* Manual of Style and Usage.

26. *Encarta Online,* http://encarta.msn.com/, accessed 7/23/03.

27. National Education Association, *Student Portfolios,* Washington, D.C.: NEA, 1993, p. 41.

28. Danielson, Charlotte and Leslye Arbrityn. *An Introduction to Using Portfolios in the Classroom,* Alexandria, VA: Association of Supervision and Curriculum Development, 1997, p. vii.

29. *Ibid.* p. 7.

30. *Ibid.* pp. 7–9.

31. *Ibid.* p. 9.

32. *Ibid.* p. 19.

33. *Science Helper K–8,* Gainesville, FL: PC-SIG, 1988.

34. The Educational Resources Information Center, http://www.eric.ed.gov, accessed 7/21/03.

35. ERIC Clearinghouse on Information and Technology, http://ericit.org/, accessed 7/21/03.

36. Information Institute of Syracuse, http://iis.syr.edu/, accessed 7/21/03.

37. ERIC Clearinghouses, http://www.eric.ed.gov./sites/barak.html, accessed 7/21/03.

38. The Educational Resources Information Center, *op. cit.*

39. Question & Answer (Q&A) Service, http://ericir.syr.edu/Qa/, accessed 7/21/03.

40. The Educational Resources Information Center, *op. cit.*

41. Resource Collection, http://ericir.syr.edu/, accessed 7/21/03.

42. The Educational Resources Information Center, *op. cit.*

43. Question Archive, http://ericir.syr.edu/Virtual/Qa/archives/, accessed 7/21/03.

44. The Educational Resources Information Center, *op. cit.*

45. Lesson Plans, http://ericir.syr.edu/Virtual/Lessons/, accessed 7/21/03.
46. Lesson Plan Submission Form, http://ericir.syr.edu/Virtual/Lessons/lpform.shtml, accessed 7/21/03.
47. The Educational Resources Information Center, *op. cit.*
48. ERIC Database, http://ericir.syr.edu/Eric, accessed 7/16/03.
49. The Educational Resources Information Center, *op. cit.*
50. Mailing Lists, http://ericir.syr.edu/Virtual/Listserve Archives/, accessed 7/21/03.
51. The Educational Resources Information Center, *op. cit.*
52. Teachnet.com http://www.teachnet.com/ downloaded 7/98.
53. Teachnet.com http://www.teachnet.com/powertools/take5/index.html, downloaded 7/23/03.
54. The Collaborative Lesson Archive. http://faldo.atmos.uiuc.edu/CLA/welcome.html, accessed 7/23/03.
55. Teachers Helping Teachers, http://www.pacificnet.net/~mandel/index.html, downloaded 7/23/03.
56. Teachers Helping Teachers, hosted by Education Orchard, http://www.edu-orchard.net/PROFESS/MANDEL/mandel1.html#anchor544843 downloaded 7/23/03.
57. Educational Resources on the Web, linked by Teachers Helping Teachers, http://www.edu-orchard.net/PROFESS/MANDEL/mandel2.html/, accessed 7/23/03.
58. Busy Teachers' Website K–12. http://www.ceismc.gatech.edu/busyt/k12wel.html, June 4, 1998.
59. Busy Teachers' Website K–12, http://www.ceismc.gatech.edu/busyt/welcome.html/ downloaded 7/23/03.
60. Akins, A.S. Virtual Reality and the Physically Disabled: Speculations of the Future, *Virtual Reality and Persons with Disabilities Proceedings*, Harry J. Murphy (Ed.), March 18–21, 1992. p. 9.
61. Negroponte, Nicholas, *Being Digital.* New York: Alfred A. Knopf, 1995. p. 117.
62. Fruchterman, James, The Age of Magic, *Virtual Reality and Persons with Disabilities Proceedings*, Harry J. Murphy (Ed.), March 18–21, 1992. p. 16.
63. *Ibid.* p. 17.
64. *Ibid.* p. 17.
65. *Ibid.* p. 17.
66. Negroponte, Nicholas. *Being Digital.* 1995, pp. 118–119.
67. *Ibid.* p. 83.
68. *Ibid.* p. 119.
69. *Ibid.*
70. *Ibid.* p. 120.
71. *Ibid.* p. 117.
72. *Ibid.* p. 117.
73. Brill, Louis M. Metaphors for the Traveling Cybernaut—Part II, *Virtual Reality World*, May/June 1994. p. 30.
74. *Ibid.* p. 31.
75. *Ibid.* pp. 30–33.
76. *Ibid.* p. 32.

77. *Ibid.* p. 33.

78. Virtual Reality in Education. http://archive.ncsa.uiuc.edu/Edu/RSE/VR/, downloaded 7/23/03.

79. Virtual Reality Resources for K–12 Education. http://www.ncsa.uiuc.edu/people/bievenue/VR,/ downloaded 7/23/03.

80. Virtual Reality for K–12 Education. http://www.npac.syr.edu/NAPC1/PUB/wojtek/hpsin/vredu.html/ downloaded 7/23/03.

81. *Ibid.* p. 1.

82. Marcus, Stephen, "Visual Realities: From the Concrete to the Barely Imaginable, *Virtual Reality and Persons with Disabilities Proceedings*, Harry J. Murphy (Ed.), March 18–21, 1992. p. 31.

83. *Ibid.* p. 31.

84. Andolsek, Diane L. Virtual Reality in Education and Training, *International Journal of Instructional Media* Vol. 22(2), 1995. pp. 145-155.

85. Criswell, E.L. *The Design of Computer-Based Instruction.* New York: Macmillan, 1989.

86. Budoff, M., T. Thorman, and A. Gras, Microcomputers in Special Education, Cambridge, MA: Brookline Books, 1985.

87. Mis, Fredrick, Computers in Education, in Hefzallah, Ibrahim M. (Ed.), *The New Learning and Telecommunications, Technologies and Their Potential Applications in Education*, Springfield, IL: Charles C Thomas, 1990, p. 75.

88. Budoff, M., T. Thorman, and A. Gras, *Microcomputers in Special Education*, Cambridge, MA: Brookline Books, 1985.

89. Hefzallah, Amani. CAI in Special Education, Unpublished Research Paper, Fairfield University, 1995.

Part Two

COMPACT DISC READ-ONLY-MEMORY (CD-ROM)

Chapter 8: Compact Disc Read-Only-Memory (CD-ROM)

INTRODUCTION

C D-ROM, a relatively new medium, became the medium of choice for storing tremendous amounts of information in multimedia formats. Chapter 8, "Compact Disc Read-Only-Memory (CD-ROM)," addresses the CD-ROM medium, the development of new CD formats such as CDI, PhotoCD, CD-RW, CDR, and Picture CD. It also tracks the development of CD-ROM software from a simple storage of large amounts of information to professionally designed multimedia, interactive CD-ROM programs.

Chapter 8

COMPACT DISC READ-ONLY-MEMORY (CD-ROM)

INTRODUCTION

CD-ROM—compact disc read only memory—was first announced by Philips and Sony in October 1983. It came about as an outcome of various inventions capitalizing on accuracy of laser technology and the foreseen quality of digital recording. The target was the consumer market, as Leonard Laub (1986) observed:

> The technology behind all of today's products for the optical storage of digital data comes not from the computer industry but the consumer electronics industry. During the late 1960s and early 1970s, television manufacturers around the world worked to develop home videodisc systems, which they intended to sell as accessories to television sets.[1]

Attention was first given to the production of an optical laser disc to store video and audio for playback on a regular home TV set. In 1978, Phillips/MCA introduced a laser videodisc player, which was followed by RCA magnetic videodisk in 1981. Laub (1986) in *CD-ROM The New Papyrus* reported that "Several mechanical and capacitance videodisc systems came to market during the 1970s, but only the optical videodisc system known as LaserVision (abbreviated LV) survived."[2] Pawha(1994) reports that Philips/MCA and RCA discontinued their products in 1984 "due to lower than expected sales."[3]

LASER VIDEODISCS

Laser videodiscs have many advantages. Videodiscs store audio and video information. Accordingly, videodiscs can be used to store and play movies. The quality of the image is better than home VHS images. Audio on a videodisc has two tracks that can be played simultaneously for a stereo effect, or one at a time. Some early use of this feature was to have the original movie sound track recorded on one track and a commentary on the different scenes on the second track.

Images and scenes on a laser videodisc can be retrieved at random. Random access makes it possible to control the operation of the laser videodisc by a computer. A great deal of interactive videodisc applications in education and in training used computers in conjunction with laser videodiscs.

O'Connor (1990) explains interactive video as "an instructional delivery system in which recorded video material is presented under computer control. Viewers not only see and hear the pictures and sound, they interact with the program by making active responses. Those responses affect the pace and sequence of the presentation."[4]

Three levels of videodisc interactivity were identified. O'Connor (1990) explains:

> By convention, interactive videodisc programs are described as falling within one of three 'Levels of Interactivity.'
>
> A Level I videodisc instructional program usually is a consumer videodisc player used to play videodisc programs with a minimum of user interactivity. Still-frame access may be possible at Level I, but generally the recorded video is played back by the user with no, or only minor, interruption.
>
> Level II industrial videodisc programs are characterized by on-board programmable memory and improved access time. Level II videodiscs are different from Level I in that they have digital coding data integrated into the videodisc itself at the time of mastering. This digital information is then "dumped" into the videodisc player's temporary memory storage area so that when the player is started (initialized), an effective random-access capability is provided on a stand-alone basis.
>
> Level III videodiscs do not contain the embedded digital control data of Level II programs but, rather, are controlled entirely by an "outboard" microcomputer. This use of a microcomputer rather than internal control data embedded on the disc itself gives more flexibility in constructing effective interactive video programming and is therefore the preferred approach of most educators today.[5]

Random access combined with the quality of the analog visual images on a laser videodisc contributed to the development of visual encyclopedias such as the *Slice of Life* Project. Based at the University of Utah, the project's primary purpose was "to encourage the development and sharing of educational multimedia applications and the integration of complementary teaching and learning technologies in health sciences and medical education."[6]

The Project started in 1986 with the production "of a videodisc containing 12,839 images from the combined visual resources of the University of Utah's Departments of Pathology, Radiology, Neuroanatomy, Anatomy, Neurosurgery, Ophthalmology, and the Medical Examiner's Office for the state of Utah."[7]

Over the span of ten years, seven editions of *Slice of Life* were produced. The seventh and the last edition (SOL VII) contained "more than 44,000 still images and 65 motion sequences related to human medicine, nursing, dentistry and allied health education."[8]

SOL VII represented "contributions from 63 institutions, two professional societies, a pharmaceutical company, and 240 individuals throughout the United States, Canada, Latin America, Europe and Australia. Subject areas on *Slice of Life* include: cardiology, cytology, embryology, gross anatomy, hematology, histology, microbiology, neuroanatomy, parasitology, pathology, radiology, gastric endoscopy, colonoscopy, dermatology, and ophthalmology."[9]

Another project similar to the *Slice of Life* was the *Slice of Brain Videodisc*, a 20,779 encyclopedia of stills and 151 motion picture sequences providing valuable resources for neuroscience education. Thirty-five institutions, one professional society, and 119 individuals contributed to the production of that videodisc.[10]

Over the years, "*Slice of Life* has evolved from just a videodisc product to an international network of health science educators and software developers mixing practical technology with education."[11]

In the spring of 2003, *Slice of Life* announced the "Grand SOL 2003 Giveaway." Qualified applicants would receive free copies of SOL editions VI and VII. The reason given was that the SOL project was cleaning its inventories of videodiscs.[12]

The SOL producers experimented with many methods of converting the analog videodisc images to digital images. They report:

> The production task proved too daunting. Each of the 44,000 analog frames from the videodisc would require individual hand-crafted image enhancement in order for it to look decent in the higher resolution world of computer digital imagery. We decided to forego this process and instead encourage the use of other, new collections in which jpegs have been digitized directly from very high quality source materials, such as original 35mm transparencies or x-rays.[13]

The SOL producers referred researchers to two alternatives: *1000 Neuroscience Images on the Web* and *A Digital Brain Atlas on CD-ROM*. In both alternatives, media other than videodisc is used.[14]

While educational and research institutions vigorously studied and experimented with creative applications of videodiscs in learning and research, the use of laser videodiscs among the general public was limited. This is possibly due to the rerecording ability of VHS tape. Laser videodiscs are read only medium. Gradually, they are being replaced by DVD.

CD-AUDIO AND THE BIRTH OF CD-ROM

CD audio has been more successful than laser videodiscs, as Pawha reports:

Unlike videodiscs, CD Audio was successful in the consumer market very quickly. Compact disc players were introduced in Japan and Europe in October 1982, at a price of $900. In March 1983, CD Players were introduced in the United States. By October 1983, the price of a CD player had dropped from $900 to $300 and it was the most successful consumer product ever marketed. In 1983, 350,000 CD players and 17 million CDs were sold.[15]

In addition to the popularity of compact disc digital audio (CD-DA), the error rates found on CD-DA were low. Pawha explains the significance of low error rate in computer devices: "Audio systems can tolerate up to a certain extent losing the semantics of the message. Computer devices have a much lower tolerance for error. If a bit is flipped on the disc, there won't be much of a difference in the quality of music, but computer data may be changed completely."[16]

Encouraged by the success of audio CD and its low error rate, Sony and Philips developed CD technology for use with personal computers using the same architecture as CD-DA.[17] A Significant value of having the same architecture for both media, CD-DA and CD-ROM, is the very low production cost for CD-ROM, as Pawha explains:

> The beauty of CD-ROM architecture is that the basic architecture of CD Audio is exactly the same as CD-ROM. Therefore, the manufacturing plants making CD Audio can also make CD-ROM without changing the manufacturing process. CD Audio was very successful, and due to its high volume, the production cost of CD audio was very low. This resulted in a very low production cost for CD-ROM.[18]

Philips and Sony first announced CD-ROM in 1983. The first commercially available disc was *BiblioFile* in 1985. The physical and logical file system for CD-ROM was announced. First the physical standards were an extension of the CD-DA. "Red Book" is the common name of CD-DA standards. The reason for calling it "Red Book" is that the standards were published in a red binder. When Sony extended the standards for CD-ROM, it was published in a yellow binder; hence the standards for CD-ROM are known as the "Yellow Book" standards.

Late in 1985, a group of industry leaders met at the High Sierra Casino and Hotel in Lake Tahoe, California, to set the standards for the structural organization of files on the CD-ROM. These standards are known as the High Sierra standards. Later they were modified and formalized by the International Standards Organization (ISO) and became known as ISO 9660.[19,20]

THE CD-ROM MEDIUM

The CD-ROM is an optical disc. Information on the CD-ROM disc is recorded and retrieved using laser technology. Laser (light amplification by stimulated emission of radiation) is an intense and highly focused beam of pure and coherent light waves. The light waves are in phase and have the same frequency. The sharply focused light beam can read and write impressions on the disc. "Since the laser beam can be focused to one micron (millionth of a meter), data can be written on a disk in a very high track density."[21] Information on the CD-ROM is recorded as a spiral track of pits with spaces between them called "lands." CD-ROM The New Papyrus (1986) describes the track:

> The pits are 0.12 μm deep and about 0.6 μm wide. The neighboring turns of the spiral pattern of pits are 1.6 μm apart. This spacing corresponds to a track density of 16,000 tracks per inch (tpi), much higher than the figures associated with floppy . . . and Winchester magnetic disks. . . . The total length of the track on a CD-ROM disc is almost 3 miles. The total number of pits on a CD-ROM disc is almost 2 billion![22]

PRODUCING CD-ROM DISCS

There are two basic processes for producing CD-ROM discs. The first is the mastering and replication method. In this method the data to be recorded on the disc are first created and organized and then saved on a computer medium such as a hard disk or a Zip drive. The saved data are then sent to a CD replication house, where a glass master is produced from which a metal stamper is made to stamp copies of the CD-ROM. Pawha (1994) explains this process:

> . . . the traditional CD manufacturing process begins by embedding the data on a glass master. A metal stamper is created from the glass master, which is then used to manufacture compact discs by an injection-molding process. Initially, compact discs are transparent, and later an aluminum coating is applied to give them a reflective property. Finally, a lacquer coating is applied to protect the aluminum.[23]

This process is usually used for the production of a large number of CDs. For small quantities, CD-Recordable (CD-R) is another option. A blank CD disc is used with a CD recorder to burn the data on the blank disc. Once recorded, the disc can be read like any CD produced through the mastering and replication process.

CD-ROM UNIQUE CHARACTERISTICS

Huge Disc Capacity

A CD-ROM disc can hold over 700 MB of information. This is equivalent to information recorded on 500 high-density microcomputer floppy disks. A 20-volume adult encyclopedia might occupy about 20 MB of the 700-MB capacity of a CD-ROM, leaving enough room for images, video and sound clips, animation, graphs, charts, games, and search software. The huge disc capacity makes it feasible to store on one disc large amounts of interrelated information. It is also feasible to integrate with the text information multimedia segments to enhance the presentation of the information, and to enrich the integrated material on the disc.

A Searchable Medium of Vast Information

Information is growing at a tremendous rate. In any professional field, the mushrooming information is published in hundreds of professional and technical journals, as well as in a growing number of web sites. Inundated with information, one must identify pertinent information in one's discipline as well as in related disciplines to make a sound judgment on any issue and to stay abreast of new developments. Hence, there is a need for a system to provide access to vast amounts of interrelated information that can be easily searched to locate pertinent information. The CD-ROM is quite a feasible option due to its huge storage capacity and its user-friendly search software.

Hundreds of searchable databases in almost every field are currently installed on CD-ROM. For instance, *CINAHL* Database* contains more than 837,647 records from 1982 to July 9, 2003, with abstracts to articles published in more than 1,637 nursing and allied health journals.[24]

Business & Industry® Database (B&I) covers more than 900 major U.S. and international trade journals, general business publications, and national, regional, and international newspapers and newsletters from 1994 to the present, updated daily. Coverage is 50% U.S. content and 50% international and includes all industries and companies with over 340,000 records added each year. Approximately 60% of the database is full-text.[25]

The Complete YEARBOOK Collection CD combines the contents of 39 individual volumes published by Mosby-Yearbook, Inc., to give physicians access to expert information covering every field of medicine. "Citations listed are drawn from an information base of nearly 900 worldwide journals in medicine, surgery, dentistry, allied health, and other health sciences." The database combines the contents of the entire print series of Yearbooks from Mosby.[26]

---

*Cumulative Index to Nursing and Allied Health Literature.

ProQuest Newspaper Abstracts provides comprehensive coverage for articles published in leading international, national, and regional papers such as *The New York Times, USA Today, The Wall Street Journal, The Atlanta-Journal Constitution, Barron's, The Boston Globe, The Guardian, Christian Science Monitor, The Chicago Defender,* and *The Washington Post.*

> Each issue of every newspaper is indexed thoroughly, so researchers have access to not only top news stories but also detailed information on the arts, sports, business, and popular culture. Even such items as editorials, editorial cartoons, obituaries, and letters to the editor from well-known people are indexed.
>
> For each item cited in the database, an abstract of up to 75 words helps the researcher know almost instantly if the complete article will meet his or her needs.
>
> The database is updated several times each day. Archival coverage dates from 1989. Back files are available from 1985 to 1988.[27]

PsycLit is another database that contains abstracts of international literature in psychology and related behavioral and social sciences. It covers over 1400 journals and monographic series in 30 different languages from over 45 countries. The records of the *PsycLit* database are from 1974 to the present. It is updated quarterly, and 52,000+ records are added annually. The number of records exceeds 760,000.

Psyclit consists of two databases. One provides access to the international literature of psychology and material relevant to psychology in the related disciplines of education, medicine, business, sociology, and psychiatry. The second covers English-language books and book chapters published worldwide from 1987 to the present.[28]

ERIC on SilverPlatter is a U.S. national bibliographic database sponsored by the U.S. Department of Education,

> (It) blends two files: Resources in Education (RIE), covering the fugitive document literature, and Current Index to Journals in Education (CIJE), covering the published journal literature from over 775 periodicals. The database also includes the full text of *ERIC Digest* records. These one- to two-page full-text records, targeted specifically to teachers, administrators, and other practitioners, provide an overview of information on a given topic and supply references with more detailed information. The current disc covers the most recent 4 years; the archival disc set covers data from 1966 to the present. Subscription includes the thesaurus on disc and a separate tutorial.[29]

Zoological Record on Compact Disc provides comprehensive coverage of worldwide zoological literature. The database has:

> Over 6,500 international journals, review annuals, monographs, meeting proceedings, books and reports are monitored for inclusion. All major areas of

zoology are represented, including: behavior, ecology, evolution, habitat, nutrition, parasitology, reproduction, taxonomy, and zoogeography. The thesaurus in *Zoological Record on Compact Disc* provides an easy-to-use means of viewing a subject, geographical, palaeontological, and taxonomical hierarchical vocabularies, so users can select the controlled terms best suited for their searches. Updated annually, the thesaurus unifies sixteen years of database vocabulary for easy, effective searching. Current subscribers who have complete backfile will also automatically receive a free replacement backfile that incorporates the most current thesaurus.[30]

Some of the databases available on CD-ROM are also available on the Internet for a subscription charge. Six factors are considered when deciding to select databases on CD-ROM or the Internet. These factors are (1) cost of purchasing the CD-ROM, (2) subscription cost to the database through the Internet, (3) potential networking of the CD-ROM, (4) number of potential users, (5) expected time of utilization, and (6) degree of prompt access to the database and subsequent rate of data transfer. These factors change from one organization to another and from one database to another.

CHARACTERISTICS OF CD-ROM SEARCH

Efficient Search Options

CD-ROM technology employs a variety of search options that make searching for information on the disc fast and efficient. Among the common search options on a CD-ROM are:

1. Word, phrase, and proximity search.
2. Boolean search to target narrowly the area of interest.
3. Bookmarks that the researcher can use and save to identify locations in the database.
4. Use of Wildcards in word search for items that have common letters and for finding an item using a keyword that is either misspelled or spelled differently.
5. Use of icons to minimize keyboard use.
6. Use of drop menus with available options to the researcher.
7. Use of hypertext and hypermedia to link to related topics.
8. Use of Quick Facts to give highlights of the item located.
9. Use of an "outline" view to navigate through a long record.
10. Exporting marked text or media to the computer clipboard and saving the exported item as a text or media file.
11. Establishing a search log to keep track of the session's history.

Hyperenvironment

Electronic publications have the advantage of employing a hypersearch environment. The hyperenvironment affords the user the freedom to question the database in any way desired and in any order needed without losing track of where the search is heading. CD-ROM databases can offer these search strategies to the user.

With the growth and popularity of the World Wide Web, a great deal of recent CD-ROM publications contain pointers to relevant sites on the web. Some of these sites offer up-to-date information on the topics presented in the CD-ROM, and others contain related information to the CD-ROM topics.

Many CD-ROM programs can keep track of the history of the search conducted. This is especially useful in hyperenvironment to assist the researcher to stay on track. Usually the temptation to go off track in searching a CD-ROM is very high, similar to searching the WEB. A record of the steps in a search can help the researcher to refocus his or her search.

Immediate Assessment of Search Efforts

In electronic searches the researcher receives immediate feedback on the results of the query. This allows the researcher to redesign the search strategy or to search other databases.

Efficient search options, a hyperenvironment, and providing the researcher with immediate results of his or her search make the CD-ROM an ideal training environment for inquisitive minds. As discussed in Chapter 1, educated persons in the information age have to be able to think clearly and logically about accessing information that will satisfy the search for answers to relevant needs. First, they have to learn how to ask questions and to formulate hypotheses. Second, they have to design an inquiry to locate pertinent information. Third, they have to evaluate the accuracy and relevance of the located information. Fourth, based on the analysis of the information gathered, they draw conclusions, one of which is redesigning the search strategy. Electronic search, such as CD-ROM searches, can provide the environment, which can foster the development of the search skills.

A Choice Medium

The CD-ROM is considered by many as a choice medium for the aforementioned reasons and for the following reasons:

1. It is a durable medium. It is not affected by magnetic fields or temperature(within reason); however, more significant is that the user

cannot alter the information on the disc. Accordingly, no virus can be introduced to the disc.

2. It is an acceptable form of publication that is expected to increase in its efficiency through technological developments, which will increase its storage capacity, develop better search software, and decrease information access and transfer time.

3. More and more publishers will be mastering databases on CD-ROM. CD-ROM became an acceptable format for publishing vast amounts of information. In addition, its hyperenvironment and capability to link to the web entice authors and publishers to publish their material in CD-ROM format.

4. In certain situations the CD-ROM can be more economical than an online search. The cost for a CD-ROM is up-front, and the user is not faced with telephone costs or cost of being online.

5. CD-ROM networking allows more than one user to simultaneously use the same CD-ROM disc. As computer and CD-ROM technologies advance, both access and data transfer times of a networked CD-ROM will improve tremendously.

6. CD-ROM technology is currently integrated into personal computers. A CD-ROM drive is no longer considered a luxury. It is an essential component of all new PCs. This practice has increased the base of CD-ROM workstations.

7. CD-ROM burners (recorders) are affordable and are common accessories on many desktop computers, allowing the user to produce and use the medium of the CD-ROM.

NEW DEVELOPMENTS IN CD-ROM TECHNOLOGY

Research has improved the efficiency of the CD-ROM medium by:

1. Minimizing information access and transfer time.
2. Achieving smoother video segments and lip synchronization.
3. Developing the technology of a "writeable" CD-ROM (a "writeable" CD-ROM allows the production of a CD-ROM at the desktop).
4. Developing multisession CD-ROM recording technology (multisession CD-ROM allows adding information to a prerecorded disc).
5. Networking the CD-ROM (networking technologies make it easy for more than one user to access information from one CD-ROM at a relatively fast speed).

As a result of these creative and innovative efforts, the CD-ROM has become a viable medium of multimedia interactive databases. During the

1990s, other research efforts explored technologies for bringing the CD-ROM to the home user. The CD-R, CD-RW, compact disc interactive (CD-I), and photo CD became major CD-ROM technologies targeting the home user, educational institutions, and the corporate world.

CD-R and CD-RW

The CD-R (compact disc recordable) allows for blank discs to be used in a CD burner to record digital information. The disc may then be used in any regular CD-ROM drive to read the recorded information. CD-R is usually used to back up or distribute large files to interested parties and to make copies of an audio CD. In making copies of CD-ROMs or audio CDs, the user has the responsibility to respect and follow copyright guidelines.

Four different sizes of CD-R are supported by most current CD-ROM drives. These sizes are (1) the 74-minute CD-R (650 mb); (2) the 80-minute CD-R (700 mb); (3) the mini CD-R (180 mb); and (4) the business card CD-R (50 mb).

The CD-RW (compact disc rewriteable) is a disc that may be used to record, erase, and rewrite files. To make the CD-RW readable by any CD-ROM drive, the user has the option before ejecting the CD-RW from the burner to prepare it to be read by any CD-ROM drive. It is also possible to return the CD-RW to its original burner to convert it back to a rewritable disc.

For producing CD-Rs and CD-RWs, the computer must have the necessary software such as Adobe CD Creator or iSimplex CD.

CD-I, Compact Disc Interactive

On October 18, 1992, *The New York Times* carried a full-page advertisement for the Philips CD-Interactive (CD-I). The copy read: "The Imagination Machine: a new generation of compact disc technology for your television and stereo." By connecting this machine to a TV set, the advertisement claimed the product to be the first family-oriented entertainment system that would bring the world on a disc and put the consumer in control.

The CD-I player can play either an audio CD or the Philips-produced CD-I. The CD-I stores motion video, quality color graphics, and audio. Using a menu, the user can select what he or she wants to view or listen to. The viewer also can determine the order of the presentation of the different events stored on the disc.

The CD-I is one form of CD-ROM. The CD-I has been in the making for a number of years. The objective was to engineer a CD-ROM interactive system that would not require the use of a computer. The proposed system had to have a built-in microprocessor, and instead of a keyboard and mouse, a remote control pad would be used to access information from the disc. Since the unit would be designed primarily for home use, the consumer could connect the new CD-I player to a regular TV set to display the CD-I's information.

The interactive aspect of CD-I promised putting the user in control of the program on the disc. Using a menu to select items of interest in a hypermedia environment, the user can navigate through the information by using the remote control pad. When the system is turned on, an arrow appears on the screen of the TV set. The arrow's movement on the screen, up, down, right, and left is controlled by a button on the pad that acts like a joystick. Once the arrow lands on an icon on the screen, the user clicks another button on the remote pad to select that icon. Although the operation of the remote pad might feel awkward to some users, for others intimidated by a keyboard and mouse, the remote pad would be a good substitute. However, as more people gain experience in using computers, especially in navigating the web, apprehension associated with operating a keyboard and a mouse will diminish. To replace the pad with touchscreen technology makes the CD-I system an excellent medium for operation in a kiosk.

Another advantage of CD-I is that of providing alternate selections through which the consumer can tailor his or her viewing according to interest. In an entertainment program, for instance, let us assume that a mystery movie has been specially prepared for a CD-I recording. At different stages of the story development, the viewer is presented with options from which to select. An option is a decision point in the building of the story, which a character has to take, resulting in a series of events, which are different from those if the character chose a different option, that is, made a different decision. Movies especially prepared for a CD-I can have a variety of endings. The viewer determines the ending by selecting an option(s). Accordingly, the unfolding of the story is determined by the viewers' option(s) selection. This is different from a VCR recording of a movie. A movie recorded on VCR has a linear delivery format in which event "a" leads to event "b," and event "b" leads to "c," until one reaches the end of the story. In a CD-I format, the viewer interacts with the recorded material by selecting a different route of events. Thus event "a" might lead to event "d," and event "d" might lead to event "m." The question becomes how many conclusions are there in one program, and the answer is several.

The same idea has a great potential for education and training. In education, a CD-I in the field of ethics can present to the student a situation in which he or she must choose an action after which the student views the effect of that choice on the characters in the situation.

In training, a CD-I designed to teach a skill could present the consequence of performing a skill in a certain manner and with a certain degree of proficiency. It also can direct the student to improve performance by showing him or her, step by step, the "how" of performing a complex skill.

One of the titles used by Philips to demonstrate the advantages of CD-I is a CD-I golf program. In this program the user can freeze the frame, adjust the speed and the angle of the swing, and then observe the ball's path. The action can be repeated using different sets of speed and angle of swings with the result of each combination shown immediately on the screen.

The extent of interactivity depends on the number of options available on the disc. The user cannot change the programming of the disc because the manufacturer encodes the programming permanently on the disc.

Despite the promise of CD-I technology to provide different levels of interactivity, its use in education has been very limited. There may be many reasons why, among which is the growing ease of producing interactive programs that would meet the specific needs of a certain group of students. Authoring systems such as HyperStudio and PowerPoint are affordable and are relatively easy to learn to use in producing interactive educational multimedia programs.

The real growth in CD-I technology has been in the production of games. (For more information, refer to The New International CD-I site at http://www.icdia.org and The Black Moon Project at http://www.classicgaming.com/blackmoon/)

Development of Photo CD

In September 1990, Kodak introduced the photo CD system as the first affordable digital system for storing photographs.[31] For the first time it became possible for people who enjoy taking photographs to have an efficient system for storing their favorite pictures. Once stored on a photo-CD, they can view them on a regular home TV set by using a photo CD player. If they desire to incorporate their images in a computer application they can easily do that.

The new photo CD technology established a link between traditional photography and digital photography. It made use of the fact that picture taking using 35-mm films is common and universal. According to Georgia L. McCabe (1992), director of marketing at the Integration and Systems Products Division, Eastman Kodak Company, there are "250 million 35-mm cameras in use today, taking over 50 billion photographs per year."[32] The photo CD offers these users a digital way of storing photographs taken with a regular 35-mm camera and, of course, all the benefits associated with optical digital recording and retrieval.

In the summer of 1992, the photo CD system and photo CD player were introduced in North America, western Europe, and Japan, and in 1993, the professional photo CD imaging station 4200 was introduced. In the same year, Photo CD Portfolio format was improved, which allowed the user to create discs combining photographic images, audio, graphics, text, and programmed access.[33]

Quality of Photo CD Images

The quality of photo CD images is far superior to what a present-day TV set can display. It is also far superior to digital pictures produced by consumer-type digital cameras. Kodak offers three categories of photo CD disc formats: (1) Photo CD Master disc, (2) Pro Photo CD Master disc, and (3) Photo CD Portfolio II disc format.

The **Photo CD Master** disc is designed for 35-mm photography. It can hold about 100 images. The disc stores images at five levels of resolution. The highest resolution, 2048   3072 pixels, is 16 times that of current TV images and four times the standard recommended for high-definition TV (HDTV). The second level, 1024   1536 pixels, is the same as HDTV resolution. The third level, 512   768 pixels, is the same resolution as regular TV. The fourth level, 128   102 pixels, is known as the small thumbnail.[34]

The **Pro Photo CD Master** disc adds an optional higher level of resolution, 4096   6144 pixels. "Professional photographers use these discs to store images from larger film formats, including 120 and 4   5 inch, as well as 35 mm. Depending on the film format and/or the resolution of the scan, the discs can hold from 25 to 100 images."[35]

The third format, **Photo CD Portfolio II** disc, can store digitally originated images and can contain other digital content such as text or audio. This format provides a single-disc type to meet the needs of customers in prepress, presentations, image archiving, and other applications. Along with photo CD images, users can write other data to the discs such as CMYK (four-color) image files for prepress applications, indexes and retrieval software, or digital audio for a "still-image multimedia" presentation.[36]

Kodak Photo CD and Kodak Picture CD

There are differences between the aforementioned **Kodak Photo CD** and **Kodak Picture CD**. Picture CD is an option that one has when delivering a roll of film for processing. The option is to process the film and produce photographs on paper or to digitally record the images on a CD or both. Table 8-1 explains the differences between Kodak Photo CD and Kodak Picture CD.[37]

Values of Photo CD to the Consumer

To explain the value of photo CD, let us assume that you used your 35-mm camera to take 24 slides or prints. After you got your developed prints or slides, you choose the ones that you like to transfer to a photo CD. For the ones selected, you return the negatives or the slides to the camera store, which in turn sends them to a Kodak photo. CD processing laboratory to

Feature	Picture CD	Photo CD
Intended For	The average picture-taker who wants to view pictures on a computer.	Professional and commercial environments.
Resolution	1 resolution at 1024 1536 pixels	5 resolutions ranging from 128 192 pixels up to 2048 3072 pixels A 6th resolution is available with *Kodak Pro Photo CD* Discs (4096 6144 pixels)·
File Format	JPG	Image Pac (.pcd)
Computer Compatibility	Macintosh or Windows based operating systems	
Input Quantity	Single roll of color negative film (C41 Process)	Multiple rolls of film
Film Type and Size	• Advanced Photo System (15, 25, and 40 exposure) • 35 mm color negative film (24 and 36 exposure)	• Black and White, Color Negative, or Color Reversal Film (existing slides or negatives) • Kodak Digital Science Photo CD Master Disc • 35 mm or Advanced Photo System film • Kodak Pro Photo CD Disc • 35 mm through 4 5 in. film
Software Availability	Software is included on the CD. Features include: • easy access to pictures on your computer. • convenient organization and storage of memories. • picture enhancement features: zoom, crop, and red-eye reduction. • e-mail capability. • viewing pictures on-screen, creating slideshows, wallpaper, and more. • ability to make reprints and picture gifts (Windows based operating systems only).	Software is needed to review and use the images. See the *Photo CD Software Download* page.[38]
Ability To Add Images	No. The CD is created at the time of film processing (one roll of film per CD).	Yes. Up to approximately 100 images can be added to a Photo CD Disc at any time.
Turnaround Time	Determined by the service provider.	
Cost and Services	Determined by the service provider.	

Table 8–1 Comparison between Picture CD and Photo CD

transfer these images to a CD-ROM disc called a photo CD. The slides or the negatives, along with your photo CD and an index print similar to a color proof sheet that shows a small print of the images imprinted on the CD are returned to you. The procedure can be repeated until you record about 100 images on the photo CD. To view the images on the CD, you may use your CD-ROM on your desktop or you may use a photo CD player.

Attaching the photo CD player to your TV set, you may view the images on the CD in any order you choose and for as long as you like. The player allows you to zoom in on sections of your photo and rotate or crop your pictures.

Taking into consideration the growing number of entertainment centers in American homes, which usually include a VCR, a large TV set, and a stereo system, a photo CD player is a welcomed addition since it not only shows images on the TV screen but also plays audio CDs. Consumers will most likely accept the idea of viewing personal photos on their TV screen. A study conducted by Kodak showed that 50% of the people sampled by Kodak indicated that they would like to view their photos on their TV set.[39]

Photo-CD has other values for the home consumer. These include:

1. Image enhancement prior to the production of prints from the CD.
2. Customized services that could include cutting and pasting of images to create a composite image.
3. Zooming in to enlarge a section of an image.
4. Use of text superimposed onto an image to create a photo enhanced with text such as a greeting card.
5. Incorporating photo CD images in computer applications, such as inserting family images into a word processing document or e-mailing an image of a new member of the family to other relatives.

Using Photo CD with Computers

A photo CD offers excellent means to include imaging in desktop applications. Photo CDs require a CD-ROM XA drive in the computer workstation. All of the new CD-ROM drives in multimedia computers are CD-ROM XA type and, thus, allow reading the photo CD images, provided the computer is loaded with graphic software that can read photo CD images.[40]

A wide range of software can read Photo CD images, such as Adobe PhotoShop, Adobe PageMaker, Microsoft PowerPoint, and Microsoft Photo Editor. It is also possible to import a photo-CD image into any of the Microsoft Office Suite documents.

Using graphic software, pictures on the photo CD can be retrieved, and, once shown on the computer monitor, the editing tools of the graphic software can be used to add special effects, edit, enlarge, and color-correct the retrieved image. Such modification has great potential in desktop and multimedia applications. The consumer may use photographs taken by a camera, edited using graphic software, and imported as an integral component of a visual on the computer screen or in a page of a document.

Photo CD and Maintaining Picture Archives

At the rate of 50 billion photographs taken every year,[41] maintaining picture archives becomes very difficult, especially if climate conditions must be sustained to preserve the quality of photographs. Using the medium of the photo CD, the problem can be controlled. Depending on the quality desired in preserving the images, a Kodak CD format is selected to store the images. The 4.72" circular photo CD can withstand a fluctuating climate better than regular photographs. At the same time, the CD can store a large number of photographs ranging from 100 to 4,400. Accordingly, storing a large number of photographs in a climate-controlled environment is tremendously simplified. Moreover, the ease of locating a desired image from a huge collection makes the photo CD an extremely valuable medium for archiving pictures.

Since the archived pictures are digital images, they can be accessed from a distance; therefore, the photo CD is also valuable in the Internet age.

For some time, producing an electronic image required advanced graphic desktop software. The photo CD can change the emphasis from creating electronic imaging to enhancing applications through the use of relatively easy to produce electronic imaging using the photo CD technology. This is a step in the right direction of making the medium of CD-ROM a transparent medium, or as the cliché says "a user-friendly" medium.

THE EVOLUTION OF CD-ROM SOFTWARE

Introduction

Within a decade since the introduction of the first CD-ROM software, CD-ROM technology has evolved into an acceptable medium of publication, an efficient and cost-effective medium for research, and a multimedia vehicle through which interrelated information having different formats can be located and examined. Since the mid 1990s, a new generation of CD-ROM software has emerged. This new generation enhances the advantages of using CD-ROM in information storing, sorting, retrieval, and presentation. It also eliminates cumbersome procedures a user has to master before getting the benefit from information stored on a CD-ROM. Ease of operation and the ability of the user to interact with multiformat information on a CD-ROM at a relatively low cost are welcomed features of the new generation of CD-ROM technologies. They bring new entertainment and information media to homes, schools, and corporate environment.

In the following few pages, we retrace the development of CD-ROM software using selected titles to show milestone achievements in CD-ROM software design.

CD-ROM Early Products

The first CD-ROM product for the school market was *Grolier's Electronic Encyclopedia*. Grolier announced its upcoming release in 1986, and the CD-ROM encyclopedia became available in 1987. The same year, Microsoft released Microsoft CD-ROM Bookshelf. Educators anticipated that the release of *Microsoft Bookshelf*[42] would accelerate the growth of databases and general references on CD-ROM. In the words of Harvey (1990):

> The rate of adoption of CD-ROM technology may increase even more rapidly as a result of the recent release of the *Microsoft Bookshelf*, a CD-ROM with the entire contents of the *American Heritage Dictionary*, *Roget's Thesaurus*, the *World Almanac and Book of Facts*, *Bartlett's Familiar Quotations*, the *Chicago Manual of Style*, a spelling verifier and corrector, and a variety of business forms and letters. Some feel that the **Microsoft Bookshelf** could be the "VisiCalc of CD-ROM;" that is, the software product which makes acquiring CD-ROM hardware both desirable and respectable, just as the original **VisiCalc** spreadsheet program bestowed respectability on microcomputers. The **Microsoft Bookshelf** disc could be used in offices, in homes, or in middle and secondary school classes as a component of language arts and communications instruction.[43]

Microsoft Bookshelf (1989) did demonstrate a viable application of CD-ROM as a desktop authoring tool. What accelerated the rapid growth of CD-ROM applications, however, were the introduction of well-designed multimedia programs on CD-ROM and the development of more powerful personal computers and faster CD-ROM drives. Wide ranges of interactive multimedia applications were produced. Searching for information on these applications became more user-friendly than that of earlier applications. All of these contributed to making the CD-ROM an essential component of a PC system and not just an accessory as it was in the early days of CD-ROM technology. The following is a review of the progress in software design during the relatively short history of CD-ROM technology.

Progress in Software Design

Fascinated with a unique characteristic of a new invention, attempts are usually directed to make use of that unique characteristic. For instance, when motion pictures were first introduced, the inventor and the public were fascinated by its ability to show motion. Accordingly, the early motion picture films were long strips of film that depicted motion. Simple day-to-day events and activities became the subject of 1- to 2-minute films. *The Arrival of a Train into a Station* (1895) depicted a train arriving at a railroad station in Paris. It was reported that the audience was "disturbed by the approach of the train."[44] When George Miles discovered motion picture tricks, he enchanted the public by his films that used deception techniques.

More recent was the early use of television in education. Mass distribution of information enticed educators to view television as a medium of overcoming the shortage of qualified teachers. One expert teacher can simultaneously teach many classes in different locations. The Airborne Television was an ambitious project in which a DC10 flying studio was used to telecast educational programs to school systems in three Midwest states.

When the CD-ROM was first introduced, its capacity to store tremendous amounts of information was at the top of the unique characteristics that captured the interest of publishers and the users. This was especially significant because hard drives on personal computers then ranged from 20 to 30 MB of storage capacity. Accordingly, emphasis in producing the CD-ROM was placed on storing a huge amount of information on one disc. *BiblioFile*[45] and *Books in Print*[46] became natural applications for CD-ROM technology. Storing a 22-volume encyclopedia on one CD attracted librarians' and educators' attention, especially since a CD-ROM cannot be torn or defaced.

Hand in hand with huge storage was the design of search and retrieval systems. One of the ultimate goals was designing a "transparent system" that would not require the user to remember many commands to search and retrieve information. On the path to achieving this goal, the industry has used a variety of creative approaches. For instance, *Science Helper K–8*[47] contained 919 lesson plans for grades K to 8. The lesson plans were selected from eight elementary science curriculum projects funded by the National Science Foundation. The disc includes abstracts of each lesson, the full contents of each lesson plan, the philosophy of each curriculum project, and retrieval software that allows the user to locate lessons for a certain grade to address a certain curriculum objective (see Chapter 7). This type of retrieval system requires the user to interact with the software to locate lesson plans that satisfy specific teaching needs.

Interactivity became a mode of operation for CD-ROM software. The ideal design of CD-ROM software was to put the user in command of the program and to provide assistance for the user in learning how to use the program. One of the early programs that attempted to achieve these objectives was the World Book, *Information Finder.*

The opening screen of the World Book, *Information Finder* (1991)[48] shows a colorful diagram of a computer keyboard. Three options are illustrated: ESC Key to "Exit," Space Bar to see the "Tutorial," and Enter to "Search." Pushing the space bar brings the user to a dialogue box overlaid on top of the first item in the World Book, Letter A. The dialogue box's headline, "Learn About," has eight topic listings: Topic Searching, Keyboard Searching, Dictionary, Quick Facts, Navigation, Bookmarks, Goto, and Notepad. Highlighting any of these items, and pushing "Return" starts a systematic tutorial on the topic.

To put the user in command of the program, functions available to the user of *Information Finder* include bookmarks; dictionary; Goto, which linked cross-referenced words typed in capital letters to more information; and a complete topic index and an index of related topics. Two search options are available: "topic search" and "key word" search. Under the "Keyword Search," available functions include bookmark, dictionary, Goto, a full index of Keyword Titles, a Search Log, Proximity Search, and Wildcards.

The Layout of Information Finder screen is very functional. The screen is divided into two panes. The left pane displays the "Outline" of the text displayed in the right pane. Clicking on a topic in the outline brings the corresponding section of the article in the right pane.

Proximity Search assists the user in refining search strategies, such as locating information including keywords in the same paragraph, under the same heading, or in the same article.

The *Electromap World Atlas* (1989)[49] employa a different search interface. The start screen shows the map of the world and a menu bar. The menu bar has eight items: Text, World, Region, Index, StatMap, TopoMap, Flip, and Print. To search the database, moving the mouse to Index, a drop box is shown with space to fill in the name of the city or the country. Hitting "Return" produces another drop box. The drop box has two columns: the one on the left has the names of the cities of the world, and the one on the right lists the corresponding countries. Hitting Return brings to the screen the map of that country. Moving the mouse to the Text item on the menu bar produces a drop menu with seven items: Geography, People, Government, Economy, Communications, Defense, and Travel. Clicking any of these items produces a text information box. The user can choose to print or to save to a file any or all of these items, in addition to the map.

Birds of America (1990)[50] added a delightful element: sound. Once the text of a bird is retrieved, the user can push a function key (F9) to show a colorful image. Accompanying the bird's picture, the bird's call plays for roughly 15 seconds. Pushing ESC can stop the bird's call.

Birds of America is one of the early CDs that employed sound. It is an intelligent application simply because no one can explain the call of a bird better than playing back a recorded call. There was not one person out of dozens who attended my presentations on CD-ROM software who had not expressed fascination, delight, and an appreciation of that creative application.

Multimedia treatment in CD-ROM became the norm of storing information on CDs. IBM and National Geographic *Mammals, Multimedia Encyclopedia* (1990)[51] was a great success. *Mammals*, still running on a DOS platform, employs navigation icons. Video clips are used to show how the animal moves. To view the video clip of an animal, the user clicks the motion picture icon. Sound is also used to achieve two functions. The first is to present the pronunciation of the name of the mammal. The second is to play back a recording of the characteristic sound of the animal.

Mammals also uses "games" as a self-assessment option. After studying the various animals, the user may opt to play a game. Prerequisite to winning the game is mastering the information of the CD. In the event that the user discovers a lack of knowledge, he or she may use the disc to supplement that lack of knowledge.

3-D Body Adventure (1994)[52] brings us one step closer to virtual reality on CD. Wearing red and green glasses, the user explores video segments in which a 3-D effect is used. In addition, in the game component of the CD, moving the mouse simulates traveling into the scene.

Improvement in technology introduces sharper and larger images, better sound quality, faster access and retrieval of information, smoother motion, and better lip synchronization. The popularity and development of the web added a new dimension to the CD-ROM medium. Links to related sites on the web are now implanted on the CD-ROM to retrieve up-to-date information on the topic of study.

Students today are lucky to have at their hands well-designed, attractive, and up-to-date multimedia topics stored on CDs. Searching the CD-ROM is much easier than early products. Point and click, search by word, Boolean searches, and timeline search are among the common methods for retrieving information from a CD-ROM. Children at the age of three can start using that interactive medium to listen and to watch stories unfold on the screen. They learn to be in control of what they watch, a step in the right direction from passive TV entertainment.

There are thousands of different CD-ROM titles. They include encyclopedias, dictionaries, bibliographic materials, atlases, desktop tools, educational applications, medical applications, engineering, business, graphic art, modern languages, games, problem-solving software, children's stories, publishing tools, talking dictionaries, news CD-ROMs, electronic magazines, phone numbers, computer software, and so forth. Periodicals in different disciplines and multimedia magazines usually feature reviews of current CD-ROM titles. These reviews are helpful for students in selecting appropriate titles.

REFERENCES

1. Laub, Lenoard. What Is a CD-ROM? in Lambert, Steve and Suzanne Popiequet (Eds.). *CD-ROM The New Papyrus, The Current and Future State of the Art.* Redmond, WA: Microsoft Press, 1986, p. 52.

2. *Ibid.* p. 52.

3. Pahwa, Ash. *The CD-Recordable Bible*, Wilton, CT: Eight Bit Books, 1994, p. 171.

4. O'Connor, Richard. Interactive Videodisc Applications in Education, in Hefzallah, Ibrahim M., (Ed.), *The New Learning and Telecommunications Technologies and Their Potential Applications in Education*, Charles C Thomas, Springfield, IL: 1990, p. 129.

5. *Ibid.* p. 129.

6. The University of Utah. *Slice of Life*, http://medlib.med.utah.edu/sol/aboutus/index.html, downloaded 7/21/03.

7. *Ibid.*

8. *Ibid.*

9. *Ibid.*

10. *Ibid.*

11. *Ibid.*

12. *Ibid.*

13. The University of Utah. *Slice of Life*, http://medlib.med.utah.edu/sol/soldigital/index.html, downloaded 7/21/03.

14. *Ibid.*

15. Pahwa, Ash, *op. cit.* p. 173.

16. *Ibid.*

17. *Ibid.*

18. *Ibid.* p. 174.

19. *Ibid.* pp. 15–24.

20. CD-ROM Standards, http://homepage.interaccess.com/~ehilborn/cdrom/cd-9660.html, downloaded 11/10/98.

21. Pahwa, Ash, *op. cit.* p. 171.

22. Laub, Lenoard, *op. cit.* p. 58.

23. Pahwa, Ash, *op. cit.* p. 2.

24. The CINAHL Database, http://www.cinahl.com/prodsvcs/cinahldbbody.htm, p. 4, downloaded 7/21/03.

25. Temple University Libraries, Resources for Business, Management and Economics, http://www.library.temple.edu/ELECRES/cdbusin.htm, p. 1, downloaded 7/21/03.

26. The Complete YEARBOOK Collection-CD, SilverPlatter, http://sunsite.nus.edu.sg/bibdb/pub/silverplatter/silverplatter043.html, downloaded 7/21/03.

27. ProQuest Products, http://www.il.proquest.com/products/pt-product-News Abstracts.shtml, downloaded 7/21/03.

28. PsycLit, http://www.tau.ac.il/soclib/psyc.html, downloaded 7/21/03.

29. SilverPlatter, ERIC on SilverPlatter, http://sunsite.nus.edu.sg/bibdb/pub/silverplatter/silverplatter088.html, downloaded 7/21/03.

30. SilverPlatter, Zoological Record on Compact Disc, http://sunsite.nus.edu.sg/bibdb/pub/silverplatter/silverplatter224.html, downloaded 7/21/03.

31. von Buelow, Heinz and Dirk Paulissen. *Photo CD Book*, Grand Rapids, MI: Abacus, 1994, p. 4.

32. McCabe, Georgia L. The Photo CD Strategy: A Revolution in Imaging, *CD-ROM Professional*, vol. 5, no.1, January 1992, pp. 18–24.

33. *Ibid.* p. 7.

34. Kodak Professional, Photo CD Disc Formats, http://www.kodak.com/global/en/professional/products/storage/pcdMaster/aboutPCD5.jhtml?id=0.3.8.34.17.4&lc=en, downloaded 7/21/03.
35. *Ibid.*
36. *Ibid.*
37. Kodak, Comparing Kodak Picture CD and Kodak Photo CD Discs, http://www.kodak.com/global/en/service/professional/tib/tib4164.jhtml?id=0.3.8.34.17.8.9&lc=en, downloaded 7/21/03.
38. Kodak, Service and Support, Drivers, Software and Firmware, Photo CD Software, http://www.kodak.com/global/en/service/software/photoCDSoftware.jhtml?id=0.3.26.18.17&lc=en, downloaded 7/21/03.
39. McCabe, *op. cit,* p. 20.
40. You could visit Kodak, Service and Support, Drivers, Software and Firmware, Photo CD Software, http://www.kodak.com/global/en/service/software/photoCDSoftware.jhtml?id=0.3.26.18.17&lc=en to download software.
41. *Ibid.*
42. Harvey, Francis A. Interactive CD-ROM Databases, The Keys to Personal Information Access and Use, in Hefzallah, Ibrahim M. (Ed.). *The New Learning and Telecommunications Technologies and Their Potential Applications in Education.* Charles C Thomas, Springfiled, IL: 1990, pp. 162–194.
43. *Ibid.* pp. 171–172.
44. Dickison, Thorold. *A Discovery of Cinema,* London: Oxford University Press, 1971, p. 38.
45. *BiblioFile,* Noosa Heads, Australia: Tom Milledge & Associates.
46. *Books in Print,* New Providence, NJ: R.R. Bowker.
47. *Science Helper K–8,* Gainesville, FL: PC-SIG, 1988.
48. *Information Finder* by World Book, Chicago, IL: World Book, 1991.
49. *World Atlas,* Fayetteville, AR: Electromap, Inc., 1990.
50. *Multi-Media Birds of America,* Portland, OR: CMC Research, 1990.
51. *Mammals,* A Multimedia Encyclopedia, Washington, D.C.: National Geographic Society, 1990.
52. *3-D Body Adventure,* Davidson, 1994.

Part Three

THE INTERNET

INTRODUCTION

The Internet and the World Wide Web's (WWW)growing popularity is changing the way we live, conduct business, communicate with each other, teach, search for information, and spend our leisure time. Three chapters in this book are dedicated to the study of the Internet and the WWW and their applications in education. Chapter 9, "The Internet—Its Early Development and Accelerated Growth," traces the Internet's early development, the creation of the WWW, the growing interest in Internet utilization in education, and the importance of preparing teachers to infuse Internet use in their teaching.

Chapter 10, "Unique Characteristics of the Internet and Its Potential Applications in Education," focuses on the Internet as the first electronic global library. Four unique characteristics of this amazing new library are recognized: (1) universal borderless access, (2) richness in multimedia resources, (3) a self-publishing medium, and (4) an interactive medium of communication. Each of these features has significant applications in education, which are discussed in this chapter.

Chapter 11, "Commonly Used Internet Resource Tools and Their Potential Applications in Education," addresses the most commonly used Internet tools, including e-mail, newsgroups, web discussion forums, file transfer protocol, and the most popular Internet tool, the web browser. Applications of these resources in education are discussed. The chapter also addresses the issues of children and youth's safety on the Internet.

Chapter 9

THE INTERNET—ITS EARLY DEVELOPMENT
AND ACCELERATED GROWTH

INTRODUCTION

During the 1960s educators and researchers realized the potential impact of computers on teaching and on training. Use of computers to deliver interactive step-by-step programmed instruction led to the development of computer assisted instruction (see Chapters 6 and 7). The potential use of computers to link people together and to provide them with access to information when they need it led to the development of the Internet.

The Internet revolutionized how information can be stored, sorted, accessed, shared, and distributed. Comparing the Internet to the printing press, Stanek et al. wrote:

> Five centuries ago the printing press with movable type brought society past an impasse with elitist control of knowledge and caused a revolution. It made possible the spread of knowledge to anyone with a passion to learn, and what is more important, it gave society an information base independent of a limited number of scholars. Today, the Internet is again causing a revolution in the way knowledge and information can be accessed.[1]

WHAT IS THE INTERNET?

A simple definition of the Internet is derived from its physical components: a network of networks. A comprehensive definition of the Internet, however, encompasses more than its physical structure. A frequently-asked-questions file gives the following definition of the Internet:

> The Internet is a global network of networks enabling computers of all kinds to directly and transparently communicate and share services throughout much of the world. Because the Internet is an enormously valuable, enabling capability for so many people and organizations, it also constitutes a shared

151

global resource of information, knowledge, and means of collaboration, and cooperation among countless diverse communities.[2]

From this definition we can see three interrelated components of the Internet: the physical network of networks, a shared global resource of information, and the people who use the Internet. The Federal Networking Council (FNC), in the following resolution that was passed on October 24, 1995, gave a more technical definition of the term *Internet*:

> The Federal Networking Council (FNC) agrees that the following language reflects our definition of the term "Internet."
> "Internet" refers to the global information system that:
> (i) is logically linked together by a globally unique address based on the Internet Protocol (IP) or its subsequent extensions/follow-ons;
> (ii) is able to support communications using the Transmission Control Protocol/Internet Protocol(TCP/IP) suite or its subsequent extensions/follow-ons, and/or other IP-compatible protocols; and
> (i) provides, uses or makes accessible, either publicly or privately, high level services layered on the communications and related infrastructure described herein."[3]

While this resolution outlined protocol standards, it made clear that the Internet is a global information system that includes the three aforementioned components. Hahn and Stout (1994) emphasized the information and people components of the Internet: "It would be a mistake . . . to think of the Internet as a computer network, or even a group of computer networks connected to one another. From our point of view, the computer networks are simply the medium that carries the information. The beauty and utility of the Internet lie in the information itself."[4] They further explained the "people" component of the Internet indicating that the Internet is a people-oriented society. It allows millions of people all over the world to communicate and to share ideas and information and to use many free programs and information sources available on the Internet:

> The Internet is much more than a computer network or an information service. The Internet is living proof that human beings who are able to communicate freely and conveniently will choose to be social and selfless. The computers are important because they do the grunt work of moving all the data from place to place, and executing the programs that let us access the information. The information itself is important because it offers utility, recreation, and amusement.
> But, overall, what is most important is the people. The Internet is the first global library forum and the first global library.[5]

The people component is also explained in a statement made by a Supreme Court judge. Considering the first amendment rights for Internet users, he stated, "The Internet may fairly be regarded as a never-ending worldwide conversation."[6]

To summarize, *the Internet is a global information system that uses networks of computers to enable people all over the world to interact with one another, and to share a vast and diversified body of information.* Figure 9-1, "A Triangular Model of the Internet," illustrates the three necessary components of the Internet: people, information, and connectivity.

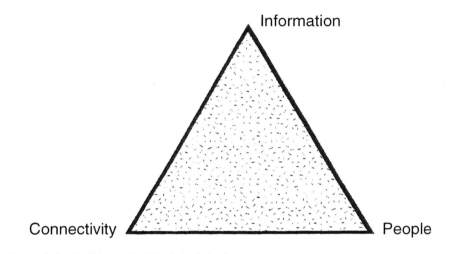

Figure 9-1 A Triangular Model of the Internet

EARLY DEVELOPMENTS

In the late 1960s, the U.S. Department of Defense decided to fund an experimental computer network "that would allow remote research and development sites to exchange information."[7] This network, named ARPAnet, began in 1969 with funds from the Advanced Research Project Administration (ARPA). ARPAnet was "designed to support military research—in particular, research about how to build networks that could withstand partial outages (like bomb attacks) and still function."[8] This meant that communication on the network would not be seriously impaired if physical sections of the network were lost.[9] Charles M. Herzfeld, the former director of ARPA, claimed that ARPAnet was not created as a result of a military need, "it came out of our frustration that there were only a limited number of large, powerful research computers in the country and that many research investigators who should have access were geographically separated from them."[10]

ARPAnet also aimed at allowing the addition and removal of new terminals and the use of different types of computers. A network protocol standard had to be developed to allow all types of computers on the network to communicate with each other. With this new protocol, *Internet Protocol* (IP), every computer on the network has its own address, a series of four number segments. To make computer addresses easier to remember, the domain name system is used. A domain name uniquely identifies an "Internet host." The Internet host is the computer that connects directly to the Internet. The host runs a program "domain name service" (DNS) that converts the domain name into the series of four numbers constituting the IP address, for example, www.fairfield.edu = 198.138.14.76.

The last segment in an address is called the top-level domain (TLD). The Internet domain address includes a second level domain such as "fairfield" in www.fairfield.edu.

TLDs with three or more characters are called "generic TLDs (gTLDs). In the 1980s, seven gTLDs were created: .com, .edu, .gov, .int, .mil, .net, and .org. Domain names may be registered in three of these generic gTLDs, .com, .net, and .org, without restrictions. However the other four gTLDS, .edu, .gov, .int, and .mil, have limited purposes.[11]

Seven new gTLDs were introduced in 2001–2002: .biz, .info, .name, .pro, .aero, .coop, and .museum.[12] Four of these new gTLDs, .biz, .info, .name, and .pro, are unsponsored. The other three new gTLDs, .aero, .coop and .museum, are sponsored. An unsponsored TLD operates under policies established by the global Internet community directly through the Internet Cooperation for Assigned Names and Numbers (ICANN) The sponsored TLD is a "specialized TLD that has a sponsor representing the narrower community that is most affected by the TLD."[13]

Table 9-1 is derived from the gTLDs table published on the ICANN web site, http://www.icann.org/tlds/

Table 9.1   Generic Top Level Domains[14]

No.	TLD	Introduced	Sponsored/ Unsponsored	Purpose
1	.aero	2001	Sponsored	Air-transport industry
2	.biz	2001	Unsponsored	Businesses
3	.com	1995	Unsponsored	Un-restricted but intended for commercial registrants
4	.coop	2001	Sponsored	Cooperatives
5	.edu	1995	Sponsored	United States educational institutions
6	.gov	1995	Sponsored	United States government
7	.info	2001	Unsponsored	Unrestricted use
8	.int	1998	Unsponsored	Organizations established by international treaties between governments
9	.mil	1995	Sponsored	United States military

(continued on next page)

Table 9.1   Generic Top Level Domains[14]

No.	TLD	Introduced	Sponsored/ Unsponsored	Purpose
10	.museum	2001	Sponsored	Museums
11	.name	2001	Unsponsored	For registration by individuals
12	.net	1995	Unsponsored	Unrestricted, but intended for network providers
13	.org	1995	Unsponsored	Unrestricted but intended for organizations that do not fit elsewhere
14	.pro	2002	Unsponsored	Accountants, lawyers, physicians and other professionals

In addition to the gTLDs, two letter country codes such as ca, de, eg, au, and jp have been established for over 240 countries.[15] They are referred to as country codes TLDs or ccTLDs.[16] (For more information on country codes, refer to http://nw.com/zone/iso-country-codes.)

In addition to the gTLDs and ccTLDS, under the guidance of the Internet Architecture Board, ICANN in cooperation with the Internet community operates for technical infrastructure purposes one special TLD, .arpa.[17]

To transfer information from one computer to another, the data are segmented into pieces called "packets." The size of the information in a packet ranges from one to 1,500 characters long.[18,19] Transmitting packets of information is much faster than transmitting the whole data as one chunk. The process of packaging and shipping electronic information became known as the Internet protocol (IP). Andy Carvin (1997) explains this process:

> With this new technology, the data from one computer could be put into an electronic "envelope" and then be addressed to another computer. The originating computer would then direct the envelope by way of the ARPAnet to the receiving site. This method of packaging and shipping electronic information became known as the **Internet Protocol** or **IP** for short. If a computer had the software for implementing IP, it could conceivably talk to any other computer in the world, as long as that other computer had similar IP software and was on the ARPAnet.[20]

On the receiving end, the receiving computer gets the information in segments, which when assembled form a copy of the original data. To make sure that the packets are correctly assembled to reflect the original order of the message, the computer has to remember the sequence of these packets.[21] A second protocol, called transmission control protocol (TCP), checks and corrects any errors in the received data.

The development of the transmission control protocol/Internet protocol (TCP/IP) is considered "one of the major impacts of ARPAnet research, and the one that led to today's Internet."[22]

ARPAnet started in 1969 with four computers connected over a long distance. In 1972, ARPAnet was publicly demonstrated.[23] Under ARPAnet major innovations occurred: e-mail (1971); telnet—a remote connection for controlling a computer (1972); and file transfer protocol (FTP), which allows files to be transferred from one computer to another (1973).[24]

> During the early 1980s, all the interconnected research networks were converted to the TCP/IP protocol and the ARPAnet became the backbone (the physical connection between the major sites) of the new Internet. . . . This conversion to TCP/IP was completed by the end of 1983—and the Internet was born.[25]

Stanek et al. (1995) reported that "By the end of 1980s, over 80,000 computers were connected through a series of networks."[26] As more and more people gained access to the Internet, it was no longer safe for military uses, and in 1983 MILnet, a military-only network, started.[27]

Using IP software, universities and research groups began using in-house networks known as local area networks, or LANs. These LANs could connect with each other using the IP software.[28] In 1986, one of the LANs branched out to form a new network, the National Science Foundation Network (NSFnet). "NSFnet first linked together the five national supercomputer centers, then every major university, and it started to replace the slower ARPAnet (which was finally shut down in 1990.) NSFnet formed the backbone of what we call the Internet today."[29]

THE ACCELERATED GROWTH OF THE INTERNET

The Creation of the World Wide Web

The introduction of the World Wide Web (WWW) accelerated the growth of the Internet. In 1989, Berners-Lee of the European Particle Physics Laboratory (CERN) in Switzerland proposed the WWW. The first prototype was developed in 1990. The developers aimed at creating an easy-to-navigate seamless network that could be accessed by any type of computer in any country. To realize this end, they developed an addressing system, uniform resource locator (URL), which can reference any type of documents on the Internet.

To facilitate navigating through documents on related topics they developed the hypertext markup language (HTML) coding language. When the mouse pointer lands on a marked text, it changes its shape from an arrow to a small hand indicating that a link exists between the marked text or graphics and other section of the document itself or a related document. Clicking the mouse connects the user with the linked document. Thus, pointing and clicking the mouse moves the user in and out of almost endless connections and links.

Alfred and Emily Glossbrenner (1996) noted that Berners-Lee concept of the WWW "didn't take off until the National Center for Supercomputing Applications (NCSA) began a project to create a *graphical* user interface for the web. That happened in 1993 to 1994, and the program was called 'Mosaic.'"[30] Mosaic allowed the user to navigate through the web by pointing and clicking the mouse. The retrieved documents included more than text. The attractive graphic design of the retrieved pages and the ease of using a graphic interface (Mosaic) to search for information made the Internet world "user-friendly" to many computer novices.

The graphic interface for searching the web is known as a "web browser." At present, Netscape, from Netscape Communications, and Internet Explorer, from Microsoft, are the two most widely used web browsers. The team that created Mosaic created Netscape. The Mosaic team, according to Alfred and Emily Glossbrenner, "broke away to establish a separate company. They named the new entity Netscape Communications, and they called their 'Web browser' software product Netscape Navigator."[31]

As the number of people logging on the Internet started to increase, businesses looked favorably at the Internet to enhance their performance. From 1969 to 1991, scholars, researchers, and the military used the Internet. There was a ban prohibiting the use of the Internet by business.[32] This ban was lifted in 1991 by the formation of the Commercial Internet Exchange (CIX). At present, the commercial sector is the fastest growing sector of the Internet.[33]

Evidence of the Internet Accelerated Growth

The U.S. Department of Commerce stated that "the Internet's pace of adoption eclipses all other technologies that preceded it. Radio was in existence 38 years before 50 million people tuned in; TV took 13 years to reach that benchmark. Sixteen years after the first personal computer (PC) kit came out, 50 million people were using one. Once it was opened to the general public, the Internet crossed that line in four years."[34]

The accelerated growth of the Internet is demonstrated by the following indicators:

1. The growing number of the Internet users.
2. The growing number of Internet domains.
3. Current trends of Internet use.
    a. Growing interest in the use of the Internet;
    b. People's growing expectations of what the Internet can offer;
    c. The Internet use in politics;
    d. The establishment of the Internet as an alternative resource for news; and
    e. Advocating Internet use in education.

The Growing Number of Internet Users

The Internet revolutionized how information can be stored, sorted, accessed, researched, shared, and distributed. It is causing a revolution in the way we conduct research, spend our leisure time, correspond with others, do business, and virtually travel the world.

The number of people using the Internet is on the increase. Due to its accelerated growth in various countries, it is difficult to determine the exact number of active online users. An educated guess puts online users worldwide at 605.60 million as of September 2002.[35] Nielsen NetRatings put it at 580 million as of 2002, with 165.7 million in the United States alone.[36,37]

The infiltration of Internet technology in schools is also on the increase. According to the National Center for Education Statistics (NCES), *Digest of Education Statistics, 2002*, 99% of American schools had access to the Internet in 2001.[38] In the world of work, the percentage of workers 18 years old and over using computer on the job rose from 45.8% in 1993 to 49.8% in 1997 and to 54.2% in 2001 (amounting to 71,782,000 workers.) The percent of on-the-job computer workers using specific computer applications was 72.2% for e-mail and the Internet, 67.2% for word processing, 62.5% for spreadsheets and databases, 53.2% for calendar schedule, 28.9% for graphics and design, 15.3 for programming, and 13% for other uses. The percentage of the workers that used four or more categories was 43.9%.[39] These figures indicate without doubt that computer skills and skills associated with the Internet are desirable, if not required, in the world of work today.

With the rapid technological developments in microprocessors, telecommunications, optical recording of information, technology of storing, sorting, and retrieving information, learning outside a traditional classroom will increase. The availability of alternative delivery and distribution systems of information through the Internet changes the practice of formal education to include online education. Moreover, the concept of the library as a place to store cataloged print and nonprint material has changed to include providing access to a variety of data and information banks through the Internet. That access is available from within a library building or from anywhere in the world provided the user has the privilege of using the library's online resources.

The WWW also has made it easy for many to access information from the vast Internet resources for more than educational reasons. The Pew report, *Getting Serious Online* (2002) reported: "As Americans gain experience, they use the Web more at work, write emails with more significant content, perform more online transactions, and pursue more activities online."[40] The report further indicated:

> The status of the Internet is shifting from being the dazzling new thing to being a purposeful tool that Americans use to help them with some of life's important tasks. As Internet users gain experience online, they increasingly turn to the Internet to perform work-related tasks, to make purchases and do

other financial transactions, to write emails with weighty and urgent content, and to seek information that is important to their everyday lives.[41]

With proper education, people learn efficient ways of using the Internet, resulting in spending more fruitful time in cyberspace; and that, too, leads to an increase in Internet users.

The Growing Number of Internet Domains

The Internet Software Consortium reported that, "It is not possible to determine the exact size of the Internet, where hosts are located, or how many users there are."[42] The Consortium further reported that, "There is no way to determine how many users are on the net, besides making guesses and estimates."[43]

One method of estimating the size of the Internet is to survey the number of Internet hosts and Internet domains. An Internet host is any computer system connected to the Internet and having an IP address.[44] A domain name is an IP address that has been given a name. Earlier, a host used to be a single machine with one domain name. Now a single machine could act "like multiple systems (and has multiple domain names and IP addresses.)[45]

Table 9.2 is derived from the Internet Software Consortium's Internet Domain Survey.[46] The Consortium believes that "the numbers presented in the domain survey to be fairly good estimates of the *minimum* size of the Internet."[47]

Table 9.2 Growth of Internet Hosts

Date	Number of Hosts
August 1981	213
May 1982	235
January 1992	727,000
October 1992	1,136,000
January 1996	9,472,000
January 1997	16,146,000
January 1998	29,670,000
July 1998	36,739,000
January 1999	43,230,000
July 1999	56,218,000
January 2000	72,398,000
July 2000	93,047,785
January 2001	109,574,429
July 2001	125,888,197
January 2002	147,344,723
July 2002	162,128,493
January 2003	171,638,297
January 2004	233,101,481*

*ISC, Internet Domain Survey. January 2004, http://www.isc.org/ops/ds/reports/2004-011/, downloaded 2/29/04.

Studying this table, one notices the following:

- The increase in the number of hosts from August 1981 to May 1982 was insignificant; it rose from 213 to 235.
- By January 1992, the number of hosts reached 727,000; however, the accelerated growth in the number of hosts started late in 1992, jumping from 1,136,000 in October 1992 to 9,472,000 in January 1996, and to 16,146,000 in January 1997, and 29,760,00 in January 1998.
- By January 2004, the number of Internet servers reached 233,101,181.

As the number of people using the Internet increases, the ensuing traffic poses a significant problem: delay to the Internet users. There is nothing more frustrating for a WWW researcher than pointing and clicking the mouse and waiting a long time for a response. Internet II will be 10-fold faster than the present Internet. It will allow for the fast transfer of video and audio files, as well as establishing interactive sessions in real time among users—a dream of everyone interested in using the Internet for distance teaching and video-conferencing. *The Chronicle of Higher Education*, February 7, 1997, reported that, with 98 colleges taking part, Internet II might start within six months.[48] Internet II site reported 202 university members as of September 2003. This is in addition to a large number of corporate partners, corporate sponsors, corporate members, affiliate members, and international partners.[49]

Current Trends of Internet Use

GROWING INTEREST IN THE USE OF THE INTERNET. The Internet is widely used in education and business. In K–12 education, 99% of American schools had access to the Internet in 2001.50 As more teachers become educated in the viable uses of Internet in teaching, more and more creative applications of the Internet will be integrated in K-12 education.

"College students are heavy users of the Internet compared to the general population," reports *The Internet Goes to College*.[51] The Internet is a part of college students' daily routine to enhance their education and their social interaction. *The Internet Goes to College* reported that students "use the Internet to communicate with professors and classmates, to do research, and to access library materials. For most college students the Internet is a functional tool, one that has greatly changed the way they interact with others and with information as they go about their studies."[52] Some of the interesting findings of that report are:

- Nearly four-fifths of college students (79%) agree that Internet use has had a positive impact on their college academic experience.
- Almost half (46%) of college students agree that e-mail enables them to express ideas to a professor that they would not have expressed in class, but

some interactions are still primarily face-to-face; only 19% of students said they communicate more with their professors via e-mail than they do face-to-face.

- Nearly three-quarters (73%) of college students say they use the Internet more than the library, while only 9% said they use the library more than the Internet for information searching.
- About half of all college students (48%) are required to use the Internet to contact other students in at least some of their classes.
- Two-thirds (68%) of college students reported subscribing to one or more academic-oriented mailing lists that relate to their studies. They use these lists to carry on e-mail discussions about topics covered in their classes.
- More than half (58%) of college students have used e-mail to discuss or find out a grade from an instructor.
- Nearly two-thirds (65%) of college students who e-mail professors say they report absences via e-mail.[53]

The report further indicated that college experience is more than learning in the classroom. "It is also about encountering new social situations and gaining new social skills. College students use the Internet nearly as much for social communication as they do for their education. But just as they use the Internet to supplement the formal parts of their education, they go online to enhance their social lives."[54] To this end, the report findings are:

- 42% of college students say they use the Internet primarily to communicate socially.
- Only 10% of college students use the Internet primarily for entertainment.
- Nearly three-fourths (72%) of college students say most of their online communication is with friends.
- Over two-thirds (69%) of college students said they are more likely to use the phone than the Internet to communicate socially.
- But 85% of college students consider the Internet to be an easy and convenient choice for communicating with friends.
- The most popular online social activity is forwarding messages to friends or family, with 37% of college students reporting doing so.
- A significant number of college students use publicly accessible computers on campus for social purposes even when they have their own computer at their disposal; 33% find that the majority of their computer use occurs at school and outside their homes or dorm rooms.

In the world of work, corporations are enhancing their Intranet sites and Internet applications for training, communicating with their employees worldwide, and advertising their products and services to the Internet users. Individuals, not-for-profit organizations, and groups of individuals with common interests are using the Internet as a platform for sharing ideas, conversing with each other, and posting messages of interest to the various users of the Internet.

David Moursund's *The Future of Information Technology in Education,* an ISTE publication, referred to a report by Forrester Researchers. The researchers reported the increase in e-mail users in 1997 to be 15% of the U.S. population, compared with 2% in 1992. They predicted that within five years that number would rise to about 50%. They explained that "Growth will be fueled by the increase in home PC penetration and the growth of Internet access in corporations. Furthermore, the emergence of personalized services and tools that let ordinary people combine graphics and attachments will help make e-mail a preferred means of communication."[55]

Five years later, The Pew Internet and American Life Project (2002) reported:

> Email is an integral part of American workers' lives. About 62% of all employed Americans have Internet access and virtually all of those (98%) use email on the job. That translates into more than 57 million American adults. . . . Most of them use email daily for work tasks. But contrary to the perception that wired American workers are buried in email, the large majority of those who use email at work say their experience with email is manageable. They say they spend a modest amount of their typical workday reading and writing email. A portion of those emails probably replace telephone calls or faxes or traditional mail.[56]

Use of e-mail outside the workplace is also becoming more popular, with more and more people using e-mail to socialize, share information, and shop. *Holiday Online* (2002) reported:

> More than three quarters of the nation's Internet users (78%) did some form of holiday activity via email and the Web this holiday season. They used email to socialize and arrange holiday gatherings, reconnect with old friends, and plan religious activities. They browsed online malls and bought gifts in higher numbers than last year. In all, 71% of Internet users went online for some kind of social or spiritual activity and 53% did some kind of e-commerce— either online window-shopping or purchasing gifts.[57]

PEOPLE'S GROWING EXPECTATIONS OF WHAT THE INTERNET CAN OFFER. *Counting on the Internet* (2002), a Pew Internet and American Life Project publication, reports, "The Internet has become a mainstream information tool."[58] A growing number of people expect to find information online, and many turn to the Internet first in searching for information.[59] This phenomenon is best explained by the following quotation from *Counting on the Internet*:

> With over 60% of Americans now having Internet access and 40% of Americans having been online for more than three years, the Internet has become a mainstream information tool. Its popularity and dependability have raised all Americans' expectations about the information and services avail-

able online. When they are thinking about health care information, services from government agencies, news, and commerce, about two-thirds of all Americans say that they expect to be able to find such information on the Web. Internet users are more likely than non-users to have high expectations of what will be available online, and yet even 40% of people who are not Internet users say they expect the Web to have information and services in these essential online arenas.[60]

INTERNET USE IN NATIONAL AND INTERNATIONAL POLITICS. The Internet has become a powerful medium of communication in both national and international politics. More and more people are searching government web sites for information.[61] "Web presence is not optional for governments in the United States," reports Pew Internet and American Life Project, *The Rise of the E-Citizen*.[62] The report (April 2002) states that 68 million American adults have used government agencies web sites. This is a sharp increase over the March 2000 figures (40 million). Their uses covered a wide range of available services, including finding information, applying for benefits, and communication with public officials. The Report concludes:

- 42 million Americans have used government Web sites to research public policy issues.
- 23 million Americans have used the Internet to send comments to public officials about policy choices.
- 14 million have used government Web sites to gather information to help them decide how to cast their votes.
- 13 million have participated in online lobbying campaigns.[63]

Political activists have used the Internet to ". . . mobilize interested citizen, and to handle the logistics of organizing such mass demonstrations as the 1999 protests at the World Trade Organization talks in Seattle and the Million Mom March in Washington, DC."[64] Conservative activists also use the Internet as a platform for expressing their opinions. Jonathan Garthwaite, editor of Townhall.com, a site dedicated to conservative views, explained the purpose of Townhall.com in the following:

Townhall.com is the first truly interactive community on the Internet to bring Internet users, conservative public policy organizations, congressional staff, and political activists together under the broad umbrella of "conservative" thoughts, ideas and actions. Townhall.com is a one-stop mall of ideas in which people congregate to exchange, discuss and disseminate the latest news and information from the conservative movement. Townhall.com is committed to inform, educate and empower the public through this emerging electronic medium.

The member organizations and columnists that we have chosen to feature on Townhall.com do not necessarily agree on every issue, yet that is why Townhall.com believes our community is of value. An interactive, open and honest debate of the issues within the conservative community will help us all in the fight against those who would sacrifice the individual and freedom for political gain and big government.[65]

THE INTERNET AS A MAJOR SOURCE OF NEWS. According to Jim Clark (1996), former president of Netscape, the Internet "represents the first fundamental change since the telecommunications system was invented. The biggest change up to now was when the telephone moved from a rotary dial to Touch-Tone . . . that's really a small change compared to this."[66]

More and more news agencies, newspapers organizations, TV and radio stations, and networks are using the Internet to extend their news services to the public. News on the Internet includes text information, audio bits, video clips, animation, and a wide range of graphics. Archiving news provides the user with search options to locate previously published items and/or related items.

Many of the news stories that are carried live on TV networks have Internet supplements for those who are interested in examining the news more closely and/or getting background information on the feature story of the news program.

The Internet has thus expanded news programming beyond what print and broadcast media can do. Through the Internet, news programming can be interactive through which an individual tailors the news of the day according to his or her interests. It is almost like providing the option to the individual to compose his or her news magazine that might include text, audio, animation, video clips, and various graphics.

Studies focusing on TV audience indicated that around 65% of the American public rely heavily on TV for news. With the growing popularity of Internet news, one wonders how long this figure will remain unchanged. In discussing the Internet as an alternative news source, *One Year Later, September 11th and the Internet,* (September 5, 2002), addressed the concept of "watershed moments"—the events that could define the Internet as an alternative news source. TV was defined as a news medium by events such as the Nixon-Kennedy debate (90 million viewers) and the Kennedy assassination and its aftermath. Attempting to define the events that might provide a turning point for the Internet and news broadcasting, the researchers of *One Year Later* wrote:

> It may be that only hindsight will provide us with the perspective required to identify similar turning points for the Web, but that hasn't stopped some from putting potential events in the running. The night of the 1996 election, the broadcast of the Mars Pathfinder mission, the breaking of the Lewinsky scandal and subsequent release of the voluminous Starr report—these and other events have each been singled out as *the* moment at which the Web came into its own.[67]

The researchers further indicated that "In practice, there will probably be no single defining moment for Web, but these events all have elements in common. In each case, large numbers flocked to the new medium, and some were looking *to fulfill a need that was not being met by the traditional news media.*"[68]

Addressing the reasons for Americans and the rest of the world turning to the Internet after September 11, 2001, the researchers pointed out:

For some, computer networks provided alternative interpersonal communication channels that allowed families and loved ones to stay in touch when the telephone and cellular networks were damaged or overloaded. Others used the Internet to collaboratively search for those lost in the confusion after the World Trade Center collapse. The vast majority of users, however, went to the Web in search of news.[69]

ADVOCATING THE USE OF THE INTERNET IN EDUCATION—A NATIONAL AGENDA. The authors of *Internet Homework Helper* (1997), a K–12 publication, made a very interesting and strong statement regarding the importance of the Internet in life today. They said, "Soon, not being on the Internet will be equivalent to not having a telephone or TV. . . . Employers and college recruiters want high school graduates with computer and Internet experience. Knowledge of computers and the Internet helps many people get (and keep) their jobs."[70] Today, hard evidence supports these two claims.

Providing computers to schools and connecting classrooms to the Internet has become a national concern that is expressed by politicians, corporations, educators, and parents. In the State of the Union Address, January 23, 1996, President William Clinton highlighted an agenda for connecting American schools with the Information Superhighway. He said:

In our schools, every classroom in America must be connected to the information superhighway, with computers and good software, and well-trained teachers. We are working with the telecommunications industry, educators and parents to connect 20 percent of California's classrooms this spring, and every classroom and every library in the entire United States by the year 2000. I ask Congress to support this educational technology initiative so that we can make sure this national partnership succeeds.[71]

Getting America's Students Ready for the 21st Century—Meeting the Technology Literacy Challenge (1996) outlined the vision of the future based on President Clinton's educational initiative challenge.[72] The report stated that, in acknowledging the challenges facing education, President Clinton and Vice President Gore announced on February 15, 1996, "The Technology Literacy Challenge, envisioning a 21st century where all students are technologically literate. The challenge was placed before the nation as a whole, with responsibility for its accomplishment shared by local communities, states, the private sector, educators, parents, the federal government, and others."[73]

The report went on to outline four concrete goals of that vision:

- All teachers in the nation will have the training and support they need to help students learn using computers and the information superhighway.
  Upgrading teacher training is key to integrating technology into the classroom and to increasing student learning.
- All teachers and students will have modern multimedia computers in their classrooms.
  Computers become effective instructional tools only if they are readily accessible to students and teachers.
- Every classroom will be connected to the information superhighway.
  Connections to networks, especially the Internet, multiply the power and usefulness of computers as learning tools by putting the best libraries, museums, and other research and cultural resources at our students' and teachers' fingertips.
- Effective software and on-line learning resources will be an integral part of every school's curriculum.
  Software and on-line learning resources can increase students' learning opportunities, but they must be high quality, engaging, and directly related to the school's curriculum.[74]

WEB-BASED EDUCATION COMMISSION.   Since November 1999, the Web-Based Education Commission[75] has investigated the full range of issues and ideas related to the Internet and education. Testimonies and dialogue with experts from different disciplines and with parents formed the basis of the Commission's report.[76] The Commission wrote:

For education, the Internet is making it possible for more individuals than ever to access knowledge and to learn in new and different ways. At the dawn of the 21st Century, the education landscape is changing. Elementary and secondary schools are experiencing growing enrollments, coping with critical shortages of teachers, facing overcrowded and decaying buildings, and responding to demands for higher standards. On college campuses, there is an influx of older, part-time students seeking the skills vital to success in an Information Age. Corporations are dealing with the shortage of skilled workers and the necessity of providing continuous training to their employees.

The Internet is enabling us to address these educational challenges, bringing learning to students instead of bringing students to learning. It is allowing for the creation of learning communities that defy the constraints of time and distance as it provides access to knowledge that was once difficult to obtain. This is true in the schoolhouse, on the college campus, and in corporate training rooms."[77]

The report outlined the promise of the Internet in three concise points:

1. To center learning around the student instead of the classroom.

2. To focus on the strengths and needs of individual learners.
3. To make lifelong learning a practical reality.

Considering these three points, the Commission wrote:

> We heard that the Internet enables education to occur in places where there is none, extends resources where there are few, expands the learning day, and opens the learning place. We experienced how it connects people, communities, and resources to support learning. We witnessed how it adds graphics, sound, video, and interaction to give teachers and students multiple paths for understanding. We learned that the Web is a medium today's kids expect to use for expression and communication—the world into which they were born.[78]

Based on the evidence presented by hundreds of people, the Commission issued a seven-point call-to-action to government, industry, and the education community that forms the framework of a national e-learning agenda:

1. Make powerful new Internet resources, especially broadband access, widely and equitably available and affordable for all learners (broadband networks, which have the capacity to carry huge amounts of data many times faster than traditional telephone lines, enable the use of full motion video and audio in education programs and real-time interaction over the Internet).
2. Provide continuous and relevant training and support for educators and administrators at all levels.
3. Build a new research and development framework around learning in the Internet age.
4. Develop quality online educational content that meets the highest standards of educational excellence.
5. Revise outdated regulations that impede innovation and replace them with approaches that embrace anytime, anywhere, any pace learning.
6. Protect online learners and ensure their privacy.
7. Sustain funding via traditional and new sources that are adequate to the challenge at hand.[79]

The Web-Based Education Commission called upon the new Congress and administration:

> . . . to embrace an "e-learning" agenda as a centerpiece of our nation's federal education policy. . . . This e-learning agenda should be aimed at assisting local communities, state education agencies, institutions of higher education, and the private sector in their efforts.
>
> We urge the new President and the 107th Congress to seize this opportunity and to focus on ways in which public law can be modified and changed to support, rather than undermine, the technology that is so dramatically changing education.[80]

CEO Forum on Education and Technology. The CEO Forum on Education and Technology was founded in 1996 as a four-year partnership between business and education leaders to assess and monitor progress toward integrating technology in America's schools.[81] Its organizing principles are:

1. All students must graduate with the technology skills needed in today's world and tomorrow's workplace.
2. All educators must be equipped to use technology as a tool to achieve high academic standards.
3. All parents and community members must stay informed of key education technology decisions confronting policymakers, administrators, and educators.
4. All students must have equitable access to technology.
5. The nation must invest in education technology research and development.

In 1997, the CEO Forum issued its first report focusing on the importance of integrating hardware and connectivity to professional development and content.[82] It also introduced StaR, School Technology and Readiness Chart for School, Colleges and Departments of Education. StaR is "a self-assessment tool for schools to gauge progress toward integrating technology to improve education. The STaR Assessment offers a benchmark measure of national progress toward integrating technology in schools."

The second report, *Professional Development: A Link to Better Learning*[83] (February 1999) focused on educator professional development. It outlined ten principles for effective professional development and presented an update of StaR Chart and StaR Assessment.

In June 2000, the Forum published its third report, *The Power of Digital Learning: Integrating Digital Content.* The report defined a vision for digital learning:

The Need For Digital Learning

There is consensus among business leaders, educators, policymakers and parents that our current traditional practices are not delivering the skills our students will need to thrive in the 21st century. As part of our efforts at school reform, we should apply technology's resources to develop the full academic abilities of all our students. The CEO Forum believes that only through the integrated approach of digital learning will our nation's schools, each operating under distinctive circumstances, opportunities and constraints, fully utilize technology in all its forms to promote student achievement and develop the essential skills.

We must make the necessary adjustments and shifts to ensure that our schools become digital learning environments. Adopting this integrated approach addresses the problems facing schools and can improve student performance. Today, a record 95 percent of schools and 72 percent of classrooms are connected to the Internet.

However, while 86 percent of teachers report using the Internet in teaching for e-mail and finding curricular materials, only 66 percent of teachers use the Internet to enhance classroom instruction. Additionally, only 30 percent leverage the Internet for student research, only 27 percent use it to solve problems or analyze data and a meager 16 percent employ these tools for lesson planning.

In short, we have placed so much focus on hardware, connectivity and rudimentary technology skills that our schools and students have not yet begun to realize the full potential of digital learning. We have also tended to discuss these components separately, when they must be seamlessly integrated to be most effective. Therefore, we must redouble our efforts to integrate digital content into the curriculum in order to ensure we apply these powerful tools in the creative ways that enhance student learning.

We recognize that our efforts to promote digital learning exist in an educational climate in which school systems and teachers are by necessity focusing on accountability structures. For both school systems and teachers this complicates the ability to implement digital learning. However, digital learning is critical if we are dedicated to preparing students with the necessary technology and critical thinking skills. We must extend accountability to the digital environment and link digital content and learning processes to student performance standards.[84]

In spring 2001, the CEO Forum released its final report, *Key Building Blocks for Student Achievement in the 21st Century*,[85] focusing on educational outcomes and assessments.

PREPARING TEACHERS TO INTEGRATE TECHNOLOGY, INCLUDING THE INTERNET, IN THEIR TEACHING. Realization of the importance of educating citizens in the skills of using information technologies, including the Internet, is also expressed in documents addressing the required qualification of K–12 teachers. This realization has been expressed by many organizations, including the National Council for Accreditation of Teacher Education (NACTE) and the International Society for Technology Education (ISTE). Recommendations of both organizations are discussed in more detail in Chapter 15.

SUMMARY

The Internet is a global information system that uses networks of computers to enable people all over the world to interact with one another and to share a vast and diversified body of information. Its origin goes back to late 1960s, when the U.S. Department of Defense decided to fund an experimental computer network that would allow remote research and development sites to exchange information. This network, named ARPAnet, began in 1969 with funds from the Advanced Research Project Administration.

The introduction of the World Wide Web in 1989 and the graphical user interface for the web in 1993–1994 accelerated the growth of the Internet. Lifting the ban that prohibited the use of the Internet by business in 1991 accelerated the growth of the Internet even further. At present, the commercial sector is the fastest growing sector of the Internet.

The growth of the Internet is reflected in the growing number of Internet users and Internet domains and current trends of Internet use in business, government, politics, entertainment, news, and education. Its use in education is advocated by various organizations, statesmen, politician, parents, and educators.

In the next two chapters we address the unique characteristics of the Internet and commonly used Internet resource tools and their applications in education.

REFERENCES

1. Stanek, William R., et al. *Electronic Publishing Unleashed.* Indianapolis, IN: Sams Publishing, 1995, p. 418.
2. *What is the Internet,* gopher://info.isoc.org/00/isoc/faq/what-is-internet.txt, updated 2/23/95.
3. FNC Resolution: Definition of Internet, http://www.fnc.gov/Internet_res.html, downloaded 10/24/95.
4. Hahn, Harley, and Rick Stout. *The Internet Complete Reference.* Berkeley, CA: Osborne McGraw-Hill, 1994, p. 2.
5. *Ibid.* p. 10.
6. *What You Need to Know About Inventors,* Inventors of the Modern Computer, ARPAnet—The First Internet, http://inventors.about.com/library/weekly/aa091598.htm, p. 1, downloaded 7/31/03.
7. Pike, Mary Ann, et al. *Using the Internet,* 2nd ed., Indianapolis, IN: Que, 1995, p. 10.
8. Carvin, Andy, *The Internet: From ARAPAnet to the NII,* http://edweb.gsn.org/ibahn/history.html, 7/14/97.
9. Hahn, *op. cit.,* p. 10.
10. *What You Need to Know About Inventors,* Inventors of the Modern Computer, ARPAnet—The First Internet, http://inventors.about.com/library/weekly/aa091598.htm, p. 3, downloaded 7/31/03, last updated 03/01/03.
11. The Internet Cooperation for Assigned Names and Numbers (ICANN). Top-Level Domains, http://www.icannn.org/tlds, p. 1, downloaded 7/31/03.
12. *Ibid.*
13. *Ibid.* p. 2.
14. Derived from ICANN, http://www.icann.org/tlds, last updated 03/01/03.
15. RIPE Network Coordination Centre, http://nw.com/zone/iso-country-codes, downloaded 7/31/03.
16. ICANN, *Ibid.* p. 1.
17. ICANN, *Ibid.* p. 1.

18. Krol, Ed. *The Whole Internet Users Guide and Catalog*, Sebastopol, CA: O'Reilly and Associates, 1992, p. 22.

19. *What You Need to Know About Inventors*, http://inventors.about.com/library/weekly/aa091598.htm, p. 2, downloaded 5/20/03.

20. Carvin, Andy. *The Internet: From ARAPAnet to the NII*," http://edweb.gsn.org/ibahn/history.html, downloaded 6/12/97.

21. Krol, Ed, *op. cit.* p. 10

22. Pike, Mary Ann, et al. *op. cit.* p. 10.

23. Krol, Ed, *op. cit.* p. 11.

24. What You Need to Know About Inventors,, http://inventors.about.com/library/weekly/aa091598.htm, p. 2, downloaded 5/20/03.

25. Pike, Mary Ann, et al. *op. cit.* p. 10.

26. Stanek, William R., et al. *Electronic Publishing Unleashed*. Indianapolis, IN: Sams Publishing, 1995, p. 418.

27. What You Need to Know About Inventors, http://inventors.about.com/library/weekly/aa091598.htm, p. 2, downloaded 5/20/03.

28. *Ibid.*

29. *Ibid.*

30. Glossbrenner, Alfred and Emily Glossbrenner. *The Little Web Book*. Berkeley, CA: Peachpit Press, 1996, p. 15.

31. *Ibid.*

32. Stanek, William R., et al. *op. cit.* p. 418.

33. *Ibid.* p. 419.

34. U.S. Department of Commerce, *The Emerging Digital Economy*, http://www.ecommercecommission.org/document/EmergingDig.pdf, 1998, p. 7, downloaded 7/31/03.

35. NUA Internet, "How Many Online," http://www.nua.ie/surveys/how-many-online/, p. 1, downloaded 7/14/03.

36. CyberAtlas, Population Explosion! http://cyberatlas.internet.com/big_picture/geographics/article/0,,5911_151151,00.html, downloaded 7/1/03.

37. Nielsen NetRatings, http://www.nielsen-netratings.com/, downloaded 7/14/03.

38. U.S. Department of Education, National Center for Education Statistics. *Digest of Education Statistics, 2002*, NCES 2003-060, by Thomas D. Snyder, Washington, D.C.: 2003, p. 485.

39. *Ibid.* Table 424, p. 495.

40. Pew Internet & American Life Project, *Getting Serious Online*, http://www.pewinternet.org/, p. 1, accessed 3/3/02.

41. *Ibid.* p. 2.

42. Internet Software Consortium, *Internet Domain Survey FAQ*, http://www.isc.org/ds/faq.html, downloaded 7/14/03.

43. *Ibid.*

44. For more information on the definition of terms used in the survey, see *Domain Survey Definitions http://www.isc.org/ds/defs.html*, accessed 7/14/03.

45. *Ibid.* Internet Domain Survey FAQ, 7/14/03.

46. Internet Software Consortium, Internet Domain Survey Number of Internet Hosts, http://www.isc.org/ds/host-count-history.html, downloaded 7/14/03.

47. *Ibid.* Internet Domain Survey FAQ.

48. *The Chronicle of Higher Education,* Washington: The Chronicle of Higher Education, Inc., February 7, 1997, p. A25.

49. *Internet 2,* http://www.internet2.edu/resources/Internet2MembersList.PDF.

50. U.S. Department of Education, National Cener for Education Statistics, *Digest of Education Statistics,* 2001, NCES 2002–130, by Thomas Snyder, Charlene M. Hoffman. Washington, D.C.: 2002.

51. Jones, Steve, The Pew Internet & American Life Project, *The Internet Goes to College,* Washington, D.C., September 15, 2002.

52. *Ibid.* p. 3.

53. *Ibid.*

54. *Ibid.*

55. *The Future of Information Technology in Education An ISTE Publication,* http://www.iste.org/publish/future/Chapter1.html, accessed 11/21/97.

56. Deborah Fallows, *Email at Work, Few feel overwhelmed and most are pleased with the ay email helps them do their jobs,* Pew Internet and American Life Project, Washington, D.C., http://www.pewomtermet.org, December 8, 2002.

57. Rainie, Lee, John Horrigan, and Pew Internet & American Life Project, *Holidays online—2002, Email grows as a seasonal fixture and e-shopping advances,* Washington, D.C., January 7, 2003.

58. Horrigan, John B., Lee Rainie, and Pew Internet & American Life Project , Counting on the Internet, *Most Expect To Find Key Information Online, Most Find The Information They Seek, Many Now Turn To The Internet First,* Washington, D.C., December 29, 2002.

59. *Ibid.*

60. *Ibid.*

61. Larsen, Elena, Lee Rainie, and Pew Internet & American Life Project, *Digital Town Hall: How Local Officials Use the Internet and the Civic Benefits They Cite from Dealing with Constituents Online,* Washington, D.C., October 2, 2002.

62. Larsen, Elena, Lee Rainie, and Pew Internet & American Life Project, *The rise of the e-citizen, How people use government agencies' web sites,* Washington, D.C., April 3, 2002.

63. *Ibid.* p. 2.

64. Pew Internet & American Life Project, *Digital Town Hall, op. cit.*

65. Garthwaite, Jonathan (Ed.), *Townhall.com,* About Us, http://www.townhall.com/about/ downloaded 8/11/03.

66. Investor's Business Daily. (1997, January 15). p. A6 quoted by David Moursund, *The Future of Information Technology in Education, An ISTE Publication,* http://www.iste.org/Publications/Books/Future/Chapter2.html.

67. Rainie, Lee, Susannah Fox, Mary Madden, and Pew Internet & American Life Project, *One Year Later: September 11 and the Internet,* Washington, D.C., September 5, 2002.

68. *Ibid.* (Italics added)

69. *Ibid.*

70. Classroom Connect. *Internet Homework Helper.* Lancaster, PA: Wentworth Worldwide Media, 1997, p. 2.

71. President William Jefferson Clinton, State of the Union Address, U.S. Capitol, January 23, 1996, http://www1.whitehouse.gov/WH/New/other/sotu.html.

72. *Getting America's Students Ready for the 21st Century: Meeting the Technology Literacy Challenge,* http://www.ed.gov/Technology/Plan/, last updated 8/25/96.

73. *Ibid.*

74. *Getting America's Students Ready for the 21st Century: Meeting the Technology Literacy Challenge:* Executive Summary—June 1996, http://www.ed.gov/Technology/Plan/NatTechPlan/execsum.html, 6/25/03, pp. 1–2.

75. The Web-Based Education Commission was established by the Higher Education Act Amendments of 1998. President Clinton, Education Secretary Richard Riley, and the Democratic and Republican leadership of Congress appointed its 16 members.

76. The Web-Based Education Commission issues urgent Call-to-Action to Harness Internet's Power for Learning, *Broadest Report To Date on E-Learning Recommends Investment, Regulatory Reform,* http://www.hpcnet.org/cgi-bin/global/a-bus_card.cgi?SiteID=203877/ 12/19/2000, accessed 1/25/01.

77. *Ibid.* p. i

78. *Ibid.* p. iii

79. *Ibid.*

80. Excerpts from Report of the Web-Based Education Commission to the President and the Congress of the United States, Senator Bob Kerrey, Chair, Representative Johnny Isakson, Vice Chair, The Power of the Internet for Learning—Moving from Promise Practice, December 2000, http://www.ed.gov/offices/AC/WBEC/FinalReport/, accessed 1/25/01.

81. CEOs issue challenge to higher education's 2.2 million teachers must have technology skills, http://www.ceoforum.org/news.cfm?NID=9 January 10, 2000. Its members are representatives from Advanced Network & Services, Inc., America Online, Inc., Apple Computer, Inc., Bell Atlantic Network Services, Inc., BellSouth, Classroom Connect, Compaq Computer Corporation, Computer Curriculum Corporation, Dell Computer, Discovery Communications, Inc., Flextronics International, IBM, Jostens Learning Corporation, Julian J. Studley, Lucent Technologies, Inc., McKinsey & Company, NEA, National School Boards Association, NewCourt Credit Group, Quality Education Data, and The Washington Post Company.

82. CEO Forum, *From Pillars to Progress,* October 1997, http://www.ceoforum.org/reports.cfm?CID=1&RID=1, accessed 8/11/03.

83. CEO Forum. *Professional Development: A Link to Better Learning,* 1999, http://www.ceoforum.org/downloads/99report.pdf, accessed 8/11/03.

84. CEO Forum. *The Power of Digital Learning,* http://www.ceoforum.org/downloads/report3.pdf , Summer 2000, pp. 11–12, accessed 8/11/03.

85. CEO Forum. *Key Building Blocks for Student Achievement in the 21st Century,* http://www.ceoforum.org/downloads/report4.pdf, accessed 8/12/03.

Chapter 10

UNIQUE CHARACTERISTICS OF THE INTERNET AND ITS POTENTIAL APPLICATIONS IN EDUCATION

INTRODUCTION

There are different approaches to addressing the potential applications of the Internet in education. One approach is to examine different sites as resources for teaching a subject matter. In such an approach, one can research the use of the Internet in teaching mathematics, sciences, social studies, Spanish, French, English as a second language (ESL), and so forth.

A second approach is to discuss the Internet tools and their use in teaching. Implementing this approach could result in papers addressing, for example, the use of e-mail to enhance education for cultural diversity or use of discussion forums to complement distance-teaching projects on the Internet.

A third approach is to compare different search engines and strategies on the Internet and the application of selected engines in teaching.

It is beyond the scope of this chapter to outline all feasible approaches to the study of the potential applications of the Internet in education. However, the chosen approach is to focus on the major unique characteristics of the Internet and briefly explain the potential educational values of each.

The unique characteristics of the Internet stem from its nature as a global information system. The Internet has its roots in connecting people to share ideas and information and in connecting people with sites that store information. These are the reasons for its existence and tremendous growth. Pike (1997) explained, "In a very real sense, information is the reason the Internet exists."[1]

Key to connecting people together or with sources of information is interactivity. People interact with each other, and they interact with information. A triangular model for the Internet thus emerges. The triangle's apexes are information, people, and connectivity. These three dynamic components form the Internet, which has become the first electronic global library. This library has the following unique features:

1. Universal Access. The Internet can be accessed simultaneously by millions of people in different parts of the world. It is a borderless library with access to its resources extending beyond the physical boundaries of any nation.
2. Rich in Multimedia Resources. The Internet is the first global library that disperses information in integrated multimedia formats.
3. A Publishing Medium: the Internet is the first library in the history of civilization to which any client can add a document.
4. An Interactive Medium. The Internet is the first and the only library whose patrons can interact with each other in real or asynchronous time, resulting in collaborative work among Internet users.

A brief discussion of these unique features of the Internet and their implications to education follows.

UNIVERSAL BORDERLESS ACCESS

Access to the Internet is universal. The Internet enables "computers of all kinds to directly and transparently communicate and share services throughout much of the world."[2]

Accessibility to the global network is not limited to computer wizards or researchers in their laboratories. The personal computer equipped with a modem has become a communication tool to send and receive messages and to browse and search the vast global information residing on computer networks forming the Internet.

Universal accessibility is crucial to effective living in today's fast-moving global environment. For the professional, the amount of information needed to make a sound judgment is growing exponentially. Accordingly, fast access to current information is not only necessary but also essential. Addressing the business needs for immediate access to current information, Heslop and Budnick (1995) said, "In the fast-moving, global, competitive business environment, it is crucial that current information is available to the consumer who needs it."[3] Up-to-date and comprehensive information is needed to make rational decisions. As David Vine put it, "A good business strategy demands intelligence as input for the decision-making process."[4]

In business, universal access to information that is crucial for a company is available not only to the top managers through their traditional information personnel but also to all of the employees through their desktop computers. Mary Cronin explains: "With management support, information gives employees a vital tool for solving problems, taking initiative to major improvements in their work, and understanding how their job and their company fit into the larger picture. It transforms workstations into unlimited information generators."[5]

This type of access to information enforces a new strategy for managing information in the corporate world. Mary Cronin explains: "By encouraging managers to move away from traditional approaches to controlling information toward a coherent strategy for using expanded access opportunities for competitive advantage. Therein lays the real potential of the Internet."[6]

For decades, educators advocated that the teacher is not and should not be the sole source of information to students. The Internet is a powerful vehicle through which students can seek information. In addition to the value of discovering information, their search of information can help individualize learning since the students are making decisions on the breadth and the depth of information they gather. Moreover, extending the learning environment beyond the physical boundaries of any nation could help foster respect and understanding of cultural diversity among people of the world, a necessary condition for achieving world peace.

RICH IN MULTIMEDIA RESOURCES

The Internet is rich in multimedia resources. Searchers of the Internet can locate vast amounts of multimedia information, including audio, charts, graphs, photographs, animated sequences, video clips, paintings from museums, news of the day from TV news agencies, radio broadcasts, TV broadcasts, and thousands of other items. These rich multimedia resources enhance the information retrieved from the web.

A great deal of the multimedia resources on the Internet is available free of charge to the public to incorporate in personal and/or professional publications.[7,8,9] For some items, the researcher must pay a fee for downloading and incorporating them in publications. In either case, copyright guidelines have to be observed.

The Internet is a rich library of published material that can be accessed free of charge. For example, Project Gutenberg is based on the premise that "anything that can be entered into a computer can be reproduced indefinitely . . . what Michael Hart (Michael Hart is the initiator of the project) termed 'Replicator Technology.'"[10] The concept of Replicator Technology is that if a text publication can be stored on a computer, then any number of copies can be made available to everyone in the world. Based on this premise, Electronic Texts (Etexts) created by Project Gutenberg are made available in plain ASCII files, which can be read by the majority of users. The collection can be searched by author or by title.

Some of the multimedia resources on the web are interactive. For example, the interactive Frog Dissections Kit states:

The purpose of this lab activity is to help you learn the anatomy of a frog and give you a better understanding of the anatomy of vertebrate animals in general, including humans. This program provides still and motion visuals of preserved and pithed* frogs, in addition to text. *A pithed frog has had its central nervous system destroyed (its spinal cord has been severed). It is technically dead, but some of its organs continue to function for a brief period. Visuals of pithed frogs are found in the section on "Internal Organs."[11]

Net Frog, created November 7, 2002, is available along with the original, The Interactive Frog Dissection created in 1994. Net Frog is an improved version of the original Frog Dissection. It requires QuickTime plug-in and Image Map capability.[12] It is expected that more and more of this kind of interactive multimedia site will be introduced, especially as Internet II becomes accessible to a wider range of the public.

Publications on the web are in hypertext and hypermedia format. Hypertext and hypermedia have in common linking capability to related text or related media. *The Concise Columbia Encyclopedia, Encarta Encyclopedia* gives a clear definition of hypertext:

The technique for organizing computer databases or documents to facilitate the nonsequential retrieval of information. Related pieces of information are connected by predefined or user-created links that allow a user to follow associative trails across the database. The linked data may be in a text, graphic, or audio format, allowing multimedia presentations. Hypertext applications offer a variety of tools for very rapid searches for specific information.[13]

According to the 2001 edition of Microsoft *Encarta Encyclopedia*, "The term *hypertext* was coined by American computer scientist Ted Nelson in 1965 to describe textual information that could be accessed in a nonlinear way. He used the prefix *hyper* to describe the speed and facility with which users could jump to and from related areas of text."[14]

Hypertext and hypermedia—hyper learning environment—empower the learner to learn. A learner can set up his or her goal and proceed in a nonlinear progression through rich, interesting, attention holding, and interrelated units of information stored in different formats to satisfy his or her learning needs and self-planned query.

Hypermedia provides the learner with a nonthreatening environment, which encourages self-discovery. Hypermedia provides the learner with an efficient means to learn how to search for information—an extremely essential skill in the age of information. Hypermedia affords the user the freedom to question a database in any way that seems desirable and in any order needed without losing track of where the search is heading. The "history" option in web browsers can help the researcher trace steps taken in a web session. Immediate evaluation of query results can help the researcher refine search strategies, including refining questions asked and locating pertinent information.

Finally, hypermedia allows the learner to be in relatively greater control of the learning process. Gradually, individuals become seekers of information, not just recipients.

PUBLISHING MEDIUM

As stated earlier, the Internet is the first global library that any client can add to its collection. For the first time in the history of education, students' written assignments, term papers, multimedia products such as PowerPoint presentations can be published for potential reading and viewing by any member of the Internet community. Having access to the Internet through Internet providers, individuals can develop their own personal web pages. Personal home pages range from the simple to the sophisticated. Simple home pages may include the author's biographical information and favorite sites on the Internet. Sophisticated personal home pages usually include more information, such as one's opinion regarding community or national issues, news of particular interest to colleagues, and links to favorite sites that have pertinent information on topics of interest. An example of a sophisticated personal page is Kathy Schrock's home page.[15]

Publishing on the Internet has unique values for both the author and the reader. These values are summarized in the following:

1. Through the use of e-mail, the author can receive readers' feedback. A dialogue can ensue between the readers and the author. This type of feedback can be helpful to the author to edit his or her publication for better readership and clearer communication.

2. Internet publications can integrate graphs, pictures, clipart, video, and audio. The nontext component of the published material not only can enrich the published articles but also can provide a vehicle through which paintings, sound recordings, experimental video, and so on get published on the Internet.

3. Internet publications can also employ hypertext coding. Hypertext coding facilitates the nonlinear retrieval of information. Related pieces of information are predefined by the author or searched for by the reader. Predefinition of related pieces of information can be done in different ways such as establishing links between keywords in the article and other related information that appears in the article or in other sources.

    The user can search for related information by using search options. A publisher might provide a search from within the published article for the reader to locate certain information by typing keywords.

4. Publications on the Internet can provide access to some of the references cited in the publication. Many times a reader becomes interested in a reference cited by an article. If that reference is available online, the author can establish a link between the title of the reference and the Internet location of that reference. Clicking that link takes the reader to the site where the whole reference is published. One can look at this feature as a way of expanding the desktop to open a number of related resources to a topic of study.

5. A published article on the Internet can be updated more readily than a printed article. Whenever new information is made available, the author can retrieve the published article to update and to report it. The same can happen if feedback from readers requires editing the article for better readability. The ease with which Internet articles can be updated and republished is a tremendous challenge to print publishers. A few weeks or months can lapse from the time an article is submitted for print to the time the article appears in print. During that time information could change drastically, rendering the published printed article out-of-date the day it appears in print.

6. The reader of an Internet publication is empowered not only to decide the nonsequential order of items he or she selects for reading but also to save all or some sections of a publication for future reference.

INTERACTIVE MEDIUM

The Internet provides a global platform for sharing ideas with others. This is usually done through messaging, user groups, chatting, conferencing, and posting and retrieving information on a variety of topics. In many of these instances, the Internet provides an interactive communication environment. Accordingly, it has the potential of enhancing human communication, since central to the enhancement of human communication is interaction among senders and receivers of messages.[16]

In face-to-face communication, there are many factors such as class, race, physical challenges, and learning disabilities that could hinder interactivity. These factors are usually removed from the Internet environment. Gianocavo et al. observed:

> . . . what a thrill to see first-hand the sense of excitement and empowerment that students feel as they receive comments and field questions from Internet-using students in other states, provinces, and countries. Consider this sense of accomplishment, but magnify it many times, when a special needs, handicapped, or learning-disabled student is involved. When these students realize that millions of Internet users are prepared to accept them solely for their words, ideas, and opinions, they feel accepted and empowered in a new way.[17]

Interactivity among people can go beyond the geographical boundaries of nations. *Friends and Partners* was jointly established in 1994 by citizens of the United States and Russia to promote better understanding between the citizens of both nations. The goal as stated by the site is to "create and link together information on our nation's histories, our art, music, literature, and religion, our educational and scientific resources, our geography and natural resources, our languages, and our opportunities for communicating, traveling, and working together."[18]

According to the *Friends and Partners* web site, "Friends and Partners now represents a community of people all over the world who provide information and communications services to promote better understanding, friendship and partnership between individuals and organizations of the United States (and, more broadly, 'the west') and countries of the Former Soviet Union."[19]

Another example of interactive homepages is the *United Nations CyberSchoolBus*.[20] The site features the Model UN Discussion Area (MUNDA). MUNDA provides a place for young people to exchange and discuss ideas and request information. Students have to register in MUNDA at no charge.[21] The web site features a variety of excellent and interesting up-to-date materials, among which are school curricula covering peace education, poverty, human rights, cities of the world, and world hunger.

Another powerful example of an interactive site is *The Diary Project*.[22] Students are encouraged to submit their thoughts and experiences "as freely as they would in their own journals."[23] Entries may be posted anonymously or with first name and age. "There are thousands of entries in 24 categories posted on the site. (The) purpose is to encourage essential dialogue and communication among teens and for them to know they are not alone in the challenges they are experiencing throughout adolescence."[24]

This *Diary Project* was launched in 1995. "It was inspired by the visit to San Francisco of the young Bosnian diarist, Zlata Filipovic, author of *Zlata's Diary*, the story of her life growing up in Sarajevo amidst a raging war. The book was internationally acclaimed, and Zlata became a role model for young people all over the world."[25]

The goal of the project is to make the site interactive and to encourage young people to communicate about inspiring matters and issues. Young people can submit their entries from the site. A very touching example of the entries is entitled "Mother," submitted August 12, 2003:

Mother

by irish stalker, Over 21, female

August 12, 2003

Dear Diary,

This is an ode to my mother ... I know I wasn't the most pleasant daughter you could've had while I was growing up . . . I know I was really mean and cruel to you all my life . . . I know I made you responsible for every stupid thing I did (including my father). I know I wasn't there when you needed me but still . . . You were there every step of the way, encouraging me the best way you could. You were there when I needed to talk to someone. You still love me no matter what and I can't believe just how much you forgave but at least, now I know what love is . . . God has shown me, through you, just what love is: it is forgiving, never failing, always hoping for the best and it just does miracles!!! Thank you for being so incredibly loving to everyone, including me. I love you!!! XOX[26]

The site is monitored by a group of teen volunteers who are overseen by Diary Project staff. Teens are advised that the site does not offer professional therapy or counseling and that they seek out an adult whom they trust (teacher, friends, parents, relative, school counselor, psychologist, medical doctor, clergy, etc.) for guidance and support for things that are overwhelming in the teen's life.[27]

Diary Deck Night is an event sponsored by the Diary Project. The goal is to get parents and teens from a community to talk and share insights "relating to what it feels like to be a teen or the parent of a teen. The goal of the evening was to enhance communication and understanding between the two generations through dialogue and discussion—to share out loud some of the things they don't know about each other and to spend a couple of hours walking in each other's shoes."[28]

Diary Deck Night puts to use entries written by parents and teens involved in the project as well as The Diary Deck a recently published collection of 75 flash cards, featuring a teen's anonymous entry excerpted from the website. Along with each entry the cards offer related questions to promote discussion. It is a resource designed to open new lines of communication between parents, teachers and teens. It offers adults a way to engage in dialogue with teens about difficult topics so they can better understand the issues they confront on a daily basis.[29]

Collaborative Medium

Providing the environment for interaction among Internet users, various forms of collaborative work take place. For instance, different projects have been initiated among schools and between schools and organizations interested in supporting quality education in K–12 schools. These projects can be categorized under three headings: collecting data, extending the learning environment beyond what any school can afford, and providing experts to interact with the students on up-to-date projects.

Collaboration in Collecting Data

The Global Attraction Project ran from February 1996 to June 1996. The purpose of the project was to bring "students in grades 4–12 around the world together to compare and contrast data on gravitational attraction in their specific locations." Participants would calculate the acceleration due to gravity in their areas and send their reports via e-mail for publishing on the project's web site. Coordinators of the project felt that it would be "a great opportunity to integrate math, science, English, and computer education."[30]

International Collaborative Boiling Point Project is similar to The Global Attraction Project. The objective is to study the effect of air pressure on the boiling point, and since air pressure changes with the elevation, the boiling point changes too.[31] The site explains the purpose of the project:

> In this experiment, students will boil distilled water and record the following information:
>
> • temperature at which the water boils (boiling point)
> • room temperature
> • volume of water
> • elevation
> • heating device
>
> The purpose of this project is to determine which factor in the experiment (room temperature, volume of water, elevation, or heating device) has the greatest influence on boiling point. Students will analyze all of the data submitted by participants to determine this.[32]

Enticing the students to participate in the collaborative project, the site poses the following question:

> **Ever Wonder What Causes a Pot of Water to Boil?**
> **If you have, this project is for you!**
>
> We have people all over the world boiling water! In the past we've had climbers on Mt. Everest, school children in La Paz, Bolivia and college professors in Cheyenne, Wyoming all participating in the project. The purpose of this project is to discover which factor in the experiment (room temperature, elevation, volume of water, or heating device) has the greatest influence on boiling point. Anyone can participate in this year's project. All you have to do is boil a bit of water, record a bit of information, and send it along to us to include in the database of results. Then, students can analyze all of the data to reach an answer to the question: What causes a pot of water to boil? It's that simple![33]

Students all over the world are invited to submit their observations. Students have the option to submit their results to the site to be included in the list of results. They also have the option just to do the experiment. Steps for doing the experiment and the forms to submit observations or results to the site are included. Explanation of how air pressure affects the boiling point is given, and the students are requested to submit what they think. The background information page includes that explanation:

If you *graphed* all the variables vs. boiling point, you probably saw that elevation had the biggest correlation to boiling point. Why did this happen? We hope to get *feedback* from others out there, but here's our understanding of what's going on.

As water boils, the water turns into steam (also known as water vapor or water gas.) You can probably watch this happen if you pay close attention while you boil your pot of water. First the water begins to form bubbles at the bottom near the heating device (see if this happens for you). Then, the bubbles begin to rise until the bubbles begin to pop off the surface of the water and seemingly evaporate into the air. What's happening here?

The energy from the heating device first raises the temperature of the water. At a certain temperature, that energy is used to transform the water from its liquid state to its gaseous state (that's when you start seeing the bubbles form). As the energy from the heating device goes into heating the water, the water temperature rises. You'll notice this happening on your thermometer. But at a certain temperature, the heating energy goes only to turning the water into a gas. When that point is reached, your thermometer will not get any higher and you will have found the boiling point of your water. Interestingly, no matter how much longer you keep the pot of water on the stove, it will get no hotter, because at this point all the energy from the heating unit is being dedicated to changing the water into gas and not into raising the heat. Why did it make this change?

As you heat up the water, you are breaking down the liquid molecule so that it can turn into a gas. Bubbles begin to be created in the base of the heating water first. But the pressure of the outside air will squash those bubbles at first because they don't have enough pressure inside them to stand up to the outside air pressure. As more energy goes into making those bubbles though, they will begin to be able to stand up to the outside air pressure. When they get to the point where they can stand up to the outside air pressure, you'll see massive bubbles coming off of your water, the temperature of your water will top off and your boiling point will be reached.

Why then, might you find that at a different elevation (where the air pressure were lower) that the boiling point were lower? I believe it's because the water gas bubbles have an easier time forming. The air pressure isn't quite as heavy on them, so they can withstand the pressure at a lower temperature, and, thus the boiling point is lower. What do you think?[34]

An Extended Learning Environment

There are a number of web applications that provide rich, creative, and interactive learning experiences employing facilities and personnel that are not readily available to any school. In the following, we briefly review some of these applications.

The Jason Project

The JASON Project began as the dream of Dr. Robert Ballard, the scientist and oceanographer who discovered the wreck of the RMS Titanic in 1986. Dr.

Ballard believed that enabling students and their teachers to do field work from the classroom was a powerful concept. The JASON Project was born on the basis of this powerful idea and has since grown into the world's premier real-time science teaching and learning program.[35]

In 1989, Dr. Ballard used a remotely operated vehicle called Jason and a submarine called Alvin to explore the wreck of the RMS Titanic. Other Jason expeditions have ensued. They "have involved students and teachers in current research that have taken their minds and imaginations to some of the most exciting places on Earth—and even to the very outer limits of our solar system!"[36]

The Jason Project site explains the project as:

. . . a multi-disciplinary program that sparks the imagination of students and enhances the classroom experience. From oceans to rain forests, from polar regions to volcanoes, the JASON Project explores Planet Earth and exposes students to leading scientists who work with them to examine its biological and geological development.

From the depths of dark oceans to the heights of wet rain forests, from icy Polar Regions to red-hot volcanoes, the JASON Project travels the world, taking students and teachers on an exciting educational adventure. The JASON Project brings adventure and the thrill of discovery into the classroom, exploring the following questions:

1. What are nature's dynamic systems?
2. How do these systems affect life?
3. What technologies do we use to study these systems and why?[37]

Information on previous,[38] current,[39] and future expeditions[40] is available through the Jason Project sites.

NASA Quest

NASA Quest is a rich resource for educators, kids and space enthusiasts who are interested in meeting and learning about NASA people and the national space program. NASA Quest allows the public to share the excitement of NASA's authentic scientific and engineering pursuits like flying in the Shuttle and the International Space Station, exploring distant planets with amazing spacecraft, and building the aircraft of the future.[41]

NASA Quest includes a full suite of online resources:

- Profiles of NASA experts and stories about their work days.
- Several live interactions with NASA experts per month.
- Audio and video programs over the Internet.
- Lesson plans and student activities
- Collaborative activities in which kids work with one another.

- Background information and photo sections.
- A place where teachers can meet one another.
- A searchable question and answer area with over 3,000 previously asked questions.
- An e-mail service in which individual questions get answered.

In addition, "Frequent live, interactive events allow participants to come and go as dictated by their own individual and classroom needs. These projects are open to anyone, without cost. To get involved, simply select your area of interest or take a look at our calendar of events, and jump in. Welcome aboard!"[42]

Sharing NASA

Sharing NASA is part of the NASA Quest project.

It focuses on the enthusiastic people of NASA who live and breathe the space program every day. Over the Internet, these people come alive for K–12 classrooms. Students feel like they've not only read about exciting events, but that they've met the people involved. Also, classrooms work together over the Internet and teachers plug into a support network of peers. Lots of online curriculum supplements help teachers integrate science and technology issues into their lessons. These projects also offer many opportunities to enhance reading, writing, and creative expression activities.[43]

According to Sharing NASA's sites, projects change over time. On August 12, 2003, the following projects were listed with links to pages giving more information on the projects.

Shuttle Team Online. Blast off with the people who make the shuttle fly.
Live From Mars. Follow NASA's current missions to Mars, including Pathfinder's July 4th landing.
Women of NASA. Amazing females at NASA as role models for young students.

For teachers to stay abreast of new offerings, Sharing NASA suggests joining Sharing NASA mailist by sending an e-mail to listmanager@quest.arc.nasa.gov. The body of the message should read exactly "**subscribe sharing-nasa.**" Also the site suggests visiting the web site at http://quest.arc.nasa.gov/interactive.

In addition to these two NASA programs, NASA's home page at http://www.nasa.gov/home/index.html has many excellent resources for kids, students, and educators. NASAKids at http://www.nasa.gov/audience/forkids/home/index.html is a fascinating page with links to very valuable and interesting resources.

Communication with Experts

Communication with experts on the Internet takes various forms. The Jason Project, NASA Quest, Sharing NASA, and the Diary Project include in their design communication between experts and students and teachers. The Electronic Emissary, based at the College of Education, University of Texas at Austin, http://emissary.ots.utexas.edu/emissary/index.html, is an online matching service that helps teachers locate experts in different disciplines who can contribute to the curriculum. Judi Harris (2003) explained the concept and how this project works.

> There are literally millions of people in the world who use Internet-based tools and resources. . . . Many are subject matter specialists whose knowledge encompasses a wide spectrum of expertise. What if electronic teams could be formed so that volunteers from among this group could communicate directly with K–12 students and teachers who are studying about these experts' specialties?
>
> **What Is the Emissary?**
>
> . . . the *Electronic Emissary*, is an Internet-based service that has been in operation since February of 1993. It is global in scope, but is coordinated from the University of Texas at Austin. The Emissary is a "matching service" that helps K–12 teachers and students with access to the World Wide Web locate other Internet account-holders who are experts in different disciplines, for purposes of setting up curriculum-based, electronic exchanges among the teachers, their students, and the experts. In this way, the interaction that occurs among teachers and students face-to-face in the classroom is supplemented and extended by exchanges that occur among teachers, students, and experts online, via electronic mail and desktop teleconferencing. The Emissary is also a research project, which focuses upon the nature of telementoring interactions in which K–12 students are active inquirers.[44]

Examples of Emissary-matched services include students from various school systems communicating with experts in different fields and located nation wide. The following are some examples of recent curriculum-related work conducted via Emissary-arranged "matches" listed in the site:

- High school students in Delaware who were studying Nathaniel Hawthorne's *The Scarlet Letter* communicated with the character Arthur Dimsdale, who was actually an American literature professor at the U.S. Naval Academy. During the following semester, the students communicated with the professor himself about Mark Twain's *Huck Finn*, culminating their exchange by creating a newspaper that they called *The Mississippi Times*, an idea first suggested by the expert. The teacher and the professor shared instructional ideas, resources, and perspectives about Mark Twain's works and views.
- Students in the "upper room" of a country school in a rural and mountainous region of northern California (11 students, ranging from 4th to 8th grade in the same classroom) learned about bones and skeletons by study-

ing their own skeletal systems and the bones found in owl pellets in the woods near their school. Their teacher, along with a biological researcher at Michigan State University, guided the students' hypothesis formation and testing as they extracted the bones from the pellets, measured them, labeled them, then reconstructed the skeletons, and deduced what kinds of animals the bones supported.

- Jannah, a 10-year-old student in Connecticut, corresponded frequently with Dr. Eisner, a professor in Arizona. They continued their study of Arthurian legends that began in the spring semester of 1995 for more than three years. Jannah, Dr. Eisner, their online facilitator, and the Emissary's director, co-authored *an article describing their online educational experiences*[45] that appeared in the May 1996 issue of the professional journal, *Learning and Leading With Technology*.[46]

- An Advanced Placement Spanish Literature class in Ross, California communicated with Bob Fritz, a professor of Spanish at Ball State University. All communication was conducted in Spanish. Topics addressed included the nivolas of Miguel de Unamuno and how these works fit into the cultural and historical context of Spain.

- 19 4th- and 5th-grade students in McAllen, Texas compared the experiences of their families on the Texas "La Frontera" to colonial life in the original 13 U.S. colonies, with the help of the director of a historic preservation center and museum in Fredericksburg, Virginia.

- Eight groups of four girls each, studying in an honors science program at a New England high school, communicated with a graduate student at the University of Minnesota about DNA & infantile leukemia (the topic of the subject matter expert's thesis), cancer research & therapy, and professional careers for women in science. The teams discussed both scientific and ethical issues online with the university-based genetics expert.

- A computer scientist at the State University of New York–Potsdam with interest and expertise in American history posed as a young Union soldier to help gifted and talented fifth-grade students in Omaha, Nebraska learn about the Civil War. He answered the students' questions in character. The students used what they learned from his responses to write a play about the Civil War, which was performed at their school.[47]

All of these unique features of the Internet, The first global electronic library, make the Internet a significant and a viable medium for distance education. They provide the components necessary to establish virtual interactive classrooms that transcend the geographical and time zones of traditional classrooms. This topic is discussed in more detail later in this book.

REFERENCES

1. Pike, Mary Ann. What is the Internet? gopher://gopher.isoc.org:70/00/isoc/faq/what-is-internet.txt, accessed 6/12/98.

2. *Ibid.*

3. Heslop, Brent, and Larry Budnick. *HTML Publishing on the Internet.* Chapel Hill, NC: Vintage Press, 1995, p. 3.

4. Vine, David, Using the Internet as a Strategic Business Tool, *Internet World*, January 1995, Volume 8, No. 1, pp. 44–45.

5. Cronin, Mary J. *Doing Business on the Internet.* New York: Van Nostrand Reinhold, 1994, p. 16.

6. *Ibid.*

7. Vincent, Patrick. *Free Stuff From the Internet, 2nd ed..* Scottsdale, AZ: The Coriolis Group, 1996.

8. Berinstein, Paula. *Finding Images Online, Online User's Guide to Image Searching in Cyberspace.* Wilton, CT: Pemberton Press, 1996.

9. Turlingtom, Shannon R. *Walking the World Wide Web, Your Personal Guide to the Best on the Web.* Chapel Hill, NC: Ventana Press, 1995.

10. Hart, Michael, *What is Project Gutenberg,* http://www.promo.net/pg/list.html, last updated 5/13/02, downloaded 8/12/03.

11. *The Interactive Frog Dissection,* http://curry.edschool.virginia.edu/go/frog/Frog2/, downloaded 8/5/03.

12. *Net Frog,* http://curry.edschool.virginia.edu/go/frog/, downloaded 8/5/03.

13. *The Concise Columbia Encyclopedia, Microsoft® Encarta® Encyclopedia 1998.*

14. Hypertext. *Microsoft® Encarta® Encyclopedia 2001.* © 1993–2000 Microsoft Corporation.

15. Welcome to Kathy Schrock's Home Page, a portal of possibilities for effective infusion of technology into the curriculum! http://kathyschrock.net/, downloaded 8/12/03.

16. Berlo. David K. *The Process of Communication—An Introduction to Theory and Practice,* New York: Holt, Rinehart and Winston, 1960, pp. 130–131.

17. Classroom Connect. *Educator's Internet Companion—Classroom Connect's Complete Guide to Educational Resources on the Internet.* Lancaster, PA: Wentworth Worldwide Media, 1995, p. ix.

18. *Friends and Partners,* http://www.friends-partners.org/friends/, downloaded 8/12/03.

19. *Ibid.*

20. The United Nation Publications, 1998, http://www.un.org/Pubs/CyberSchoolBus/, downloaded 8/12/03.

21. The Model UN Discussion Area (MUNDA) http://www.un.org/Pubs/CyberSchoolBus/modelun/index.asp, downloaded 8/12/03.

22. *he Diary Project, About the Diary Project,* http://www.diaryproject.com/, downloaded 8/12/03.

23. *Ibid.*

24. *Ibid.*

25. *Ibid.*

26. *The Diary Project, Mother,* http://www.diaryproject.com/entries/?68438, downloaded 8/12/03.

27. *The Diary Project, Submit an Entry,* http://www.diaryproject.com/submit/, downloaded 8/12/03.

28. *The Diary Project, Diary Deck Night,* http://www.diaryproject.com/entries/?-25, downloaded 8/12/03.

29. *Ibid.*
30. *Classroom Connect*, February, vol. 2, no. 5, p. 8.
31. *International Collaborative Boiling Point*, http://k12science.stevens-tech.edu/curriculum/bp/background.html, accessed 6/11/98.
32. *Boil, Boil, Toil & Trouble, The International Boiling Point Project, Project Purpose*, http://www.k12science.org/curriculum/boilproj/purpose.html, accessed 8/12/03.
33. *Boil, Boil, Toil & Trouble, The International Boiling Point Project*, http://www.k12science.org/curriculum/boilproj/index.html, accessed 8/12/03.
34. *International Collaborative Boiling Point*, http://k12science.stevens-tech.edu/curriculum/bp/background.html, accessed 6/11/98.
35. *The Jason Project*, http://www.jason.org/jason_project/jason_project.htm, accessed 8/14/03.
36. *The Jason Project, Past Expeditions*, http://www.jason.org/expedition/past_expeditions/past_expeditions.htm, accessed 8/14/03.
37. *The Jason Project*, http://www.jason.org/jason_project/jason_project.htm, accessed 8/14/03.
38. *The Jason Project, Past Expedition, op. cit.*
39. *The Jason Project, Current Expedition*, http://www.jason.org/expedition/current_expedition/current_expedition_.htm, accessed 8/16/03.
40. *The Jason Project, Future Expedition*, http://www.jason.org/expedition/future_expedition/future_expedition_j ason15.htm, accessed 8/14/03.
41. NASA Quest, http://quest.arc.nasa.gov/about/index.html, accessed 8/12/03.
42. *Ibid.*
43. *Sharing NASA*, http://iita.arc.nasa.gov/products/k12/ames_sharing.html, downloaded 8/12/03.
44. Harris, Judi, *About the Electronic Emissary Project*, http://emissary.ots.utexas.edu/emissary/about.html, pp. 1–2, last updated 2/28/03, accessed 8/16/03.
45. ftp://emissary.ots.utexas.edu/pub/emissary/studies/LLT.May.96.pdf, accessed 8/16/03.
46. *Learning and Leading with Technology*, http://www.iste.org/L&L/index.html, accessed 8/15/03.
47. Harris, Judi *op. cit.* pp. 3–4.

Chapter 11

COMMONLY USED INTERNET RESOURCE
TOOLS AND THEIR POTENTIAL
APPLICATIONS IN EDUCATION

INTRODUCTION

Information is exchanged and shared on the Internet in many ways. The first resource tools widely used were e-mail, Newsgroups, File Transfer Protocol (FTP), and Telnet. Additional resource tools such as Archie and Gopher were introduced as the Internet increased in its size, and the need to speed up the process of finding, retrieving, and transmitting information became crucial to the increasing number of users. However, the major breakthrough in the development of a user-friendly Internet environment has been the World Wide Web and its graphic web browsers.

The following is a brief discussion of the most commonly used Internet tools. It concludes with the most popular Internet tool, the web browser.

E-MAIL

Deutsch (1997) defines e-mail, or electronic mail, as "an automated message processing service that allows you to exchange messages with other users."[1] E-mail is the most widely used service on the Internet. In the world of work, the percentage of on-the-job computer workers using specific computer applications was 72.2% for e-mail and the Internet, 67.2% for word processing, 62.5% for spreadsheets and databases, 53.2% for calendar schedule, 28.9% for graphics and design, 15.3% for programming, and 13% for other uses.[2]

In schools, according to NCES, *Digest of Education Statistics, 2002*, there has been a widespread introduction of computers into the schools. In 2001, the average public school contained 124 instructional computers, and the proportion of instructional rooms with Internet access increased from 50 percent in 1998 to 85 percent in 2001. About 99 percent of schools had access to the Internet in 2001.[3]

Parker (1995) reported that "many studies have shown that recipients are much more likely to reply to an e-mail message than a written request, primarily because of the ease of formulating the response."[4] Through e-mail individuals can communicate on a one-to-one or on a group basis, provided that participants have e-mail addresses. Interested individuals can subscribe to a mailing list. An Internet mailing list is a list of the e-mail addresses of a group of people who are interested in corresponding about a topic of interest or concern.

In e-mail, one also has the option of copying a message to a number of other recipients, including him- or herself. Attachments, such as files, or received e-mail from other sources can be transmitted along with the e-mail. E-mail technology also permits the transfer of multimedia files such as audio, photographs, animation, and video clips.

E-mail is an asynchronous form of communication. A sender e-mails a message whenever appropriate. A recipient of that message gets to read that message at a convenient time. After reading the message, the recipient can decide on a response and when it is to be mailed. Also, the recipient decides whether to save the message, print it, or erase it.

E-mail may be used to enrich and to enhance the educational experience of students. In the following section, the educational values of e-mail are presented.

The Educational Values of E-mail

Enhancing Communication

Through e-mail, communication between the teacher and his or her students can be enhanced. A teacher can communicate classroom assignments to the whole class or to certain individuals. Students can e-mail their term papers, multimedia projects, and completed assignments to the teacher. Almost any type of student report that can be made in class can be e-mailed to the teacher. The teacher, after reviewing student's work, can e-mail his or her feedback. Accordingly, e-mail extends the communication between the teacher and the students beyond the boundaries of the classroom to wherever the students have access to send and receive e-mail. For this reason, e-mail is a significant component of any distance teaching project.

Distance Teaching

Internet Roadmap 1996 is a complete introductory course on the Internet offered through e-mail.[5] In the words of Patrick Crispen (1996), the author of *Internet Roadmap*, the objectives of the Roadmap 1996 are to:

- Show you around the Internet.

- Give you some basic commands that will help you use the tools of the Internet more effectively.
- Point you in the direction of people who can help you if you ever get lost.
- Give you a glimpse of what the coming Information Superhighway may actually look like.[6]

Including the Welcome Page, or "Map" as it was called by the author, there are a total of 27 maps. Among the topics discussed in this course are Levels of Internet Connectivity, E-mail, Listservs, Netiquette, Usenet, Spamming, Internet Security, Telnet, FTP, Gopher, Bookmarks, Veronica, WWW, and the Future. In addition to the 27 maps, the course includes three extra maps: Neat Stuff to Check Out, Advertising on the Internet, and a Guest Lecture.

The course is offered free of charge and lasts for six weeks. Interested individuals can subscribe to the Roadmap 96 list. This is done by sending an e-mail letter to Listserv@Lists.Internic.net with Subscribe Roadmap96, Yourfirstname, Yourlastname in the body of the letter.

The story of posting RoadMap96 on the Internet is very interesting. At the time of posting the course, the summer of 1994, the author, Patrick Douglas Crispen, was a senior at the University of Alabama majoring in economics through the College of Arts and Sciences. Self-taught, he started with using the Internet for e-mail and then continued learning more about the Internet. His workshop "Roadmap" started accepting participants in July 1994, and by October 1994 over 62,000 people from 27 countries had enrolled in the Roadmap distribution lists. The total number of people receiving the original version of the workshop was over 500,000 persons around the world, "making the Roadmap workshop the most popular Internet training workshop in history."[7]

In Crispen's words he authored the workshops to "give new users free training on how to use the Internet, to give the University of Alabama some positive publicity, and to ensure that I can get a *JOB* when (and if) I graduate. The Career Center told me that the most important part of a job search is 'networking'. So, I networked. :)"[8]

Cooperative Projects

Noon Shadow Observation Project, by Kenneth Cole of Faubian Middle School in McKinney, Texas describes the origin and the continuation of this interesting project:

The Noon Shadow Project is based on the method that Eratosthenes, the Librarian of Alexandria, Egypt, used to calculate the circumference of the Earth over 2000 years ago. Educators began the Noon Project in the late 1980s to demonstrate the possibilities for collaborative educational opportunities using electronic mail. The results of that initial effort are published at http://lrs.ed.uiuc.edu/Guidelines/LRWS.html.

One of the originators of the project, Kathleen Smith, continued to recreate the project yearly at the Vernal Equinox from her classroom at Central Academy in Champaign, Illinois. Ihor Charischak of the Stevens Institute of Technology in Hoboken, New Jersey has written some great lessons about the Noon Observation Project. He posted them on his site called the Noon Day Project. Ángela Núñez of IEP Alberto Pico in Santander, Spain translated the lessons into Spanish. Hans Fries of Schulzentrum Im Ellener in Bremen, Germany wrote lessons for the project in German.[9]

Kenneth Cole describes the project as a collaborative project done by schools worldwide. Throughout the world students measure the length of a noon shadow at the vernal equinox, and the results are submitted using an Internet form. A spreadsheet is used to analyze the data.[10]

In addition to learning scientific information related to the project, students have the opportunity to communicate with other students worldwide and learn about countries participating in the project.

Kenneth Cole maintains a home page[11] on which results from 1997 to 2001 may be obtained. Additional Noon Shadow resources are available through the Internet by doing a search using "Noon Shadow Observation Project" as a search string. Resources include lesson plans, contributions from worldwide countries, history of the project, as well as information on the first mathematician, Eratosthenes, the chief librarian of the Library in Alexandria, Egypt, who estimated the circumference of the earth over 2000 years ago using the same methods applied in the project today.

Patricia Charnay's *Newsletters Across the World*[12] was an invitation "to join a French project of a monthly pupil-written e-mail newsletter among ten secondary classes throughout the world. Each school would receive letters from the other participants in return for its own contribution during the whole school year."[13] Participating classes had to commit to e-mailing a newsletter on the 15th of each month for eight months addressing themes chosen for the year. The project aimed at developing students' knowledge of the world and its people through reading, writing, social studies, and technology. The project was scheduled to begin September 1998 through June 1999.

Donna Dintelman explains *Zooming through Zoos for Zip*:[14] "We are looking for classrooms who will be visiting a local zoo during the school year. The class will be required to videotape a portion of their zoo and submit their tape to the project organizers. In return you will receive a composite tape of all the zoos submitted to us for use in your zoo unit the following school year."[15]

E-mail would be used to correspond with the participating schools. Dintelman stated that her goal was to receive at least eight videotapes. The best portions of the tape would be assembled into one tape, which would be mailed to each of the participating schools. The project was scheduled to begin January 1999 and end May 1999.

Using e-mail, *Write On!* is a creative collaborative writing project involving ten second-grade classes from around the world.[16] Ann Farmer, the teacher of the sponsoring class explains the process.

> The sponsoring class will write one paragraph beginning a story. That paragraph is then e-mailed to the next participating class. That class has one week to write a second paragraph, and e-mail both paragraphs to the third class. A copy is also sent to Ms. Farmer's class. This process continues with each class adding their paragraph and e-mailing the entire story on to the next class. The final class to receive their copy is responsible for writing a conclusion. The final story will then be e-mailed back to Ms. Farmer's class.
>
> After receiving the final paragraph the story will be published on the web page. Participating classes will then be able to read the entire story, print it out, and illustrate their section. Each class will choose one illustration, and e-mail it in gif format to Ms. Farmer's class. The illustration will then be included with the story published on the Web page![17]

Reflecting on the above projects, first, the success of the projects depended on the cooperation of students and teachers from around the world. They all shared in the ownership of the final product.

Second, to participate effectively, students had to compose their messages based on work done locally at their schools and then e-mail them. In doing that, they learned and practiced creative and accurate reporting. They also experienced acceptable correspondence etiquette.

Third, all of the collaborative projects described contributed to the development of students' appreciation of other cultures. They had unlimited possibilities for learning about the history, geography, political structure, climate, native language, native heritage, and so on of participating countries.

Fourth, some projects, such as *Noon Shadow Observation Project*, were interdisciplinary. Information from various disciplines has to be learned to successfully complete the project.

Fifth, participation in collaborative projects enhanced participants' self-esteem as they received recognition from a national and/or international audience.

Sixth, worldwide collaborative projects contribute to the development of participants' understanding and appreciation of world citizenship. Such understanding helps nurture positive attitudes and skills for peaceful and collaborative living in culturally diverse communities, nations, and the world.

Seventh, in all of the collaborative projects, e-mail was not an added feature in the plan. E-mail is woven and integrated into the project plan. When e-mail is an add-on, "there is usually neither the time nor the academic credit for sustaining a commitment over time to the project."[18]

Experts' Visits through E-Mail

Experts, community leaders, corporation and businesses interested in K–12 education, national and international nonprofit organizations, and educational associations and institutions can provide rich resources to students and teachers through e-mail communication. The Emissary Program,[19] discussed in Chapter 10, is a well-organized effort to "match" experts with particular groups of students. Individual schools can identify experts within the community or on a national level to provide consultation, response to students' curriculum inquiries, and up-to-date information on various topics.

Relationships between experts and students through e-mail could develop into electronic mentoring. Through this relationship, the classroom expands to involve human resources beyond the geographical boundaries of the school. In addressing the values of "telementoring," The Emissary Program stated:

> We have learned that students and teachers exploring real-world, many-faceted, curriculum-based topics need to actively build deep and sophisticated understanding. One of the most effective ways to do this is by engaging in ongoing dialogue with knowledgeable others, as the students form, refine, and expand their comprehension. Classroom teachers typically serve as the subject matter experts with whom students interact in such complex areas of inquiry. Yet when the issues being explored are multidisciplinary, technically and conceptually sophisticated, or dependent upon current and highly specialized research and theory, additional expertise must be made directly available to students and teachers longitudinally, and on an as-needed basis. This is what telementoring offers to learners and educators today, and what the Electronic Emissary Project brings to students and teachers worldwide.[20]

Cross-Cultural Communication

Almost at no cost, young people can use e-mail to communicate with their peers anywhere in the world. Since e-mail is multimedia, keypals can send messages in text as well as in nontext formats such as audio and video clips. They can also include in their messages pointers to their favorite sites on the web, or to sites that carry information related to their e-mail messages. There are many sites on the web that provide information on who, where, and how to connect with keypals.

Intercultural E-Mail Classroom Connections (IECC), a free public service offered by <u>teaching.com</u>[21] links students, teachers and classes interested in cross-culture. IECC was originally created in 1992 by three professors from St. Olaf College in Minnesota. It was one of the first services on the Web to facilitate international pen-pal exchanges between teachers and classrooms around the globe.[22]

At present, list services available for free subscription are:

IECC-K12. For teachers in primary and secondary classrooms who are seeking partner schools.
IECC-HE. For teachers in higher education who are seeking partner schools.
IECC-Discussion Forums. General discussion about issues related to the use of e-mail in intercultural classroom activities.
IECC-Surveys. For students and teachers looking to gather information and opinions from a global audience.
IECC-Intergen. A new service for teachers and 50+ aged volunteers seeking intergenerational exchanges.[23]

Special Internet Mailing Lists

An e-mail message can be simultaneously sent to multiple addresses by using "listserv." Listserv is an automated form of e-mail, which includes the e-mail address of each of the members composing the list. Mailing list server automatically routes the message posted by the mailing list coordinator or by any member of the group to all the members of the group.

To subscribe to a mailing list, one has to send an e-mail to the administrative address of the list. The body of the message should read "Subscribe Listname Lastname Firstname." To remove one's name from a list another e-mail is sent. In this case the body of the message reads "Unsubscribe Listname Lastname Firstname."

There is a growing number of listservs in a wide range of topics and fields. Mary Hricko noted, "With the growing number of topic-oriented listservs, discussions on classroom topics are easy to find and offer a great way to enrich the educational experience."[24] Listservs are an excellent communication form through which teachers can share ideas, discuss instructional issues, debate different points of view, or just simply request information on topics of study.

Listservs can also be used to locate references. Mary Hricko noted that "LIBREF-L, a Listserv organized by reference librarians, often responds to queries and assists members with locating hard-to-find information. ". . . LIBREF-L also lists useful web sites for research purposes and can help instructors set up bookmarks for a specific topic".[25] Such a service is especially beneficial when the school library does not have access to a specific reference material. "Students can post their query to the list and in a matter of minutes retrieve not only the answer, but the place where the answer was found."[26]

Use of listservs as resource tools has also been observed by Ronald E. Clock and Wilbin M. Gelter (1998), who "encouraged their students to subscribe to various listservs based on specific course content."[27] They remarked that "Normally, subscription to these listservs is nearly instantaneous, and often students are chatting and retrieving library information before the first class begins."[28] The authors concluded, "Listservs have indeed proven to be an extremely valuable academic tool."[29]

Based on the educational values of e-mail in education, Robert H. Anderson, et al. (1995) advocated that the "nation should support universal access to e-mail through appropriate public and private policies."[30] This recommendation is based on their finding that the "use of electronic mail is valuable for individuals, for communities, for the practice and spread of democracy, and for the general development of a viable National Information Infrastructure (NII).[31] The authors warned against an increasing gap between those who have access to e-mail and those who haven't. Some of the recommendations to remedy this situation is the provision of access in libraries, community centers, and other public venues.[32] Based on their analysis of e-mail on a global level, the authors concluded:

> Democracy in the nations of the world is positively correlated with interconnectivity. For nations emerging into democracy, or attempting to, connectivity is likely to have a positive influence on democratization. We conclude that, "The United States should support increase interconnectivity abroad, since this may aid the spread of democracy."[33]

USENET

USENET is a network that provides access to electronic bulletin boards where individuals post, read, and reply to messages focusing on specific topics or issues. These electronic bulletin boards are commonly referred to as newsgroups. Newsgroups are open forums. When a person chooses to post a message to a particular newsgroup, anyone surfing the Internet can read the message and can also respond to it.

Google Groups, Google Inc. which acquired the well-known Deja News in February 2001, gave the following account on the history of Usenet:

> Before the Web and web browsers, and before e-mail became ubiquitous, online communication meant posting text messages on electronic bulletin boards where others could read and reply to them. Usenet began as a collection of these bulletin boards (now called discussion forums or newsgroups) started in 1979 by Steve Bellovin, Jim Ellis, Tom Truscott, and Steve Daniel at Duke University. Over the years, the number of such newsgroups has grown to the thousands, hosted all over the world and covering every conceivable topic about which humans converse.
>
> While there was incredibly valuable information available in the discussions taking place on newsgroups, finding that information could be an exercise in frustration and futility. Someone would start a topic with a posting on a bul-

letin board. Someone else would reply. This initial post and response now constituted a "thread" on the topic. The thread might grow to include dozens or even hundreds of individuals responding to the first post or any that came after it. They might start threads of their own as offshoots of the original discussion. Think of that initial post as a single cell dividing again and again, mutating and expanding geometrically with no predefined direction. The result is likely something you'd find in a low budget horror movie. Finding a specific bit of information in Usenet was an equally horrific task. To make it more complex, almost all newservers expire messages after a few days or, at most, a few weeks. Expired messages are deleted from the live discussion forums and aren't viewable or searchable by users.

In 1995, Deja News was created to provide a user-friendly interface to Usenet. Deja began archiving and indexing messages so they could be searched and sorted, turning an ephemeral and unmanageable resource into a reference tool that was fairly easy to use.

In February 2001, Google Inc., a company dedicated to providing access to all information online, acquired the Usenet discussion service from Deja.com, including its entire Usenet archive of more than 500 million messages—over a terabyte of human conversation. Google has expanded accessibility to the Usenet database through deployment of improved search and browsing tools and integration of the full archive with more recent postings. The combined database of more than 650 million messages already constitutes the largest collection of Usenet data on the Web and is growing at a rapid pace.[34]

Usenet newsgroups are categorized by topics, and subtopics. Deja News explained:

> Usenet Newsgroups are categorized into several large topics, each of which is broken down into more and more specific topical sub-topics, sub-sub-topics, etc. The different parts of a newsgroup name are always separated by "." (period). Within each newsgroup are postings (also called "articles") which are the real content of Usenet—they look like e-mail between one user and another, but instead of just being sent between people, they're available for anyone in the world with Usenet access to read![35]

There are over 15,000 different newsgroups. Originally USENET was "developed for UNIX systems in 1979. It has become a worldwide network of thousands of USENET sites, known as *news hosts* or *news servers*, running many operating systems (such as UNIX, MS-DOS, Windows NT) on various types of computers."[36]

USENET is a popular method of distributing information to a large number of hosts on the Internet. "The advantage of USENET is that information can be transmitted to thousands of users across the world quickly. USENET, however, usually does not stay on a particular system for very long unless it is archived separately from the USENET system."[37]

Messages posted to a particular newsgroup are called *threads*.[38] It is possible to organize these threads chronologically so that one can know the place of each in an ongoing discussion. Web browsers enable the user to sort the threads by date, subject, or the sender.[39]

Google Groups explains how to navigate Usenet in the following:

> Usenet is like a river with thousands of tributaries. The main forks in the river lead to the top-level discussion categories (such as "alt"). Follow one of the river's forks and you'll come to smaller branches (such as alt.animals), which lead to tributaries containing messages divided into even more specific topics (such as alt.animals.dogs). Ultimately, your journey will take you to the smallest part of the data stream; the part containing messages from people who are interested in one particular topic (such as alt.animals.dogs.beagles).
>
> The different parts of a newsgroup's name are always separated by a period, a traditional categorization symbol in the computer world. Each newsgroup contains threads made up of messages (also referred to as 'articles' or 'postings') that look like e-mail between one user and another, but can be read by anyone accessing that particular newsgroup.[40]

Most newsgroups are unmoderated. This means that any message that might be considered inappropriate could be posted on the Net. This fact emphasizes the need to develop young people's discrimination skills and the need to promote acceptable Internet protocol and etiquette. With thousands of newsgroups to choose from, Phil James (1996) suggested browsing through several newsgroups and reading the messages but not responding. This practice is known as *lurking*.[41] The Google Groups page at http://groups.google.com/ seems to be user-friendly and efficient in searching for Usenet information.

WEB DISCUSSION FORUMS

Web discussion forums differ from newsgroups in that they are closed forums. Using special discussion forum software or web course design software such as WebCT,[42] the web discussion forum can be established as a platform for classroom discussion. Any student in the class with access to the web can participate in the discussion forum. Students and teachers can be separated in time and place; however, through discussion forum they can interact and share ideas and information.

Discussion forums can be organized around topics of study either by the teacher or by the students. "This organization more closely imitates how a classroom discussion takes place," explained Diane J. Goldsmith (1998). "Students can click on a specific topic, read the discussion taking place on that topic and contribute to it. New topics can be added when necessary, and old ones removed when they are finished."[43]

New technologies usually resolve specific problems, and present new challenges. Some of the issues posed by discussion forums are well-articulated by Goldsmith:

> As more of us become comfortable using these asynchronous forms of computer mediated communication, we have begun to discuss some of the issues posed by this new methodology. Some of these are similar to the issues face-to-face teachers consider, but have a different slant due to the different modality. How do we pose questions that provoke good responses? How often should we enter the conversation and in what ways? How do we handle those students who seem uncomfortable with this format? Will students' excitement about these technologies wear off as they become widely used? How else can we use these forms of communication? And finally, how do we evaluate whether they do in fact enhance our students' learning?[44]

FILE TRANSFER PROTOCOL (FTP)

"When the Internet started, some applications were written that were explicitly designed to transmit information between hosts. The first, and still one of the most important applications, was the FTP program."[45] FTP provides the means of moving files around the Internet from one computer to another. Files can be transferred regardless of their platform or operating system, if the two computers can talk the FTP protocol. Compressed and uncompressed files, whether they are text, audio, graphic, video, and/or operating systems can be transferred on the Internet. Once the file is transferred to the user's computer, the user can manipulate the file according to his or her needs, using the appropriate software loaded on his or her computer. For instance, a resident word processing program on the user's computer can open a transferred text file. From that point on, the user can reformat the document, insert other pertinent information, and resave it as a document of the word processing program used to read it. In all of these activities, credit should be given to the source of information and procedures and guidelines for copyright have to be strictly observed.

In addition to text file, the Internet has rich resources of images, paintings from museums, clipart, video segments, animation sequences, and audio bites. These resources, after securing the right to use—and many of them are offered free to the public—may be used to enhance documents and/or presentations. Again, copyright laws and guidelines have to be strictly observed.

The Internet "Anonymous FTP" is a service that allows users to visit public sites on the Internet and download files without any charge. Information in different formats is available for the user's benefit. The more you search, the more will you find exciting material at no cost.

One of the interesting uses of FTP is downloading files to update software, fix a software problem, and allow interested parties to participate in assessing new features of software. With more computers having access to the Internet, software producers are adding online registration features, which the user can use to register the product with the software producer. The advantage of online registration is that the producer can inform the user on any new developments, updates, creative uses of some features of the product, and/or the availability of some files, which can be transferred using FTP.

Another interesting use of FTP is downloading a beta-version of new software. This makes it possible for the producer to test the product with prospective users, and to make the users share in the development of the software. Using e-mail, users can write their comments and their reaction to the test product.

Tools to Enhance Searching for Files Containing Specific Information

As the size and scope of information on the Internet increases, two problems emerge with the use of FTP. First, to know what is stored in an FTP site, one has to connect to the site and browse through the directories of files on that site. The second, to know whether a file has the sought after information, the user has to open that file. Since file names cannot give a descriptive summary of the content of the file, the user might take the time to open a file to find that it does not contain pertinent information to the topic he or she is searching. To alleviate these problems, two tools were introduced: Archie and Gopher.

The Development of Archie

Archie "was originally formed to be a quick and easy way to scan the offering of the many anonymous FTP sites that are maintained around the world."[46] "The Archie service began as a project for students and volunteer staff at the McGill University School of Computer Science. It is now offered as a network resource by a number of sites."[47] The same reference lists 36 ARCHIE public servers in 20 countries around the world. Pike (1995) explains Archie:

> Archie is a system that maintains a database of the contents of FTP sites across the Internet. This database is updated periodically by a program that connects to participating FTP sites and lists the directories and files on these sites. The Archie system also supports several different programs that allow users to search the database for files that match a specified search pattern. The information that is returned to the user is the FTP site(s) where the matching files can be found and the directory where the files are located, along with information about the size and date of the file.[48]

Kehoe (1996) reported that "Currently, Archie tracks the contents of over 1200 anonymous FTP archive sites containing over five million files stored across the Internet. Collectively, these files represent well over 50 gigabytes of information, with new entries being added daily."[49] "The Archie databases are accessible through an interactive Telnet session, e-mail queries, WWW forms."[50] Moreover, "The design of the Archie system was orchestrated so it could be easily extended to include other databases—not just lists of FTP sites. Hence, in addition to the anonymous FTP database, the Archie system also has a Gopher database, which is populated by index- ing registered sites. Not every Archie server offers the Gopher database."[51]

The Development of Gopher

The Gopher program addresses the second major problem with FTP: describing the contents of files on FTP sites. "Gopher allows users to graphi- cally look through an FTP site with descriptions of the contents of the files and directories."[52] The University of Minnesota developed Gopher. It is named after the school's mascot. Gopher is three entities: a network protocol, a serv- er type, and one of many client applications used to access information.[53]

Gopher differs from FTP and e-mail in that it does not require an exact address. In FTP, you have to know the name of the FTP server that stores the file in which you are interested. In e-mail, one has to know the exact address of the receiver. Gopher is different in that it can allow the user to browse for the information he or she is seeking without knowing on which server the intended information resides. However, the user must know the address of a Gopher server before starting. Once connected to a Gopher server, the user gains links to other Gopher servers.

Another value of Gopher is that it presents the result of the search in a table of contents format with description of the content of the file. This makes it easy for the user to browse and select the files of interest. Also, Gopher makes it possible to locate information without worrying about where it might reside.

TELNET

Telnet is the Internet's remote logging-in application. It makes it possible to access computers on the Internet using a laptop or a desktop PC from a remote location. Through this Internet resource, a desktop PC keyboard can manipulate files and information stored on a remote computer. For instance, through Telnet you can open the card catalog of an academic library or access a variety of databases on remote computers providing that you have the privilege of accessing these databases.

THE WEB BROWSER

The ease of using the web browsers has been a major reason for the growing interest of the public in the Internet. Web browsers are used to navigate the web servers and to connect the user with other available services on the Internet such as FTP, Gopher, and Telnet. Eileen Giuffré Cotton (1997) observes: "Gopher, FTP, and Telnet will soon be things of the past. It's nearly that way now."[54] She further explains why a web browser is better than other programs put together:

> If you want to access a file in GopherSpace, you do not need to change navigation programs—stay in your browser. At the URL prompt type gopher:// in lower case letters, followed by the address you want in GopherSpace. When you hit Return, a familiar looking set of gopher files will appear, and you can surf away in GopherSpace using your browser.
>
> The same is true for ftp. At the URL prompt, type ftp:// and the address you want from ftp to fetch. The same prompts for ftp will appear, and you take it from there. This is so much easier than having to work with three or four different navigation programs. The beauty of a Web browser is the ease with which you can go anywhere on it.[55]

The most common web browsers are Netscape and Internet Explorer. A great deal of features is common among browsers. Accordingly, skills learned in using one browser can be transferred to the other.

A wide selection of books and reference materials explaining both Netscape and Internet Explore are available, for example, *Microsoft Internet Explorer 6,*[56] *Internet Explorer 6 for Dummies,*[57] and *Microsoft Internet Explorer 6: Introductory Concepts and Techniques.*[58]

In addition to printed materials, the Help option on any browser can be used to search for information on how to use the browser. Clicking on the "Help" option for Internet Explorer, for instance, a drop menu appears. Among the items in this menu are Content & Index, Tip of the Day, For Netscape Users, Online Support, and Send Feedback.

Contents of "Content & Index" include:

- Getting Started with Internet Explorer
- Finding the Web Pages You Want
- Browsing the Web Offline
- Printing and Saving Information
- Sending Information over the Internet Safely
- Understanding Security and Privacy on the Internet
- Controlling Access to Inappropriate Internet content
- Customizing Your Browser
- Accessibility

From the Help Menu, one may click on "Web Help" to go to Microsoft Support Online site.[59] This site is very rich with pointers to valuable information and resources. It includes:

- Microsoft Database of Support Articles
- Downloading Software (software updates, service packs, patches, device drivers, and downloadable Microsoft products)
- Contacting Microsoft to get assistance online or by phone
- Product Support Centers—Support information and FAQs related to various Microsoft products
- Customer Service
- Posting a question to a Microsoft Public Newsgroup

Searching for Information

There are different options for searching for information on the web. All of them point to URLs that might contain the information.

Printed References

It is becoming very common that printed references contain URL listings of sites related to the information presented in print. Typing the URL in the "Address," "Location," or "GoTo" box in the browser's window and clicking on "Return" takes the user to that site.

Electronic Internet Guides

Microsoft Internet Directory[60] consists of a printed directory and a CD-ROM. The user can search the electronic directory by typing a keyword in a search box. As the keyword is being typed, the keyword list displayed in the left windowpane scrolls up or down to match the typed keyword or ones that are close to it. Clicking on a keyword in the list, the corresponding information—a description of the site and a link to that site—is displayed in the right pane.

Captured Web Sites on a CD-ROM

There are CD-ROMs that contain a variety of web sites selected for their classroom suitability and relevance to subject areas of study. These sites are captured and saved on the CD-ROM: thus, students don't have to be on the Internet to study these sites. *Classroom Connect iCD*[61] (1998) was designed so that the teacher can easily bring the rich content of the World Wide Web to the classroom, whether the class has a live Internet connection or not. If the class is connected, the iCD can be used as "a launch pad" to the Internet.[62] *Classroom Connect* explains the design of the iCD in the following:

> On your CD-ROM, you will find a variety of Web sites chosen for classroom suitability and relevance to the major subject areas of language arts, social studies, math, and science. These sites have been captured on CD-ROM, so you get all the sights, sounds, and information without the necessity of going online. Enter the "Faculty Room" on your CD-ROM for the Lesson Plans and Activity Sheets that have been written especially for the sites on this CD-ROM. All these materials offer clickable links to both the CD and the Internet. In the same "Faculty Room" you will also find a password-protected Answer Bank.[63]

Electronic Resources with Embedded Links to the Web

Encyclopedias, atlases, and other electronic publications published on a CD-ROM have embedded links to sites on the web. These sites are selected to update the information on the CD-ROM and/or to provide access to related material. For instance, *Microsoft Encarta* on CD has links to the *Encarta Online*. The following briefly describes benefits of *Encarta Online*:

> Most everyone will find something of interest at the Encarta Encyclopedia Web site. The Schoolhouse section here enables students and teachers to explore specific topics by providing detailed information and links to related sites. Students can also submit questions in the Ask an Expert area of this section, or browse questions and answers in the Expert Archive. An associated Learning Activity area includes complete activity plans for teachers. In the Teacher's Lounge, educators can communicate with colleagues or explore other educational sites.[64]

Site Reviews and Links on CD-ROM

Microsoft *Internet Solutions for K–12 Education*[65] and Classroom Connect, *School Web Page Survival Kit*[66] are two examples of CD-ROM programs intended to assist the user with locating educationally sound sites. The reviewed sites have links to their locations on the web as well as related sites.

CD-ROM Companions to Printed References

Many published books come packaged with a companion CD-ROM, for example, Eileen Giuffre Cotton's (1997) *The Online Classroom, Teaching and Learning with the Internet*.[67] The companion CD-ROM contains a variety of software and links to many of the online sites discussed in the book. As an example, Professor Cotton compiled a list of 29 sites addressing the topic "Virtually Together in D.C." It contains the following valuable sites:

- National Capital Parks
  URL: http://www.nps.gov/nacc/
- The Washington, D.C. Fun and Recreation Home Page
  URL: http://www.his.com/~matson/
- The White House
  URL: http://www.whitehouse.gov
- Old Executive Office Building
  URL: http://www.whitehouse.gov/WH/Tours/OEOB/
- The White House Collection of American Crafts
  URL: http://www.nmaa.si.edu/whc/whcpretourintro.html
- The Department of Defense
  URL: http://www.dtic.dla.mil/defenselink/
- The House of Representatives
  URL: http://www.house.gov/
- The Senate
  URL: http://www.senate.gov/
- CapWeb
  URL: http://policy.net/capweb/congress.html
- Other Sources of Government Information
  URL: http://www.senate.gov/other/gov_other.html
- Other Departments of Government
  URL: http://www.law.vill.edu/Fed-Agency/fedweb.exec.html#feddept
- Library of Congress Virtual Tour
  URL: http://www.loc.gov/
- The Smithsonian Institution
  URL: http://www.si.edu/newstart.htm

Subscribing to a Web Service

Major newspapers, magazines, TV channels, TV networks, radio stations, Internet providers, and so forth have sites that can be visited and searched free of charge. In some of those sites, the subscriber has the option to select the type of news in which he or she is interested. This option provides the subscriber with a personalized page that contains selected items. This personalized configuration minimizes the time for searching for certain information.

In addition to free subscription to information sites, there are sites that require paid subscription. As an example, *Infogate for Education* provides interactive digital libraries for students. *Infogate* explains its service:

Technology now enables national education authorities, schools and universities to provide students and educators the opportunity to access a new world of information.

This information is not just text and simple graphics, but consists of rich multimedia content such as live lessons, movies, edutainment, TV broadcasts, interactive learning games and other content.

The planning, development and control over the distribution of the content is managed through the national or local department of education. The Infogate solution enables the education system to meet its national goals of

- Providing equal opportunity to education to all students throughout the country
- Reduce the digital gap among the student population in the country
- Provide a rich learning experience for all grades from elementary level to high school and university level.[68]

Searching Homepages of Professional Organizations and Learning Institutions, and Government Agencies

Many professional organizations' home pages serve as a launch pad to navigate the web for information of significant interest to the members of that organization, as well as to the organization's mission. Libraries of major universities, such as The UC Berkeley Libraries[69] and Columbia University Library Web,[70] have well-designed sites rich with resources for web researchers. Government agencies have extensive web sites that contain a great deal of information. For instance, *The U.S. Department of Education Reports and Studies*[71] has very valuable reports that can be downloaded, saved on a diskette, and/or produced in a hard copy format.

It is beyond the scope of this publication to list all of the rich resources that the web researcher can visit and study. However, there is a variety of references that point to valuable educational and learning sites. For example, *The Rough Guide to the Internet, 2003,* by Angus J. Kennedy (2002) and *Online! A Reference Guide to Using the Internet,* by Andrew Harnack and Eugene Kleppinger (2000) are valuable sources of information on a variety of Internet topics and selected sites.

Subscription to Online Periodicals and Journals

Subscription to the *Syllabus* magazine,[72] from Syllabus Press Inc., is free. The magazine is also available online.[73] The online site presents news, reports, and features of the current issue. The visitor can search the magazine archives from the web site.

All of the aforementioned options can be employed by the Internet researcher to locate information by either using the embedded links or by typing the URL. Sometimes, however, it becomes imperative to conduct an original web search.

Original Search

Basically, there are two methods for searching the Web. The first is known as concept search, category search, or directory search. This method is based on reviewers classifying the material on the web under directories similar to a library classification. The second method is known as keyword search or index search.

In the first method, directory search, sites are reviewed by professional people and classified under directories. The directories are organized hierarchies of subject matter categories. Under each category there are subcategories. Numbers between parentheses are displayed after each subcategory. These numbers indicate how many links to web pages are available under the respective category.

Going from the general to the specific, knowing the category of the topic one is interested in searching, can be very effective. If one cannot determine the category under which an item is categorized, the search engine provides the option of searching the directories with a keyword that can be typed in the search box.

Directory servers on the Internet include only the materials that have been reviewed and categorized by the professional reviewers. Accordingly, directory search delivers a fewer number of hits than the keyword search, unless the option of searching the entire web through the directory search is chosen. Researchers advocate using directories for categorical searches and the search engines for keyword searches.[74]

The keyword or index search method is based on computer-generated indices of the content of the web sites. Robots periodically scan the web sites and form massive indices of web pages. Using a search engine, the user enters a keyword or a phrase in its search box. Then, the search is done by searching the indices accumulated by these robots and returns a list of hits, name of the site and a link to it, that the search engine thinks match the request of the searcher. A rating posted by the hit is based on how many words in the search match the words in the headers and in the titles of the web sites it returns.

Google, AllTheWeb, Hotpot, AltaVista, MSN Search, and WebCrawler are among the widely used search engines. All of them provide tips in their help options on how to do the search.

With the rapid expansion of the web bases of information, there is concern about how up-to-date the indices of the search engines are. Karla Haworth et al. (1998) report that six major search engines, then, had indexed a relatively small percentage of the estimated 320 million worldwide web pages on the Internet.[75] The following table is based on the findings of their study.

Search Service	Percentage of Material Indexed
HotBot	34
AltaVista	28
Northern Lights	20
Excite	14
InfoSeek	10
Lycos	3

The researchers also "computed the percentage of documents that were reported by each service but were no longer valid." These results showed how recently the search services have updated their indices. Invalid links ranged from 1.5% (Lycos) to (5.3%) (HotBot). The researchers concluded, "The nature of the Web brings up important questions as to whether the centralized architecture of the search engines can keep up with the expanding number of documents, and if they can regularly update their databases to detect modified, deleted and relocated information."[76]

More recent studies (2003) put the size of the web at 17 billion web pages vs. 320 million pages in 1998. Only around 18% of those web pages are indexed.[77,78] Since sites that are not indexed are invisible to the researcher, the concern expressed by Haworth et al. regarding the up-to-date and accuracy of web research is still valid.

For the aforementioned reasons, first, it is always advisable to employ more than one search engine. MetaCrawler.com conducts the search simultaneously on several search engines indices. Naturally, it takes a little bit longer, but it has the probability of yielding more information.

Second, the web is a tremendous information library, but it is not the only resource available to the researcher. Books, periodical, magazines, human resources, and original field work could provide information unavailable through the web.

Searching Instead of Surfing

The American Heritage Dictionary defines surfing as "The sport of riding on the crest or along the tunnel of a wave, especially while standing or lying on a surfboard." *The Concise Columbia Encyclopedia* defines surfing as the "sport of gliding toward the shore on a breaking wave, done on a board from 4 to 12 ft. (122 to 366 cm) long. . . . The surfer paddles toward the beach until an incoming wave catches the board, then stands up and glides along or just under the crest of the wave." "Surfing requires balance, timing and agility. The surfer challenges to read the oncoming wave so as to catch it as it peaks before it passes beneath him."[79]

Reflecting on these definitions, one could see that the starting point is the shore, and the end point is the shore. There is fun for skilled surfers who enjoy performing this sport. The fun is generated from the challenge of the wave; the exuberant feeling as the surfer is carried on the peak of an incoming wave rushing at a tremendous speed to the shore.

Surfing the Internet is similar to the surfing sport. There is excitement generated from exploring uncharted territory and not knowing what one might find interesting. A serendipitous experience might occur, as one discovers by accident, something of particular value.

Without a search plan and a well-defined search objective, one can easily wonder aimlessly through the Internet without progressing through the vast sea of knowledge, similar to the surfer who after having fun from riding the waves, returns to the same shore where he started.

Prior to the Internet, television viewers have been using television remote controls to surf the channels looking for something that might be interesting, or for the most unobjectionable program to watch. Studies in media awareness have warned us against surfing television channels. Instead, they encourage viewers to study television guides and reviews to select programs that enrich, entertain, and inform them.

Media scholars know that it takes time to learn how to use a new medium. Usually people working with a new medium become fascinated with the new invention and what it can offer that other media cannot. From that view, emphasis is put on capitalizing on the new dimensions the new invention brings forth. To illustrate, when motion pictures were discovered, people were fascinated with the ability of the new medium to preserve and present moving images. Early 1895 movies focused on filming moving objects and events such as *The Arrival of a Train at a Station.* Moviemakers needed a few years to develop the art of telling a story through the motion picture medium. When this happened, with the first action documentary film, *The Life of the American Fireman* (1902), movies began a spiral growth. From that date on, the art of communication through silent movies began flourishing, and a large number of beautifully produced classical movies were produced.

Late 1920s brought in a newcomer. Sound was introduced to moviemaking. As the earlier moviemaker and the public were fascinated with the element of motion, so the moviemakers and the public of late 1920s and early 1930s were fascinated with the new invention, "sound." Movies during that period were advertised as 100% talkies, meaning that every scene had sound. For years, the art of communication through motion pictures developed during the silent era suffered. For almost a decade, moviemakers developed the art of communication through sound movies. They discovered, for instance, that "silence," the absence of sound, could be very effective in communicating a particular scene's message.

The Internet is a new technology that is mushrooming at a tremendous rate. Again, like any new medium, we are fascinated by its potential offerings. How we can harness the Internet for enriching the lives of our students is a very important question.

There are four major parts for answering this question. First, as the Internet grows in size and in complexity, speed and ease of accessing the desired information have to improve. There is nothing more frustrating than waiting for a long time to link with a site or to discover that the information you are seeking is not there or to be overwhelmed with hundreds of sites that might carry the information you are seeking. Search technology has to improve to assist the user in defining and pinpointing his or her strategies to reach the desired information.

Second, provide access to everyone who is interested. Otherwise, the gaps between the haves and have-nots would increase, and equality among our student population will suffer.

Third, develop the ability of the citizens to intelligently use the Internet. This requires schools to integrate the use of the Internet in their curriculum. Prerequisite to this activity is developing teachers' understanding of the place of the Internet in education and developing their skills in using it.

Fourth, in using the Internet, children and youth are liable to encounter inappropriate material, as well as communication with predators that could threaten their well-being and safety. Accordingly, addressing children and youth's safety on the Internet is an essential component of our discussion in harnessing the Internet for quality education of our children and youth. In the following few pages we address this issue.

CHILDREN AND YOUTH'S SAFETY
ON THE INTERNET

Crimes Against Children Research Center at the University of New Hampshire conducted a survey of a national sample of 1,501 youth, ages 10 through 17, who used the Internet regularly (at least once a month) to assess possible online victimization.[80] The survey addressed three main issues: sexual solicitations and approaches, unwanted exposure to sexual material, and harassment. The survey revealed that:

- Almost one in five (19%) of the young Internet users surveyed received an unwanted sexual solicitations in the past year.
- Five percent of the surveyed youth received a distressing sexual solicitation (i.e., the solicitation made them feel very or extremely upset or afraid).
- Three percent of the youth received an aggressive solicitation involving offline contact or attempts or requests for offline contact.
- None of the solicitations led to an actual sexual contact or assault.[81]

The survey also showed that two-thirds of the solicitations took place in chat rooms, and 24% were received through instant messages. Seventy-five percent of the incidents were described by youth as not distressing, and 25% were described as very or extremely upsetting or frightening. The youth didn't tell anyone about 49% of the sexual solicitations, and 24% were disclosed to parents. However, more than one third of aggressive incidents were not disclosed.[82]

The survey also showed that youth are exposed to sexually explicit pictures on the Internet without seeking or expecting them. The great majority of these exposures involved pictures with nudity, 38% showed people having sex, and 8% included violent images. Seventy-one percent of these exposures occurred while youth were surfing or searching the web, and the rest occurred through e-mail or Instant Messages.[83] Forty-four percent of these incidents were not disclosed. The survey also showed that some youth (6%) are victims of online harassment.

Only a few of the above offenses in the three categories were reported to authorities. (Only 18% of aggressive solicitations were reported, mostly to the Internet providers.)[84]

Two important facts stand out. First, youths are exposed to unwanted indecent and sometimes aggressive material on the Internet. Second, in many of these instances, the occurrences are not disclosed to parents or authorities. Consequently, due to their limited experience, youths and especially children could become easy prey for harmful information and harmful web users. Accordingly, it becomes imperative to develop their Internet safety skills.

Developing children and youth's Internet safety skills is a joint responsibility between parents, schools, and the Internet community.

Putting Parents in Control

There is a need to educate parents in the basics of the Internet. Age or lack of interest in computers and the Internet are lame excuses. The Internet is a reality, and more and more homes are gaining access to the Internet. Becoming intelligent and discriminating consumers of the Internet is imperative for parents to assume their parental guidance of their youth in the information age.

Fortunately, first, the basics of the Internet are not that difficult to learn. If their young children are capable of using e-mail and surfing the net for information, so their parents should be capable of the same. Second, there is abundance of self-teaching material that is available free of charge on the Internet, and a wide selection of reference books that are especially written for the Internet novice.

Basics of the Internet for parents include the following components:

1. **Basic information on starting one's Internet experience.** *Parents Guide to the Internet*, published by the U.S. Department of Education, is available online free of charge.[85] In addition, many public and private organizations have special Internet tutorials that parents could access. An example is *Internet Basics* posted by the Public Broadcasting Service (PBS).[86]

2. **Understanding the good and the bad sides of the Internet.** Parents should be aware of the excellent Internet resources, especially those designed with youth and children in mind. They also should be aware of the inappropriate sites and the attempts of predators to sexually harass innocent youth and children.

3. **Parents should be aware of detecting signs of their children being at risk online.** *A Parent's Guide to Internet Safety* posted online by the Federal Bureau of Investigation(FBI) lists some of these signs:

   - Your child spends large amounts of time online, especially at night.
   - You find pornography on your child's computer.
   - Your child receives phone calls from men you don't know or is making calls, sometimes long distance, to numbers you don't recognize.
   - Your child receives mail, gifts, or packages from someone you don't know.
   - Your child turns the computer monitor off or quickly changes the screen on the monitor when you come into the room.
   - Your child becomes withdrawn from the family.
   - Your child is using an online account belonging to someone else.

4. **Parents should be also knowledgeable on what to do if they observe any of those signs.** Many sites propose actions to be taken by parents in the event they suspect that their children are being exploited or harassed by online predators. *A Parent's Guide to Internet Safety*[87] recommends the following:

   - Consider talking openly with your child about your suspicions. Tell them about the dangers of computer-sex offenders.
   - Review what is on your child's computer. If you don't know how, ask a friend, co-worker, relative, or other knowledgeable person. Pornography or any kind of sexual communication can be a warning sign.
   - Use the Caller ID service to determine who is calling your child. Most telephone companies that offer Caller ID also offer a service that allows you to block your number from appearing on someone else's Caller ID. Telephone companies also offer an additional service feature that rejects incoming calls that you block. This rejection feature prevents computer-sex offenders or anyone else from calling your home anonymously.
   - Devices can be purchased that show telephone numbers that have been dialed from your home phone. Additionally, the last number called from your home phone can be retrieved provided that the tele-

phone is equipped with a redial feature. You will also need a telephone pager to complete this retrieval.

- This is done using a numeric-display pager and another phone that is on the same line as the first phone with the redial feature. Using the two phones and the pager, a call is placed from the second phone to the pager. When the paging terminal beeps for you to enter a telephone number, you press the redial button on the first (or suspect) phone. The last number called from that phone will then be displayed on the pager.

- Monitor your child's access to all types of live electronic communications (i.e., chat rooms, instant messages, Internet Relay Chat, etc.), and monitor your child's e-mail. Computer-sex offenders almost always meet potential victims via chat rooms. After meeting a child online, they will continue to communicate electronically often via e-mail.

- Should any of the following situations arise in your household, via the Internet or online service, you should immediately contact your local or state law enforcement agency, the FBI, and the *National Center for Missing and Exploited Children*:[88]

    1. Your child or anyone in the household has received child pornography.
    2. Your child has been sexually solicited by someone who knows that your child is under 18 years of age.
    3. Your child has received sexually explicit images from someone that knows your child is under the age of 18.

    If one of these scenarios occurs, keep the computer turned off to preserve any evidence for future law enforcement use. Unless directed to do so by the law enforcement agency, you should not attempt to copy any of the images and/or text found on the computer.

5. **Parents Should Know What to Do to Minimize The Chances of an Online Exploiter Victimizing Their Children?** In the event that parents suspect that there is a chance of their children being exploited or victimized, the FBI guide offers the following suggestions:

- Communicate, and talk to your child about sexual victimization and potential online danger.
- Spend time with your children online. Have them teach you about their favorite online destinations.
- Keep the computer in a common room in the house, not in your child's bedroom. It is much more difficult for a computer-sex offender to communicate with a child when the computer screen is visible to a parent or another member of the household.
- Utilize parental controls provided by your service provider and/or blocking software. While electronic chat can be a great place for children to make new friends and discuss various topics of interest, it is also prowled by computer-sex offenders. Use of chat rooms, in particular, should be heavily monitored. While parents should use these mechanisms, they should not totally rely on them.
- Always maintain access to your child's on-line account and randomly check his or her e-mail. Be aware that your child could be contacted

through the U.S. Mail. Be up front with your child about your access and reasons why.

- Teach your child the responsible use of the resources online. There is much more to the on-line experience than chat rooms.
- Find out what computer safeguards are used by your child's school, the public library, and at the homes of your child's friends. These are all places, outside your normal supervision, where your child could encounter an on-line predator.
- Understand, even if your child was a willing participant in any form of sexual exploitation, that he or she is not at fault and is the victim. The offender always bears the complete responsibility for his or her actions.

Instruct your children:

- To never arrange a face-to-face meeting with someone they met online.
- To never upload (post) pictures of themselves onto the Internet or online services to people they do not personally know.
- To never give out identifying information such as their name, home address, school name, or telephone number.
- To never download pictures from an unknown source, as there is a good chance there could be sexually explicit images.
- To never respond to messages or bulletin board postings that are suggestive, obscene, belligerent, or harassing.
- That whatever they are told online may or may not be true.

The Guide responds to frequently asked questions such as 1) My child has received an e-mail advertising for a pornographic website, what should I do? (2) Is any service safer than the other? and (3) Should I just forbid my child from going online?[89] To these questions the Guide gives the following responses, respectively:

1. Generally, advertising for an adult, pornographic website that is sent to an e-mail address does not violate federal law or the current laws of most states. In some states it may be a violation of law if the sender knows the recipient is under the age of 18. Such advertising can be reported to your service provider and, if known, the service provider of the originator. It can also be reported to your state and federal legislators, so they can be made aware of the extent of the problem.
2. Sex offenders have contacted children via most of the major online services and the Internet. The most important factors in keeping your child safe online are the utilization of appropriate blocking software and/or parental controls, along with open, honest discussions with your child, monitoring his or her online activity, and following the tips in this pamphlet.
3. There are dangers in every part of our society. By educating your children to these dangers and taking appropriate steps to protect them, they can benefit from the wealth of information now available on-line.[90]

In answering the last questions Yahooligans states: "Parents have always had to balance the tough issues of letting their kids explore the world while maintaining their safety. The best results usually come from educating yourself and your children so that everyone can make smart decisions."[91]

6. **Parents should be able to set up with their children rules for using the Internet safely.** By taking responsibility for their children's online computer use, "parents can greatly minimize any potential risks of being online," wrote Larry Magid, author of *Child Safety on the Information Highway* and creator of the **SafeKids** and **SafeTeens** web sites, which may be accessed from http://www.larrysworld.com/. He advises the parents to make it a family rule to:

- Never give out identifying information—home address, school name, or telephone number—in a public message such as chat or bulletin boards (newsgroup), and be sure you're dealing with someone that both you and your child know and trust before giving out this information via e-mail. Think carefully before revealing any personal information such as age, marital status, or financial information. Do not post photographs of your children on web sites or newsgroups that are available to the public. Consider using a pseudonym, avoid listing your child's name and E-mail address in any public directories and profiles, and find out about your ISP's privacy policies and exercise your options for how your personal information may be used.

- Get to know the Internet and any services your child uses. If you don't know how to log on, get your child to show you. Have your child show you what he or she does online, and become familiar with all the things that you can do online.

- Never allow a child to arrange a face-to-face meeting with another computer user without parental permission. If a meeting is arranged, make the first one in a public place, and be sure to accompany your child.

- Never respond to messages or bulletin board items that are suggestive, obscene, belligerent, threatening, or make you feel uncomfortable. Encourage your children to tell you if they encounter such messages. If you or your child receives a message that is harassing, of a sexual nature, or threatening, forward a copy of the message to your ISP, and ask for their assistance.

- Instruct your child not to click on any links that are contained in e-mail from persons they don't know. Such links could lead to sexually explicit or otherwise inappropriate web sites.

- If someone sends you or your children messages or images that are obscene, lewd, filthy, or indecent with the intent to harass, abuse, annoy, or threaten, or if you become aware of the transmission, use, or viewing of child pornography while online, immediately report this to the National Center for Missing and Exploited Children's CyberTipline at 1-800-843-5678 or www.missingkids.com/cybertip.

- Remember that people online may not be who they seem. Because you can't see or even hear the person it would be easy for someone to misrepresent him- or herself. Thus, someone indicating that "she" is a "12-year-old girl" could in reality be a 40-year-old man.

- Remember that everything you read online may not be true. Any offer that's "too good to be true" probably is. Be very careful about any offers that involve your coming to a meeting, having someone visit your house, or sending money or credit card information.
- Set reasonable rules and guidelines for computer use by your children. Discuss these rules and post them near the computer as a reminder. Remember to monitor your children's compliance with these rules, especially when it comes to the amount of time your children spend on the computer. A child's excessive use of online services or the Internet, especially late at night, may be a clue that there is a potential problem. Remember that personal computers and online services should not be used as electronic babysitters.
- Check out blocking, filtering, and ratings.
- Be sure to make this a family activity. Consider keeping the computer in a family room rather than the child's bedroom. Get to know their "online friends" just as you get to know all of their other friends.[92]

Magid developed a set of rules of Internet safety, *My Rules for Online Safety*, based on the aforementioned family practice:

- I will not give out personal information such as my address, telephone number, parents' work address/telephone number, or the name and location of my school without my parents' permission.
- I will tell my parents right away if I come across any information that makes me feel uncomfortable.
- I will never agree to get together with someone I "meet" online without first checking with my parents. If my parents agree to the meeting, I will be sure that it is in a public place and bring my mother or father along.
- I will never send a person my picture or anything else without first checking with my parents.
- I will not respond to any messages that are mean or in any way make me feel uncomfortable. It is not my fault if I get a message like that. If I do I will tell my parents right away so that they can contact the online service.
- I will talk with my parents so that we can set up rules for going online. We will decide upon the time of day that I can be online, the length of time I can be online, and appropriate areas for me to visit. I will not access other areas or break these rules without their permission.[93]

GetNetWise is a valuable site for parents. *The Online Safety Guide* states: "Keeping children safe on the Internet is everyone's job." The Guide gives the following rules to maximize the safety of children on the Internet.

- Parents need to stay in close touch with their kids as they explore the Internet.
- Teachers need to help students use the Internet appropriately and safely.
- Community groups, including libraries, after-school programs, and others should help educate the public about safe surfing.

- Kids and teens need to learn to take responsibility for their own behavior—with guidance from their families and communities.
- It's not at all uncommon for kids to know more about the Internet and computers than their parents or teachers. If that's the case in your home or classroom, don't despair. You can use this as an opportunity to turn the tables by having your child teach you a thing or two about the Internet. Ask her where she likes to go on the Internet and what she thinks you might enjoy on the Net. Get your child to talk with you about what's good and not so good about his Internet experience. Also, no matter how Web-literate your kid is, you should still provide guidance. You can't automate good parenting.[94]

Again and again, the above guides emphasize the need for parents to assume their responsibilities of providing guidance to their children in using the Internet. If parents feel unprepared to deal with the Internet two options are suggested. First, they could educate themselves in the basics of the Internet. This could be done either by using online resources or adult education programs in their towns. The second option is to allow their children to teach them something about the Internet.[95] The most important aspect of this option is creating opportunities to talk with their children about what they like and dislike about the Internet and about danger that they might have encountered.

7. **Parents should be aware of filters that they could use to block inappropriate Internet material, and/or to monitor their children's sessions on the Internet.** There are different types of filters that allow parents to monitor their children's use of the Internet, block certain sites or even block the Internet entirely on the home computer. For example, *CyberPatrol* can filter web sites, block or filter chat, help manage the child's time on line, and protect personal information. It can also create personalized filtering profiles for many users. The CyberPatrol site explains these features:

- **Filtering harmful websites.** Filter offensive words and phrases from web-based e-mail. Block or allow sites based on specific CyberList categories using combined filtering technologies.
- **Block or filter chat.** Filters both inbound and outbound chat as well as filter, block or allow any chat or instant messaging program.
- **Manage time online and access to local programs.** Set limits on your child's online activities as well as block or limit their access to local programs such as computer games and home finance packages, based on time of day, daily and weekly periods.
- **Protect personal information.** Monitor inbound and outbound chat sessions to filter out inappropriate language and help prevent kids from inadvertently divulging personal information online, such as names, address, phone numbers.
- **Customize filtering for each user.** Create personalized filtering profiles for an unlimited number of users. Customize filtering according to

age, interests, needs and family belief, providing users with their own personal User Profile that's password protected.[96]

NetNanny 5.0 claims that it "can prevent access to inappropriate sites, limit the amount of time your children spend online, prevent them from revealing private information via e-mail or IM, and generally control their Internet experience." In addition to customizing the software setting for up to 12 different users, it allows the parents to view and edit Net Nanny's lists of websites, newsgroups and chat rooms, and to add others that parents might choose for children not to see.[97]

Other filters such as *SentryCam* and *Cyber Sentinel* capture screenshots of what the child is watching. *SentryCam* claims that the program may be run in a stealth mode, that it is capable of capturing screenshots of games, chat rooms, websites, e-mail read and written online, and that it can follow the child into private chat rooms or private message windows.[98]

Cyber Sentinel claims: "In addition to blocking objectionable material Cyber Sentinel has the ability to capture the screen when questionable material is accessed. This data is stored in a secure database for review. When a screen capture is taken, Cyber Sentinel's e-mail notification feature will alert you (parents)."[99]

Other parents might choose a hardware locking device such as *NetProtect*,[100] which disables all Internet access with the turn of a key. The device is a tamper-resistant clip that prevents the unit from being unplugged and does not require software to install or to update.[101]

In addition to using filters, parents might choose to use browsers that are configured for safe use by children such as *The Children's Browser*,[102] and *SurfMonkey*.[103]

The use of filters on home and school computers has opponents who base their argument on two points. (1) filters might block good educational sites, if the computer senses one word in the text that is not permissible, and (2) safe navigation of the Internet should be taught and not forced.

Regarding these claims, first, with continuous upgrading of filtering software, this problem will be eventually minimized. The damage that could happen to children from landing on inappropriate material outweighs the lack of retrieving an article that might be useful. Second, it is true that Internet safety should be taught and not forced. However, achieving this important objective requires well-planned learning activities. Accordingly, parents and teachers should determine whether filters are to be used or not depending on whether their children have already developed discriminating abilities to make the right decisions in choosing their Internet sites and contacts, if any.

Schools and Children's/Youth's Internet Safety

The challenge educators face in developing discriminating consumers of information and entertainment is an old one. In the early 1930s, the power of motion pictures and their effects on youth were recognized. Based on the intensive and comprehensive Payne Fund Studies conducted at Ohio State University, 1930 to 1933, a textbook, *How to Appreciate Motion Pictures*, focusing on teaching motion pictures discrimination, was published in 1935.[104] "The intent was to teach the adolescent how to judge pictures for himself by setting standards, and to teach him how to apply them. It was believed that a discriminating audience would be a constructive power for control of what would be produced."[105]

More recently, Dale (1969), the author of *How to Appreciate Motion Pictures*, explained the difference between a critical-minded person and a sponge-minded person:

> The "sponge-minded" absorb with equal gullibility what they see at the movies, what they read in the newspapers, what they hear over television and radio. They are the passive viewers, readers, and listeners. Fair game for advertisers, they spend huge sums for patent medicines each year. Even in their student days, they accepted without a flicker of distrust what the textbook said or what they heard from the lecture platform. Porous as sponges, their minds absorb for a brief time but do not assimilate.
>
> The "critical-minded" are active, not passive, in their reception of the printed and spoken word or the motion picture, television, and radio. They constantly ask: "Is it true? Where's your evidence?" and "What do you mean by 'true'?" They search out hidden assumptions, unwarranted inferences, false analogies. They are the good-natured skeptics and sometimes, unfortunately, the soured cynics. They give the ill-informed and inaccurate teacher many a bad moment. And they are our greatest hope for progress.[106]

Education has to strive to cultivate the critical-minded citizen. Regardless of the medium of information, emphasis should be put on developing the questioning mind when the students receive information from radio, TV, motion pictures, street posters, magazines and newspapers, sound recordings, and the Internet.

Developing a questioning mind of information media is an outcome of planned activities in which thinking about one's relationship with the medium and what it offers is examined.[107] Considering this, it is recommended that educators develop and offer units of study that instill in students critical awareness of the Internet. Specific objectives of these units could include:

1. **Understanding one's relationship with the Web.** A series of questions should be presented to children and youths in the form of a ques-

tionnaire to assist them in articulating their personal relationship with the Web. Some of these questions could be: How often do you use the Internet? Do you use the web primarily for entertainment, education, or e-mail? When looking for information do you surf the net or do you have a search plan to locate the information? Do you have access to the Internet from your bedroom or from the family room? Are you willing to give up the use of the net to spend some time reading, socializing with peers or family members, or just going for a walk?

The preceding questions are examples of the content that ought to be covered and not as examples of definitive questions for such a questionnaire. Appropriate techniques for designing these questions to ensure true and accurate responses should be used.

2. **Understanding types of services available through the Web.** Children and youth should have adequate understanding and knowledge of the different services available through the Internet. They should know that entertainment, downloading music, instant messaging and e-mail, and shopping are some but not all of the services available. They should gain training in designing simple search strategies to learn how to formulate questions, locate answers, and assess the validity of the answers retrieved.

3. **Developing an appreciation of what is a good site with emphasis on the credibility of the source.** Children and youth must understand that not every published piece of information has to be true. Two important criteria they should learn to consider: who is the author of the information, and when was it last updated. They should also learn how to cross-reference the information they locate with other references such as books, periodical, newspapers, encyclopedias, and so forth to determine its validity. This practice helps develop students' discerning abilities to judge the accuracy of the information retrieved by comparing it with information from reputable sources. Schools publishing their home pages can help by providing pointers to exciting and credible sources of information including libraries holdings.

4. **Participating in collaborative projects with peers under the monitoring of their schools.** Students must realize the value of doing collaborative projects with peers, including international peers. Such an activity, however, should be supervised by a mature mentor.

5. **Participating as authors of school web pages.** In doing this activity they will learn the basics of designing and producing web pages and the accuracy of information posted. From the skills they learn they will become more appreciative of good sites, and they would be more willing to use the school home page to further pursue their education.

THE INTERNET COMMUNITY AND YOUTH'S
SAFETY ON THE INTERNET

As discussed in Chapter 9, the Internet has three necessary components: people, information, and connectivity. The people component has been emphasized by authors of scholarly material on the Internet. For instance, Hahn and Stout (1994) wrote, "The Internet is much more than a computer network or an information service. The Internet is living proof that human beings who are able to communicate freely and conveniently will choose to be social and selfless.[108]

The people component is also explained in a statement made by a Supreme Court judge. Considering the first amendment rights for Internet users he stated, "The Internet may fairly be regarded as a never-ending worldwide conversation."[109] However, there is a negative side to the people component represented by those individuals who use the Internet as a stage to manifest their delinquencies causing problems to children and youth. This fact puts more demand on community-conscious people, organizations, and Internet commercial enterprises to exert extra effort to provide children and youths with safe use of the Internet. One could see some of these efforts reflected in monitored chat rooms and sites designed especially for children and youth. Schools in particular have special responsibilities along this track by producing their own school home pages that children and youth may use as a portal for safe Internet navigation.

THE SCHOOL HOME PAGE

An area of web publishing that is gaining momentum is school home pages. The number of schools posting their home pages is on the increase. According to Web66 International School Web Registry (1998),[110] the total number of K–12 school home pages worldwide increased from 6,200 in January 1997 to 10,500 in January 1998 and to 13,373 in July 1998. At present, almost every K–12 school in the United States has its own home page. Some of them are well developed, and others are more or less a place holder.

The growth of school home pages is also true in two- to four-year colleges and universities. Corporation, businesses, not-for-profit national and international organizations, and governmental departments have long realized the importance of maintaining a presence on the web.

Primarily there are three major functions of the school home page: administrative, instructional, and an outreach to the learning community worldwide. The administrative functions include informing students, parents, teachers, and the community at large on a wide range of information including school bulletins, community, national and international news of particular interest to education, K–12 in general, and to the individual school in particular. At the college level, the home page is used to communicate pertinent information to potential students who visit various college home pages to locate a school that fits their interest.

Instructional applications of the home page target the enrichment of students' learning experiences through expanding their learning resources by providing links to sites of particular significance to the curriculum. The selected sites are preassessed by teachers with respect to their potential contribution to the curriculum.

The school home page is also a global platform through which students' creative multimedia work may be posted. Writing and composing work for publishing on the home page could have significant positive effects on students' learning. First, the student experiences a sense of self-worth as he or she knows that other people are reviewing the material. Second, knowing that the material is being reviewed by other people outside the school community could motivate the student to work hard to ensure quality of submitted material prior to posting it. Third, publishing students' work on the homepage helps extend the geographical boundaries of the school to include local, national, and international learning communities.

To enhance interaction with worldwide students, the school home page should be designed to encourage feedback from its visitors. For instance, the school home page of University Park Elementary School in Fairbanks, Alaska invites the visitor to share student-developed stories about life in Alaska and at their school. It also invites the visitor to share their "microcopia." The students define "microcopia" as "a large collection of information about a small topic, especially a topic that might be hard to find out about in much of the world."[111] They further explained the choice of that name and the purpose of developing "microcopia." The home page states:

> We invented the term "Microcopia" to describe many of our projects. Think of it as a lot of information about a small or obscure topic, but one that we know a lot about because it affects our lives here in Fairbanks. For example, the Chena River is a very small river as world rivers go, but to us it is a unique ecosystem and a very important part of our economy. We think that we can create microcopia that can teach people around the world about life in Alaska, and we like the idea that elementary school students can create and publish information that is not available anywhere else.[112]
>
> A long list of published "microcopia" includes:

- Alaska Gold
- A Visit from the Oregon Museum of Science and Industry (OMSI)
- A Walk Through Early Fairbanks
- The Changing Chena
- Graphing 'Round Our School

- Making Traditional Dogsleds with Elder Howard Luke
- Salmon from A to Z
- Moose Tales: Close Encounters of the Antlered Kind
- Traditional Native Wood Mask Carving
- Transformation Myths and Masks
- The 1996 Yukon Quest Sled Dog Race
- The History and Restoration of The Riverboat Nenana
- The World Wide Web Storybook Library
- Baking Bread and Experimenting with Yeast
- Traditional Athabascan Fiddling
- A Visit to Mystic Seaport
- A Denali Adventure
- HyperCard Stacks
- Writers' Workshop
- Ice Art '95: A Spectacular Ice Carving Exhibition
- Dog Mushing in the '95 Open North American Championships[113]

A Walk Through Early Fairbanks is one of the books written and illustrated by a third grade class. The editor noted that this web site is "constructed to resemble as closely as possible the remarkable hard-cover book published by Mrs. Kaltenbach's class in May, 1997. . . . The photographs were scanned at 72 dots per inch and saved as high-quality JPEGs."[114]

A book cover, a forward, 14 pages of text and photographs, a page for students' paintings, a reference page, and a page introducing the authors constitute an interesting, well-illustrated book. The forward stated the purpose and the procedure of developing the material for the electronic book:

> This project was about community. Third-grade students researched current sites of old buildings to learn the history of their community. Fairbanks, Alaska was established in 1902, not long after E.T. Barnette started a trading post to supply the miners who searched for gold in the hills and streams of the Tanana Valley. Students used photographs as visual starting points and books on local history to begin their research about this town begun on the banks of the Chena River. Later, Rene Blahuta, President of the Fairbanks Historical Society, kindly visited our class. Mrs. Blahuta emphasized that what made Fairbanks a community was that people really cared. Buildings reflect the attitude of hardy people who stayed around to build a life amid their search deep in the bedrock for precious gold.
>
> Students, accompanied by many parents, also went "out into the field" to explore the old downtown section of Fairbanks, a city whose current population exceeds 33,000. On this trip, parents shared memories and stories that made history come alive. For example, Karen Brauser, a nurse at the Fairbanks Memorial Hospital, related how the nuns of St. Joseph's Hospital guarded the door at night from intruders in the early days.
>
> As you read our work, you will learn about the rugged, creative pioneers of our far-north community by the buildings they left behind. We hope you enjoy your "walk through early Fairbanks."[115]

While the students at University Park Elementary School learn about their own community, they are also reaching out to the learning community worldwide, the third function of the school home page. Their "micro-copia" concept and material are interesting and informative and may engage the visitor to explore the school's site and to communicate with the students. Starting with an interesting question, the site is structured to point the visitor to retrieving more information pertaining to that question. For instance, one of the interesting lines on their first page reads, "Some people think that all Alaskan schools have moose walking around on their play-grounds. They're right."[116] Clicking on "They're right" brings you to the Bill the Moose page.

Bill the Moose . . .

These pictures are of Bill, a young male moose who, with his mother and a twin sister, has been hanging around University Park for the past few years. This is probably the last year that Bill will travel with his mother and sister.

We give Bill and his family a wide berth when they are on the school grounds. Moose can be unpredictable and may charge you. Most of the time, though, they munch on willow bushes and will walk away when humans approach.

University Park builds a banked "luge run" every winter on the sledding hill. Last year, Bill was at the top of the hill and accidentally stepped on the ice. His legs went out from under him and he slid all the way down the luge run at a very high speed. Too bad we didn't have a camera then.[117]

The page concludes with giving pointers to sites that have related material on the moose:

Do you want to learn about some U Park third graders' first-hand experiences with moose? Check out "Moose Tales: Close Encounters of the Antlered Kind."

For anything you could ever want to know about moose, check out The Magnificent Moose Project from Anne Wien Elementary.[118]

Before ending this chapter, three words of caution are in order. The Internet is constantly changing its three basic and integrated components: connectivity, information and people. As a result of that constant change, it is common that a site changes its address. Typing the URL of a site could result in an error if the browser fails to locate the site. Some sites extend the courtesy of establishing a link in their old home page to lead the visitor to the new site.

Second, technology of the web is developing rapidly. There always will be better software, faster loading of pages, and other measures that will ensure more effective communication on the web. Users of the Internet should become aware of the availability of refinement software that can improve their browser's performance.

Third, publishing on the web is becoming easier to learn and to handle. Accordingly, more individuals venture to publish their material on the web. Since there are no criteria for selection of what goes on the web, anything can get published. It is extremely important, therefore, to examine information received from the web to determine its validity. In addition, guiding young students to educationally sound sites can make their Internet experience rewarding.

REFERENCES

1. Deutsch, Peter. *The Internet as Service Provider*, http://services.bunyi.com/com.reading/articles/service_provider/, accessed 6/11/97.
2. U.S. Department of Education, National Center for Education Statistics. *Digest of Education Statistics, 2002*, NCES 2003–060, by Thomas D. Snyder. Washington, D.C.: 2003, p. 485.
3. *Ibid.* Table 424, p. 495.
4. Parker, Tim. How Internet E-Mail Works, in Pike, Mary Ann, et al. *Using the Internet*, 2nd ed. Indianapolis, IN: Que, 1995, pp. 283–299.
5. Crispen, Patrick, *Internet Roadmap 1996*, http://netsquirrel.com/roadmap96/, accessed 3/10/04.
6. Crispen, Patrick. *Internet Roadmap 1996 Objectives*, http://netsquirrel.com/roadmap96/map01.html, accessed 3/10/04.
7. Crispen, Patrick, *Internet Roadmap 1996, Map 27*, http://netsquirrel.com/roadmap96/map27.html/, accessed 3/10/04.
8. *Ibid.* p. 3.
9. Cole, Kenneth, *Noon Shadow Observation Project*, Copyright ©2000 by KERA, North Texas Public Broadcasting, All rights reserved. Funding provided by a grant from Lucent Technologies, available online at http://erc.kera.org/pdf/lessonlibrary/NOON_PRINT.PDF, accessed 8/13/03.
10. *Ibid.* pp. 2, 3.
11. McKinney High School North's *Noon Project 2002*, http://www.kencole.org/noon/, accessed 8/13/03.
12. Charnay, Patricia. *Newsletters Across the World*, http://www.qesnrecit.qcc.ca/cc/projects/98-99/newswrld.htm, accessed 8/11/03.
13. *Ibid.*
14. Dintelman, Donna. *Zooming through Zoos for Zip*, http://www.gse.harvard.edu/~library/onedu-1098.htm, accessed 8/12/03.
15. *Ibid.*
16. *Write On!* http://www.stolaf.edu/cgi-binmailarchivesearch.pl?directory=/var/spool/ftp/pub/iecc&listname=archive.projects&location=53273, accessed 9/19/98.
17. *Ibid.*
18. http://www.stolaf.edu/network/iecc/discussion/what-works.html/, p. 2, accessed 9/19/98.
19. Harris, Judi. *About the Electronic Emissary Project*, http://emissary.ots.utexas.edu/emissary/about.html, accessed 8/3/03.

20. *Ibid.* pp. 3–4.
21. *Teaching.com,* http://www.teaching.com/, accessed 8/26/03.
22. *About IECC,* Teaching.com, http://www.teaching.com/iecc/AboutIECC.cfm
23. IECC Homepage, http://www.teaching.com/iecc/, accessed 8/26/03.
24. Hricko, Mary. Listservs as Instructional Tools: The Latest Trend in Teaching Aids, *Stop Surfing, Start Teaching, 1998 National Conference,* February 22–25, 1998, Sponsored by University of South Carolina, Conference Proceedings, pp. 74–77.
25. *Ibid.* p. 75.
26. *Ibid.* p. 75.
27. Clock, Ronald E., and Wilbin M. Gelter, Enhancing Instruction Through the Use of Liserver Subscriptions and Accompanying WWW Libraries, *Stop Surfing, Start Teaching, 1998 National Conference,* February 22–25, 1998, Sponsored by University of South Carolina, Conference Proceedings, pp. 72–74.
28. *Ibid.* p. 72
29. *Ibid.* p. 74
30. Anderson, Robert H. et al. *Universal Access to E-Mail: Feasibility and Societal Implications,* Santa Monica, CA: RAND, 1995, p. xiv.
31. *Ibid*
32. *Ibid.* p. xv
33. *Ibid.* p. xxii
34. *Google Groups—Basics of Usenet,* http://groups.google.com/googlegroups/basics.html, accessed 8/20/03.
35. *Deja News—What is Usenet?* http://dejanews.com/help/dnusenet_help.html/ downloaded summer 1998.
36. James, Phil. *Official NETSCAPE Navigator 2.0 Book, The Definitive Guide to the World's Most Popular Internet Navigator, Windows Edition,* Research Triangle Park, NC: Ventana Communications Group, 1996, p. 202.
37. *Ibid.* p. 533.
38. *Ibid.* p. 202.
39. *Ibid.* p. 213.
40. *Google Groups. op. cit.*
41. James, Phil. *op. cit.* p. 205.
42. WebCT, http://www.webct.com/, accessed 9/2/03.
43. Goldsmith, Diane J. Beyond Listservs—Discussion Forums for Beginners: Issues of Interaction, Access, and Training, *Stop Surfing, Start Teaching, 1998 National Conference,* February 22–25, 1998, Sponsored by University of South Carolina, Conference Proceedings, pp. 93–96.
44. *Ibid.* pp. 93–94.
45. Parker, Tim, How Internet E-Mail Works, in Pike, Mary Ann, et al. (Eds.) *Using the Internet,* 2nd ed. Indianapolis, IN: Que, 1995, p. 533.
46. Kehoe, Brendan P. *Zen and the Art of the Internet.* Upper Saddle River, NJ: Prentice Hall, 1996, p. 35.
47. Bunyip Information Systems, Inc. *ARCHIE Homepage,* http://services.bunyip.com:8000/products/archie, 8/19/96.
48. Pike. *op. cit.* p. 536.
49. Kehoe, Brendan P. *Zen and the Art of the Internet. op. cit.* pp. 35–36.
50. Kehoe, Brendan P. *op. cit.* p. 35.
51. *Ibid.*

52. Pike, Tod, "How Information is Stored on the Internet," in *Using the Internet, Second Edition*, Mary Ann Pike (Editor), Indianapolis, IN: Que Corporation, 1995, p. 535.

53. *Ibid.* p. 603.

54. Cotton, Eileen Giuffré. *The Online Classroom*, Lancaster, PA: Wentworth Worldwide Media, 1997, p. 20.

55. *Ibid.*

56. Microsoft Corporation, *Microsoft Internet Explorer 6 Resources Kit,* paperback and CD-ROM, Redmonth, Washington: Microsoft Press, 2001.

57. Lowe, Doug. *Internet Explorer 6 for Dummies.* New York: John Wiley & Sons, 2001.

58. Shelly, Gary B., et al. *Microsoft Internet Explorer 6: Introductory Concepts and Techniques*, Cambridge, Mass: Course Technology, 2002.

59. Microsoft Support Online, http://support.microsoft.com/default.aspx

60. Microsoft Press. *Microsoft Internet Directory.* Redmont, Washington: Microsoft Press, 1998.

61. Classroom Connect, *Internet CD*, vol. Two, no. One, Classroom Connect, Inc., http://www.classroom.net, 1998.

62. *Ibid.*

63. *Ibid.*

64. MSN. *Encarta Online.* http://encarta.msn.com, accessed 9/8/03.

65. Microsoft. *Internet Solutions for K–12 Education*, Redmont, Washington: Microsoft Press, 1997.

66. Classroom Connect. *School Web Page Survival Kit.* Classroom Connect, Inc., http://www.classroom.net, 1997.

67. Cotton, Eileen Giuffré. *The Online Classroom*, Lancaster, PA: Wentworth Worldwide Media, 1997.

68. *Infogate*, http://www.infogateonline.com/C1.htm, accessed 8/11/03.

69. *The UC Berkeley Libraries.* http://www.lib.berkeley.edu/, accessed 3/10/04.

70. *Columbia University Library Web*, http://www.columbia.edu/cu/web/, accessed 3/15/04.

71. *The US Department of Education Reports and Studies*, http://www.ed.gov/index/.html/, accessed 3/10/04.

72. *Syllabus.* San Jose, CA: Syllabus Press.

73. *SyllabusWeb*, http://www.syllabus.com/mag.asp, downloaded 8/15/03.

74. Cotton, *op. cit.* p. 61.

75. Haworth, Karla, et al. Scholars Find That Internet-Search Tools are Inaccurate, Incomplete, and Outmoded," *Academe Today, The Chronicle of Higher Education*, Washington: The Chronicle of Higher Education, Inc., April 3, 1988.

76. *Ibid.*

77. SearchEngineWatch.Com. *Search Engines Sizes,* http://www.searchenginewatch.com reports/article.php/2156481, accessed 8/12/03.

78. Metamend. *How Big is the Internet? How fast is the Internet Growing?* http://www.metamend.com/internet-growth.html, accessed 8/12/03.

79. Microsoft. *Microsoft Bookshelf,* 1998 (soundtrack), Redmont, Washington: Microsoft Corporation, 1997.

80. Finkelhor, David, Kimberly J. Mitchell, and James Wolak. *Online Victimization: A Report on the Nation's Youth*, National Center for Missing & Exploited Children, 2000.

81. Office of Juvenile Justice and Delinquency Prevention, Office of Justice Program, U.S. Department of Justice, *Highlights of the Youth Internet Safety Survey*, Fact sheets, March 2001, #4.
82. *Ibid.* p. 1
83. *Ibid.* pp. 1–2
84. *Ibid.* p. 2.
85. U.S. Department of Education. *Parent Guide to the Internet*, http://www.ed.gov/pubs/parents/internet/index.html , accessed 10/2/03.
86. PBS Parents. *Internet Basics*, http://www.pbs.org/parents/quickstart/browser.html/, accessed 10/2/03.
87. FBI Publications. *A Parent's Guide to Internet Safety*, http://www.fbi.gov/publications/pguide/pguidee.htm, downloaded 10/2/2003.
88. National Center for Missing and Exploited Children, http://www.missingkids.com/, accessed 10/2/03.
89. National Center for Missing and Exploited Children, p. 5.
90. *Ibid.* p. 6.
91. Yahooligans! *Staying Street Smart on the Web!* http://www.yahooligans.com/docs/safety, p. 2, accessed 10/2/03.
92. Lawrence J. Magid. *Child Safety on the Information Highway* ©1998, National Center for Missing and Exploited Children, http://www.safekids.com/child_safety.htm, accessed 10/2/03.
93. *Ibid.*
94. FBI Publications. *A Parent's Guide to Internet Safety*, op. cit.
95. GetNetWise. *Online Safety Guide*, http://kids.getnetwise.org/safetyguide, accessed 10/2/03.
96. *Ibid.*
97. Parental Control Software. CyperPatrol, http://cyberpatrol.com, accessed 10/2/03.
98. NetNanny Software. *Keeping Kids Safe Online*, http://www.net-nanny-software.com, accessed 10/3/03.
99. SentryCam. *Guarding Against the Dangers of the Internet*, http://sentrycam.com/fam/specs.htm, accessed 10/3/03.
100. Security Software Systems. *Cyber Sentinel 2.0 Home Edition*, http://securitysoft.com/new601/cs home.htm, accessed 10/3/03.
101. NetProtector, http://modemlock.com, accessed 10/3/03.
102. *Ibid.*
103. ChiBrow. *The Children's Browser*, http://chibrow.com, accessed 10/3/03.
104. *SurfMonkey*, http://surfmonkey.com/, accessed 3/15/04.
105. Charters, W. W. *Motion Pictures and Youth: A Summary*. New York: Macmillan, 1935, p. 59.
106. *Ibid.*
107. Dale, Edgar. *Audio Visual Methods of Teaching*, 3rd ed. New York: The Dryden Press, 1969, p. 418.
108. Hefzallah, Ibrahim M. *Critical Viewing of Television—A Book for Parents and Teachers*. Lanham, MD: University Press of America, 1987.
109. Hahn, Harley, and Rick Stout. *The Internet Complete Reference*. Berkeley, CA: Osborne McGraw-Hill, 1994, p. 10.

110. What You Need to Know About Inventors. *Inventors of the Modern Computer, ARPAnet—The First Internet,* http://inventors.about.com/library/weekly/aa091598.htm, p. 1, downloaded 7/31/03.

111. Web66, http://web66.coled.umn.edu/schools.stats.stats.html, accessed 6/10/98.

112. The Falcon's Nest, University Park Elementary School, Fairbanks, AK, http://www.northstar.k12.ak.us/schools/upk/upk.home.html, accessed 10/15/03.

113. *Ibid.*

114. The Falcon's Nest, University Park Elementary School, Fairbanks, AK, *Micropium,* http://www.northstar.k12.ak.us/schools/upk/upk.home.html, accessed 10/15/03.

115. The Falcon's Nest, University Park Elementary Sdchool, Fairbanks, AK, *A Walk Through Fairbanks,* http://northstar.k12.ak.us/schools/upk/walk/title.html, accessed 10/15/03.

116. The Falcon's Nest, University Park Elementary School, Fairbanks, AK. *Foreword to A Walk Through Fairbanks,* http://northstar.k12.ak.us/schools/upk/walk/foreword. html, accessed 10/15/03.

117. The Falcon's Nest, University Park Elementary School, Fairbanks, AK. *Bill the Moose,* http://northstar.k12.ak.us/schools/upk/upk.home.html, accessed 10/15/03.

118. *Ibid.*

119. *Ibid.*

Part Four

VIDEO TELECOMMUNICATIONS

Chapter 12: Television in Education
Chapter 13: Satellite Communications for Learning

INTRODUCTION

Chapter 12, "Television in Education," reviews the proven advantages of using the television medium in education. It reviews current developments in television services including cable television, satellite television, WebTV, and the use of television in distance education. It indicates the need to develop children and youths' critical viewing skills of television and reviews selected critical viewing curricula and strategies.

Chapter 13, "Satellite Communications for Learning," indicates that the use of satellites in communication transcends the world of entertainment as they are consistently used to enhance communications among people from different nations and to support educational activities of a wide range of learning organizations. The chapter addresses the basics of satellite communications and their potential and innovative uses in learning.

Chapter 12

TELEVISION IN EDUCATION

PROVEN ADVANTAGES OF TELEVISION
AS A MEDIUM OF INSTRUCTION

From television's early days of development, its promise to entertain and its easy accessibility helped make the rate at which TV invaded American homes faster than any other invention. The following table shows the speed at which TV and other modern inventions entered 80% of the American homes.[1]

Invention	Years to Enter 80% of American homes
Telephone	80
Electricity	62
Cars	49
Electric washing machines	47
Refrigerators	37
Radio	25
TV	10

Over the span of three decades, the 1950s through the 1970s, television occupied a prime place among media and technologies of instruction. Hundreds of research projects were conducted to assess the advantages of using television and video recordings in education. In 393 comparison studies using experimental and control groups, Wilbur Schramm (1962), a noted communication scholar reported teaching with television as being superior in 21% of those studies, inferior in 14%, and with no significant difference between the experimental and control groups in 65% of the cases.[2]

In the early days of using television in education, the emphasis was put on telecasting lessons offered by an experienced teacher to classrooms across a wide geographical area. The underlying principle was to offer quality teaching to schools lacking the expertise of qualified teachers. When the nation realized the need to improve science and mathematics education in the late 1950s, TV was viewed as a vehicle through which quality science instruction and in-service science education programs could be offered.

Continental Classroom was a pioneering science education program broadcast to science teachers on some commercial channels at 6:30 A.M. Facing the loss of audience of commercial programs if educational programs were telecast during prime hours, broadcast of educational TV on commercial channels tended to be early morning or late evening.

Instructional television programs were generally tailored in the same fashion as classroom instruction. To use the visual dimension of the television medium, some demonstrations and film clips were used, especially with lower grades. For college level and adult education, the pattern was what has been described as the "talking head," a presenter talking to the camera most of the time.

In late 1960s, the use of television in instruction had evolved into an efficient instructional and educational tool. This major achievement has been the outcome of the following inventions and practices.

1. **Portable video production and playback.** The introduction of the 1/2" videotape machine and portable B&W television cameras at a price affordable by individuals and schools, eliminated the problem of scheduling classes to coincide with the telecast of instructional television programs. Schools and individuals can now afford to record the program and play it back when scheduling permitted. Also, students and teachers are able to select certain segments for viewing as many times as needed. The ability to produce video segments to meet local and specific instructional needs encouraged educators to experiment with a medium that may be controlled and directed.

2. **Creation of national Public Broadcasting Service for radio and television.** The Public Broadcasting Act of 1967 created the Corporation for Public Broadcasting (CPB). CPB began to function in 1968. It was charged with the responsibility of:

    a. Assisting new stations in getting on the air.
    b. Establishing one or more systems of interconnection.
    c. Obtaining grants from federal and other sources.
    d. Providing funds to support program production.
    e. Making grants to stations to support local programming.
    f. Conducting research and training projects.

    The Public Broadcasting Service (PBS) was created by CPB in 1969 to select, schedule, and distribute programming through the widespread system of public TV stations. The public TV stations produce the majority of the programs distributed by PBS. PBS also seeks and obtains programs from a variety of local, regional, overseas, and other sources. Both CPB and PBS have significantly contributed to the development of quality educational television programs.

The National Public Radio (NPR) was established by CPB in 1971 as a source of programs to be distributed nationally and as manager of the interconnection service for public radio stations. NPR serves the stations through acquisition, production, distribution, and promotion of public radio programs.

3. **Production of excellent educational TV programs.** Starting with the first broadcast of "The Ascent of Man" (1975) over PBS stations nationwide, several series with excellent video and academic qualities have been made available to institutions. The success of these series in terms of student enrollment has been phenomenal.

Forty-thousand students in 420 institutions in the United States have used "The Ascent of Man." "Classic Theatre: The Humanities in Drama" was viewed by 11,000 students in 275 institutions. Fifteen thousand students enrolled in 300 institutions saw "The Adams' Chronicles." "The Age of Uncertainty" (1977), "The Long Search" (1978), and the first selections of "The Shakespeare Plays" demonstrated the possibility of reaching and teaching a large number of students.

4. **A "new breed" of telecourse producers.** By 1974, a "new breed" of telecourse producers had emerged. Several institutions began producing telecourses that were visually more exciting than earlier educational TV material. Some of the new producers were Miami-Dade Community College District, Coast Community College, Southern California Consortium for Community College Television, and University of Mid-America (UMA). The State University of Nebraska created UMA in 1974. UMA is a consortium of Midwestern universities for the design and production of courses for adult learners.

5. **A Systems Approach in Teaching.** With the adoption of a systems approach in teaching, educational media experts started treating TV as a medium to be integrated in a teaching/learning system in which other media formats are used. Adopting this approach freed the educational television designer from "televising a course." The emphasis shifted to designing a course in which print, TV, and other nonprint media are integrated. That concept has been in practice in the Open University in England with great success.[3]

6. **Cooperative Telecourse Use.** Through a consortium representing many institutions, college adoption telecourses became financially feasible. In addition, public television stations found it easier to deal with requests for programming and scheduling from one agency rather than from dozens of colleges.

7. **Satellite Educational Consortia.** The number of schools and organizations interested in originating and distributing information

through a satellite network has been on the increase since the early part of the 1980s. Interactive television teleconferences are becoming more common, adding the dimension of immediate feedback, which open broadcast lacked. NUTN is an example of satellite consortia for learning (see Chapter 13, Satellite Communications for Learning.)

8. **Abundance of TV channels.** By the advent of cable television, more channels became available. The concept of "broadcasting" started to take a new meaning. A new term, *narrow casting*, was introduced to describe transmission of specific programs to specific audiences. Specialized channels carrying educational programs came into existence. In addition, schools were assigned cable channels for their use.[4]

All of the aforementioned innovations have contributed to making television an efficient medium of instruction. Whether it is open broadcast, video playback, or local productions, educators have found a variety of ways to strengthen and enliven their instruction. Studies on the use of television in education proved, then, that home-bound students welcome TV as an educational medium.[5] With growing emphasis on self-improvement through continuing education, educational television became a friendly source of information to the adult learner and a convenient means of gaining college credits.[6,7,8]

In addition, from the 1960s to the 1980s developing students' critical awareness of media (especially television) was a hot topic that engaged many educators as well as authors of K–12 textbooks. *Coping with Mass Media,*[9] *Coping with Television,*[10] *Getting the Most out of Television*[11]; *Critical Television Viewing: A Language Skills Work-A-Text,*[12] *Television Literacy: Critical Viewing Skills,*[13] *Inside Television: A Guide to Critical Viewing,*[14] and *New Seasons: The Positive Use of Commercial Television with Children*[15] were some titles popular among schools attempting to develop their students' critical awareness of television. Some school systems introduced courses in television production with the objective of cultivating critical viewers of television.

THE SHINING STAR OF TECHNOLOGIES TAKES A BACK SEAT

In the early part of the 1980s, the shining star of technologies of instruction lost its prime place among technologies of instruction. The advent of computer technologies shifted the emphasis from television to the application of computers in education. Even with the current renewed interest in television as an educational medium, studies addressing standards of literate teachers and students do not give television the emphasis it deserves. Current studies, however, show that children and youths spend the most time with television. *Media in the Home, 2000, The Fifth Annual Survey of Parents and Children* reported:

> For the fourth consecutive year, television is the medium with which children spend the most time. According to parents of children aged two to seventeen, children spend nearly two and-a-half hours (147 minutes) with television each day. Overall, parents report children spend an average of almost six and-a-half-hours (382 minutes) in some form of mediated communication each day, be it watching television or video tapes, playing video games, using a computer, talking on the telephone, browsing the Internet, or reading a book, magazine or newspaper. It is important to note that children often engage these media simultaneously, for example, reading while watching television or using the computer while talking on the phone. In terms of time spent in front of screens, children reportedly spend over four and-a-half hours (281 minutes) watching television or videotapes, playing video games, using the computer, or browsing the Internet each day. This is up 21 minutes from the time reported spent in front of screens last year.[16]

The report further indicated that: "Television has an even stronger presence in homes with children. The average U.S. household has 2.4 television sets while the average household with children age two to seventeen has 2.8 sets."[17]

Kids & Media @ the New Millennium, November 1999, also indicated that TV viewing occupies more time than any other type of media. The report gave the following figures of the average amount of time children spend with different types of media:

Watching TV	2:46 hours
Listening to CDs or tapes	0:48 hours
Reading	0:44 hours
Listening to the radio	0:39 hours
Using the computer for fun	0:21 hours
Playing video games	0:20 hours
Using the Internet	0:08 hours[18]

With the increasing access to the Internet, children probably spend more time with the Internet than reported in the 1999 study. However, it is far less than the 2:46 hours spent in front of the television set. Television and video clips have their growing presence on the Internet, which increases the time children and youth interact with television material, whether on the Internet or in front of their television set in their living room.

Based on viewing estimates, children spend more time in front of the TV than they spend in regular schooling; and based on the frequency of television commercials, a person by the age of 65 years will have watched the equivalent of one and one-half years of TV commercials alone! Quite a popular medium! The advancement of television technologies helps make the most popular medium of communication even more popular. The following section discusses some of the major reasons why television is and will continue to be the most popular medium of communications.

TELEVISION, THE MOST POPULAR MEDIUM OF COMMUNICATION

Easy Accessibility

The process of accessing information or entertainment programs on television is simple and easy. Turning on the TV set requires no skill. According to Nielsen Media Research, of the 99.4 million American homes that owned at least one TV set in 1999 (98.2% of U.S. households), 99% had color television sets, 35% had two television sets, and 41% had 3 or more TV sets.[19]

Home videocassette recorders were introduced in the late 1970s. During the past 20 years VHS machines have become common appliances in all schools and in the majority of American homes. Two legislations helped foster the spread of VCRs in schools and in homes.

First, in 1981, the Congressional House Subcommittee approved guidelines for "off-the-air recording" of broadcast television programs for educational use.[20] These guidelines state that a broadcast program can be taped off-the-air for viewing in a classroom, up to two times during the first ten consecutive school days following its recording. The instructor can keep the tape for reference up to the 45th day following the date of the broadcast, after which it should be erased. However, the school may obtain a long-term retention agreement at a very reasonable fee. These guidelines have encouraged schools to use broadcast material to enrich classroom teaching and learning.

Second, on January 17, 1984, the Supreme Court ruled (5–4) that the use of video recorders to tape television programs at home does not violate copyright laws.[21,22] This encouraged the public to use videocassette recorders to record programs off-the-air to watch at their own leisure, and eventually develop their own videocassette libraries.

In addition to such legislation, other factors helped popularize VHS with the public, not only in the United States but also all over the world. These factors include the decreasing cost of purchasing home video cameras and VHS machines. In a short time, many have become home video producers capturing family events on tape and playing them back on their TV set. In many instances the video camera, the VHS machine, and the home TV set replaced the still picture camera, the slide projector, or the photo album.

Home video recorders have become more popular day by day. In 1983, *The New York Times* reported that the sales of videocassette recorders totaled 4.2 million units. This figure was twice that of 1982. The sales of blank cassettes were 57 million units in 1983 compared to 24.7 million units in 1982.[23] Today, VCRs are found in 90% of the American homes. According to *2001, The New York Times Almanac:*

> In twenty years, the videocassette recorder (VCR) has gone from a curiosity to a luxury to an appliance found in more than 90% of American homes. The vast majority of people continue to use their VCRs simply to watch prerecorded videos from their local rental store. 742 million pre-recorded cassettes were sold in 1999, more than twice as many as in 1993. But a sizable number of owners have figured out how to program their VCRs and were responsible for the sale of 425 million blank cassettes in 1999.[24]

Abundance of Television Channels

Prior to cable and satellite television, television channels were limited to a small number. For instance in Fairfield County, CT, the maximum number of channels received by a roof antenna didn't exceed eight on the VHF band and two on the UHF band. In many regions of the country, the number of TV channels received was far less than that. In some areas, even the reception of available channels was poor.

Cable TV is a giant that was born of the necessity to provide a clear signal to households that could not receive a clear signal with home antennas. During its early years (1950–1970), cable's growth was very slow. In 1970, 7.5% of the nation's households were wired for cable.[25] During that time, the emphasis was put on providing clear signals to homes deprived of good reception due to distance from TV transmitters or geographical obstruction to the broadcast signal.[26] By mid-1970s, two developments put cable growth on an accelerating curve.

First, the introduction of satellite transmission has provided centralized, cost-effective distribution of programs such as movies on movie channels.[27] This development invited large companies to enter the field of cable operation and production of software. At present, the cable industry has several large corporations that own a number of cable systems throughout the United States. These companies, called "multiple system operators," (MSO)[28,29] benefit from the size of their operation by purchasing programs on a group basis and by the availability of capital to help finance the construction and the expansion of their systems.

Second, the Federal Communications Commission (FCC) relaxed its rules to allow cable companies to import distant signals. This led to the availability of more programs for the viewer to choose from and to the emergence of the first superstation, WTBS in Atlanta.[30] The superstation transmitted its signal via satellite to cable operators in other markets around the country. These developments increased the popularity of cable television. No longer is poor reception the reason for hooking to cable. Attractive alternative programming and other electronic services appeal to the public.

In December 2002, the National Cable and Telecommunications Association (NCTA) reported that 96.6% (100,174,200 homes) of the U.S. television households (103,700,000 homes) were passed by cable. Cable penetration of TV households in May 2003, was 67.4% of households passed by cable (71,897,250 basic cable customers).[31] Competing with the cable television industry for a share in TV households are companies using direct broadcast satellite (DBS), and telephone companies. As a result of this competition, 22.31 million consumers subscribe to noncable multichannel video programming.[32] Regardless of the pipeline that feeds the home TV set, the fact remains that the consumer has an abundance of television channels from which to choose.

New Information Services

To provide customers high-quality pictures and sound, more programming, and two-way technology, such as connection to the Internet through cable modems, the cable companies invested a total of $12.43 billion in 2000.[33] Industry analysts in May 2001 estimated that by the end of 2001, "60% of all cable homes will be passed by activated two-way plant, allowing for the deployment of interactive online services and telephony."[34] Interactive services include "interactive program guides (IPGs), TV-based web access, and video on demand (VOD).[35] In addition, two-way communication on cable provides the customers with access to the Internet. Fiber optics makes that connection a high-speed connection. In April 2003, NCTA reported that there were 12 million cable modem customers.[36]

All of the aforementioned and other projected developments have transformed cable TV from a facility providing good reception and a variety of TV channels into an information utility that, in addition to providing high quality picture and sound, provides interactive digital and video services. No wonder the National Cable *Television* Association has recently changed its name to the National Cable *Telecommunications* Association, using the same abbreviation, NCTA.

Television in Distance Education

Use of television in distance education has been common in American institutions. Educational agencies, PBS, universities, or commercial institutions produce telecourses (courses taught by television). Two options are usually used to telecast telecourses to participating schools: satellite transmission and educational television channels. Copies of some courses are recorded on cassette format available to participating schools along with printed and other course supplementary materials.

One of the main providers of telecourses is PBS Adult Learning Services. PBS provides, in addition to telecourse material, professional development programs, live satellite events, *Going the Distance* project, and web-based courses.[37]

There are three options for institutions to use the television segment of a telecourse. First, the television programs could be used to enrich the library resources. Students would be advised to review the programs on their own. In addition, segments of the programs could be screened during class time.

In the second option, institutions wrap around the scheduled broadcasts, whether on satellite or on educational or public television channels, a course primarily designed by the faculty of the institution. The telecourse material is usually used to pace the course and to provide audiovisual information prepared by experts. Usually in this option, the number of classroom meetings is reduced, sometimes by 50%. Class time is usually devoted to discussing key information in the course, assessing students' progress in the course, and introducing course topics and assignments. In this option, students get the better of two worlds.

In the third option, the telecourse is adopted in its entirety as designed and produced by the course originator. Students are usually asked to attend the course opening session, a midterm, and final test sessions on campus. At one time, this model was known asthe 30/30 model, i.e., 30 programs, 30 minutes each. When students need help, they are given a phone number to call. This model has been popular in community college education.

Cable in the Classroom

Cable in the Classroom, CIC, is a television education initiative. Launched in 1989, CIC is a $420 million public service effort supported by 38 national cable networks[38] and over 8,500 local cable companies.[39] CIC provides a free cable connection and over 540 hours per month of commercial-free educational programming to schools across the country.[40] According to NCTA, in December 2001, 81,654 schools (43,676,577 students) were served by CIC.[41]

Through this project, local cable TV companies provide a cable conenction into every school in their service areas. The monthly magazine, *Cable in the Classroom*,[42] is also available to schools. The magazine lists CIC programming by subject area. The magazine is also available online from the CIC home site at http://www.ciconline.com/home.htm/.[43]

The participating national cable networks telecast, usually during off-hours, commercial-free educational programming that teachers and students tape for use according to the teaching and learning needs of the teacher and students. Supplementary materials to the broadcast are also published on the web site of the cable networks. For instance, lesson plans that accompany the daily broadcast of CNN Newsroom are available from the CNN web site at http://learning.turner.com/newsroom.[44]

Cable in the Classroom provides training workshops for teachers using television in teaching. CIC has already expanded its training mission to include training teachers on effective use of the World Wide Web. This expanded mission is based on a study conducted by CIC focusing on the use of cable and the Web in teaching. The study showed that "almost half of all elementary and secondary school teachers in the U.S. use the Web in their teaching, but most do not believe they are adequately prepared to use it well and need additional training." To address this need, CIC provided online web-based training for teachers: *Web Teacher, Your Resource for Web Knowledge.*[45] In addition, four computer labs in the Washington, D.C. area were established to train teachers, administrators, and parents. The labs were cosponsored by the D.C. Public Schools, the Smithsonian Institution, and George Mason University.[46]

Finally, *Cable in the Classroom Comes Home* is a CIC initiative that was launched in 1997 to encourage parents and other volunteers to help schools build free, noncommercial, educational video libraries. "The project provides families with information about cable's commercial-free educational programming that can be taped and donated to a school's video library or used at home."[47]

Educational Television Collaboration Among K–12 Schools

To meet their instructional needs, schools within one system or across other school systems collaborate on offering educational programs, which would be difficult for one school to do alone. The Cable Classroom Project is a good example of this type of activity.

The Cable Classroom Project is a distance learning project that started in Connecticut in the late 1980s among three towns: Somers, East Windsor, and East Granby. The project uses two educational access channels made available to the schools from the local cable TV system. Two schools interact orally and visually, and the third school watches the interaction between the two schools on two TV monitors. During scheduled broadcast times, the three schools share classes in different two-site combinations.

Each of the three sites is equipped with three video cameras, one directed at the teacher, the second directed at the students, and the third mounted on a copy stand to transmit the image of a visual placed on the copy stand. Sitting at the teaching station, the teacher can use a simple switch to select the camera that will transmit to the receiving site.

Each site also has three large TV monitors. One monitor displays the copy stand image, the second displays the image received from the remote site, and the third displays the signal put out by the originating site. Microphones are mounted on the students' desks to transmit students' questions. In addition to the components of the two-way audio and video transmission, each site has a phone line equipped with a fax machine for transmitting hard copy documents between the sites.[48]

Continuous Introduction of New Technologies

With the rapid technological developments in microprocessors, telecommunications and visual recording and retrieving, the medium of television will become even more popular. Future uses of television will increase through the availability of alternative delivery systems. For instance, digital video players are an excellent medium not only for entertainment but also for education. The technology of DVD makes it a user-controlled medium. Since the information is encoded digitally, its access could be easily controlled either by hand-held devices or by a program especially designed on a computer. The DVD will definitely replace the videodisc technology in training, and development, and it could possibly replace VHS.[49] At present, video rental stores carry VHS and DVD copies of the same movies.

Technological advances continue rapidly. High definition television and large TV screens help reinforce TV as a favorite medium of communication. Quality digital video cameras and recorders, selling at affordable prices, may encourage many to become home and school video producers. Video editing using desktop computers will assist them in constructing quality programs.

TV on the WEB

TV on the web provides three services:

1. To support text by providing video segments to show an event, a demonstration, an advertising of a product, announcement of a service, a current news item, etc.
2. To provide additional information in relation to regular or special broadcast programs. The interrelated site in this case provides text, video segments, audio bites, databases on information related to the broadcast, interactive chat during and after the broadcast of the program.
3. To broadcast and rebroadcast TV programs. This presence is currently limited due to the bandwidth required for live and video broadcasts. Eventually, with the projected Internet high-speed communication, more television broadcast will be available on the web.

The presence of TV on the web providing any of the services outlined above not only makes communication on the web more effective but also reinforces human communication through the medium of moving images and sound. Many surfers of the web expect to see video segments on sites they visit. TV signals are not only becoming more and more acceptable means of communications but also recommended.

THE NEED TO DEVELOP K–12 STUDENTS' TELEVISION CRITICAL VIEWING SKILLS

Never before has there been a medium of communication as popular as TV. Nor has there been a medium that captures the attention of millions of viewers for long viewing hours every day. Moreover, television's effects on its viewers, especially children and youth with limited frame of reference to unfamiliar things they watch on television, are well documented.

Television programs that generate a great deal of concern among parents and educators are those preoccupied with the portrayal of violence and misinformed sex. Despite the concern about children's exposure to TV violence, for instance, "American children and adolescents are being exposed to increasing amounts of media violence," reports the American Academy of Pediatrics. In a policy statement on Media and Violence, the American Academy of Pediatrics (1996) indicated:

> American children and adolescents are being exposed to increasing amounts of media violence, especially in television, movies, video games, and youth-oriented music. By age 18, the average young person will have viewed an estimated 200,000 acts of violence on television alone. Video game violence, children's cartoons, and music lyrics have become increasingly graphic. In movies, action films depict anatomically precise murders, rapes, and assaults; with each sequel, the number of deaths increases dramatically.[50]

Despite concern about misinformed sex, The American Psychological Association (1999) estimated that teenagers were exposed to 14,000 sexual references and innuendoes per year on television.[51] More recently, The American Academy of Pediatrics, Committee on Public Education, Policy Statement, *Sexuality, Contraception, and the Media (RE0038)* (January 2001), stated, "In film, television, and music, sexual messages are becoming more explicit in dialogue, lyrics, and behavior. In addition, these messages contain unrealistic, inaccurate, and misleading information that young people accept as fact."[52]

In addressing the effects of media on young people, Matt James, Senior Vice President of the Kaiser Family Foundation, said: "Television clearly makes an impression on kids today, whether it's in what they think they should look like or the qualities they associate with women and men. The media is a powerful tool that can either reinforce negative stereotypes or present strong role models for young girls and boys today."[53] In her article

"Does Your Patient Have Sleep Problems? Ask about TV First," Joanne Cantor wrote:

> If a patient you are seeing isn't getting enough sleep, television programs and movies are likely culprits. Beyond keeping children up later to watch, mass media are a potent source of nightmares, sleep disturbances and intense anxieties. Several recent reports in medical journals support this contention.
>
> A survey of third- through eighth-graders revealed that as the number of hours of television viewing per day increased, so did the prevalence of symptoms of anxiety, depression and post traumatic stress.
>
> Similarly, a different survey of parents of children in kindergarten through fourth grade revealed that the amount of children's television viewing (especially at bedtime) and have a television in their own room were significantly related to the frequency of sleep disturbances. Indeed, 9% of the parents' survey reported that their child experienced TV-induced nightmares at least once a week.[54]

Documented effects of television programs on children and youth, viewed in the light of long hours of viewing everyday, make it extremely essential for education to aim at developing K–12 students' television critical viewing skills. To be a critical viewer is to stay in control of one's television viewing. Critical viewers of television are capable of:

1. Analyzing what they see and hear on television.
2. Distinguishing between reality and the world of television.
3. Making informed judgments and expressing a thoughtful evaluation of programs they watch.
4. Making intelligent use of their leisure time in which television viewing is one among other enjoyable activities.[55]

Critical viewing comes from within. It is not imposed. It is an outcome of planned activities in which understanding the medium of television and what it offers and thinking about one's relationship with television are underlined. It is a skill that can and should be taught.[56]

During the 1980s, a few textbooks were developed targeting the development of students' critical viewing of television. The following is a brief account of four of those textbooks (programs).

Critical Television Viewing: A Language Skills Work-A-Text (1980)[57] was developed by WNET-13, a New York City public television station, with funding from the U.S. Office of Education and Welfare. The curriculum defines critical viewing of television as "the ability to analyze, evaluate and express what is seen and heard on television—orally, in writing or in choice of reading materials." The target students were grades 5 to 9. Two *Work-A-Text* books are available. One was designed for students, and the second one was the Teachers' Annotated Edition.

Work-A-Text contains activities, charts, games, logs, illustrations, and photographs to introduce and reinforce basic skills and concepts. The following is a list of the ten chapters and the objectives of each.

1. How Does Television Fit into Your Life? The objective is to examine different media and the ways in which the students use them so that they may begin to be aware of how the media, especially television, influence their lives.

2. What Are The Ingredients for a Television Story? The objective is to examine television stories in terms of character, setting, conflict, plot, theme, and logic so that viewers may begin to understand the difference between television's fiction and life's reality.

3. Who Puts a Television Program Together? The objective is to learn about some of the production elements in a TV program and to learn to read a TV script.

4. How Do Different Types of Television Programs Compare to Each Other? The objective is to become aware of different types of television programs and their identifying characteristics so that viewers might become aware of why they prefer one type of program over another.

5. How Does Television Persuade Us? The objective is to become aware of persuasion techniques on television so that viewers might become aware of how commercials and regular programming could affect viewers' opinions and behavior.

6. How Do You Analyze TV News? The objective is to understand the elements of TV news compared with other media.

7. How Does a Television Program Get on the Air? The objective is to experience reading a TV script and become aware of how some kinds of programming decisions are made.

8. What Do You Like About the Television Program You Watch? The objective is to analyze the individual program elements and develop the skills necessary to form and support opinions of television programs.

9. How Do You Review a Television Program? The objective is to examine and organize opinions of individual program elements into a cohesive written review.

10. How Can You Become a More Critical Television Viewer? The objective is to make judicious use of television viewing time.

Inside Television—A Guide to Critical Viewing (1980)[58] is a joint production of WGBH Educational Foundation, Office of Radio and Television for Learning, Boston, Massachusetts, and Far West Laboratory for Education Research and Development, San Francisco, California. It aims at teaching high school students to become more sophisticated, discriminating viewers of television and more sophisticated, discriminating thinkers in general. The program may be used as the basis for a full-semester course or as a supplement to certain standard high school subjects. It is divided into seven units:

1. *You & Television* (An introduction to television as a medium, and to the way Americans use it).
2. *The Television Industry* (A comprehensive explanation of television as a business, its history and regulations).
3. *Programs and Production* (Dramatic form, characterization, production techniques).
4. *Selling* (Commercials, public service announcements, political advertising, and packaging).
5. *That's The Way It Is? TV News* (News and information programming).
6. *The Television Environment* (Television's subtle messages and the effects of viewing).
7. *A Saving Radiance?* (Future technology and a reexamination of the issues raised in Unit 1).

   Each unit, in turn, has four interrelated components:
   - *The Text* provides information about television and its role in society.
   - *The Activities* suggest writing assignments of varying lengths; others call for a general discussion and responses to specific questions. Some activities are done individually, others are done in small groups or by the class as a whole, and some are designed as homework assignments.
   - *The Readings* encompass a variety of reprinted material. They follow the text in each unit. Assignments for readings are given in the *Teacher's Guide*. Some of the readings entitled "In Conversation with . . ." are edited interviews (especially commissioned for this course) with prominent people in television including producers, directors, actors, and advertisers.
   - *The Worksheets* are provided separately and may be duplicated using copying equipment. They provide the students with the opportunity to perform a wide variety of brief written exercises for class or homework and role-playing activities such as interviewing, scheduling programs, and writing the student's own news show.

Television Literacy: Critical Viewing Skills (1980)[59] was developed by the School of Public Communication at Boston University, under contract with the Department of Education. The main objective of the curriculum is to educate and sensitize the adult population to the powerful effects of television on society. The curriculum includes a text, an instructor's guide, and a student workbook. It consists of four modules:

1. *Behind the Scenes* focuses on the inner work of television: the structure, techniques, creative process, business, politics, and the effects of television.
2. *Persuasive Programming* examines persuasive techniques in presenting information in commercials, public service announcements, and institutional documentaries to sell products or ideas. The basic concepts studied in this module included appeals, effects, methods, claims, forms, structure, and research.
3. *Entertainment Programming* focuses on the structure and ingredients of prime-time shows; entertainment themes on television; social behavior on television; characteristics of talk, fun, and game shows on television; and television as a popular culture.
4. *Informational Programming* studies the origins and constraints of informational programming; gathering, assigning, and selecting news; organizing the news; selling the news; documentaries and special news programs; and the impact of TV news.

Getting the Most Out Of Television (1983)[60] is a curriculum designed by Drs. Jerome and Dorothy Singer of the Yale University Family Television Research Center and Diana M. Zuckerman, Radcliffe College, Harvard University. The primary target students are in grades 3 to 6. The authors list the objectives of the curriculum to assist students to:

1. Understand how the television medium works, from its basic technology to its total communication impact.
2. Develop vocabulary, writing, and critical thinking skills.
3. Explore personal and social values conveyed by television news, drama, and documentaries.
4. Become discriminating consumers by learning how and why television commercials are made.
5. Distinguish between fact and fiction, fantasy and reality, and actual and staged violence.

Eight lessons were designed to teach children about television so that they may be less passive viewers and more discriminating consumers (p. ix). The primary objectives of the eight lessons are to teach children:

1. How television works.
2. To distinguish between reality and fantasy on television programs.
3. About the purpose of commercials and the techniques used for product enhancement.
4. To discuss television characters as a way of helping them to understand themselves.
5. Not to generalize about minority group members from the few examples portrayed on television.

6. That the violence on television should not be imitated;
7. That they can become more in touch with the world events by watching television; and
8. That they can get more out of television by being discriminating viewers and consumers.

The lessons are written in conjunction with seven programs available on both videotape and 16-mm films from ABC Wide World of Learning. However, the authors indicate that the lessons can be easily taught without the use of the tapes or the films. The seven programs are:

1. *The Technical Side of TV:* how television pictures are made and broadcast and what a television studio, set, and control room look like.
2. *People Make Programs:* the television team members who plan and produce shows.
3. *The Magic of Television:* special effects, dissolves, and slow motion; how one distinguishes fantasy from reality on television.
4. *Characters We See on Television:* how do television characters become role models? How do stereotyping and fictional conventions ignore the complexities of human nature?
5. *Action and Violence:* the difference between fantasy action and the real-life action of news and sports. How is TV violence staged, and why is it dangerous to imitate?
6. *The Real World of Television:* various forms of news programs available on television; how does television news relate to magazines, newspapers, and other news formats?
7. *Commercials:* why are commercials made, and how do they influence us? How can we become more discriminating consumers?

Hefzallah (1987) addresses the issue of developing children's and youth's critical viewing of television. He first indicates that: "To help our children use television in an intelligent manner, we ourselves have to use it in an intelligent manner. Before we can foster good taste in others, we have to develop that taste ourselves and believe in its necessity."

Second, he identifies seven basic steps of becoming a critical viewer of television:

1. Understanding one's relationship with television.
2. Understanding television programming policy.
3. Analyzing the structure of news programs.
4. Analyzing entertainment programs.
5. Analyzing commercials.
6. Collecting information on viewers' interaction with television.
7. Being an activist: becoming aware of organizations and learned communities interested in advocating intelligent use of television by K–12

students, and learning to whom one could write to voice concern about bad programming.

Each step includes a worksheet, or a self-questionnaire, for the reader to complete. Certain chapters in the book are recommended for reading prior to the completion of the worksheet. He also indicates that the worksheets may be used as guidelines in interviewing children, with the consent of their parents, to assist them in becoming aware of their television viewing habits, as well as to develop their understanding of the medium of television.

In studying all of these curricula designs for developing K–12 students' critical viewing of television, important questions come to mind. Do we develop critical viewing skills in a unit of study or a course that is offered once? If so, in what grade level do we offer that unit or course? Or, is the aim of developing students' critical viewing skills an ongoing objective that should stay current in every grade level?

I believe that the answer to these questions is threefold. First, teachers and parents have to develop this ability before they are able to teach it. Second, a basic unit on the television medium should be introduced as early as possible in the elementary school (second- and third-grade students were able to comprehend the basics of TV advertising and to write short scripts for imaginary products). Third, critical viewing of television is one facet of critical thinking, an objective that must be emphasized in every grade level. We just have to be aware and convinced of its vital importance.

REFERENCES

1. Schramm, Wilbur. *Responsibilities in Mass Communications,* New York: Harper & Brothers, 1957, p. 23.
2. Schramm, Wilbur. *Educational Television the Next Ten Years.* Stanford, CA: The Institute for Communication Research, 1962.
3. *How the Open University Teaches,* http://www.open.ac.uk/OU/Intro/Teaching.html/
4. Hefzallah, Ibrahim M. *The New Educational Technologies and Learning— Empowering Teachers to Teach and Students to Learn in the Information Age.* Springfield, IL: Charles C Thomas Publisher, 1999, pp. 256–259.
5. Chu, Godwin C., and Wilbur Schramm, *Learning from Television: What the Research Says.* NAEB, Washington, D.C., 1967.
6. Randolf, Deborah A. Colleges Offer More Courses Through *TV. The Wall Street Journal,* Nov. 20, 1980.
7. National University Consortium for Telecommunications in Teaching, University of Maryland, University Park, MD, Videotape featuring students' comments on directed study, viewed 1980.
8. Community Junior Colleges. *Extravaganza* (videotape), viewed 1990.

9. Littell, Joseph F. (Ed.). *Coping with the Mass Media.* Evanston, IL: McDougal & Little & Company, 1979.

10. Littell, Joseph F. (Ed.). *Coping with Television.* Evanston, IL: McDougal & Little & Company, 1973.

11. Singer, D.G., et al. *Getting the Most Out of TV.* Santa Monica, CA: Goodyear Publishing Co., 1981.

12. WNET, *Critical Television Viewing: A Language Skills Work-A-Text,* Student Edition and Teachers' Guide. New York: Globe Book, 1980.

13. School of Public Communications. *Television Literacy: Critical Viewing Skills,* Boston, MA: Dendron Press, 1980.

14. White, Ned. *Inside Television: A Guide to Critical Viewing,* Palo Alto, CA: Science and Behavior Books, 1980.

15. Potter, Rosemary Lee. *New Seasons: The Positive Use of Commercial Television with Children,* Columbus, OH: Charles E. Merrill, 1976.

16. The Annenberg Public Policy Center of the University of Pennsylvania. *Media in the Home, 2000, The Fifth Annual Survey of Parents and Children,* http://www.appcpenn.org/mediainhome/survey/survey7.pdf/ p. 19, accessed 7/6/01.

17. *Ibid.* p. 8.

18. Roberts, Donald F., Ulta G. Foehr, Victoria J. Rideout, and Mollyann Brodie. *Kids & Media @ the New Millennium, A Comprehensive National Analysis of Children's Media Use,* The Henry J. Kaiser Family Foundation, http://www.kff.org/content/1999/1535/KidsExecSum%20FINAL.pdf/, p. 8, accessed 9/20/01.

19. Nielsen Media Research. *The World Almanac & Book of Facts 2001.* Mahwah, NJ: World Almanac Education Group, 2000, p. 314.

20. *Congressional Record,* October 14, 1981.

21. *Sony Corporation of America vs. Universal City Studios,* N. 81-1687, *U.S. Law Week,* January 17, 1984.

22. For more information on the issue, refer to Wallace, Jr., Paul S., Copyright Law: Legalizing Home Taping of Audio and Video Recordings, Issue Brief Number IB82075, The Library of Congressional Research Service, Major Issues System, Washingon, D.C.

23. *The New York Times,* Sunday, January 22, 1984, Sec. 4, p. 1.

24. Wright, John W. (Ed.). 2001, *The New York Times Almanac, The Almanac of Record.* New York: The New York Times, 2000, p. 395.

25. Robb, Scott. *Television/Radio Age Communications Coursebook,* 1978–1979 edition. Englewood Cliffs, NJ: Communications Research Institute, pp. 4–20.

26. Baldwin, Thomas F., and D. Stevens McVoy, *Cable Communication.* Englewood Cliffs, NJ: Prentice-Hall, 1983, p. 9.

27. *Ibid.* p. 127.

28. Robb, Scott. *op. cit.* pp. 4.13–4.14.

29. Baldwin, Thomas F. *op. cit.* pp. 243-244.

30. *Ibid.* p. 112

31. NCTA. *Industry Overview,* http://www.ncta.com/Doc/PageContent.cfm?pageID=86/, downloaded 7/26/01.

32. *Ibid.*

33. NCTA. *Cable TV Handbook, Overview of the Cable Television Industry,* http://www.ncta.com/pdf_files/Ind_Ovrvw_060801.pdf/, p.11, downloaded 7/26/01.

34. *Ibid* p. 2
35. *Ibid.* p. 10
36. NCTA. *Industry Overview,* http://www.ncta.com/Doc/PageContent.cfm?pageID=86/, downloaded 7/26/01.
37. *PBS ALS Agenda on Line,* http://www.pbs.org/als/agenda/index.html, accessed 9/24/03.
38. Cable Networks. *Cable in the Classroom,* http://ciconline.com/nets.htm, accessed 7/12/98.
39. Cable Companies. *Cable in the Classroom,* http://ciconline.com/mso.htm, accessed 7/12/98.
40. *What Is Cable in the Classroom?* http://www.ciconline.com/about.htm/, accessed 7/12/98.
41. NCTA. *Industry Overview,* http://www.ncta.com/Doc/PageContent.cfm?pageID=46/, accessed 10/10/03.
42. *Cable in the Classroom* (ISSN #1054-5409) is published monthly, except July/August. Combined by CCI/Crosby Publishing, 141 Portland Street, Suite 7100, Cambridge, MA 02139, (617) 494-4997; (617) 494-4898 (Fax).
43. *Cable in the Classroom Online Homepage,* http://www.ciconline.com/home.htm/, accessed 8/20/98.
44. CNN Newsroom. http://learning.turner.com/newsroom, accessed 3/7/04.
45. National Cable Television Association & TECH CORPS. *WebTeacher, Your Source for Web Knowledge,* http://webteacher.org/winexp/indextc.html/ or http://www.webteacher.org/home-windows/index.html/, downloaded 7/10/98.
46. Cable in the Classroom Institute. Cable in the Classroom Professional Development Institute, http://www.ciconline.com/inst.htm/, 1996–1998, downloaded 7/10/98.
47. Cable in the Classroom. *Cable in the Classroom Comes Home,* http://www.ciconline.com/CICCH.htm/, 1997–1998, downloaded 7/10/98.
48. Stone, Peter. The Cable Classroom Project, in Hefzallah, Ibrahim M (Ed.), *The New Learning and Telecommunications Technologies, Their Potential Applications in Education.* Hefzallah. Springfield, IL: Charles C Thomas Publisher, 1990, pp. 88–90.
49. Wright, John W. (Ed.). *2001, The New York Times Almanac, The Almanac of Record, op. cit.* p. 396.
50. American Academy of Pediatrics. *Media Violence* (RE9526), Policy Statement, http://www.aap.org/policy/00830.html/, June 1996, downloaded 8/13/01.
51. Issues Briefs. *Teens, Sex, & the Media.* Studio City, CA: Mediascope Press, http://www.mediascope.org/pubs/ibriefs/tsm.htm, downloaded 3/15/00.
52. American Academy of Pediatrics, *Sexuality, Contraception, and the Media (RE0038), op. cit.*
53. Children Now. *Reflections of Girls in the Media,* http://www.childrennow.org/media/mc97/ReflectSummay.html, 1997, p. 8, downloaded 8/9/01.
54. Cantor, Joanne. Does Your Patient Have Sleep Problems? Ask about TV First. *American Academy of Pediatrics News,* September 2000.
55. Hefzallah, Ibrahim M. *Critical Viewing of Television, A Book for Parents and Teacher.* Lanham, MD: University Press of America, 1987.
56. *Ibid.*

57. WNET. *Critical Television Viewing: A Language Skills Work-A-Text,* Student Edition and Teachers' Guide. New York: Globe Book Co., 1980.

58. White, Ned. *Inside Television: A Guide to Critical Viewing,* Palo Alto, CA: Science and Behavior Books, 1980.

59. School of Public Communications. *Television Literacy: Critical Viewing Skills,* Boston, MA: Dendron Press, 1980.

60. Singer, D.G., et al. *Getting the Most Out of TV,* Santa Monica, CA: Goodyear Publishing Co., 1981.

Chapter 13

SATELLITE COMMUNICATIONS FOR LEARNING

INTRODUCTION

In 1982, Elliot Richardson said, "There was a time when the seas seemed endless and the skies vast enough to swallow any of the mistakes and errors of man. The world used to be big and men could afford to be small. Now the world is small and men must be big."[1] Today, satellites are making the small world even smaller. Satellite systems provide the fastest and most efficient ways of sending and retrieving video information to and from any location on earth. Business, industry, and education are discovering the benefits of satellite communications. Speed, cost-effectiveness, and flexibility of satellite communications have intrigued professionals in training and development in corporations and in continuing education in schools and universities. Educators on campuses around the country are studying and experimenting with the potential uses of satellite communication to enhance universities' missions. Public schools with installed satellite reception antennas reap the benefits of receiving staff development programs and special courses for their students from satellite consortia.

Prior to the planning for effective use of satellite communication in education, educators must develop a basic understanding of satellite communication, become familiar with a variety of satellite consortia and the kind of programming and services they offer, and learn about some innovative use of satellite communication in enriching students' learning experience. This chapter addresses each of these points in turn.

BASICS OF SATELLITE COMMUNICATION

A decade ago laymen were not accustomed to terms like *URL*, *HTML*, *spam*, *instant messaging*, and *chat rooms*. Today, however, they are household words because the consumer and educator soon recognized and began to take advantage of the enormous potential of the Internet. Likewise, the satellite and all that it promises is ushering us into an age in which words like *downlink* and *KU-Band* are becoming part of our everyday vocabulary. We are in a new age in which satellites shrink the distance between people and facilitate the interaction among them. Common understanding of the basics of satellite communication and knowledge of the following basic terms often used in talking about satellite communications are essential to the achievement of that goal.

1. *Satellite.* In 1945, Arthur Clarke, author of *2001: A Space Odyssey*, introduced the idea of satellite communications. Clarke theorized that if a satellite were positioned high enough above the equator and its speed were controlled to match that of the earth's rotation, it would appear stationary in the sky. Such a geostationary orbit, however, would be possible only if the satellite were positioned directly above the equator at a distance of 22,300 miles.[2] A satellite's main function is to receive the signal from an earth station and rebroadcast it on a new channel. From its position high in space it can "see" one-third of the earth's surface.[3]

2. *Satellite Transponders.* Every satellite has at least 24 channels. With new technological developments, the number of satellite channels will increase. Each of these transponders can transmit one television signal or thousands of simultaneous telephone calls.

3. *C-Band and KU-Band.* Satellite signals use a high-frequency band ranging from 3.7 to 4.2 GHz. This band is called the C-Band. A new generation of satellites is using a higher frequency ranging from 11.7 to 12.2 GHz called the KU-Band. More and more satellites are expected to be operating on the KU-Band.

4. *Footprints.* The satellite's antenna directs its signal to all designated reception areas on the ground in a particular shape called a footprint.[4] The signal is strongest at the center of that area, which makes it possible to use smaller dishes for reception. The signal diminishes in its intensity, as one moves away from the center, so larger dishes are needed.

5. *Uplink and Downlink.* An uplink is simply a ground station that sends a signal up to the satellite. The satellite changes the signal's frequency and retransmits it to a downlink, a ground receiving station.

6. *TVRO.* Television-receive-only refers to satellite-receiving stations or homes. The two primary components of this system are the dish and the receiver. By directing the dish toward the satellite and tuning the receiver, one can receive a single channel at a time.

7. *The Satellite Dish.* The satellite dish is mainly an antenna that collects and focuses the satellite signal. Satellite signals are weak signals, almost as weak as a CB radio signal. For this reason, the satellite dish must be relatively large in diameter for good reception. With new developments in telecommunications, the size of the dish is getting smaller and smaller.

8. *Clarke Belt/Satellite Parking Lot.* The band of outer space above the equator at a distance of 22,300 miles is called the "Clarke Belt" in recognition of Arthur Clarke's pioneering vision.[5] Spacing between satellites in the Clarke Belt, or as it is also called the "satellite parking lot," is crucial. Satellite spacing is calculated in degrees. One degree, as measured from the earth, is equivalent to 460 miles between satellites. How far apart satellites are "parked" from each other depends on the transmission power of the satellite and frequency used. For example, C-Band satellites are spaced two degrees apart, while higher frequency KU-Band satellites are spaced three degrees apart.[6]

9. *Direct Broadcast Satellite.* Direct broadcast satellite (DBS) refers to the technology of sending direct satellite signals to homes. With this technology, the satellite signal is strong enough to allow for the use of smaller dishes, which mean lower cost for individuals to receive satellite signals directly in their homes.

EDUCATIONAL SATELLITE CONSORTIA

The world of satellite communications is gaining ground in education, especially in higher and continuing education. A considerable amount of programming is available through satellites. Most of those programs provide the participants with learning and training experience unavailable through other means. An alphabet soup has emerged: acronyms of satellite and distant learning consortia. Brief reviews of four major educational satellite consortia follow.

National University Telecommunications Network (NUTN)

NUTN was founded in July 1982. Its coordinating office was located on the campus of Oklahoma State University in Stillwater, Oklahoma. Today's NUTN coordinating office is at Old Dominion University. NUTN describes its mission in the following:

> The National University Telecommunications Network (NUTN) provides dynamic professional development opportunities in support of emerging and current technology applications to professionals involved in higher education.
> As a premier higher education organization in the educational telecommunications field, NUTN provides vision and experience in a highly personal setting. It utilizes numerous channels to facilitate and promote networking, mentoring, and collaborating among higher education institutions, administrators managing technology and content delivery, teaching faculty and educational technology professionals.[7]

NUTN is a coalition of two- and four-year colleges joined to develop the use of satellite technology to share expert knowledge and special events happening on their respective campuses. NUTN is involved in satellite videoconferencing for higher education. The scope of videoconferencing has expanded to national audiences. Nationally recognized experts share their expertise in a wide variety of disciplines through videoconferencing with audiences on campuses, corporations, and governmental and other organizations.

NUTN has been recently structured "to provide greater assistance to its members and a broader mandate of applications and technologies." The *NUTN Experience* explains the new mandate:

> In the past two years, as a result of intense planning, a series of "think tanks," membership forums at the annual conference, and a series of meetings by the Advisory Board, Today's NUTN has been restructured to provide greater assistance to its members and a broader mandate of applications and technologies. All of this has been designed to meet the challenges of the developing digital world, as well as the burgeoning demands of distance education on our nation's campuses.

To meet the new mandate, Today's NUTN outlined its new agenda. The following points are some of the highlights of that agenda:

1. Today's NUTN will focus on the use of new and emerging technologies in videoconferencing and distance education.
2. The NUTN structure will include sources of information and points of contact for its members through a broad array of Resource and Special Interest Groups. Resource Groups include:
   - Technology and Application
   - Distance Learning
   - International
   - Corporate
   - Research
3. Professional development remains a key component of the organization and will be augmented in a variety of new and strengthened ways.
4. Online assistance utilizing the World Wide Web will provide reports and resources on an extensive variety of related subjects.
5. While NUTN plays an important role in providing higher education institutions and professionals critical and timely access to experts, quality programming and media materials not otherwise readily available, it has another more profound function to fulfill. NUTN will also be a leader in testing new ways of accomplishing higher education's goals, and the changing roles of faculty and staff as new technology makes available resources at unprecedented levels of access. NUTN institutional and professional members will be positioned to take full advantage of both opportunity and change prompted by these developments of the information age.
6. The National University Telecommunications Network, Today's NUTN, is committed to providing the highest level of programming/production, delivery and professional development for its members. NUTN intends to

be the premier association in higher education's applications of new and emerging communications technologies.[8]

Public Broadcasting Service Adult Learning Service (PBS ALS)

Using satellite and Internet technology, PBS Adult Learning Service provides distance education programming for higher education. Originally, Adult Learning Satellite Service (ALSS) started telecasting telecourse material and special programming in 1981. A telecourse is an integrated package of instructional material that includes print, video, CD-ROM, and Internet components.

"From its very beginnings, public television has considered the delivery of learning services to be at the core of its vision," said Jinny Goldstein (1997), PBS senior vice president for learning services.[9] Commenting on the creation of ALS, Goldstein explained three trends that came together at the end of the 1970s, "to make the creation of ALS not only logical but inevitable." She said:

> First, there was a growing recognition that adult learners (people beyond the traditional college ages of 18–22) were fast becoming a major force in higher education. Second, it was becoming clear that a larger number of potential students would enroll in college if they could overcome the barriers of time and distance that kept them from conventional on-campus courses. Third, the quality of telecourses was steadily improving.[10]

In addition to telecourses, PBS ALS offers other learning services through satellite distribution. These services include professional development programs, live satellite events, and ready to earn resources.[11]

Professional development programs are especially designed satellite telecasts for faculty and staff development focusing on current educational issues. Curriculum enrichment programs are designed to present rich TV programming that enhances the undergraduates' learning experiences. The range of the programs covers many college disciplines.

Live satellite events are telecasts of special programming addressing current educational issues. They provide the opportunity for the audience to listen to experts discussing important issues. Usually, the audience has the option to call in questions and make comments.

Ready to Earn® provides students and workers with resources they need to develop workplace skills and pursue rewarding careers. PBS defined the role of *Ready to Earn®* as to "help a new generation of workers become 'ready to earn,' properly prepared, educated, and capable of competing successfully in today's high-performance, global economy."

Ready to Earn® services are available to colleges and to the workplace. They include *Educational Resources, Going the Distance* initiative, and PBS *LiteracyLink®*.

Educational resources include a wide selection of video programs, CD-ROMs, and live satellite events that help in teaching "essential workplace competencies such as team work, problem solving, creative thinking, as well as many of the SCANS* skills identified by the U.S. Labor Secretary's Commission on Achieving Necessary Skills."[12]

Going the Distance® (GTD), the first major project of the PBS Adult Learning Service's *Ready to Earn*® initiative was launched in 1994 providing a leadership role in developing distance degree programs. ALS PBS GTD's goal is to "serve as a catalyst for change in the higher education community."[13] PBS ALS explains:

> The PBS Adult Learning Service's Going the Distance (GTD) degree program offers a virtual campus to your college. GTD responds to the growing number of adults who are eager to earn college degrees, but who require more flexibility than traditional on-campus courses allow.
>
> The GTD Project offers you a wide array of information, references, and tools to develop, enhance, and promote your institution's distance degree program. Whether you're interested in establishing a distance degree program at your institution or are working to enhance the program you already offer, GTD provides you with the resources you need.[14]

In 1998, PBS ALS reported that the goal of GTD was to enable colleges to offer two-year degrees entirely through distance education.[15] A partnership was developed among colleges, public TV stations, and ALS to broadcast telecourses to meet the needs of homebound students and students who could not take the courses on campus. Usually materials for these courses are block-fed by satellite transmission to public TV stations and to campuses with satellite reception facilities. In 1998, 62 public television stations, 187 colleges, and 37 states participated in GTD. The majority of distance learning courses were telecourses. and from 1995 to 1996 alone more than 400,000 students nationwide enrolled in PBS-distributed telecourses. From 1981 to 1997, more than four million students have earned college credit through ALS-distributed telecourses. The project's overall objective was for a degree to be available at a distance in each state by the year 2000.[16]

Fifteen years after the initiation of ALS in 1981, Jinny Goldstein, Senior Vice President of PBS Learning Services, reflecting on the success of ALS telecourses, said:

> . . . numbers don't come near to telling the whole story. We discovered, for example, that telecourse students are very serious learners. They are women and men, who want and need a degree and are willing to work (to) get it. The ability to receive a quality education without the need to commute to a campus at a particular time has opened up a whole new constituency, the adult

---

*Secretary of Labor's Commission on Achieving Necessary Skills (SCANS), 1981.

learner. In fact, colleges cite significant increases in overall enrollment as a result of their ALS participation.

So I would say that we know that we have succeeded by two measures, one numeric and one made up of fifteen years worth of experience and knowledge about what telecourses have meant to students. We know that 3.5 million students have taken ALS telecourses. We know that a remarkable proportion of American colleges and universities are ALS participants. We know of the thousands of learners who are now enrolled in complete telecourse-based degree programs. And, equally important, we know the stories of individual students: we know of the worker who is learning new skills, of the handicapped person who is completing her degree, and of the parent who finally has a chance to begin an education because of distance learning opportunities. These are the real measures of success—in human terms—of any educational endeavor, and these are what make ALS so worthwhile.[17]

In 1998, more than 2,000 colleges and universities used telecourses distributed by ALS. Annual student enrollment in these courses was more than 400,000 students.[18]

LiteracyLink® provides adult literacy resources that integrate online interactivity, computer technology, and video programs. The LiteracyLink® project "prepares adults with the reading, writing, math, and communication skills necessary to be successful in the workplace and to pass the GED test."[19]

"*Ready to Earn* services are unique in that they are designed for learners and workers whose needs are often unmet in traditional educational and business settings," explains ALS.[20]

Public Broadcasting Service The Business Channel (PBS TBC)

PBS The Business Channel is especially designed to provide an "interactive workplace education." Timely topics to business workforces are delivered by satellite and web technologies. The TBC home page claims: "We guarantee access to "the best and brightest" in the business world. You'll have opportunities to interact with leading experts, creative business thinkers, and faculty members from the nation's most prestigious colleges and universities."[21]

Satellite Communications for Learning International (SCOLA)

SCOLA is an internationally based consortium of educational institutions. SCOLA's mission is "to help people of the world learn about one another; their countries, their cultures, their languages, and their ideologies. SCOLA emphasized the importance and effectiveness of modern information technology as a tool in overcoming barriers to global understanding and will remain at the forefront of its application."[22]

SCOLA utilizes satellite technology to bring news, educational, and a variety of television programming unedited in their original languages to member institutions. Broadcasting digitally on four satellite channels, it reaches educational institutions, businesses and organizations, special interest groups, and interested viewers of educational channels on local cable systems. SCOLA's channels include:

1. **SCOLA Channel I.** This 24-hour-a-day channel rebroadcasts international news from 35 countries in their original languages. Through these programs, viewers "see the countries of the world as the countries see themselves. They learn how the people look and sound and what kinds of events make up the news."[23]
2. **SCOLA Channel II.** This channel rebroadcasts a variety of programs including documentaries and entertainment and the arts from 10 countries in their respective native languages.
3. **SCOLA Channel III**, China Channel. This channel broadcasts a variety of programming from the People's Republic of China. A team of SCOLA resident Chinese broadcasters edits and transmits programs on this channel including documentaries, entertainment, tours of China as well as Chinese language courses. SCOLA launched this 24-hour channel on November 1, 1996, featuring Chinese programs produced by 40 TV stations from all over China who joined together under the name China Yellow River TV, CYRTV. The Chinese State Education Commission supplies special educational television productions to SCOLA.[24]
4. **SCOLA Channel IV**, On September 23, 2003 SCOLA announced the launch of Channel IV effective September 29, 2003. This channel will "allow viewers to see news from their favorite countries an additional three to four days per week. Some countries now are only shown a few days per week due to space limitations."[25] Starting January 1, 2004, the following countries line up this new channel: Azerbaijan, Basque, Belarus, Bosnia and Herzegovina, Egypt, Estonia, Georgia, Kazakhstan, Kurdistan, Kyrgyzstan, Lebanon, Macedonia, Moldova, Nepal, Pakistan, Peru, Portugal, Qatar, Serbia and Montenegro, Tajikistan, Thailand, Ukraine, Uzbekistan, and Vietnam.[26]

In addition to the four channels, SCOLA offers programming over the Internet using live video streaming.[27]

The Insta-Class services offered by SCOLA are very interesting. Insta-Classes are a 5- to 10-minute weekly transcript in the official or native language of the selected country and an English translation of that transcript. The Insta-Classes also contain key words, quizzes, and vocabulary.[28] The Insta-Class transcripts and the English translation with vocabulary notes and quizzes, along with RealAudio clips, are available through SCOLA's Web site http://www.SCOLA.org/.

SCOLA developed a list of suggested uses for Channels I, and II. The uses are grouped under different study disciplines.

FOREIGN LANGUAGE
- Practice standard pronunciation, rhythm, gesture, expression.
- Observe protocol and vocabulary for governmental, business, and formal occasions.
- Prepare for study or work abroad with a direct view of current events and culture.
- Learn conversational usage such as slang and regional accents.

POLITICAL SCIENCE
- Learn current events as they happen, reported from the scene.
- Gain political perspectives other than our own.
- Practice the language of your specialty.
- Understand more deeply current challenges and conflicts in the world.
- Explore the cultural context for area studies.

CULTURAL DIVERSITY CLASSES
- See cultural events as they happen, reported in native perspectives.
- Learn firsthand the variety of our world views.
- Watch documentary series on specific topics such as art, history, and technology.
- See the customs, conditions, and concerns of the peoples of the world.

MEDIA
- Study production techniques as developed throughout the world (camera angles, set design, lighting, editing).
- Examine the variety of direction styles, through aspects such as expectations, program, and pacing.
- Observe worldwide technological levels and standards.

COMMUNICATIONS
- Study the world's variety of communication techniques through our panoramic view.
- Observe mannerisms, etiquette, topics discussed in particular countries, cultures, or languages.
- Extend your fluency in your specialty language, as well as your understanding of each nation and its culture.

BUSINESS
- Learn about the global market—Prepare to enter it
- Learn the work habits, politics, laws, and protocol in international and foreign settings.
- Practice the modern world languages.

HISTORY
- Learn about historical sites, sagas, and events through our documentaries and current reports.

- Show the importance of historical causes by relating them to current events; illuminate current events through understanding their historical causes.
- Delve into the culture and languages of area studies

SOCIOLOGY/ANTHROPOLOGY
- Gain live access to other societies—their historic traditions, modern conditions, future directions
- Use documentaries on archeological sites and expeditions, cultural studies.
- Gain contact with the world culture—The modern combination of unity and diversity.

INTERNATIONAL STUDIES
- A transitional link for international students upon entering the U.S. keeping them apprised of current events from their home country.
- Used to ease the return of the international student to their native country.
- Tool for a U.S. exchange student to better understand the country, customs and culture.

GEOGRAPHY
- Geographic locations pinpointed and observed firsthand.
- The study of a region's current product output and climatic changes.
- Learning the natural features of each region.

DRAMA
- Observation of the individual character, and background.
- Study of personal reaction to various situations such as beliefs in:
  - Family
  - Customs and Culture
  - Humor
  - Government/law
  - Education
  - Health
  - Entertainment
  - Work habits

LITERATURE
- Presentations of new and old works of literature, poetry, and prose.
- Observation of the original presentation and the acceptance of the work.

HEALTH
- Medical methods and technology.
- Innovative health care:
  - Medical breakthroughs.
  - Hospital settings and their differing aspects.
  - Clinical and surgical observations.
- Ideas and views of health care from many nations.

GOVERNMENT AND LAW
- Study of the governmental infrastructure of the individual countries.
- Gain a broader understanding through viewing a country's application of the law.
- Information regarding current changes in the laws and governmental structure.

RELIGIOUS STUDIES
- Study of religions viewed directly from the country.
- Observe religious ceremonies as they are practiced.

COUNSELING
- Understanding the cultural behavior and insights of the people of the country to maintain an effective counsel for the international students.[29]

POTENTIAL USES OF SATELLITE COMMUNICATION IN LEARNING

Reception of Specialized Cultural and Instructional Programs

In addition to educational and cultural programs available through educational satellite consortia, there is a wide variety of interesting and highly specialized programs available through satellite communication. These programs can be used to enrich education in history, science, communication, political science, Latin American studies, fine arts, and modern languages.

Distribution of School-Based Television Programs on a Satellite Network

As a member of a satellite consortium, an educational institution can choose to send videotaped programs for satellite distribution to the uplink facilities of the consortium. There is a difference between producing a television program for distribution through open broadcast or cable television and producing video programs for distribution through a satellite consortium. Open telecast distribution requires that the program should appeal to a relatively large audience. With satellite communication, programs can be designed to appeal to a narrower audience, yet reach a large population of that specific audience. For instance, a program featuring a new approach in teaching physics does not attract a public television audience; however, by telecasting the same program through a satellite consortium, it can attract a relatively large number of those concerned about teaching physics. A sample of potentially feasible programs follows.

1. Enrichment programs to public schools in science, mathematics, computers in education, and foreign languages.

2. Special courses to schools that lack trained teachers, and required facilities. For instance, Arts and Sciences Teleconferencing Service (ASTS) of the College of Arts and Sciences of Oklahoma State University (OSU) was established in 1984 to provide "equal access" to educational resources to rural high schools. Rural educators and the OSU. administration and faculty recognized that rural schools often could not offer foreign languages and upper level mathematics and science courses due to personnel, financial, and geographic restriction. OSU's College of Arts and Sciences, the Oklahoma State Department of Education, the Oklahoma Legislature, and the Oklahoma rural superintendents of education across the state worked together to develop ASTS. The first course, German I by satellite, was broadcast in the fall of 1985. During 1987 and 1988, ASTS served 170 schools across 14 states. Other courses have been added including physics by satellite, advanced placement calculus, trigonometry, and German II by satellite. (For more information on current distance education projects at OSU, see Chapter 14.)

3. In-service programs to teachers and administrators and special programs focusing on new trends and problems facing education. Professionals within an educational institution find satellite communication an attractive and efficient medium for sharing their expertise with other professionals in member institutions of the consortium.

In all of these examples, providing the technology for feedback, such as toll-free telephone numbers, can ensure the necessary interaction between the originator of the program and the recipients of the program.

Participation in a Growing Teleconferencing Activity

Capitalizing on the expertise of faculty, administrators, and professional people within a university, college, or school, video teleconferencing can be produced and transmitted for distribution to colleges and other teleconferencing sites through a satellite consortium.

The number of organizations and schools becoming interested in originating and distributing information through a satellite network is on the increase. Each consortium has its advantages. Which consortium would yield maximum benefit to one particular school has to be determined based on the needs of the school and available human expertise within the school.

To transmit a teleconference, an uplink arrangement is necessary. The uplink carries the signal from the originating site to a designated uplink facility to be distributed to the participating teleconference sites. Three uplink methods are possible. First, a transmitting dish may be rented for the day of the teleconference. Second, arrangements could be made with AT&T

to carry the signal through its telecommunication system. Third, arrangements may be made with public television or cable television uplink facilities. Various factors have to be considered in deciding which method is the most appropriate and economical. One of those factors is the determination of the receiving and participating sites. Determination of the participating sites depends on which teleconferencing consortium a school joins and on the topic of the teleconference. Most of the satellite consortia have coordinating offices, which provide marketing surveys, program coordination, and access to high-quality technical consultation at a reasonable cost. Usually they charge a fee to conduct a survey to determine interest in programs. One must plan topics that will attract enough people to cover the cost of the marketing survey, the cost of the print-related material, and the rental of an uplink device.

In addition to gaining exposure for the originating school on many campuses and corporate headquarters, students on campus would have free access to the teleconferencing. They would also gain exposure to some of the uses of telecommunication technology in education, business, and industry.

Becoming active in teleconferencing activities may be participating only as a recipient of teleconferences. Schools and universities should study the variety of teleconferences available through the aforementioned consortia to downlink the appropriate conferences for their needs. Acquiring the rights to videotape the conference can help increase the educational video collection of a school library.

Programming a Special Campus Channel

A channel can be programmed to carry entertainment and cultural programs especially selected for a specific student body. Programs can be either locally originated or received from different satellites or rented from film and video rental houses.

In addition to providing special cultural and entertainment programs for a specific student body, having a television channel on a campus provides the opportunity for students to gain firsthand experience in programming a television channel and in marketing commercial spots.

INNOVATIVE USE OF SATELLITE
COMMUNICATION IN LEARNING

Visiting with Experts in Their Research Working Environment

Regardless of where the experts are, a live video interview between them and students in other locales can be established through satellite communications. *Fairfield University's Link with Endeavour* is an example of this innovative educational experience.

March 9, 1995, became a milestone in the academic development of college and high school honor students who participated in a live interview with Endeavour astronauts as they were orbiting the earth. Satellite, television, and telephone communications were used in this event. The event was viewed by an audience of 600 people seated in the Oak Room of Fairfield University's Barone Campus Center. The event was also telecast live on Cablevision system in 16 towns in Fairfield County.

Ten students from Fairfield University and two honor students from the Fairfield public school system prepared for the event under the guidance of Dr. Evangelos Hadjimichael, Professor of Physics at Fairfield University. Students followed the mission's daily report posted by NASA on the Internet and read related material to the mission's goals. They prepared scientific questions to ask the astronauts.

Phone lines carried students' voices to Houston, Texas, and from there they were relayed to *Endeavour* in its orbit. The audio/video signal of the astronauts from inside *Endeavour* was uplinked to NASA's satellite. This signal was then downlinked by Fairfield University's satellite reception system and was carried through Fairfield University's Campus Television Network to be viewed on large screens strategically placed in the Oak Room. From the Oak Room, Cablevision of Connecticut carried a live program centered on the astronauts' interview. This program, *Fairfield University's Link with Endeavour*, lasted from 5:30 P.M. to 6:30 P.M. on March 9, 1995. The interview of the astronauts lasted from 6:03 P.M. to 6:18 P.M.

Tom Appleby, Cablevision News 12 anchorperson, hosted the show. Prior to the interview, an 18-minute video program, *Endeavour Countdown*, was projected to the audience in the Oak Room as well as to the audience of Cablevision Channel 12. *Endeavour Countdown* was produced by the Media Center by compiling video footage from NASA's satellite. The program explained the goal of *Endeavour's* mission, introduced the astronauts, and showed crew training and the exciting takeoff of the rocket carrying *Endeavour* to study the invisible universe. The program was followed by introduction of the student panelists and a dialogue between the host of the program and Professor Hadjimichael until the time of the interview. After the interview, 12 minutes of wrap-up questions and answers followed. The scenario of that exciting event is presented below.

Scenario of Fairfield University's Link with Endeavour

5:00 Link with Astronauts Logo.
5:25 *"Standby for live broadcast. Please be silent."*
5:30 Broadcast begins with Tom Appleby.
     Tom explains the program, then he introduces Dr. Hadjimichael.

5:35   Tom introduces *Endeavour Countdown*, a program produced by the Media Center.

5:53   End of *Endeavour Countdown*, back to Tom. Tom asks Dr. Hadjimichael to introduce the panelists.

5:54   Dr. Hadjimichael introduces the student panelists.

6:02   ***"Standby for link with Endeavour."***
            Satellite signal on large screen and monitors.

6:03   Live Interview with Endeavour.

Establishing Contact:

Capcom:	*Endeavour*, this is Houston. Are you ready for the event?
Orbiter:	Houston, *Endeavour*. We are ready.
Capcom:	Fairfield, this is Houston. Please call *Endeavour* for a voice check.
Hadjimichael:	*Endeavour*, this is Fairfield. How do You hear me?
Orbiter:	(Reports voice quality. If not Acceptable, stand by for instruction from Houston.) If acceptable, we will hear: "Fairfield we are ready for questions."
Hadjimichael:	(Introduces himself, the number of students from FU and Fairfield High, and begins the questions. Every student identifies him- or herself and his or her school before addressing the astronauts.)

6:18   *Hadjimichael*:   Houston, Fairfield. That concludes the event.
            Capcom: Thanks, Fairfield.

6:18:30 Back to Tom for comments on the interview, and to respond to presubmitted questions.

6:28   (Tom's concluding remarks.)

6:29   (Roll credits.)

Eight years later, I still have a vivid memory of the audience's excitement as the image of the large screen changed from a local shot of the host to a shot of the earth taken from *Endeavour*. The excitement reached its peak when the shot of the earth was replaced by a shot of the interior of the vessel showing three astronauts posing for the interview. The thrill and excitement that the students experienced as they realized that they were talking with the astronauts in space will stay with them for years to come.

Home, Away From Home

In the summer of 1996, 15 Egyptian professors from three universities in Egypt came to the Fairfield University campus to attend a Fulbright Summer Enrichment Program. Their charge was to develop a four-year curriculum for the preparation of English teachers in their respective colleges. The duration of the workshop was over five weeks.

The scholars were to reside in the campus townhouses. The media center staff searched the satellite line-up to locate the Egyptian satellite channel. Having the campus connected through a closed-circuit TV system, it was possible to feed the Egyptian Space Channel to the townhouses.

To our visiting scholars, the Egyptian Space Channel provided a bit of home while they were away from home. To colleagues on campus, the channel provided a window on Egyptian TV and Egyptian culture. All of this was achieved through satellite technology.

Experiential Learning

An innovative approach targeting the cultivation of future journalists can be implemented through affiliation with programs such as CNN Newsource in the Classroom.[30] CNN Newsource every day feeds its affiliates 17 feeds of timely mix of news stories. CNN explains the "feed material" in the following:

> The 17 daily CNN Newsource news feeds are rich in a variety of national and international pieces, medical, sports, entertainment, weather, business, science/technology, travel, environmental, fashion features and topical graphics, fed in package and vo/nat sound (voice-over/natural sound) formats. This material is provided by our 35 bureaus worldwide, and our broadcast licensees throughout the country that provide CNN with reciprocal news-gathering capabilities. It is also our hope that occasionally your school might be able to provide us with material to be aired on the CNN networks and repackaged for the Newsource feeds.[31]

In addition to the feeds that could be tapped by the school each day, CNN Newsource in the Classroom provides "live generic reports" and "look live" reports that may be used at no charge and incorporated into students' productions. Both reports are generated and produced by CNN Newsource, which "sends its own correspondents to cover live breaking news for affiliates who can't send crews to cover the story."[32]

Students learning television journalism could excerpt all the material fed via CNN Newsource and include it in their productions for campus use. In the event that the school plans to air the piece off campus, CNN requires the school to adhere to the in-market embargo policy outlined in the license agreement between the school and CNN Newsource.[33]

Time-coded final "rundowns" providing numerical listing of the pieces transmitted are fed after the video feed to make it easier for the user to locate stories of interest. The text portion of the service is posted on the Internet. Licensed affiliates receive a password allowing them to get to the text site.[34]

Such rich up-to-date resources, which are used by professional television journalists, provide future television journalists with first-hand experience in developing newscasts based on "real news items." In the following, CNN Newsource summarizes the potential benefits of this type of experiential learning in the study of journalism:

By having such a valuable resource at your fingertips, your students can learn the following:

- to write stories to today's video—today
- to produce packages using vo/nat sound elements
- to edit down packages with reporter tracks
- to localize national and international stories
- to incorporate state-of-the-art topical and weather graphics
- to handle wire copy and use valuable script and rundown information
- to produce student newscasts
- to practice editorial skills
- to develop and sharpen tape production skills

In addition to the obvious applications within the broadcast journalism curriculum, your students can use CNN Newsource video to aid in the production of programming for other departments within the school, such as Business, Pre-Med, Science, Home Economics.

Applications for the use of CNN-provided material and the disciplines to which they can be applied are endless.[35]

Interactive Communication Among People from Different Nations

The following example, although dating back to 1987, is chosen to show how satellite communication can overcome the barriers of space and language to provide a vehicle for interaction among people from different cultures. This innovative use occurred in the spring of 1987 to bring interested American and Soviet Union parties to talk about how media affects the relationships between the two countries. *US/USSR Spacebridge: The Role of the Media in Current Relations* was produced by the Center for Communication and Gostelradio in conjunction with the American Society of Newspaper Editors.[36]

Originally the following material appeared in the *Instructional Development Newsletter*, published by the Media Center of Fairfield University under the title "You Were There, . . . and Also Here," in May 1987.[37]

On April 8, 1987, the media center was the site of an exciting video teleconference between American and Russian journalists and university students. About 50 universities in the United States received the teleconference through satellite downlinks. In Connecticut, Fairfield University was the participating university in this venture. Fairfield University graduate and undergraduate students attended the teleconference, along with representatives of the news media. This was not the first time a television program originated from two nations; however, it was one of the most exciting programs. Focusing on media in shaping US/USSR relationships, the telecommunication medium was used intelligently.

How did the system work? Each country had two interactive studios. All studios were interconnected, allowing the person talking to be seen on receiving television sets. Set design and color schemes were complementary, yet different enough to allow viewers to identify immediately the location from which the person was speaking. In the United States, the main studio was in San Francisco and the second interactive studio was in Boston. In the USSR, the main studio was in Moscow and the second interactive studio was in Tbilisi, Georgia. The Masonic Auditorium in San Francisco housed a five-camera mobile production unit. Peter Jennings moderated a panel of three American journalists: Stuart Loory, Senior Correspondent, Cable Network News; Seymour Topping, Director of Editorial Development, *The New York Times*; and Elizabeth Tucker, Staff Writer, *The Washington Post.*

On the other side, in the TV studio of Gostelradio (the USSR's State Committee for TV and Radio), Vladimir Pozner, a commentator for the Soviet State Television and Radio, moderated a panel of three Russian journalists: Alexander Shalnev, commentator, *Izvestia* newspaper; Tengiz Sulkhanishvilly, TV Correspondent, Tbilisi, Georgia; and Yurii Tschekochikhin, Staff Writer, *Literary Gazette.*

Each main studio received two signals, one from the interactive site in its country and the feed that was sent from the other country. At the same time, each main studio transmitted two signals. The first was its feed to the other country, and the second was its composite signal for broadcast in its own country (see Figures 13.1 and 13.2).

The two interactive sites in Boston and in Tbilisi transmitted one signal to their main studios via Westar IV, and Ghorizont, respectively. They also received the broadcast composite signal through the same satellites on different channels.

Four satellites were involved in this event: Westar IV, Satcom 1R, Intelstat, and Ghorizont. The first two are American domestic satellites. Intelstat is an international satellite operated by Intelstat Consortium, and Ghorizont is a Russian domestic satellite.

The signal received by the viewers at teleconferencing sites traveled a half-million miles at the speed of light. Since the American TV signal is different from the European and Russian systems, en route to its destination, the American signal in NTSC was converted to SECAM standard, and the Russian signal in SECAM was converted to NTSC standard.

Figure 13.3 shows the complete route of all signals involved. From the Masonic Auditorium in San Francisco, the American feed to Russia was transmitted via microwave to a Satcom 1R uplink facility outside the city. The feed was downlinked from Satcom 1R by a Comsat earth station near Etam, West Virginia, and then was uplinked to an Intelstat satellite.

The feed was then received by a Russian earth station near Dubna, 150 miles from Moscow. There the signal was converted from the American television standard (NTSC) to the Russian format (SECAM). Finally, the signal was transmitted to the Gostelradio television studios in Moscow.

The Russian feed to the United States followed the same route and was converted at Dubna from SECAM to NTSC standard. The American com-

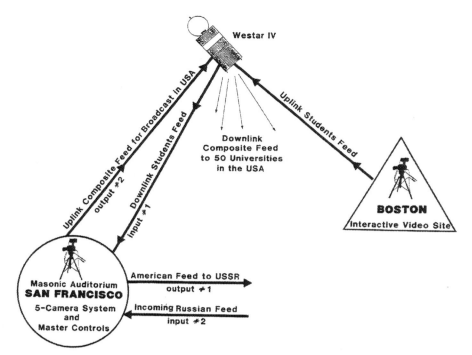

Figure 13.1 The American Site

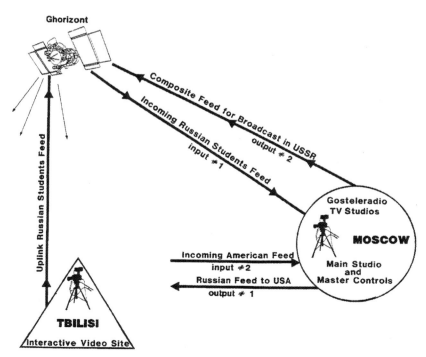

Figure 13.2 The Russian Site

272

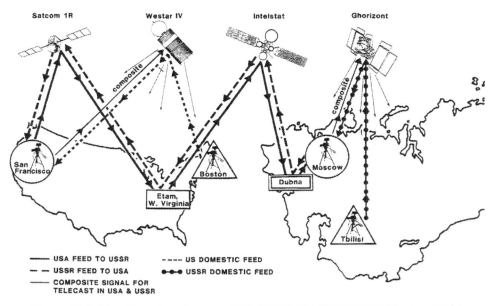

Figure 13.3 The Complete Route of US/USSR SPACEBRIDGE (Spring 1987)

posite signal was transmitted to Westar IV for downlinking at approximately 50 American universities. The Russian composite signal was uplinked to Ghorizont for downlinking at Russian viewing sites.

In each main studio there were two directors. The lead director selected the shots for the composite signal for transmission on domestic satellites. This signal was recorded and edited into a one-hour program and given to PBS and commercial TV. The second director selected the shots of the country's feed to the other country.

The producers and directors in the control rooms in San Francisco and Moscow were in constant direct communication via an audio channel.

Spacebridge technology provided the channels through which nations could talk to each other. This is one of the bright sides of the new telecommunications technology.

CONCLUSION

Satellite communication is an important learning technology providing innovative and rich learning experiences to students of various age levels. To summarize, satellite communication can:

- Enrich educational offerings through the integration of highly specialized learning and teaching material unavailable on conventional channels.
- Share educational experiences with other colleges, universities, and the corporate world.

- Extend school boundaries to reach distant sites of learning and teaching.
- Expose students and teachers to viable and cost-effective uses of telecommunication technology.
- Provide students in communication with the opportunity to gain first-hand experience in television programming and in marketing commercial spots.
- Open the classroom to the world by incorporating well-designed interactive teleconferences with other nations of the world.

REFERENCES

1. Richardson, Elliot. Telefutures. *The Futurist*, April 1982, p. 62.
2. Long, Mark, and Jeffrey Keating. *The World of Satellite Television*. Mendocino, CA: Quantum Publishing, 1986.
3. Whitehouse, George E. *Understanding the New Technologies of the Mass Media*. Englewood Cliffs, NJ: Prentice-Hall, 1986, p. 148.
4. Long, Mark. *op. cit.* p. 16.
5. *Ibid.* p. 13.
6. Whitehouse, *op. cit.* p. 157.
7. National University Telecommunications Network. *NUTN, Mission*, http://www.odu.edu/dl/nutn/mission.html, accessed 7/25/03.
8. National University Telecommunications Network. *The NUTN Experience*, http://www.odu.edu/dl/nutn/nutn_experience.html, accessed 7/25/03.
9. PBS. *Agenda*, Washington, DC, Fall/Winter 1997.
10. *Ibid.* p. 2.
11. PBS. *Adult Learning Service Information Package*, June 1998. See also, PBS Adult Learning Service online at http://www.pbs.org/als, accessed 9/24/03.
12. In 1990, the Secretary of Labor appointed a commission to determine the skills our young people need to succeed in the world of work. The commission's fundamental purpose was to encourage a high-performance economy characterized by high-skill, high-wage employment. Although the commission completed its work in 1992, its findings and recommendations continue to be a valuable source of information for individuals and organizations involved in education and workforce development. Please refer to http://www.ttrc.doleta.gov/SCANS/. You can obtain the full report from http://www.ttrc.doleta.gov/SCANS/Blueprnt.htm.
13. PBS ALS. *Going the Distance*, http://www.pbs.org/als/gtd/index.html/, accessed 7/30/03.
14. *Ibid.*
15. PBS, ALS, *Going the Distance*, http://www.pbs.org/learn/als/gtd/project/short.html/, downloaded Summer 1998.
16. *Ibid.*
17. PBS Adult Learning Service. The Adult Learning Service at Fifteen—An Interview with Jinny Goldstein, Senior Vice President, PBS Learning Services, *Agenda Online Magazine*, http://www.pbs.org/als/agenda/articles/2f67.html, accessed 9/21/03.

18. PBS. *Agenda*, Fall/Winter, 1997. See also *PBS ALS Agenda OnLine*, http://www.pbs.org/als/agenda/index.html, accessed 09/24/03.

19. PBS. Adult Learning Service Information Package, June 1998. See also PBS Adult Learning Service Online at http://www.pbs.org/literacy/, accessed 09/24/03.

20. PBS ALS. *Ready to Earn*, http://www.pbs.org/als/agenda/articles/nssb.html, accessed 09/24/03.

21. PBS. *The Business Channel*, http://www.pbsthebusinesschaneel.com/main/about/, downloaded Summer 1998. See also *PBS The Business Channel,®* http://www.pbs.org/als/agenda/articles/tbc.html, accessed 09/24/03.

22. *About SCOLA*, http://www.scola.org/about/index.html, accessed 9/26/03.

23. SCOLA. *Information Package*. See also SCOLA web homepage at http://www.scola.org/, accessed 09/26/03.

24. SCOLA. *Information Package*. See also SCOLA web page: Welcome to SCOLA at http://www.scola.org/about/Lee/index.html/, accessed 09/29/03.

25. *SCOLA TV Network Adds 4th Channel*, http://www.scola.org/whatsnew/channel4.html, accessed 9/29/03.

26. *Ibid.*

27. *SCOLA Live Video Streaming*, http://www.scola.org/streaming/index.html, accessed 09/29/03.

28. SCOLA, FAQ. *Insta-Class Service*, http://www.scola.org/about/faq.html/, p. 3. See also Insta-Class Service at http://www.scola.org/insta-class/index.html, accessed 09/29/03.

29. *How can I make best use of SCOLA?* http://www.scola.org/about/faq.html#sec7, accessed 09/29/03.

30. CNN Newsource Sales. http://classroom.cnn.com/, accessed 09/26/03.

31. CNN Newsource Sales. CNN Newsource Feed Material, http://classroom.cnn.com/feed_material.html, accessed 09/26/03.

32. CNN Newsource Sales. CNN Newsource Live, http://classroom.cnn.com/live.html, accessed 09/26/03.

33. CNN Newsource Sales Student Newscasts on Air, In-Market Embargo Policy, http://classroom.cnn.com/newscast.html, accessed 09/26/03.

34. CNN Newsource Sales. Technical Considerations, CNN Newsource Text Rundowns & Scripts, http://classroom.cnn.com/technical.html, accessed 09/26/03.

35. CNN Newsource Sales. CNN Newsource Applications, http://classroom.cnn.com/applications.html, accessed 09/26/03.

36. U.S.A./U.S.S.R. Spacebridge was produced by The Center for Communication, 1133 Avenue of The Americas, New York, NY, and Gostelradio, Moscow, in conjunction with the American Society of Newspaper Editors. The Spacebridge Project was funded by a grant from the John D. and Catherine T. McArthur Foundation. The Center for Communication, Inc. is a nonprofit organization that provides opportunities for university students and faculty to meet leading communication professionals. The Center sponsors seminars in all areas of communications including advertising and marketing, television and radio, print and broadcast journalism, the new technologies, public relations, and publishing, and examines current communication policy issues and conducts practical career development workshops. In November 1987, the U.S.A/

U.S.S.R. Spacebridge was awarded First Prize Gold Medal by the International Teleconferencing Association.

37. Hefzallah, Ibrahim (Ed.). You Were Here, . . and Also There. *Instructional Development Newsletter*, Media Center, Fairfield University, Fairfield, CT, May 1987.

Part Five

DISTANCE EDUCATION

Chapter 14: Distance Education

INTRODUCTION

Distance education is an old teaching strategy that has recently gained new momentum and perspective due to the development of information and telecommunications interactive technologies and the need to provide a learning environment conducive to citizen's lifelong learning. Pioneering educators, statesmen, community leaders, scholars, and politicians express the need to speed up the adoption of distance education to meet adults' learning needs and to achieve educational equity among K–12 schools.

Chapter 14, "Distance Education," reviews the development of distance education practices from home study courses to the present practices that utilize new information technologies and sound pedagogical principles.

Chapter 14

DISTANCE EDUCATION

INTRODUCTION

Distance education is an old teaching strategy that has recently gained new momentum and new perspective due to the development of information and telecommunications interactive technologies and the need to provide a learning environment conducive to lifelong learning. Some scholars date the beginning of distance education around 150 years ago.[1] Others consider that cave painting and tribal talking drums were forms of distance education.[2]

THE FIRST GENERATION OF DISTANCE EDUCATION PRACTICES

Home study courses of the early 1800s have evolved into the organized and more structured correspondence-independent studies with two million Americans participating at present. The earliest documented home study course offered in the United States was shorthand in 1728. Caleb Philips, teacher of the new method of shorthand, advertised in *The Boston Gazette* on March 20, 1728, that "Persons in the country desirous to learn this art, may, by having the several lessons sent weekly to them, be as perfectly instructed as those that live in Boston."[3]

In Europe, a Swedish newspaper in 1833 publicized the opportunity to study "Composition through the medium of the Post."[4] A few years later, in 1840, after the initiation of penny post in England, which allowed the delivery of a letter anywhere in the country for a penny, Isaac Pittman offered shorthand instruction via correspondence. Holmberg reported that Pittman "reduced the main principles of his shorthand system to fit into postcards. He sent these to students, who were invited to transcribe into shorthand short passages of the Bible and sent the transcription to him for correction."[5] Three years later, in 1843, "the Phonographic Correspondence Society was formed to take over these corrections of shorthand exercises. It was the beginning of what was later to become Sir Isaac Pittman Correspondence Colleges."[6]

In 1873, Anna Eliot Ticknor established a Boston-based society, the Society to Encourage Studies at Home. "The Society offered instruction in 24 subjects organized within six departments: history, science, art, literature, French, and German. Many of her students were young women kept at home by the conventions of their time."[7] The Society attracted more than 10,000 students in 24 years.[8] Students of the classical curriculum (mostly women) corresponded monthly with teachers, who offered guided readings and frequent tests. Anna Eliot Ticknor is credited with the idea of exchanging letters between teacher and students, guided readings, and frequent tests, which formed "a vital part of the organization's personalized instruction."[9]

In 1883, "The academic respectability of correspondence teaching in the United States was formally recognized in 1883 when the State of NY authorized the **Chautauqua Institute** to award degrees through this method," reported Moore and Kearsely.[10] According to Terry Ann Mood, "Chautauqua . . . lacked the resources necessary to sustain this movement. Ultimately, universities took over the correspondence-for-credit arrangement."[11]

Another interesting development in the early days of distance education in the United States was initiated in 1891 by Thomas J. Foster, editor of *The Mining Herald*, a daily newspaper in eastern Pennsylvania. He began offering a correspondence course in mining and the prevention of mine accidents. His business developed into the *International Correspondence Schools* (ICS).[12] "As the railroad industry gained importance, ICS offered correspondence courses to workers from as many as 150 railroad companies; in fact railroad cars were sent around the country to provide hands-on instruction. Today ICS is the largest commercial provider of home study programs."[13] ICS institution is located in Scranton, Pennsylvania. Total enrollment is approximately 33,000. Popular programs offered by the ICS institution include administrative and secretarial services; computer and information sciences; child care and guidance workers and managers; and electrical and electronics equipment installers and repairers.[14]

In the late 1870s, the university extension movement in the United States promoted the correspondence method. Among the pioneers in the field were Illinois Wesleyan in 1877 and the University Extension Department of the University of Chicago in 1892.[15] Illinois Wesleyan offered bachelor, master, and doctoral degrees as part of a program modeled on the Oxford, Cambridge, and London models. "Between 1881 and 1890, 750 students were enrolled, and in 1900, there were nearly 500 students seeking degrees. However, concerns about the quality of the program prompted a recommendation that it be terminated by 1906."[16]

On the K–12 front, the Calvert School of Baltimore enrolled four pupils in its home study courses in 1906, thus becoming the first primary school in the United States to offer instruction by correspondence. More than

400,000 students worldwide have benefited from Calvert home schooling program.[17]

Reflecting on the aforementioned history of distance learning, the following points become clear:

1. The origin of distance teaching is multinational.
2. The goal of learning at a distance was to improve and update professional knowledge and to widen intellectual horizons.
3. The individuality of the learner and the flexibility in both time and place of study were emphasized.
4. The value of providing teacher feedback to the students was emphasized.
5. Providing the student with learning material packages before the start of the course was crucial.
6. The original target groups of distance education efforts were adults with occupational, social, and family commitments.
7. The public responded favorably to initiative from entrepreneurs as well as higher education institutions to study through correspondence.
8. The print medium and the postal services were crucial to the implementation of these alternative routes to learning.
9. Correspondence and independent studies vendors looked favorably on incorporating new methods of instruction.
10. The range of course offerings was wide, encompassing conventional subject matters taught in K–12, vocational schools, and colleges.
11. Simple initiatives have evolved into institutions and organizations for teaching at a distance.

CURRENT CORRESPONDENCE AND INDEPENDENT STUDIES

Millions of Americans are currently enrolled in correspondence and independent studies using primarily the print medium and conventional postal services. Today, two million Americans are enrolled in Distance Education and Training Council (DETC) accredited institutions.[18]

The *Distance Education and Training Council* (DETC) was established in 1926. Its purpose was "to foster and preserve high quality, educationally sound and widely accepted distance education and independent learning institutions."[19] The scope and the function of the Council is best described in the following:

DETC member institutions offer more than 500 different academic, vocational, and avocational courses by mail or by telecommunications. These courses often make use of specially written learning texts and quite often include audio-visual training devices, job enhancing materials, tools, computers, and other equipment. Course length ranges from a few weeks to over four years of study. Although most distance study institutions teach students entirely "at distance," some institutions offer courses which feature a combination of distance study and resident training. DETC institutions vary in size. Various Armed Forces distance study institutions have enrollments of more than 200,000 students, while other schools may have fewer than 200 students.[20]

Since its establishment in 1926, DETC institutions have attracted millions of Americans to their correspondence programs. At-home instruction in law degrees was offered as early as 1908, radio electronics in 1914, television electronics in 1935, robotics in 1975, and microcomputer repair in 1976. Most of these courses were conducted primarily through the print medium using regular mail for correspondence. The first use of online learning in DETC was in 1986.[21]

"Today, DETC is comprised of some 80+ distance education institutions located in 21 states and 7 countries. They include non-profit institutions, trade associations, for profit companies, colleges and universities, and military organizations."[22] The wide range of programs offered by these institutions is impressive. They include "tuition-free programs for the blind and for parents of deaf children, church-owned schools of theology, and schools teaching in Spanish and even a university in Japan that offers degrees in translation."[23] Currently, over 500 fields of study are offered, ranging from accounting to yacht design, to over two million students enrolled in DETC institutions.[24]

DEVELOPMENTAL PHASES OF DISTANCE EDUCATION

Over the years, distance teaching has undergone five distinct concepts of development: (1) correspondence and independent atudies; (2) broadcast media; (3) open university concept; (4) online education, and (5) integrated (blended) learning. These concepts are distinct in the technologies used to deliver the learning material and in communication between the instructor and the students. These concepts of distance education and the practices built on them coexist today side by side with more emphasis shifting toward the blended learning concept.

CORRESPONDENCE CONCEPT. Correspondence and independent studies mainly rely on print media and learning kits. The use of online activities in this type of distance teaching is relatively new. DETC reported that the first online learning in DETC was in 1986. Teaching in this phase was primarily one-way communication. Interaction between the instructor and the students was conducted by mail and sometimes by phone, and more recently by e-mail.

BROADCAST CONCEPT. With the advent of radio, some educators thought of radio as a means of spreading the expertise of a few scholars and excellent teachers to a larger student population. At one time radio was viewed as a panacea to many shortcomings in conventional schooling, in addition to its perceived benefits to distance education. Lack of immediate feedback between the radio instructor and the students, as well as the lack of the visual element undermined the success of radio in conventional education, as well as in distance education. However, in some developing countries, due to the availability of radio, a medium that may be heard and does not require reading skills, radio has found its way to inform and instruct the populace.

When television came on the scene, it became the new medium of choice for use in conventional education as well as in distance education. Television was then viewed as a multimedia medium. No longer does one hear only the sound of an object, but one also can see what it looks like and how it moves and reacts to its environment. The concept of the master teacher who might reach many students in different geographic areas took hold in educational practice. Still, broadcast television lacks feedback between the instructor and the students.

THE OPEN UNIVERSITY CONCEPT. This stage of distance education development marked the beginning of designing the learning experience based on solid recognition of the existing space and time separation between the instructor and students. In this phase, television viewing comprised only about 15% of a student's activities in a distance education course, while 65% of the student's time was devoted to completing various assignments. Radio was also used for some listening assignments. Special learning kits were provided to the students prior to the beginning of the course. Students have mentors to call during the course of study, and they attend summer sessions with classmates. No wonder the site of Open University at Milton Keane in England, a campus without students, became a place for worldwide educators and community leaders who are interested in distance education to visit and learn about the Open University concept and practice.

ONLINE EDUCATION CONCEPT. The Internet provides a dynamic medium to implement distance education practices. Students not only are able to access the learning material anytime of the day from almost anywhere in the world, but also they may communicate through e-mail, chat rooms, bulletin boards, and discussion forums with their instructor and other students taking the course. The speed of communication and transfer of information adds to the immediacy of interaction in this phase of distance education.

Moreover, the Internet is definitely a multimedia environment allowing a variety of information packaged in different formats to be available at the command of the student.

INTEGRATED LEARNING (BLENDED LEARNING) CONCEPT. This concept is the culmination of generations' attempts to perfect distance education. It is primarily a concept that is rooted in systems theory, which addresses all the components that could affect learning under different circumstances. It starts by assessing the needs of the learner and then designing course and learning materials using the most efficient means of communication between the instructor and the students. In this manner, it uses every available learning tool and medium to achieve the well-stated objectives of the course of study. It takes into consideration that the distance between the instructor and the students is a pedagogical distance and not a geographical distance, as Michael Moore and Greg Kearsley (1996) explain:

> When we speak of distance learning, we do not speak of an educational course that is not different from 'contiguous' courses except for the physical separation of learner and teachers. This distance is a distance of understandings and perceptions caused by the geographic distance, that have to be overcome by teachers, learners, and educational organizations if effective, deliberate, planned learning is to occur. The procedures to overcome this distance are instructional design and interaction procedures, and to emphasize that this distance is pedagogical, not geographic, we use the term 'transactional distance.'[25]

To put this concept into practice, multiple information technologies are used. These include electronic mail, chat sessions, bulletin boards, discussion groups, audio and video live interaction on the Internet, audio and video satellite and cable television teleconferencing, print media, phone, fax machines, prerecorded video (tape or DVD), CDs, audio cassettes, and, of course, face-to-face interaction when the design of the course calls for it.

DEFINITION OF DISTANCE EDUCATION

Based on the evolving concepts of distance education, many terms are used to describe distance education. Terms used include *distance education, distance teaching, distance learning, tele-learning, tele-teaching, tele-training, telecommunications-based education, outreach,* and more recently, *web-based teaching, web-based learning, web-based training,* and *blended learning.*

All of these terms attempt to describe the process of distance education. They all imply two major elements in distance education process: (1) separation in time and space between the students and the instructor, and (2) the intended outcomes of this process: learning, education, and/or training. Focusing on these two elements of the term, different authors defined *distance education* in a manner that might appear different from each other, yet they are the same. For instance, Willis Barry (1994) defined distance education as "the organizational framework and process of providing education at a distance," and distance learning as "the intended instructional outcome, i.e., learning that takes place at a distance."[26] A similar definition is given by Collis (1996). She defined tele-training as "making connection among persons and resources through communication technologies for learning-related purposes."[27]

In defining *distance education,* Moore and Kearsely (1996) emphasized the planning aspect of learning in places and at times that are more convenient for learners rather than teachers or teaching institutions:

> Distance education is planned learning that normally occurs in a different place from teaching and as a result requires special techniques of course design, special instructional techniques, special methods of communication by electronic and other technology, as well as special organizational and administrative arrangements.[28]

Duning (1993) defined *telecommunications-based education* as any educational offering, whether at a distance or not, that depends on four components of an educational telecommunications system:

- Hardware;
- Software that provides directions for operating and manipulating hardware;
- Transport, referring to electronic methods for receiving and sending programming among locations with educators and learners; and
- Professionals who lead, manage, support, and use the system and who respond to instructor's and learners' needs.[29]

All of the aforementioned definitions imply the following:

1. Distance education aims at achieving planned learning outcomes. It requires special techniques of course design and teaching.
2. A distance separates the students and the teacher.
3. The students would determine the time of receiving the instruction, unless the distance-teaching event is done in a synchronous mode where the communication between the instructor and the students is done in real time.
4. The interaction, synchronized or delayed, between the instructor and the students is mediated.
5. Communication technologies are vital to the achievement of the outcomes of distance teaching.

6. Organizational management is essential to the implementation of distance-teaching projects.

In some of the literature on distance education, the terms *distance education* and *distance learning* are used interchangeably. However, a distinction exists between the two terms since learning is the outcome of planned educational activities.

A second intricate difference is that between distance teaching and distance learning. Teaching is the process of achieving planned learning outcomes. Distance teaching, therefore, is the planned activity carried out by the instructor to help students achieve planned learning outcomes.

There is also a significant difference between training and education. Training is used to refer to learning specific skills. Education is a much broader process than training. Some of its components could aim at training in certain skills.

Distance education is, therefore, an educational system for providing instruction at the command of the students at times and places more convenient to them than being physically present in a regular classroom setting. In some delivery modes of distance education, interaction between the instructor and the students happens in real time and may possibly be face-to-face.

UNCERTAINTY AND PROFESSIONAL FRUSTRATION

While some faculty and educational administrators are enthused about the implementation of distance education, others are experiencing a sense of uncertainty and/or frustration. Becky S. Duning (1993) observed:

> The advent of telecommunications-based education and training turned many experienced educators and administrators into novices overnight. First, the rapid pace and unfamiliar vocabulary of the field produced confusion about when, why, and how to adopt new electronic technologies. Second, the basis from which to make decisions about introducing a new system was unclear. Was the decision primarily technical, managerial, or educational? A third source of frustration centered on the thorny questions inevitably raised concerning the relationship of the telecommunications system to the fundamental purposes of the parent organization. Most organizations confront such questions irregularly and seldom have a good strategy for doing so.[30]

Another reason for being uncertain about adopting distance education and/or objecting to its implementation are the inaccurate predictions that were made about other technologies. Professor Noem observed: "People scornful of those trends take solace by remembering the incorrect predictions about the educational roles of television or programmed instruction. But just because things haven't happened in the past doesn't mean that a vastly superior technology will not be effective in the future."[31] Today, the proper and creative use of the new learning and telecommunications technologies can help make distance education a success.

DISTANCE EDUCATION AND CHALLENGES FACING EDUCATION

Some educators, statesmen, community leaders, scholars, and politicians express the need to speed up the adoption of distance education especially on the college level. They advocate that the sound pedagogical implementation of distance education can help meet the challenges facing education today, among which are:

1. Achieving excellence in education.
2. Supporting evolving school curricula to help students meet the challenges of the modern age.
3. Meeting various needs, interests, and learning styles of individual students.
4. Educating students in the process of self-learning.
5. Educating students in the use of new communications and information delivery systems.
6. Changing career requirements and preparing citizens for a productive life.
7. Employing effective teaching methodologies that emphasize assessment and comprehension of information retrieved.
8. Providing citizens with ample opportunities for life-long learning not only in career-oriented education, but also in general education.
9. Providing educational equality for all members of the nation, and extending educational services to under-served population.

Points 1 to 5 in the previous list were discussed in Chapter 5, "Mediated Interaction." Following is a discussion of points 6 to 9.

Changing Career Requirements and Preparing Citizens for Productive Lives

Information is growing at an accelerated pace. New learning disciplines and new careers are emerging, while some of the current careers are being phased out. Consequently, preparation for assuming a career is changing.

A few years ago, the life cycle of an individual was equivalent to preparation for and assuming a career. Today, frequent retraining and retooling are necessary in the working lifetime of an individual. As Winston Hindle (1983) explained, "We can almost guarantee that a person we hire today will not be performing the same job in five years, or even two years in many cases. The problem is that the working lifetime of our employees is not very much greater than the development and support lifetimes of our products."[32] He further pointed out that "Right now a typical employee in industry or in business can look forward to a career that consists of cycles with alternating periods of training and productive contributions."[33]

Stan Davis (1996), the author of *The Monster Under the Bed*, emphasized the need for life-long learning. In an interview with *Educom*, he said:

> Today, half of what an engineer learns as a freshman is effectively obsolete by the time he or she graduates from college and enters the labor force. When you have that speed of change you must upgrade your education throughout your life cycle.
>
> For the first two decades of a person's life, that means upgrading the school system, but for the next four decades that means upgrading the person's education as an employee in the workplace and as a customer in the marketplace.[34]

Jack M. Wilson (1997), former dean of Continuing and Undergraduate Education at Rensselaer Polytechnic Institute, reported that "Christopher Galvin, president of Motorola, made the comment to the American Society of Engineering Education that Motorola no longer wanted to hire engineers with a 'four-year degree'. Instead they want employees with a '40-year degree.'"[35]

Peter J. Denning (1996), former associate dean for computing at George Mason University, discussed the concept of "business design" as it applies to universities. He explained business design as the ". . . overall framework in which a business is formulated-its style, approach and basic assumptions."[36] He went on to say:

> . . . the business design of the university is becoming obsolete and that public universities especially are slow to respond. Our customers (students, parents, and employers) are looking for cheap private alternatives and are complaining loudly to the political process. The politicians in our state capitals have been reacting by cutting budgets, micromanaging our time (more hours in the classroom), and abolishing tenure (post-tenure review).[37]

Professor Denning believes that university educators are faced with enormous threats not only to their traditional ways of doing business but also in some cases to their very existence. Yet, in his words, "At the same time, we are presented with enormous opportunities for significantly improved education that once again attains its aims of preparing people for productive careers and meaningful lives."[38] Distance education can help realize these aims.

Imparting Information vs. Assessing Information

In the age of information, K–college educational practice has to shift its focus from imparting and transferring knowledge to assessing information retrieved from vast resources available to the learners. There are two reasons for this. First, due to the information explosion in many disciplines, it is a major task for teachers to keep up with developments in their disciplines. This is especially true since information is becoming more and more interdisciplinary, requiring faculty to become more knowledgeable of related disciplines. Accordingly, to delegate the responsibility of transferring information to the teacher alone minimizes the effectiveness of educational practice. The need is for teams of experts who would prepare interdisciplinary and up-to-date learning materials. A course team in a distance education project can just do that.

Second, a few years back, educators advocated that one of the main functions of a teacher is to guide his or her students to locate information. Locating information is no longer a difficult task. Through electronic publications students have access to vast amounts of information stored in multimedia formats. Students, however, have to develop a discriminating ability to assess the validity of information retrieved. This also entails that teachers have to develop assessment tools to determine students' comprehension of information retrieved.

Minimizing the burden of imparting information, teachers can consult with their students to guide them in assessing their achievement. Contrary to the belief of some proponents of technology in education that technology minimizes human interactions, Eli Noam, director of the Columbia Institute for Tele-Information,[39] predicted that "We will . . . see, in successful universities, an expansion of the guidance function, more of the tutorial, hands-on, mentoring-type activities that direct human contact provides best."[40]

Lifelong Liberal Arts Education

The rapid change in career requirements and the introduction of new careers make both career education and liberal arts education a lifelong process for a productive and satisfying life.

Technology of the modern age dictates the need for highly specialized personnel. Accordingly, people might tend to be narrowly trained and lack a broad vision of life. Therefore, there is a need for educational institutions to offer lifelong learning opportunities in liberal arts education. The range of these offerings might be too broad for one institution to offer. Distance education consortia might help coordinate various school resources providing rich and varied educational material and courses to the public.

Providing Educational Equality

Help Overcome Lack of Teaching and Learning Resources in Some Schools

Every student has the right to an education that fosters maximum development of his or her talents. It is feared that the age of information technology is widening the gap between schools with adequate funds and resources and schools that lack those resources. This gap has to be diminished to establish harmony among the members of our society regardless of social and economic background. Well-designed distance education programs using media that are accessible to many students such as television, radio, and the Internet could help bring educational equality to students who suffer from inadequate teaching and learning resources in their schools.

Sometimes due to lack of enough students interested in taking a course in the Russian language, for instance, a school may find that offering such a course is not cost-effective. Two options to solve this problem are feasible. First, schools could cooperate to jointly offer courses. A two-way video connection can make offering the course cost-effective to both schools. Having a skilled teacher in one location with one group and interacting through cable with the other group is a viable solution to offering a variety of courses. Incorporating interactive instructional technology within this distance education strategy, such as e-mail, voice mail, discussion forums, and so on, could minimize the necessity for a teacher being present while the students are studying. An example of schools collaborating to provide a wide range of courses regardless of the size of classes is the Cable Classroom Project briefly discussed in Chapter 12.

The second option is to offer distance education courses online or through television by colleges and universities. For example, Hagerstown Community College offers a select number of courses that are broadcast live on cable television. Watching the class at home, students can interact with the instructor by telephone and can submit and receive assignments on the Internet.[41]

Oklahoma State University has been offering special courses, first by satellite and now online, to high school students. For example, *German Online* replaced *German by Satellite*, originally developed in 1984 by Harry Wolhert, Professor of German Language at the College of Arts and Sciences, Oklahoma State University, who started the innovative program. The idea was to offer high school students, in schools unable to hire a foreign language teacher, German language courses. The classes were broadcast live to schools participating in the project. A site coordinator was available at the remote site(s). He or she did not have to speak German. Tests could be graded by the site coordinator by providing him or her with a key to the correct answers or sending the tests to *German by Satellite* for grading.

To maintain the students' interest in the program, videotaped segments were interspersed every seven to nine minutes with authentic language material. This material included segments produced by *German by Satellite*, music videos and German-language commercials. "The video material is coordinated with language or cultural topics discussed during the lesson. Thus, the breaks not only help hold students' attention, but also reinforce the presented material."[42]

The current web-based *German Online* is a distance learning program that offers German I, German II, German III, German IV, and advanced placement (AP) German. The course information pages state the following description of the program:

- German Online is a distance learning made easy.
- German Online offers a complete sequence of courses for schools which cannot hire a foreign language teacher.
- The on-site coordinator does not have to know any German.
- The courses are completely online, with streamed video and audio, animated Flash clips and computer exercises. By filling in Info Sheets with information from the online material, students are actively involved in creating their own textbook.[43]
- In German III and IV, students apply the language skills they have acquired by working with authentic material and completing several projects.
- AP German prepares students for the National Advanced Placement Test administered by the College Board.[44]

Other universities use their information infrastructure to provide learning programming to schools in their communities. For example, the University of Massachusetts Lowell uses its UMass Lowell Instructional Network (UML INET) to provide programming to local school districts. The network uses microwave, satellite, broadband, and fiber transmission methods. The network is part of the statewide Massachusetts Information Turnpike Initiative (MITI), a high-speed fiber network connecting the five campuses of the UMass system.[45] "This network allows the campuses to collaborate and share resources via a high speed, private network. Numerous State and community colleges are also members of the MITI network."[46]

Design Strategies to Increase K–12 Students' Aspirations in Isolated and Poor Areas to Pursue College Education

Naomi Smoke, Project Coordinator of Hezel Associates addressed this issue:

Although postsecondary education is more accessible today than ever before, there are some students for whom college remains a distant dream. Isolation and a lack of resources present two challenges to students who want to pursue a college education. In rural areas, where higher education has not been the experience for most people in the community, expectations for education beyond the twelfth grade can be low. In some urban areas, even those students who do demonstrate interest in higher education may not have a support structure they can call upon for approaching and understanding colleges and universities.[47]

Smoke referred to efforts of teachers and school administrators from Massachusetts, the Adirondack region of New York, and Vermont to put in place an infrastructure that prepares K–12 students for higher education:

> Through guidance and support from the Foundation for Excellent Schools (FES),[48] a non-profit organization that helps low-income communities achieve academic excellence, education teams from these schools are identifying strategies for improving opportunities for their students. The Adirondack Excellent Schools Program (AESP), the Vermont Excellent Schools Program (VESP), and the Building Excellent Schools Together (BEST) II all aim to create strategic networks those schools can call upon to support their students' academic aspiration.[49]

Smoke explained the major task facing the schools involved in this challenging project. She said:

> The situation the participating schools face can be daunting: all are located in isolated areas characterized by higher than average poverty rates and lower than average student test score. By working with other schools in the consortia, reaching out to their local communities, and developing relationships with higher education institutions, AESP, VESP, and BEST partners are working towards a shared goal of helping their students "take one more step" in their lives.[50]

Distance education programs generated from universities targeting K–12 students could introduce K–12 students to colleges and could help inspire them to seek college education.

Provide Opportunities for Individuals Desirous of Completing Their High School Diploma Online

For adults and students who could not complete their high school education, independent studies are the most reasonable way of attaining their high school diplomas. Primarily there are two types of distance education institutions that can monitor, counsel, and assist prospective candidates to meet the requirements for attaining the high school diploma: (1) universities independent study high school programs, and (2) high school distance education providers.

1. *Universities Independent Study High School Programs.* A number of higher education institutions have commenced their online high schools. For instance, Indiana University, through its Independent Study Program (ISP), offers more than 100 high school courses, enrolling over 14,500 students from the 50 states and 25 countries in 2003.[51] The University of Nebraska-Lincoln Independent Study High School has been awarding high school diplomas for more than 40 years with an average of 200 diplomas per year.[52] In addition to providing an entire diploma sequence of courses, the Independent Study High School is an alternative to summer school programs, has low enrollment courses, and can alleviate a teacher shortage.[53]

2. *High School Distance Education Providers.* High school distance education providers, such as Keystone National High School, provide accredited distance learning programs for high school students. The school started in 1974. In the 2002–2003 school year, it served over 20,000 students.[54] In this school, students could schedule course work to suit their personal circumstances. However, they are allowed one full calendar year, starting with the day of enrolling in the course, to complete the course. A six-month extension is available for an additional fee. Students are also encouraged not to rush through course material and may not complete a course in less than eight weeks from the day of enrollment.[55]

LEVELS OF IMPLEMENTING DISTANCE EDUCATION PROJECTS

There are two distinct levels of implementing distance education: total and partial teaching through distance means. In total teaching, the majority of teaching and learning activities are done through mediated interaction. In partial distance teaching, components of a program are taught through mediated interaction.

Total-Distance Education

The British Open University

Since its establishment in 1969, the British Open University has opened the door to higher education for more than two million people.[56] The story of the Open University (OU) is very interesting. The following is a brief account of its history.

In 1962 Michael Young (now Lord Young of Dartington) proposed 'an open university' to prepare people for the external degrees of London University. His own energies, however, went into the foundation of the National

Extension College, and it was Harold Wilson (later Lord Wilson, then leader of the Opposition) who in a speech at Glasgow in 1963 launched the idea of a "University of the Air." He envisaged this as a consortium of existing universities using broadcasting and correspondence tuition to bring their teaching to adult students in their own homes.

At that time the idea attracted little interest. It was never official Labour Party policy and remained very much Mr Wilson's personal project. After he became Prime Minister in 1964 he asked his Minister for the Arts, Jennie Lee (later Baroness Lee of Ashridge), to take responsibility for it.

As the ideas developed, Jennie Lee made it clear that she wanted an autonomous, independent university equal to any other. She overcame the skepticism and even hostility of the educational establishment by 'outsnobbing the snobs,' as she put it herself: she brought together a Planning Committee which included five vice-chancellors, the principal of a polytechnic, and the leaders of two education authorities. Their recommendations won the support of Jennie Lee's colleagues in the Cabinet, and the Open University at last became government policy, and shortly afterwards, a reality. Funds were allocated, staff recruited, and a site found in the new city of Milton Keynes.

The first 24,000 students were admitted in 1971. By the mid-70s there were more than 50,000 undergraduates and a wide range of courses for them to study.[57]

More recent facts and figures shown below reflect the effectiveness of this unique institution not only in the UK but also worldwide.

- The majority of OU students are working towards a BA/BSc degree.
- The OU has 158,000 undergraduate students, 25,000 postgraduate students, and 5,000 students on access courses.
- In addition, 29,838 "study packs" were sold last year to people who wanted to study an OU course without formally enrolling.
- Almost 80% of undergraduates are in paid employment while studying.
- About one-third of first degree graduates since 1973 have held less than the minimum entry requirements for a traditional university
- The largest number of students falls into the 25–45 age range, but there are many outside that. The oldest OU graduate ever was 94, and the youngest was 17.[58]

Open University courses are designed for students studying in their homes or workplaces. "Courses use a range of teaching media—specially-produced textbooks, TV and radio programmes, audio and video tapes, computer software and home experiment kits. Personal contact and support comes through locally-based tutors, a network of 330 regional study centres in the UK and overseas and annual residential schools."[59]

The OU is a distance education success story for an institution totally designed for distance education. The National Technological University (NTU) is another distance education success story.

NTU—Sylvan Online Higher Education

NTU was established in 1984 "as the first accredited "virtual university" to serve the continuing education needs of engineers, scientists, and technical managers. NTU explains its beginning and projected development:

> With the support of major technology companies such as IBM, Motorola, and Hewlett-Packard, NTU was formed to deliver academic courses via unique satellite network directly to corporations' training facilities. In 1984, NTU began offering degree programs using courses supplied by seven universities. Today NTU offers several master's degree programs with courses supplied through a consortium of U.S. universities. Courses are delivered online and via CD-ROM, DVD and videotape.
>
> In 1999, NTU created a for-profit entity called National Technological University Corporation (NTUC), which acquired the assets of PBS The Business Channel from the Public Broadcasting Service. This substantially broadened the range of non-credit professional development courses offered. Beginning in 2000 and up through February 2002, all professional development courses were marketed through a new brand, PBS The Business & Technology Network. In November 2000, NTUC officially changed its name to Stratys Learning Solutions, although the courses continued to be marketed through the two brands, NTU and PBS The Business & Technology Network.
>
> In February 2002, Sylvan Online Higher Education assumed control of Stratys and NTU with a commitment to strengthen and expand the educational mission of National Technological University. With the financial backing of Sylvan, NTU is charting a new course of growth with a renewed determination to provide exceptional academic and professional development training to working professionals.[60]

Successful total distance education projects do not abandon face-to-face communication with the students. I believe that some of the ingredients for success of the British Open University are "residential achools." The OU gives the following as benefits of residential schools:

- Intensive tuition, opportunities to discuss ideas, and group activities.
- A period of concentrated study away from other pressures and distractions.
- The opportunity to carry out practical work, visit galleries or field sites and other special activities.[61]

Some courses offer an Alternative Learning Experience (ALE) to students who cannot attend the residential school. In the event that the student cannot attend the residential school he or she has to successfully participate in the ALE to receive course credit.[62]

Finally, common among students who succeed in total distance education institutions is their high degree of motivation. For economic, job-related, family, and residential concerns, total distance education is the route that they pursue to attain learning, which satisfies their career and/or liberal arts needs.

Total K–12 Distance Education

Total K–12 distance teaching has been growing with emphasis on completing high school. (Refer to the discussion entitled "Providing Opportunities for Individuals Desirous of Completing Their High School Diploma Online."

Partial Distance Education Strategies

In partial distance education, components of a program are taught through mediated interaction. These components range from total courses to units of a study within one course.

The major originators of special distance education courses for K–12 students are universities. Examples of these offerings were discussed earlier.

TECHNOLOGIES OF BLENDED LEARNING

Many schools are making use of advanced satellite and cable television technologies in offering distance education components and the increased capability of the web as a base for distance education. Educational technologists have been advocating a systems approach in teaching in which various technologies of communication and learning are integrated with the printed page to offer rich and interactive learning materials to the students. In this chapter, we focus on the use of television and the web in distance education.

Use of Television in Distance Education

In the early days of using television in education, the emphasis was put on telecasting lessons offered by an experienced teacher to classrooms across a wide geographical area. The underlying principle was to offer quality teaching to schools lacking the expertise of qualified teachers. When the nation realized the need to improve science and mathematics education in the late 1950s, TV was looked upon as a vehicle through which quality science instruction and in-service science education programs could be offered.

Continental Classroom was a pioneering science education program broadcast to science teachers on some commercial channels at 6:30 A.M. Facing the loss of audience of commercial programs if educational programs were telecast during prime hours, broadcast of educational TV on commercial channels tended to be early in the morning or late in the evening.

Instructional television programs were generally tailored in the same fashion as classroom instruction. To use the visual dimension of the television medium, some demonstrations and film clips were used, especially with lower grades. For college level and adult education, the pattern was what has been described as the "talking head," in which a presenter talked to the camera most of the time.

In the late 1960s, the use of television in instruction had evolved into an efficient instructional and educational tool. This major achievement has been the outcome of the following inventions and practices (see Chapter 12 for more details:

- Portable video production and playback
- Creation of a national public broadcasting system for radio and television
- Production of excellent educational TV programs
- A "new breed" of telecourse producers
- A systems approach in teaching
- Cooperative telecourse use
- Satellite educational consortia
- Abundance of TV channels

All of these innovations have contributed to making television an efficient medium of instruction. Whether it is open broadcast, video playback, or local productions, educators have found a variety of ways to strengthen and enliven their instruction.

Telecourses in Distance Education

Use of telecourses in distance education has been common in American institutions. Educational agencies, PBS, universities, or commercial institutions produce telecourses. Two options are usually used to telecast the telecourses to participating schools: (1) satellite transmission, and (2) educational television channels. Copies of some courses are recorded on cassette format available to participating schools along with printed and other course supplementary materials.

One of the main providers of telecourses is PBS Adult Learning (PBS ALS). PBS ALS licenses educational program rights to colleges, universities, and other organizations. These programs may be the basis for educational courses or for enriching current courses being offered. In addition, PBS ALS offers professional development programs and events such as a video conference focusing on educational issues. PBS ALS inventory of telecourses includes more than 100 telecourses and over 25 courses with some web-based components.[63]

According to PBS ALS, since its creation in 1981 more than five million students have earned college credit through telecourses distributed by ALS.[64] Distribution of courses is done through public television stations. Public television stations receive the telecourse through satellite transmission and rebroadcast the components of the telecourse on their channels.

ALS uses the web to distribute software for developing and administering online courses. Some of the video-based series of programs have web components.[65]

PBS provides, in addition to telecourse material, professional development programs, live satellite events, the *Going the Distance* project, and web-based courses (see Chapter 13).

Whether telecast or stored on videocassettes in the school library, there are three options for institutions to use the television segment of the telecourse. First, the television programs may be used to enrich the library resources. Students are advised to review the programs on their own. In addition, segments of the programs may be screened during class time. This option has been in use at Fairfield University with some modification. First, the Media Center purchases the right to telecast the programs on the Campus Television Network (CTN), which is a closed-circuit TV system. At the request of the faculty, programs are scheduled for broadcast prior to the time the professor meets with his or her class. The program is usually scheduled at four different time slots during the week. Students can view the program from their dormitory rooms or from the Media Department in the library. The professor might choose to queue the tape at certain segments, which he or she would screen in class for discussion. Reports from faculty using this strategy have been very positive. Starting with two classroom extension channels for classroom viewing assignments, CTN increased the number of channels to five within the span of three academic years to accommodate the increase in faculty requests for this service.

In the second option, institutions use the scheduled broadcasts on public television channels in a course primarily designed by the faculty of the institution. The telecourse material is usually used to pace the course and to provide audiovisual information prepared by experts. Usually in this option, the number of classroom meetings is reduced, sometimes by 50%. Class time is usually devoted to discussing key information in the course, assessing students' progress in the course, and introducing course topics and assignments. In this option, students get the better of two worlds.

In the third option, the telecourse is adopted in its entirety as designed and produced by the course originator. Students are usually asked to attend the course opening session and take a mid-term and final exam on campus. At one time, this model was known as the 30/30 model (i.e. 30 programs,

30-minutes each). When students need help, they are given a phone number to call. This model has been popular in community college education.

Web-Based Distance Education

The World Wide Web has unique characteristics that make it a magnificent medium for communication and teaching. Through the web, course authors and designers can plan, produce, and mount interactive, multimedia, and up-to-date courses accessible by any student enrolled in the course from anywhere at anytime. Since the course uses the Internet environment, it has the potential of using the unique and powerful features of the Internet, including searching tremendous information resources, communicating with others regardless of the distance or the individual culture, and exploring new avenues of information depending on one's interest and mastery level of the information sought and the interest in the topic of study. (For more details, see Chapters 9, 10, and 11.)

The process of producing web courses has been facilitated with the introduction of powerful and easy to learn course authoring systems. These new developments have encouraged more educators to consider the web for mounting distance education material. *WEB CT*[66] and *Blackboard*[67] are widely used software for posting courses online.

Some institutions might be interested in mounting web pages to support conventional teaching. In addition to web course software, other simpler software might be used. For instance, recent word processing software allows the user to save a document in an HTML format for publishing on the web. PowerPoint 2002 in the MSOffice XP suite also enables the user to save a PowerPoint presentation as an HTML file. Relatively more advanced software such as FrontPage 2002 is easy to learn. On the more professional side, is the easy-to-use web course development software referred to earlier, *WEB CT* and *Blackboard.*

Simple and more advanced web publishing software has already empowered many teachers to experiment with posting courses or components of a course on the web. As we experiment with web publishing for achieving some aspects of distance education, we will develop new insights in teaching at a distance and discover creative methods of teaching and learning.

LIVE AUDIO-VIDEO DISTANCE EDUCATION TECHNOLOGY

Two-Way Video and Audio Transmission Technologies

Technologies that are available for use with distance education projects have been discussed in the body of this book. They include open television channels, cable television, satellite TV, closed-circuit TV systems, printed material, the web, desktop videoconferencing, radio, recorded audio and video tapes, CD-ROM, and, of course, the printed page. The choice of a medium within a distance education application is determined by instructional design principles (see Chapters 3, 4, and 5). In this section, we briefly discuss audio-video distance education technology.

Sometimes a distance education project calls for interactive group sessions. A "tele-classroom" is an especially designed room that is prepared for group interactive communication with other sites participating in the distance education project. Figure 14.1 shows a typical distance teaching classroom designed as either an origination or a remote site in a two-way audio and video telecommunication. In addition to the instructor(s) and student microphones, three cameras are positioned in strategic positions in the room. A rack of equipment that includes video and audio playback equipment allows incorporating audio and/or video segments in the session. All of the outputs from the cameras, playback equipment, and a computer are fed to a control console (see Figure 14.2). The teacher manipulates the console. He or she decides which signal should be fed to the remote site. This signal is usually called the line-out signal.

Two television monitors are mounted side-by-side in front of the room. One monitor displays the other site, and the second displays the line-out signal. Thus, students at both sites may see and hear the instructor as well as each other.

Transmission between the sites may be done by cable or by satellite transmission. In many cable television franchise areas, the cable company assigns two educational access channels. Each site transmits on one of these two channels, and the dual television monitors in both sites display these two channels.

To reach a large number of sites, a two-way audio and one-way video system is used. The remote sites receive the television signal (video and audio). Individuals at the remote sites can communicate with the originating site by phone. This system is commonly used in national or regional video teleconferencing.

The web may also be used for live audio-video activities. Specific software is usually needed on both the instructor's and the students' workstations. Also, all of the workstations should have web cameras and microphones. At present the number of students receiving live audio-video interactive tutoring is limited (between 15 and 20 students).

PicturTel is another technology that may be used for synchronized audio-video distance education sessions. PicturTel is a telephone line–based video-conferencing system that is very suitable for conferencing with small groups. A basic self-contained PicturTel unit contains a video camera mounted on top of a large television set. The camera is controlled by a keypad, which allows for panning, tilting, zooming-in, and zooming-out. Another graphic camera can be mounted on a copy stand for sharing graph-

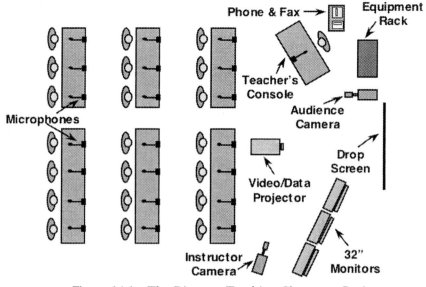

Figure 14.1 The Distance Teaching Classroom Design

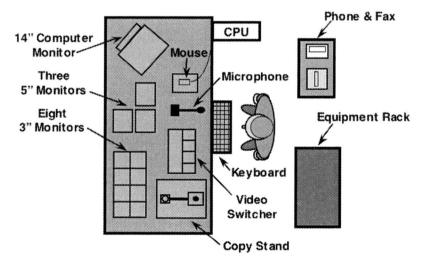

Figure 14.2 The Teacher's Console in Distance Teaching Classroom

ics with the other site. The system also incorporates necessary audio components including a conference microphone and loudspeakers.

Both conferencing sites must have identical units. The system uses an ISDN* phone line for transmission and reception. The video in this system is compressed video. The system is easy to use and does not require pre-arrangement with a video carrier such as a cable television company or a

---

*Integrated Services Digital Network (ISDN) supports the transmission of a wide range of services including audio and video signals.

satellite uplink facility. In addition, it is a closed system; it is practically like a conference phone conversation between two parties (for more information, see Chapter 5.)

SUMMARY

Distance education is an old teaching strategy that has recently gained new momentum and new perspective due to the development of information and telecommunications interactive technologies and the necessity to provide a learning environment conducive to lifelong learning.

Distance education is an educational system for providing instruction at the command of the students at times and places more convenient to them than being physically present in a regular classroom setting. In some delivery modes of distance education, interaction between the instructor and the students takes place in real time.

Pioneering educators, statesmen, community leaders, scholars, and politicians express the need to speed up the adoption of distance education, especially on the college level. They advocate that the sound pedagogical implementation of distance education can help meet the challenges facing education today, with emphasis on lifelong education.

There are two distinct levels of implementing distance education: total and partial teaching. In total teaching, most teaching and learning activities are done through mediated interaction. In partial teaching, components of a course, taught through mediated interaction, are integrated with face-to-face interaction as well as teaching and learning activities.

Distance education projects are originated and/or sponsored by universities, public sectors interested in improving education especially on the K–12 level, and commercial enterprises.

Television as a medium of distance education has been in use since its early days of telecast. Various developments contributed to changing the concept of using television in instruction from "talking head" to well-designed television programming.

Web-based teaching is gaining momentum as the software for developing courseware and publishing on the web is becoming easier and easier.

In selecting the medium or media for distance education, a systems approach is employed. In this system, the selection of the medium is done according to principles of instructional design.

REFERENCES

1. Holmberg, Borje. *Growth and Structure of Distance Education.* London: Croom Helm, 1986, p. 6.

2. Mood, Terry Ann. *Distance Education, An Annotated Bibliography.* Englewood, CO: Libraries Unlimited, 1995, p. 1.

3. Holmberg. *op. cit.* p. 6.

4. *Ibid.* p. 7.

5. *Ibid.* p. 7.

6. *Ibid.* p. 7.

7. Mood. *op. cit.* p. 1.

8. Watkins, Barbara L. A Quite Radical Idea: The Invention and Elaboration of Collegiate Correspondence Study, in Watkins, Barbara L. and Stephen J. Wright (Eds.). *The Foundation of American Distance Education: A Century of Collegiate Correspondence Study,* Dubuque, Iowa: Kendall/Hunt, National University Continuing Education, 1991, p. 3.

9. Holmberg, *op. cit* p. 8.

10. Moore, Michael G., and Greg Kearsley. *Distance Education—A System View.* New York: Wadsworth, 1996, p. 20.

11. Mood. *op. cit.* p. 2.

12. Moore and Kearsely. *op. cit.* p. 20.

13. *Ibid.* pp. 20–21.

14. *ICS, International Correspondence Schools,* http://www.ohwy.com/pa/h/hx249928.htm, accessed 8/12/03.

15. Holmberg. *op. cit.* p. 8.

16. Watkins. *op cit.* pp. 4–5.

17. *Calvert's History,* http://home.calvertschool.org/hs/welcome/history.html, accessed 8/12/03.

18. Distance Education and Training Council, DETC. The Association, DETC History, http://www.detc.org/theassociation.html, updated 8/18/03, accessed 8/12/03.

19. *Ibid.*

20. *Ibid.*

21. *Ibid.*

22. *Ibid.*

23. *Ibid.*

24. *Ibid.*

25. Moore and Kearsley. *op. cit.* p. 200.

26. Willis, Barry (Ed.). *Distance Education Strategies and Tools.* Englewood Cliffs, NJ: Educational Technology Publications, 1994, p. v.

27. Collis, Betty. *Tele-learning in a Digital World, The Future of Distance Learning.* London: International Thomson Computer Press, 1996, p. 9.

28. Moore and Kearsley. *op. cit.* p. 2.

29. Duning, Becky S., Marvin J. Van Kekerix, and Leon M. Zaorowski. *Reaching Learners Through Telecommunications, Management and Leadership Strategies for Higher Education.*San Francisco, CA: Jossey-Bass, 1993, p. 2.

30. *Ibid.* pp. 1–2.

31. Educom Staff. Eli Noam on the Future of the University. *Educom Review,* : vol. 31, no. 4, http://educom.edu/web/pubs/review/Articles/31438.html, release date: July/August 1996, accessed 6/10/98.

32. Hindle, Jr. Winston R. Educational Technology, Industrial Training, and Lifelong Learning, in *Using Technology For Education And Training.* Silver Spring, MD: Information Dynamics, 1983 pp. 9–10.

33. *Ibid.* p. 10.

34. Educom Staff. *Slicing the Learning Pie, Educom Review,* vol. 31, no. 5, http://educom.edu/web/pubs/review/review/Articles/31532.html/, release date: September/October 1996, accessed 6/10/98.

35. Wilson, Jack M., Distance Learning for Continuous Education. *Educom Review,* vol. 32, no. 2, http://educom.edu/web/pubs/review/review/Articles/32212.html/, release date: March/April 1997, accessed 6/12/98.

36. Denning, Peter J. *Business Designs for the New University. Educom Review,* vol. 31, no. 6, http://educom.edu/web/pubs/review/review/Articles/31620.html/, release date: November/December 1996, p. 1, accessed 6/20/98.

37. *Ibid.* p. 1.

38. *Ibid.* p. 2.

39. *Columbia Institute for Tele-Information,* http://www.citi.columbia.edu/, accessed 8/20/03.

40. Educom Staff. Eli Noam on the Future of the University. op. cit. p. 2.

41. Hagerstown Community College, *Distance Education Format,* http://www.hcc.cc.md.us/academics/distance/coursetypes.php, 8/18/03.

42. *German by Satellite,* Oklahoma State University, http://gbs.okstate.edu/courses/faq.html/, accessed 7/12/98.

43. *German I Online,* Outline 1, http://germanonline.okstate.edu/test_lesson.html, accessed 8/18/03.

44. *German Online, Course Information,* http://germanonline.okstate.edu/courses/courses.html, accessed 8/18/03.

45. University of Massachusetts–Lowell, Graduate School of Education. *The Instructional Network,* http://gse.uml.edu/INET/Index.htm, accessed 8/18/03.

46. *Ibid.*

47. Smoke, Naomi. How Some Schools Are Making a Post-Secondary Education Accessible to Their Students, News & Ideas for Learning Technology Strategies, Hezel Associates, http://www.hezel.com/spring_2003/going.asp, downloaded 8/25/2003.

48. *Foundation for Excellent Schools,* http://www.fesnet.org, downloaded 8/25/03.

49. *Ibid.*

50. *Ibid.*

51. *School of Continuing Studies High School, Indiana University,* http://scs.indiana.edu/hs/hs.html.

52. *Nebraska's High school, University of Nebraska–Lincoln,* http://dcs.unl.edu/ishs/students/diploma.html, accessed 8/24/03.

53. *Nebraska's High school, University of Nebraska–Lincoln,* http://dcs.unl.edu/ishs/schools_orgs/index.html, accessed 8/24/03.

54. *Keystone National High School,* http://kestonehisghschool.com/, accessed 8/25/03.

55. *Keystone National High School,* http://kestonehisghschool.com/html/policy_completion.php/, accessed 8/25/03.

56. *The Open University, Facts Sheets, Background Information,* http://www.open.ac.uk/media/factsheets/index.asp/, accessed 8/20/03.

57. *The Open University, Facts and Figures,* http://www.open.ac.uk/ou/Intro/factsAndFigures.html/, downloaded June 1998.

58. *The Open University, Facts Sheets, Background Information, op. cit.*

59. *Ibid.*
60. *NTU, About US,* http://www.ntu.edu/home/aboutus.asp#CO, accessed 8/25/03.
61. *The Open University Residential Schools, FAQ,* http://css4.open.ac.uk/residential-schools/general/faq.shtm, accessed 8/25/03.
62. *Ibid.* p. 2.
63. *PBS Adult Learning Service, The Provider for Educational Providers,* http://www.pbs.org/als/about_als/index.html, accessed 9/13/03.
64. *Ibid.*
65. *Ibid.*
66. *Web CT,* http://www.webct.com/, accessed 8/20/03.
67. *Blackboard,* http://company.blackboard.com/index.cgi, accessed 8/20/03.

SECTION IV

EFFECTIVE UTILIZATION OF THE NEW LEARNING AND TELECOMMUNICATIONS TECHNOLOGIES

Chapter 15: Empowering Teachers to Use the New Learning and Telecommunications Technologies in Their Teaching

---

INTRODUCTION

An essential element of the design of effective learning environments is ensuring the learner's interaction with models of excellence, both in human resources and in learning materials. Very often, access to models of excellence can be achieved through mediated interaction. The technology of the information age provides students and teachers with the tools and vehicles through which models of excellence can be accessed. Availability of these tools is one side of the coin; effective utilization is the second.

Chapter 15, "Empowering Teachers to Use the New Learning and Telecommunications Technologies in Their Teaching," focuses on conditions leading to the empowerment of the teachers to teach and the students to learn in the information age. It reviews major recommendations made by learning societies and organization regarding standards of technology-literate teachers and students. It also focuses on standards for the preparation of school media specialists and their emerging role as staff developers.

Chapter 15

EMPOWERING TEACHERS TO USE THE NEW LEARNING AND TELECOMMUNICATIONS TECHNOLOGIES IN THEIR TEACHING

INTRODUCTION

An essential element in the design of effective learning environments is ensuring the learner's interactivity with models of excellence, both in human resources and in learning materials. Very often, access to models of excellence can be achieved through mediated interaction. The technology of the information age provides students and teachers with the tools and vehicles through which models of excellence can be accessed. Availability of these tools is one side of the coin. Effective utilization is the second.

To implement effective utilization:

1. School curricula must be examined and restructured in light of the goals of education with special attention to what the new learning and communications technologies can offer.
2. Teachers have to be educated in the use of the new learning and telecommunications technologies and their potential applications in education.
3. There is a need to foster the new role of the school media librarian in the information age. This new role is fivefold: information specialist, teacher, instructional consultant, administrator, and staff developer.
4. There is a need to implement a partnership among schools, parents, and the community at large to provide for quality education for our nation's students.

Revision of school curricula is beyond the scope of this publication. This chapter focuses on the last three prerequisites for the effective utilization of the new learning and telecommunications technologies in education.

EDUCATING TEACHERS IN THE USE OF INFORMATION TECHNOLOGIES

The new telecommunications and instructional technologies provide educators with the tools through which they can achieve quality education for all students of our country. However, the prerequisite to reaping the benefits of these tools is the competency of teachers in using them in their teaching.

Recommendations of Legislators and Learning Communities

Getting America's Students Ready for the Twenty-First Century

Getting America's Students Ready for the 21st Century—Meeting the Technology Literacy Challenge outlined the vision of the future based on President Clinton's educational initiative challenge.[1] The report stated that in acknowledging the challenges facing education, President Clinton and Vice President Gore announced on February 15, 1996, "The Technology Literacy Challenge, envisioning a 21st century where all students are technologically literate. The challenge was placed before the nation as a whole, with responsibility for its accomplishment shared by local communities, states, the private sector, educators, parents, the federal government, and others."

The report went on to outline four concrete goals of that vision:

- All teachers in the nation will have the training and support they need to help students learn using computers and the information superhighway.
  Upgrading teacher training is key to integrating technology into the classroom and to increasing student learning.
- All teachers and students will have modern multimedia computers in their classrooms.
  Computers become effective instructional tools only if they are readily accessible to students and teachers.
- Every classroom will be connected to the information superhighway.
  Connections to networks, especially the Internet, multiply the power and usefulness of computers as learning tools by putting the best libraries, museums, and other research and cultural resources at our students' and teachers' fingertips.
- Effective software and online learning resources will be an integral part of every school's curriculum.
  Software and online learning resources can increase students' learning opportunities, but they must be high quality, engaging, and directly related to the school's curriculum.[2]

NCATE Standards for Technology Literate Teachers

On the teacher accreditation front, The National Council for Accreditation of Teacher Education (NCATE) has developed a report:

Technology and the New Professional Teacher: Preparing for the 21st Century Classroom. The report is the

> . . . culmination of a year of deliberations by an NCATE Task Force on Technology and Teacher Education. The report makes recommendations about the integration of technology into teacher preparation programs, which if implemented by NCATE, will undoubtedly foster change at accredited schools of education.[3]

The Task Force's report addressed three goals:

1. NCATE's leadership role in stimulating more effective use of technology in teacher education programs.
2. Using technology to improve the existing accreditation process and to reconceptualize accreditation for the 21st century.
3. Improving NCATE's internal operations through greater and more effective uses of technology.[4]

The first set of recommendations for stimulating effective use of technology in teacher education are:

1. NCATE should require schools, colleges, and departments of education to have a vision and plan for technology that reinforces their conceptual model for teacher education.
2. NCATE, working with other professional organizations such as the American Association of Colleges for Teacher Education (AACTE), should encourage each school, college, and department of education to establish and explore the use of modern communications technology in carrying out its various functions and responsibilities.
3. NCATE, working with other professional organizations such as AACTE, should identify and make available to all interested institutions exemplary practices of technology use in the preparation of teachers for the 21st century.[5]

On March 21, 2000, the NCATE Unit Accreditation Board adopted "Unit Standards." The Standards were ratified by the NCATE Executive Board on May 11, 2000, and are required for all visits by NCATE to accredit a teacher education institution, starting from the fall of 2001.

The conceptual framework "establishes the shared vision for a unit's efforts in preparing educators to work effectively in P–12 schools. It provides direction for programs, courses, teaching, candidate performance, scholarship, service, and unit accountability."

Six indicators for conceptual framework are:

1. Shared vision.
2. Coherence.
3. Professional commitments and dispositions.
4. Commitment to diversity.
5. Commitment to technology.

6. Candidate proficiencies aligned with professional and state standards.

The fifth indicator, "commitment to technology," reflects "the unit's commitment to preparing candidates who are able to use educational technology to help all students learn; it also provides a conceptual understanding of how knowledge, skills, and dispositions related to educational and information technology are integrated throughout the curriculum, instruction, field experiences, clinical practice, assessments, and evaluations." Technology was defined by NCATE as[6]

> What candidates must know and understand about information technology in order to use it in working effectively with students and professional colleagues in the

1. Delivery, development, prescription, and assessment of instruction.
2. Problem solving.
3. School and classroom administration.
4. Educational research.
5. Electronic information access and exchange.
6. Personal and professional productivity.*

While these competencies are required from all teachers, they are also of significant importance for the School Media Specialist. Since they outline the technology standards, which teachers have to develop to become effective teachers, they offer the School Media Specialist a framework for staff development in technology for his or her colleagues.

ISTE Standards for Technology-Literate Teachers

In 1997, the International Society for Technology in Education (ISTE) recommended, "All candidates seeking initial certification or endorsements in teacher preparation programs should have opportunities to meet the educational technology foundation standards." Three basic categories of standards are recommended:

1. **Basic Computer/Technology Operations and Concepts.** Candidates will use computer systems to run software; to access, generate and manipulate data; and to publish results. They will also evaluate performance of hardware and software components of computer systems and apply basic troubleshooting strategies as needed.
2. **Personal and Professional Use of Technology.** Candidates will apply tools for enhancing their own professional growth and productivity. They will use technology in communicating, collaborating, conducting research,

---

*NCATE, *Glossary of NCATE Terms*, http://www.ncate.org/search/glossary.htm, accessed 3/5/04.

and solving problems. In addition, they will plan and participate in activities that encourage lifelong learning and will promote equitable, ethical and legal use of computer/technology resources.

3. **Application of Technology in Instruction.** Candidates will apply computers and related technologies to support instruction in their grade level and subject areas. They must plan and deliver instructional units that integrate a variety of software, applications, and learning tools. Lessons developed must reflect effective grouping and assessment strategies for diverse populations.[7]

In a more recent study, ISTE developed the *ISTE National Educational Technology Standards (NETS) and Performance Indicators*.[8] These standards, the educational technology foundations for all teachers, include six categories:

I. **TECHNOLOGY OPERATIONS AND CONCEPTS.**
Teachers demonstrate a sound understanding of technology operations and concepts.
Teachers:
A. demonstrate introductory knowledge, skills, and understanding of concepts related to technology (as described in the ISTE *National Education Technology Standards for Students*).[9]
B. demonstrate continual growth in technology knowledge and skills to stay abreast of current and emerging technologies.

II. **PLANNING AND DESIGNING LEARNING ENVIRONMENTS AND EXPERIENCES.**
Teachers plan and design effective learning environments and experiences supported by technology. Teachers:
A. design developmentally appropriate learning opportunities that apply technology-enhanced instructional strategies to support the diverse needs of learners.
B. apply current research on teaching and learning with technology when planning learning environments and experiences.
C. identify and locate technology resources and evaluate them for accuracy and suitability.
D. plan for the management of technology resources within the context of learning activities.
E. plan strategies to manage student learning in a technology-enhanced environment.

III. **TEACHING, LEARNING, AND THE CURRICULUM.**
Teachers implement curriculum plans that include methods and strategies for applying technology to maximize student learning.
Teachers:
A. facilitate technology-enhanced experiences that address content standards and student technology standards.
B. use technology to support learner-centered strategies that address the diverse needs of students.
C. apply technology to develop students' higher order skills and creativity.

    D. manage student learning activities in a technology-enhanced environment.

IV. ASSESSMENT AND EVALUATION.
Teachers apply technology to facilitate a variety of effective assessment and evaluation strategies. Teachers:
    A. apply technology in assessing student learning of subject matter using a variety of assessment techniques.
    B. use technology resources to collect and analyze data, interpret results, and communicate findings to improve instructional practice and maximize student learning.
    C. apply multiple methods of evaluation to determine students' appropriate use of technology resources for learning, communication, and productivity.

V. PRODUCTIVITY AND PROFESSIONAL PRACTICE.
Teachers use technology to enhance their productivity and professional practice.
    Teachers:
    A. use technology resources to engage in ongoing professional development and lifelong learning.
    B. continually evaluate and reflect on professional practice to make informed decisions regarding the use of technology in support of student learning.
    C. apply technology to increase productivity.
    D. use technology to communicate and collaborate with peers, parents, and the larger community in order to nurture student learning.

VI. SOCIAL, ETHICAL, LEGAL, AND HUMAN ISSUES.
Teachers understand the social, ethical, legal, and human issues surrounding the use of technology in Pre-K–12 schools and apply those principles in practice.
    Teachers:
    A. model and teach legal and ethical practice related to technology use.
    B. apply technology resources to enable and empower learners with diverse backgrounds, characteristics, and abilities.
    C. identify and use technology resources that affirm diversity
    D. promote safe and healthy use of technology resources.
    E. facilitate equitable access to technology resources for all students

Since today's teacher preparation programs provide a variety of alternative paths to initial licensure, ISTE developed four sets of performance profiles for technology-literate teachers according to four phases, or paths, of their professional development. According to ISTE:

The Technology Performance Profiles for Teacher Preparation suggest ways programs can incrementally examine how well candidates meet the standards. The

Profiles correspond to four phases in the typical preparation of a teacher. The Profiles are not meant to be prescriptive or lockstep; they are specifically designed to be fluid in providing guidelines for programs to create a set of benchmarks in planning and assessment that align with unique program design.[10]

The four phases are: (1) general preparation performance profile, (2) professional preparation performance profile, prior to the culminating student teaching or internship experience, (3) student teaching/internship performance profile, and (4) first-year teaching performance profile. For teacher preparation programs as well as school media specialist programs, it is crucial to examine carefully these sets, and to focus more specifically on the professional preparation and student teaching performance profiles. Prior to the endorsement for teaching and school media certificates, prospective teachers and school media specialists should achieve a satisfactory level of proficiency in the areas indicated by ISTE.

ISTE Technology Foundation Standards for All Students

In addition to Technology Foundation Standards for All Teachers, ISTE also developed Technology Foundation Standards for All Students. These standards are divided into six broad categories:

1. Basic operations and concepts
   - Students demonstrate a sound understanding of the nature and operation of technology systems.
   - Students are proficient in the use of technology.
2. Social, ethical, and human issues
   - Students understand the ethical, cultural, and societal issues related to technology.
   - Students practice responsible use of technology systems, information, and software.
   - Students develop positive attitudes toward technology uses that support lifelong learning, collaboration, personal pursuits, and productivity.
3. Technology productivity tools
   - Students use technology tools to enhance learning, increase productivity, and promote creativity.
   - Students use productivity tools to collaborate in constructing technology-enhanced models, prepare publications, and produce other creative works.
4. Technology communications tools
   - Students use telecommunications to collaborate, publish, and interact with peers, experts, and other audiences.
   - Students use a variety of media and formats to communicate information and ideas effectively to multiple audiences.
5. Technology research tools

- Students use technology to locate, evaluate, and collect information from a variety of sources.
- Students use technology tools to process data and report results.
- Students evaluate and select new information resources and technological innovations based on the appropriateness for specific tasks.
6. Technology problem-solving and decision-making tools
    - Students use technology resources for solving problems and making informed decisions.
    - Students employ technology in the development of strategies for solving problems in the real world.

According to ISTE,

Standards within each category are to be introduced, reinforced, and mastered by students. These categories provide a framework for linking performance indicators within the Profiles for Technology Literate Students to the standards. Teachers can use these standards and profiles as guidelines for planning technology-based activities in which students achieve success in learning, communication, and life skills.[11]

ISTE Profiles for Technology Literate Students provide performance indicators describing the technology competence students should exhibit upon completion of grades pre-K–12.[12] These standards are available online, as well as in a recent publication of the ISTE in collaboration with the U.S. Department of Education (*National Educational Technology Standards for Students, Connecting Curriculum and Technology, ISTE, 2000*). The online reference and the book reference are both helpful to students seeking teaching or school media specialist certification.

Web-Based Education Commmission—Call-to-Action To Harness Internet's Power for Learning (12/19/2000)

The Web-Based Education Commission was established by the Higher Education Act Amendments of 1998. President Clinton, Education Secretary Richard Riley, and the Democratic and Republican leadership of Congress appointed its 16 members.

The Web-Based Education Commission investigated the full range of issues and ideas related to the Internet and education. Testimonies and dialogue with experts from education, high-tech and publishing communities, thousands of people—teachers, principals and administrators, private-sector experts, government representatives, researchers, college professors, parents, and others from urban areas, rural areas, and all areas in between formed the basis of the Commission's report.[13]

The report observed:

For education, the Internet is making it possible for more individuals than ever to access knowledge and to learn in new and different ways. At the dawn of the 21st Century, the education landscape is changing. Elementary and secondary schools are experiencing growing enrollments, coping with critical shortages of teachers, facing overcrowded and decaying buildings, and responding to demands for higher standards. On college campuses, there is an influx of older, part-time students seeking the skills vital to success in an Information Age. Corporations are dealing with the shortage of skilled workers and the necessity of providing continuous training to their employees.

The Internet is enabling us to address these educational challenges, bringing learning to students instead of bringing students to learning. It is allowing for the creation of learning communities that defy the constraints of time and distance as it provides access to knowledge that was once difficult to obtain. This is true in the schoolhouse, on the college campus, and in corporate training rooms.[14]

The report outlined the promise of the Internet in three concise points:

- To center learning around the student instead of the classroom.
- To focus on the strengths and needs of individual learners.
- To make lifelong learning a practical reality.

The report said:

We heard that the Internet enables education to occur in places where there is none, extends resources where there are few, expands the learning day, and opens the learning place. We experienced how it connects people, communities, and resources to support learning. We witnessed how it adds graphics, sound, video, and interaction to give teachers and students multiple paths for understanding. We learned that the Web is a medium today's kids expect to use for expression and communication.[15]

Based on the evidence presented by hundreds of people, the Commission issued a seven-point call-to-action to government, industry, and the education community:

1. Make powerful new Internet resources, especially broadband access, widely and equitably available and affordable for all learners (broadband networks, which have the capacity to carry huge amounts of data many times faster than traditional telephone lines, enable the use of full motion video and audio in education programs and real-time interaction over the Internet).
2. Provide continuous and relevant training and support for educators and administrators at all levels.
3. Build a new research and development framework around learning in the Internet age.
4. Develop quality online educational content that meets the highest standards of educational excellence;

5. Revise outdated regulations that impede innovation and replace them with approaches that embrace anytime, anywhere, any pace learning.
6. Protect online learners and ensure their privacy.
7. Sustain funding-via traditional and new sources that are adequate to the challenge at hand.[16]

The Web-based Education Commission called on the Congress and the Administration

> . . . to embrace an "e-learning" agenda as a centerpiece of our nation's federal education policy. . . . This e-learning agenda should be aimed at assisting local communities, state education agencies, institutions of higher education, and the private sector in their efforts.
>
> We urge the new President and the 107th Congress to seize this opportunity and to focus on ways in which public law can be modified and changed to support, rather than undermine, the technology that is so dramatically changing education.[17]

CEO Forum on Education and Technology

The CEO Forum on Education & Technology was founded in 1996 as a five-year partnership between business and education leaders "to help ensure that America's schools effectively prepare all students to be contributing citizens and productive workers in the 21st Century. To meet this objective, the Forum issued an annual assessment of the nation's progress toward integrating technology into American classrooms."[18] The Forum project closed its doors in December 2001.

Its organizing principles were:

- All students must graduate with the technology skills needed in today's world and tomorrow 's workplace.
- All educators must be equipped to use technology as a tool to achieve high academic standards.
- All parents and community members must stay informed of key education technology decisions confronting policy-makers, administrators and educators.
- All students must have equitable access to technology.
- The nation must invest in education technology research and development.[19]

In the first year (1997), the CEO Forum issued a report, *From Pillars to Progress*, focused on the importance of integrating hardware and connectivity to professional development and content.[20] It also introduced StaR, School Technology and Readiness Chart for School, Colleges and Departments of Education. StaR was "a self-assessment tool for schools to gauge progress toward integrating technology to improve education." The

STaR assessment "offers a benchmark measure of national progress toward integrating technology in schools."[21]

The second year's report, *Development: A Link to Better Learning* (February 1999) focused on educator professional development. It outlined 10 principles for effective professional development and presented an update of StaR Chart and StaR Assessment.[22]

In June 2000, the third year, the Forum published *The Power of Digital Learning: Integrating Digital Content*. The report defined a vision for digital learning:

> There is consensus among business leaders, educators, policymakers and parents that our current traditional practices are not delivering the skills our students will need to thrive in the 21st century. As part of our efforts at school reform, we should apply technology's resources to develop the full academic abilities of all our students. The CEO Forum believes that only through the integrated approach of digital learning will our nation's schools, each operating under distinctive circumstances, opportunities and constraints, fully utilize technology in all its forms to promote student achievement and develop the essential skills.
>
> We must make the necessary adjustments and shifts to ensure that our schools become digital learning environments. Adopting this integrated approach addresses the problems facing schools and can improve student performance.[23]

Addressing the issues that schools face in adopting technology in their teaching, the report went on to indicate that digital learning is critical for preparing the students with the necessary technology and critical thinking skills:

> We recognize that our efforts to promote digital learning exist in an educational climate in which school systems and teachers are by necessity focusing on accountability structures. For both school systems and teachers this complicates the ability to implement digital learning. However, digital learning is critical if we are dedicated to preparing students with the necessary technology and critical thinking skills. We must extend accountability to the digital environment and link digital content and learning processes to student performance standards.[24]

In the spring of 2001, the CEO Forum released its final report, *Key Building Blocks for Student Achievement in the 21st Century*,[25] focusing on educational outcomes and assessments.

Comments on the Studies and Recommendations

Initial Technology Competencies for Teachers

The aforementioned reports advocated the need to develop teachers' fluency in technology. Starting with a strong background in the subject matter, skilled teachers in technology can examine the applications of technology in their teaching. There is a need, however, *to determine initial technology competencies for teachers and to develop a sequential professional development program in the infusion of technology in education.*

Teachers' Knowledge of the Basics of Instructional Design

The CEO Forum reports also advocated the need to infuse technology in teacher preparation programs. However, emphasis was put on the use of computers and the Internet in instruction. Instructional technology involves more than the use of computers. Instructional technology is firmly grounded in educational technology. Educational technology is a technology of the mind, which integrates new and conventional technologies of instruction to achieve stated educational objectives. This integration requires systemic planning based on our knowledge of human learning. It examines communications and information technologies to determine the most appropriate for the achievement of the desired objective in a cost-effective manner. The choice of technology of instruction is determined not only by economic considerations but also by the unique characteristics of each technology, the purpose of using it, with whom it is used, and under what circumstances. Accordingly, for the teachers to be effective in designing educational technology learning environment, they have to be skilled in the instructional design basics.

Teachers' Critical Awareness of Mass Media

In addition to the knowledge of instructional design and skills associated with information technologies, it is important to pay attention to off-school factors that affect the students' learning and understanding of life. Television has been called the "*second school.*" On average, children from ages 3 to 18 spend more time in front of the TV than they spend in regular schooling. Simply, we cannot neglect that time or the potential effects that mass media have on our children and youths. Schools have to target developing children's critical awareness of mass media. This skill cannot be achieved unless the teachers themselves are competent in designing strategies to cultivate children's critical awareness of mass media.

The School Media Librarian

To stay abreast of developments in technologies of instruction, teachers need the professional assistance of the school media librarian. Since the first school library was established, there have been continued efforts to provide teachers and students with the resources necessary for well-rounded and meaningful teaching and learning experiences. Today, it is an accepted fact that the school library media center is an instructional center of the school and that the role of the school library media specialist is that of an information specialist, a teacher, an instructional consultant, an administrator, an information specialist, and a staff developer. It is essential for teachers to understand the new role of the school library and what the school media specialist can offer to the design and implementation of rich interactive learning resources. In addition, teachers should be competent in integrating the different library resources in their teaching.

Infusion of Technology in Teacher Preparation

Teacher-preparation institutions should support creative initiatives by faculty members who strive to integrate the tools and the products of the information age in teaching preservice and inservice teachers. Experiencing the use of technology in their training enhances prospective teachers' understanding of effective instructional design that employs the tools of the information age. This means the infusion of technology in the curricula of teacher preparation.

Necessary Conditions for Preparing Technology-Literate Teachers

To cultivate a competent K–12 teacher in the use of information technologies in teaching and to meet the standards outlined by learned communities necessitates the following:

College Professors Competent in the Use of Information Technology in Teaching

There is a tendency among teachers to use the methods of teaching through which they were taught. If teachers do not experience the effective use of information technology in their college and postcollege education, they tend to practice traditional methods of teaching in their schools. For education to prepare technology literate teachers, information technologies have to be embedded in all of the course offerings in a teacher-preparation program. This means that the faculty of colleges of education have to become competent in the use of information technology in teaching their courses.

Staff development programs in colleges of education should address this issue. A professional development program for the faculty could start with informing them about the new learning and telecommunications technologies and their potential applications in education. Providing the faculty with opportunities to examine a variety of software, media programs, and applications of the new technologies in teaching helps them in developing new insights in designing their courses and teaching plans.

Libraries, media centers, and computer centers in teacher preparation institutions must cooperatively assume leadership and catalytic roles in educating the faculty in the implementation of the new technologies in college teaching. They also have the responsibility of providing a comprehensive and up-to-date sample of information technology applications and software designed for education K–12 for the college faculty to examine.

Libraries of Teacher Preparation Institutions Rich in Information Technology

As college professors become competent in the use of information technology in their research and teaching, exposing their students to a wide range of information resources becomes natural. This can not be achieved unless libraries of teacher-preparation institutions maintain comprehensive and up-to-date reference services. With that availability in mind, professors could plan their courses in which students have to use the library's rich resources including digital access to the world of information.

In addition to resources necessary to teach college courses, libraries of teacher-preparation institutions should maintain a K–12 curriculum collection. The curriculum collection should be expanded to include, in addition to school textbooks and media programs, electronic publications designed for use with K–12 students and guides to Internet sites focusing on K–12 education.

New Requirements for Admission

Working knowledge of at least one computer operating system, word processor, spreadsheet, and a web browser should be a requirement for enrollment in a teacher-preparation program. It is assumed that a student who has developed this minimum working knowledge possesses a minimum level of computer literacy and familiarity with the basic operation of computers. Such background is necessary for the student to be able to use the computer to access information from databases and information utilities. If a student cannot meet this requirement, he or she should be given the opportunity to develop that competency without rewarding course credits.

Requiring an Introductory Course in Educational Technology for All Students Seeking a Teaching Certificate

An effective teacher-preparation program should emphasize the right of every K–12 student to a rich learning environment. Today, K–12 students cannot be taught in the fashion that was practiced years ago. A visually and computer-oriented generation cannot be denied the right to use and interact with well-designed teaching materials presented through communications technology.

For graduate teachers capable of using the new learning and telecommunications technologies in education, teacher-preparation institutions should require a basic course in the use of educational technology from all students seeking a teaching certification. A major objective of this course is the development of preservice teachers' clear understanding of educational technology (see Chapter 3).

As an example of such a course, the basic course in educational technology at Fairfield University Graduate School of Education and Allied Professions has developed the following lists of concepts.

Target Concepts in a Basic Course in Educational Technology for K–12 Teachers:

1. Education is more than what students experience in their school years.
2. Education has to develop in every student respect and appreciation of cultural diversity among citizens.
3. Education has to develop in every student a critical mind capable of examining biased messages explicitly or implicitly portrayed in mass media, especially television.
4. For students with special learning needs, schools have to provide the tools of the new information age, which can assist those students in becoming self-dependent.
5. Education aims at developing the whole person. Emphasis on memorization and mastering skills results in neglecting the whole person's needs and aspirations.
6. Learning is a continuous process that does not stop at graduation or at securing a job. There is always a need for continuous education on all levels and for all ages. Being instructional technology literate can help achieve this objective.
7. Teaching is mainly a communication process. Understanding the extended view of communication is necessary to the achievement of successful communication.
8. Teaching has to be designed as a system that targets the individual student to improve the person as a whole. It considers the specific learner, well-defined objectives, accurate and up-to-date content, alternative teaching methods, learner's involvement, continuous evaluation, and planned follow-ups.
9. Creative technology utilization can help present difficult concepts in meaningful ways, capture the attention of the learner, meet students'

individual learning styles, individualize learning, and achieve the affective domain of education.

10. New information technology makes processing, sorting, and retrieving information more efficient. It challenges both the teacher and the learner to delve more deeply in the subject they are studying.

11. New telecommunication technologies open the doors for the learners to achieve continuous growth and educational excellence.

12. When teaching is properly designed and administered applying what we know about the learner, the learning process, and the advantages and limitations of channels of learning (media), learning can be self-rewarding and teaching can be exciting and self-fulfilling.

13. Quality education is a shared responsibility among schools, parents, and the community.

14. Distant teaching is a viable strategy to achieve educational equity among schools in different districts.

15. Effective utilization of instructional technology requires retooling teachers to master the use of the new technologies. It also requires from administrators a clear understanding of educational technology.

16. The school librarian has a new title, "school media specialist." A school media specialist's role is fivefold: information specialist, teacher, instructional consultant, administrator, and staff developer.

Emphasizing Educational Equality in Teacher Preparation Programs

In the information age, the educational gap between schools with adequate funds and resources and schools that lack these resources could increase. It is crucial to the establishment of harmony among members of our society, regardless of their socioeconomic status, that this gap be closed. In their preparation years, preservice teachers have to be made aware of this problem and ways of alleviating it. That awareness is best accomplished when students of teacher-preparation institutions participate in programs that reach out to underprivileged schools. These programs should be a component of a master plan of schools of education to reach out to neighboring schools, especially underprivileged schools.

In developing this plan, consideration might be given to the establishment of a center for field services. Some of the goals of such a center are to:

- Establish strong relationships with schools and other institutions and to assess their educational and training needs, which the school of education can offer.
- Recruit students from neighboring school systems.
- Help achieve educational equity for students in less than affluent school systems by providing them with communication links to the

institution's resources (one should not overlook the possibilities of outside funds that might be allocated just to achieve this goal).

- Provide the opportunities for the faculty and the students to work more closely with school personnel in a variety of settings.

THE SCHOOL MEDIA SPECIALIST

During the past four decades, the proliferation of information resources and new developments in information dissemination technologies have broadened the concept of the school library from a place of housing and distributing print materials to an instructional center of the school. The role of the school librarian has also expanded.

In 1988, two major national organizations, the American Association of School Librarians (AASL) and the Association of Educational Communications and Technology (AECT) addressed the mission and the challenges facing the school media libraries. Their findings and recommendations, *Information Power,* were published in 1988. This was revised in 1998 as *Information Power—Building Partnerships for Learning.* The book stated its focus in the following:

> Profound changes in society and technology during the past decade have resulted in massive changes in education and school library media programs. Children and young people still look to their schools for information beyond academics, but the explosion of knowledge made possible by advances in information technology has given the schools and their library media programs more options for responding to this goal. The content of knowledge and the ways of accessing it continue to grow exponentially.
>
> Information Power approaches this twofold growth by advocating the creating of a community of lifelong learners. Information literacy—understanding how to access and use information—is at the core of lifelong learning. . . . Information Power provides broad guidelines for local professionals to adapt their individual learning situation within their school library media programs.[26]

Information Power identified the mission of the library media program "to ensure that students and staff are effective users of ideas and information." Today's mission focuses on "offering programs and services that are centered on information literacy and that are designed around active, authentic student learning." The report listed the following goals of today's library media program:

1. To provide intellectual access to information through learning activities that are integrated into the curriculum and that help all students achieve information literacy by developing effective cognitive strategies for select-

ing, retrieving, analyzing, evaluating, synthesizing, creating, and communicating information in all formats and in all content areas of the curriculum.

2. To provide physical access to information through
   a. A carefully selected and systematically organized local collection of diverse learning resources that represent a wide range of subjects, levels of difficulty, and formats;
   b. a systematic procedure for acquiring information and materials from outside the library media center and the school through such mechanisms as electronic networks, interlibrary loan, and cooperative agreements with other information agencies; and instruction in using a range of equipment for accessing local and remote information in any format.

3. To provide learning experiences that encourage students and others to become discriminating consumers and skilled creators of information through comprehensive instruction related to the full range of communications media and technology.

4. To provide leadership, collaboration, and assistance to teachers and others in applying principles of instructional design to the use of instructional and information technology for learning.

5. To provide resources and activities that contribute to lifelong learning while accommodating a wide range of differences in teaching and learning styles, methods, interests, and capacities.

6. To provide a program that functions as the information center of the school, both through offering a locus for integrated and interdisciplinary learning activities within the school and through offering access to a full range of information for learning beyond this locus.

7. To provide resources and activities for learning that represent a diversity of experiences, opinions, and social and cultural perspectives, and to support the concept that intellectual freedom and access to information are prerequisite to effective and responsible citizenship in a democracy.[27]

The report identified three sets of information literacy standards for student learning: information literacy, independent learning, and social responsibility standards. Information literacy standards include efficient and effective accessing of information, critical and competent evaluation of information, and using information accurately and creatively.[28] Independent learning standards include pursuing information related to personal interests, appreciating literature and other creative expressions of information, and striving for excellence in information seeking and knowledge generation. Social responsibility standards include recognition of the importance of information to a democratic society, practicing ethical behavior in regard to information and information technology, and participating effectively in groups to pursue and generate information.

For the media specialist to fulfill his or her role, "the effective library media specialist draws upon a vision for the student-centered library media program that is based on three central ideas: collaboration, leadership, and technology."[29] School media specialist programs must target the cultivation of a specialist who cooperates with teachers, school administrators, students, and parents to create an intellectual information environment in which students develop their abilities as well as their desire for lifelong learning.

School media specialist certification programs must focus on the expanding role of the school media library and the challenges that their graduates face. New developments and advancements in information technology emphasize the vital role that school media specialists play in assisting their students to master such information.

In an attempt to ensure the quality of school media specialist preparation programs, the AASL assigned a task force to develop performance-based standards for school media education programs

Performance-Based Standards for School Library Media Education Programs

The AASL appointed a task force, at the ALA 2000 Annual Conference, to "continue the work of developing the performance based standards for school library media education programs. These Standards are developed and approved by the AASL for the ALA and will be endorsed by the National Council for Accreditation of Teacher Education (NCATE) for use by the Specialty Area Board (SASB) Accreditation Process."[30]

On December 20, 2000, the Task Force posted on the web a request for comments on the second draft of the AASL Standards for School Library Media Specialist preparation. The proposed standards are to be applied to master's degree programs and/or to graduate certification programs.[31]

The Standards include eight components of professional preparation and 35 standards. They are:

Component 1. Proficient Information Specialist. School Library Media Specialists provide effective and efficient physical and intellectual access to information and ideas.

Standard 1.1	Candidates seek information using a variety of electronic and traditional formats and sources.
Standard 1.2	Candidates identify and respond positively to information needs and requests.
Standard 1.3	Candidates access and provide for the learning community to access information using regional, state, national, and international traditional and electronic links.
Standard 1.4	Candidates recommend and use policies and procedures that provide private, legal, ethical, and equitable access to information and ideas.

Component 2. Effective Collection Builder. School Library Media Specialists develop and maintain collections critically and competently.

Standard 2.1	Candidates select resources using valid criteria following standard professional practice.

Standard 2.2	Candidates monitor collections and plan to provide access to resources that support student achievement; the school curriculum; the school philosophy, mission, and goals; and state curriculum content standards.
Standard 2.3	Candidates critically evaluate collection resources.
Standard 2.4	Candidates seek and use input from the school's learning community when building collections and selecting resources.
Standard 2.5	Candidates recommend and use collection development policies and procedures.
Standard 2.6	Candidates are committed to the provision of free and equal access to both traditional and electronic resources and collections.
Standard 2.7	Candidates create new resources to meet specific information needs of the learning community.

Component 3. Expert Teacher. School Library Media Specialists are expert teachers who effectively integrate the library media program into the school's curriculum in order to promote student achievement.

Standard 3.1	Candidates demonstrate knowledge of how students differ in their development and approaches to learning.
Standard 3.2	Candidates use the instructional design process to create and implement teaching-learning activities based on their knowledge of human development, learning abilities, learning styles, subject matter, and curriculum goals.
Standard 3.3	Candidates plan and work collaboratively with teachers to ensure integration of information skills into the curriculum provide access to resources and promote effective use of technology across the curriculum.
Standard 3.4	Candidates are committed to promoting maximum use of the school library media services and resources.

Component 4. Accomplished Motivator. School Library Media Specialists motivate and guide members of the learning community in appreciating literature and pursuing lifelong learning.

Standard 4.1	Candidates demonstrate a sound knowledge of children's and young adult literature.
Standard 4.2	Candidates develop appropriate techniques for selecting children's and young adult literature for the library media center.
Standard 4.3	Candidates develop appropriate techniques for sharing children's and young adult literature in the school and library media center.

Component 5. Skilled Manager. School Library Media Specialists effectively plan, organize, and manage human, financial, and physical resources.

Standard 5.1	Candidates develop short- and long-range plans for the school library media program that support the mission, goals, and objectives of the school.

Standard 5.2   Candidates demonstrate knowledge of the budgetary process and skills in budget planning.

Standard 5.3   Candidates evaluate human and physical school library media program resources.

Standard 5.4   Candidates communicate effectively in a variety of ways with all members of the learning community.

Standard 5.5   Candidates recommend and use standard procedures for the organization of resources and equipment.

Standard 5.6   Candidates develop and establish policies and procedures for the efficient and effective operation of the library media program.

Standard 5.7   Candidates effectively manage the library media program including technology resources and information systems.

Component 6. Effective Leader and Inclusive Planner. School Library Media Specialists serve as leaders within the learning community, ensuring that the library media program is central to the instructional program of the school and creating a positive, technologically rich learning environment that nurtures a sense of community and a respect for diverse cultures and learners.

Standard 6.1   Candidates collaborate with members of the learning community, developing programs and managing the library media resources and services to maximize program integration into the school curriculum.

Standard 6.2   Candidates keep the learning community informed of educational trends and developments in the library media field.

Standard 6.3   Candidates demonstrate skills in the processes necessary to maintain collections diverse in format and content in order to meet the needs of a learning community with a wide range of abilities, backgrounds, needs, and learning styles.

Standard 6.4   Candidates develop appropriate techniques for introducing students and other members of the learning community to the different information access formats, print and nonprint, available in the library media center as well those available in the community and/or electronically.

Standard 6.5   Candidates recognize that students and other members of the learning community differ in their development of and approach to information literacy.

Component 7. Reflective Practitioner and Lifelong Learner. School Library Media Specialists evaluate the effectiveness of the library media program in relation to needs of the learning community and actively pursue professional development opportunities.

Standard 7.1   Candidates identify and use appropriate assessment tools to evaluate and improve library media programs.

Standard 7.2   Candidates work with other members of the learning community to improve library media programs and student achievement.

Standard 7.3   Candidates engage in self-assessment, reflect on perform-
                      ance, and share results.

Component 8. Responsible Citizen. School Library Media Specialists advocate
and plan for intellectual freedom as well as the ethical and legal use of information and ideas

Standard 8.1   Candidates demonstrate a commitment to the principles
                      of the library profession regarding intellectual freedom,
                      confidentiality, the rights of users, and other intellectual
                      property concerns.
Standard 8.2   Candidates collaborate with teachers and other members
                      of the learning community to encourage students to
                      become information literate, independent learners and
                      socially responsible in their use of information and infor-
                      mation technology.[32]

These standards describe the multiple roles that today's school library
media specialist performs. Due to the continuous need to educate teachers
in the infusion of technology in teaching, more emphasis should be placed
on effective leadership and inclusive planning, as expressed in the sixth
component. The school media specialist is the potential catalyst to motivate,
train, and provide leadership for teachers in various disciplines to infuse
technology in their curricula. Moreover, he or she could extend that role to
include school administrators to assist them in adopting practices leading to
the encouragement of the teachers to employ information technologies in
their professional development and teaching. Because of the importance of
educating in-service teachers and administrators in creative and innovative
ways of infusing technology in K–12 education, this role could be viewed as
a ninth component in the school media specialist professional practice: the
School Media Specialist, a Professional Staff Developer.

Based on a review of the print and electronic literature addressing the
necessity for improving education through the proper applications of information technologies and the preparation of the school media specialist to
assume a leading role in technology applications in education, six salient
points are presented:

1. The issue is no longer whether technology should be used in schools
    or not. The goal is to ensure effective use of technology to enhance
    and extend learning opportunities for *every* student.
2. The Internet is growing at a very fast pace not only in the number of
    people worldwide who are using it but also in its creative applications
    in various aspects of our lives including business, research, education,
    communication, entertainment, video and television broadcasts,
    radio broadcast, and newspapers publications.

3. Technology in education has gone through four major phases: (1) audiovisual aids, (2) audiovisual methods of teaching, (3) integration of technology in the curriculum, and (4) infusion of technology in education. Infusion of technology in education would result in creative curricula and more comprehensive and accurate assessment practices.

4. Teachers have to be educated in the variety of information technologies with emphasis on how the technology could be infused to enhance the educational experience of *every* student.

5. Conventional technologies, such as the tape recorder, should not be overlooked just for the sake of using new technologies. Teachers, assisted by the school media specialists, can plan effective learning environments in which technologies are selected and used for their potential contribution to the learning and teaching task and not based on their newness.

6. The school media specialist's role is expanding to include responsibilities for organizing, administering, and assessing professional development activities for the teachers as well as for the administrators in the school. The traditional fourfold role of the school media specialist as a teacher, information specialist, instructional partner, and program administrator has expanded to include a fifth role: professional staff developer. I think that more emphasis ought to be put on developing the school media specialist's abilities and skills for actual participation in rigorous professional development programs in his or her schools.

School media specialist programs will continue to be faced with complex challenges as access to increasing amounts of information expands, dictating the reexamination of the role of the school media specialist. Colleges of education preparing some of their students to assume the role of school media specialists must focus on the expanding role of the school media library and the challenges that their graduates face. Over the past two decades, state boards of education, professional organizations, and teacher training institutions have identified competencies that school media specialists must master. For instance, in the state of Connecticut, the school media specialist should be capable of:

1. Design, implementation, and evaluation of media programs. Media programs are defined as all the instructional and other services furnished to students and teachers by a media center and its staff;

2. Evaluation, selection, acquisition, organization, production, and retrieval of media (print and nonprint);

3. Teaching students, staff, and faculty to utilize media and its accompanying technology by applying valid instructional methods and techniques;

4. Assisting students in the interpretation of print and non-print materials;

5. Application of principles of administration and supervision for effective leadership and operation of the school library media center and program; and

6. Formulation of the educational specifications and contribution to the design of school library media facilities.

Schools of education around the country have translated these and similar competencies into the goals and objectives of school media specialist programs. For instance, the Educational Technology Department of the Graduate School of Education and Allied Professions at Fairfield University developed a comprehensive graduate program for the preparation of school media specialists. The statement of philosophy of the program as well as its goals, objectives, and competencies are presented in Appendix I.

COMMUNITY PARTNERSHIP

Quality education is a shared responsibility among schools, parents, and the community at large. Our economic survival and leadership role in the free democratic world rest on the educated individuals of our nation. The need to improve the quality of education and to achieve educational equity for everyone is urgent. Many communities and corporations have worked together with schools to improve education. Among collaborative work are adopting a school, providing internship programs, offering assistance in teaching, and providing resources to schools. Such cooperation could help foster the realization of the schools' goal of cultivating the educated person.

CONCLUSION

The route to achieving excellence in education has many paths. The new learning and telecommunications technologies introduced in the information age offer a vehicle through which excellence in education can be achieved. There is a need, however, to study all aspects of educational practice, including financial support for a cost-effective education; the preparation of teachers, school media specialists, and school administrators; professional development of school personnel; nourishing professional ties between faculty of colleges of education and schools; revision of school curricula to accommodate the needs of the new age; and the role of the school media library in education. Since quality education is a shared responsibility among schools, parents, and the community, there is a need to establish effective partnerships among these entities.

Educational reform should not focus only on producing a skilled work force but also on cultivating the educated person. In the concluding remarks in the television series *Learning in America*, Roger Mudd said:

> Much of the school reform appears to be driven by America's loss of her competitive economic edge and the threat to our jobs. Schooling, we would suggest, is not a preparation for earning a living. It is one of the objectives, it is not the main one. Learning is for the sake of learning and not for the sake of earning. Learning in America should not only enrich our spirit, powers, wisdom and inner-contentment, but also should enable our country to function and flourish. For a nation so diverse as ours to maintain itself, there must be intelligent discourse and common understanding. For that, education is the keystone.[33]

Our economic survival and leadership in the free democratic world rest on the educated individuals of our nation. The need to achieve excellence in education and educational equity for everyone is urgent. Only when our quest is multilateral and targets the student as a whole person will we realize excellence in education.

REFERENCES

1. *Getting America's Students Ready for the 21st Century: Meeting the Technology Literacy Challenge*, http://www.ed.gov/Technology/Plan/, last updated August 25, 1996, accessed 7/26/98.
2. *Getting America's Students Ready for the 21st Century: Meeting the Technology Literacy Challenge: Executive Summary*—June 1996, http://www.ed.gov/Technology/Plan/NatTechPlan/execsum.html, pp. 1–2, accessed 7/26/98.
3. *NCATE Report Says Schools of Education Should Increase Emphasis on Technology*, http://www.NCATE.org/specfoc/techrpt.html, p. 1, accessed 7/26/98.
   4. *Ibid.* p. 11.
5. *Ibid.* pp. 11–12.
6. National Council for Accreditation of Teacher Education (NCATE). *Professional Standards for the Accreditation of Schools, Colleges, and Departments of Education*, Washington, D.C., 2002, p. 13.
7. *ISTE Recommended Foundations in Technology for All Teachers*, http://www.iste.org/specproj/standards/found.htm, p. 1, accessed 7/26/98.
8. *National Educational Technology Standards (NETS) and Performance Indicators*, http://cnets.iste.org/teachstand.html/, accessed 11/11/00.
9. *ISTE Technology Standards for Students*, http://cnets.iste.org/index2ss.html/, accessed 11/11/00.
10. *ISTE, Technology Performance Profiles for Teacher Preparation*, http://cnets.iste.org/perfprofiles.html/, accessed 11/11/00.

11. *ISTE, Technology Foundation Standards for All Students,* http://cnets.iste.org/sfors.htm/, accessed 11/11/00.

12. *ISTE, Profiles for Technology Literate Students,* http://cnets.iste.org/profiles.htm/, accessed 11/11/00.

13. Web-Based Education Commission Issues Urgent Call-to-Action to Harness Internet's Power for Learning, *Broadest Report To Date on E-Learning Recommends Investment, Regulatory Reform,* December 19, 2000, http://www.hpcnet.org/cgi-bin/global/a-bus_card.cgi?SiteID=203877/, accessed 12/19/2000.

14. *Ibid.* p. i.

15. *Ibid.* p. iii.

16. *Ibid.*

17. Excerpts from Report of the Web-Based Education Commission to the President and the Congress of the United States, Senator Bob Kerrey, Chair, Representative Johnny Isakson, Vice Chair. *The Power of the Internet for Learning—Moving from Promise Practice,* December 2000, http://www.ed.gov/offices/AC/WBEC/FinalReport/, accessed 1/17/01.

18. *The CEO Forum on Education and Technology,* http://www.ceoforum.org/about.cfm/, accessed 9/10/03.

19. *CEO Forum Reports,* http://www.ceoforum.org/reports.cfm?CID=1&RID=6, downloaded 9/10/03.

20. *Ibid.*

21. *CEO Forum STaR4,* http://www.ceoforum.org/downloads/star4.pdf/, downloaded 9/10/03.

22. *The CEO Forum School Technology and Readiness Report,* http://www.ceoforum.org/downloads/99report.pdf, downloaded 9/10/03.

23. CEO Forum. *The Power of Digital Learning,* http://www.ceoforum.org/downloads/report3.pdf, p. 10.

24. *Ibid.* p. 11.

25. CEO Forum. *Key Building Blocks for Student Achievement in the 21st Century* http://www.ceoforum.org/downloads/report4.pdf.

26. The American Association of School Librarians and the Association for Educational Communications and Technology. *Information Power, Building Partnership for Learning,* American Library Association, Chicago and London, 1998, (pp. vi–vii).

27. *Ibid.* pp. 6–7.

28. The American Association of School Librarians and the Association for Educational Communications and Technology. *Information Literacy Standards for Student Learning.* Chiacgo, IL: American Library Association, 1998.

29. *Ibid.* p. 4.

30. ALA and AAS. Assuring Quality in School Library Media Education Programs, http://www.ala.org/aasl/aasl-nacate/draft2_into.html/ December 20, 2000, accessed 1/17/01.

31. *Ibid.* p. 1.

32. The American Association of School Librarians, *Program Standards for School Library Media Specialist Preparation; Level: Advanced; Degree or level: Post-baccalaureate or Masters Degree Programs,* prepared for presentation to the NCATE Specialty

Areas Studies Board, second draft: December 16, 2000, http://www.ala.org/aasl/aasl-ncate/draft2_rtf.rtf, accessed 1/17/01.

33. *Paying the Freight,* the fifth and the last program in the television series *Learning in America,* Produced by MacNeil/Lehrer Production and WETA, broadcast on PBS on April 24, 1989.

APPENDIX

THE SCHOOL MEDIA SPECIALIST PROGRAM AT THE GRADUATE SCHOOL OF EDUCATION AND ALLIED PROFESSIONS, FAIRFIELD UNIVERSITY

Statement of Philosophy

We believe that the goal of education in the 21st Century ought to become more focused than ever on cultivating truly educated persons. An *Educated Person* in this Age is one who is capable of maintaining a high quality of life, and of contributing to the betterment of the community and the world as a whole.

Educators have been advocating the need for individualized, flexible, interactive, interdisciplinary and up-to-date learning environments in which students control their own learning—necessary conditions to enable students to become educated persons. However, with reliance on textbooks and audiovisual supplements it was difficult, if not impossible, to implement such progressive educational practices.

Information technologies have proven to be a significant advantage to the teaching/learning process. Never before have educators had the wide and effective range of instructional and telecommunications technologies that are available to them and their students in and out of class. Today, the new learning and telecommunications technologies can help realize educators' pedagogical dreams.

Since we educate by means of the environment, special attention has to be given to the design of learning environments conducive to the cultivation of the educated person. An essential element of that design is ensuring the learner's interactivity with models of excellence, both in human resources and in learning materials. Fortunately, the technology of the information age provides students and teachers with the tools and vehicles through which models of excellence can be accessed.

To implement effective utilization of the technology of the information age in education, first, school curricula have to be examined and restructured in the light of the goals of education with special attention to what the new learning and communications technologies can offer. Second, teachers

337

have to be educated in the use of the new learning and telecommunications technologies and their potential applications to education. Third, there is a need to foster the new role of the school media specialist in the information age. This new role is five-fold: an information specialist, a teacher, an instructional consultant, an administrator, and a professional staff developer. Fourth, there is a need to implement a partnership among schools, parents, and the community at large to provide for quality education for our nation's students.

The program emphasizes theory, production, applications, and infusion of educational technology in education. It explores the effects of information technologies on the learner, the educational system, and the society as a whole.

Goals and Objectives of the School Media Specialist Program

The School Media Specialist Program aims at developing prospective school media specialists' understanding, appreciation, and basic competencies needed to implement the following concepts to achieve educational excellence and equity for all students.

Goals

The program in school media aims at assisting students to develop the following concepts related to technology and education. These concepts form the basis of the program upon which specific objectives are articulated and achieved.

1. To achieve excellence in education, the learner has to have direct access to models of excellence in his learning environment. The presence of excellent teachers and community resource people is a necessary condition for the achievement of excellence in education. In addition to models of human excellence, rich integrated use of teaching and self-learning materials are essential to stimulate the learner, and to provide him with suitable material to meet individual needs.

2. Education aims at developing the whole person. Emphasis on memorization and mastering skills results in neglecting the whole person's needs and aspirations. A variety of rich information resources can help in cultivating the whole person.

3. The library media center is an agent for educational reform which targets not only the production of a skilled work force, but most important, the cultivation of the educated person. This can be achieved through providing rich and varied learning resources, access to information in a variety of formats, in-service training to teachers and

school administrators, and orienting parents with the potential applications of the new learning and technologies in education.

4. Teachers' awareness of educational resources on the Internet and their viable uses to enrich the learning environment does not only expand the scope of learning resources available to the students, but also is essential for the preparation of the students for an effective life in the Age of Information.

5. To help students assume a productive and self-rewarding life in the Age of Information, it is essential to help them develop their competencies in exploring a variety of information resources including print, non-print, electronic publications, and the Internet to enrich their lives. This entails teachers who are skilled in searching electronically published and distributed information. The School Media Specialist can offer peer-training sessions for teachers lacking these skills.

6. In some teaching situations, use of media is treated as an afterthought, or as an addition to a teaching plan that can be executed without the use of media. In other situations, use of media in instruction is considered to be a practice of a teacher who is keeping pace with the times. Media should not be an afterthought. It is not a fad, either. Its main goal is to achieve excellence in education. It requires systematic planning based on our knowledge of human learning. The choice of technology of instruction is determined not only by economic considerations, but by the unique characteristics of each technology, the purpose of using it, with whom it will be used, and under what circumstances.

7. Every student has the right to an education that will foster maximum development of his talents. Instructional technology can help achieve educational equity to all students through providing interactive and rich learning environment, which can meet the various needs, interests, and learning styles of individual students; and through electronically connecting schools to share resources.

8. Based on the degree of modern society's dependence on mass media for information, entertainment, and for spending a large portion of leisure time, as well as on the basis of the tremendous effects that media, specifically TV has on everyone, developing students critical viewing skills should not be left to chance. Planned learning strategies to develop young people's critical viewing skills are a must in school curriculum.

9. Today, students are technology-oriented, while teachers tend to be print-oriented. The school library media center can help bridge this gap by providing students with access to new learning and information technologies, and by introducing to teachers the potential applications of these technologies in education.

10. Learning is a continuous process, which does not stop at graduation, or at securing a job. There is always a need for continuous education

on all levels and for all ages. Providing the students with access to a variety of learning resources which can meet various student needs, technology can help motivate and inspire students for self-learning. Moreover, new telecommunication technologies open the doors for the learners to achieve continuous growth and educational excellence after regular school years.

11. Teaching is mainly a communication process. Understanding the basics of this process is necessary to the achievement of successful teaching.

12. Teaching has to be designed as a system, which targets the individual student to improve the person as a whole. It considers the specific learner, well-defined objectives, accurate, up-to-date content, alternative teaching methods, learner's involvement, teaching and learning technologies, continuous evaluation, and planned follow- up.

13. Creative media utilization can help present difficult concepts in meaningful ways, capture the attention of the learner, meet students' individual learning styles, individualize learning, and achieve the effective domain of education.

14. New information technology makes processing, sorting, and retrieving information more efficient. It challenges both the teacher and the learner to delve more deeply into the subject they are studying.

15. When teaching is properly designed and administered, applying what we know about the learner, the learning process, the advantages, and limitations of channels of learning (media), learning can be self-rewarding, and teaching can be exciting and self-fulfilling.

16. Quality education is a shared responsibility among schools, parents, and the community. The three agents ought to have a clear understanding of what instructional technology can do to help achieve quality education. They should have a continuous dialogue to enhance conditions leading to educational excellence. New telecommunications technologies can help foster communication among these parties.

17. Effective utilization of instructional technology requires retooling teachers to master the use of the new technologies. It also requires from administrators a clear understanding of educational technology.

18. The school librarian has a new title, "school media specialist". A school media specialist role is five-fold: an information specialist, a teacher, an instructional consultant, an administrator, and a staff developer.

Specific Objectives of the Program Are:

1. To further develop the student's understanding of the design of an effective learning environment in which the learner becomes motivated, interested, and active.

2. To develop the student's ability to formulate realistic learning/teaching objectives and to design a systematic approach to achieve those objectives.

3. To provide the opportunity for the student to develop a system approach for a unit of study in a chosen field of interest under the guidance of a faculty member.

4. To develop the student's sensitivity and appreciation of factors hindering effective student-teacher communication especially those related to the inappropriate selection and utilization of media.

5. To develop the student's understanding of the continuous process of evaluation, and to develop his/her skill in using evaluation procedures in evaluating media programs and media hardware.

6. To develop the student's understanding of the leadership role of a school media specialist, especially in schools where a traditional approach in teaching is dominant.

7. To develop the student's understanding of the role of the media/library, and its proper design to achieve the school objectives.

8. To develop the student's understanding of planning and conducting in-service training sessions to his/her schoolteachers.

9. To develop the student's understanding of the role of supportive personnel in the school media library.

10. To develop the student's ability and understanding of the process of selection and purchase of instructional materials and equipment to enhance the effectiveness of the learning/teaching process.

11. To develop the student's awareness of sources of information on available media and computer-assisted instruction programs.

12. To develop the student's skills in using library reference tools, and in training young people to retrieve information including the use of the World Wide Web, CD-ROM databases.

13. To develop students' understanding of potential applications of the World Wide Web in research, teaching, and in classroom assignments.

14. To develop students' understanding of the viable uses of home pages in teaching and in enhancing communication between students and the school, and between the community, parents, and the schools.

15. To appreciate the viable uses of e-mail in enhancing communication among teachers, students, school administrators and community agencies.

16. To explore the use of WWW in teaching cultural diversity, and to increase students' awareness of the world as a global village.

17. To become familiar with worldwide resources on the WWW.

18. To focus on the application of WWW and the Internet in teaching one's subject matter, and to enhance the schools' mission.

19. To develop the student's understanding and skills in basic cataloging procedures of both print and non-print teaching materials.

20. To develop student's understanding and basic skills of school library automation.
21. To develop the student's understanding of and familiarity with children and young-adult literature presented in both print and non-print media formats.
22. To introduce and train the student in the visual arts of communication to increase his level of visual literacy and his ability to express himself fluently through at least one form of visuals: still pictures, motion pictures, video, and/or computer-generated visuals.
23. To develop the student's understanding of the principles and techniques of aural communication.
24. To train the students in basic production techniques and proper utilization of inexpensive teaching materials that can be made available to almost every classroom.
25. To develop the student's understanding of the state of instructional technology implementation in education and its projected development.
26. To develop the student's understanding of the present and future development in the field of telecommunications and computers and their potential effects on education.
27. To develop the student's understanding of current trends and needs in education and the potential application of instructional technology to serve educational needs.
28. To challenge the creativity of the student, and to encourage him/her to experiment with new devices and new approaches in instruction including the use of computers in multimedia presentations.
29. To develop the student's understanding of the nature of research in educational media and to apply basic research principles to identify and test a proposed solution to an educational problem in one's field of interest.

Basic Competencies

The following are basic competencies which the student will develop during his/her study. The program is designed to allow for further development of some of these competencies according to the interest and professional needs of the student.

1. Ability to define the components of a school library media program and explain their interrelationships.
2. Ability to compose a philosophy statement for a school library media program reflective of the school's mission.
3. Ability to design long-range goals for a school-library media program which will clarify and maintain the mission focus of the program, inte-

grate school library media services with curriculum planning and implementation, and keep pace with technological and theoretical changes in education.

4. Ability to describe processes for creating collegial relationships in the school, which will enable the library media specialists to be team members in instruction and curriculum design.

5. Ability to list specific professional competencies of various personnel comprising the staff of a school library media program at the school-building level.

6. Ability to design and compile manuals which explicate the functions, policies, and procedures of a school library media program at the school-building level for faculty and students.

7. Ability to plan for collection management based on documented school needs.

8. Ability to design a plan for initiating and maintaining networks to other school library media professionals, other education professionals, the community and governmental bodies and agencies.

9. Ability to use e-mail in enhancing communication with other professionals in school media in particular, and with educators in general.

10. Ability to evaluate the effectiveness of internal operations policies and procedures (e.g., evaluation, selection, and acquisition of educational media, media organization and processing and program activity development) which serve as the core functions of a school library media program at the school building level.

11. Ability to describe procedural steps in managing an annual budget system to maintain a school library media program at the school building level.

12. Ability to design the physical arrangement of furnishings and audiovisual equipment for efficient media operation.

13. Ability to effectively share in the school curriculum development through informing and advising the teachers on available media programs and new approaches in instructional technology.

14. Ability to plan, organize and conduct effective inservice training in media for teachers.

15. Ability to serve as a resource person and an advisor to both teachers and students in locating, selecting, evaluating and utilizing teaching materials, including microcomputer and CD-ROM software, and special television programs available either through satellite transmission, consortia of distant teaching or specialized channels on cable, and K-12 educational sites on the WWW.

16. Ability to retrieve information on existing media programs in different disciplines.

17. Ability to identify and use basic reference tools, online databases, and CD-ROM databases.

18. Ability to use basic search engines on the WWW such as AltVista, InfoSearch, Yahoo!, Google, and WebCrawler, and to develop skill in narrowing a search on a particular topic.

19. Ability to operate a microcomputer system, and to use existing packages to perform media/library activities.

20. Ability to teach young people how to use reference tools including on-line and CD-ROM databases to browse, sort, search and retrieve needed information.

21. Ability to perform basic cataloging practices for print and non-print teaching materials

22. Ability to perform comprehensive evaluation of teaching materials including microcomputer, CD-ROM and interactive videodisc software in terms of their content, modes of presentation, and search strategies.

23. Ability to operate and use a variety of audiovisual equipment such as projection equipment, tape recording equipment, graphic production equipment, still picture single-lens reflex cameras, and TV production equipment.

24. Ability to use seamless software on a microcomputer platform to generate multimedia documents.

25. Ability to produce different types of audiovisual materials such as: overhead transparencies, 2" 2" slide/sound presentations, video programs using single camera as well as multiple camera system, audio programs using multiple sound input, and graphic materials using both conventional graphic tools and microcomputer graphic programs.

26. Ability to use computer graphic software to produce a multimedia graphic presentation.

27. Ability to recognize the elements of visual composition and to arrange these elements to produce effective visuals.

28. Ability to recognize the elements of audio composition and to arrange these elements to produce effective audio programs.

29. Ability to visualize and produce effective conventional and computerized multimedia presentations.

30. Ability to recognize limitations of existing classrooms and to offer practical advice to minimize these limitations.

31. Ability to use at least one computer-controlled multimedia authoring package in designing and using computer multimedia presentation.

32. Ability to recognize and retrieve good quality educational and cultural television materials available through a variety of resources including educational and cultural television channels.

33. Ability to design and administer instructional units, which target the development of K-12 students' critical viewing skills of media, especially entertainment television programs, and critical consumption of WWW resources.

34. Ability to search, retrieve information, and to communicate using a Web browser.
35. Ability to author Web pages, and to initiate a school homepage that can serve his/her school learning environment's needs.

INDEX

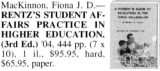

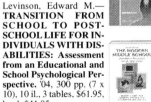